Red Spies
in America

Red Spies in America

Stolen Secrets and the Dawn
of the Cold War

Katherine A. S. Sibley

University Press of Kansas

Published by the University Press of Kansas (Lawrence, Kansas 66049), which was organized by the Kansas Board of Regents and is operated and funded by Emporia State University, Fort Hays State University, Kansas State University, Pittsburg State University, the University of Kansas, and Wichita State University

Library of Congress Cataloging-in-Publication Data

Sibley, Katherine A. S. (Katherine Amelia Siobhan), 1961–
Red spies in America : stolen secrets and the dawn of the Cold War /
Katherine A. S. Sibley.
p. cm.
Includes bibliographical references and index.
ISBN 0-7006-1351-X (cloth : alk. paper)

1. Espionage, Soviet—United States—History—20th century.   2.
Spies—United States—History—20th century.   3. United
States—History—1933–1945.   4. World War, 1939–1945—Secret
service—Soviet Union.   5. Cold War.   I. Title.

E743.5.S498 2004
327.1247′073′0904—dc22
2004   019571

British Library Cataloguing-in-Publication Data is available.

Printed in the United States of America
10 9 8 7 6 5 4 3 2 1

The paper used in this publication meets the minimum requirements
of the American National Standard for Permanence of Paper
for Printed Library Materials Z39.48-1984.

In memory of my parents, C. William Sibley (1919–1983) and
Margaret M. Walsworth-Bell Sibley (1920–2000),
who also first spied each other in World War II

CONTENTS

ILLUSTRATIONS

ACKNOWLEDGMENTS

This joy of completing this book would never have been possible without the kindly assistance of so many colleagues and friends. Among those who read the book in any one of its infinite and diverse earlier combinations, and provided much needed advice, I would like especially to thank Harvey Klehr, Arthur Hulnick, Betty Unterberger, John Earl Haynes, Bruce Craig, John Prados, Wesley Wark, Dan Leab, Randall Miller, George Sibley, Stephen Whitfield, Jessica Gienow-Hecht, and Bob Beisner. This project also benefited from the close scrutiny of members of two academic seminars, the Philadelphia International History Group at Saint Joseph's University and the Delaware Valley Russian History Seminar at Swarthmore College. I am especially grateful to PHIHG members Marc Gallicchio, Richard Immerman, John McNay, Bill Ashbaugh, Dan Aldridge, Rich Manser, Arthur Dudden, Iloyna Homeyard, and Nona Smith, as well as to Swarthmore seminarians Adele Lindenmeyr, Barbara Norton, Bruce Grant, Sibelan Forrester, Tom Bradley, Mike Hickey, and Bob Weinberg. Among those who also assisted me with research by sharing their materials, ideas, time, and hospitality were John J. Walsh, Hayden Peake, Neville Wylie, Gregg Herken, David Foglesong, Rorin Platt, Herb Romerstein, Carol Jackson Adams, Jim Ryan, Jonathan Beard, Athan Theoharis, Alexander DeConde, Melvyn Leffler, Robert Hanyok, Bill Runyon, Eduard Mark, Mike Warner, Richard Gid Powers, Sina Dubovoj, Justus Doenecke, Laura Wolfson, Mark Kramer, Charles Whittaker, Gary Speer, Kelly McClanahan, and, most memorably, Kathy Olmsted, who gave me the highlights of Nathan Gregory Silvermaster's dissertation in the waves of Oahu's North Shore.

In the archival universe, many others offered their generous aid. Guiding me in digging through the rich but often inaccessible collections at the FBI were John Fox and Linda Colton, as well as the FOIA Reading Room staff; at the National Archives, the amazing and resourceful John E. Taylor—truly a national treasure—was an immense help. At the Hoover Institution on War, Revolution, and Peace in Stanford, California, Carol Leadenham pointed me in the right direction, as did Dennis Bilger and Liz Safley at the Truman Library in Independence, Missouri. At the FDR Library in Hyde Park, New York, Verne Newton, Raymond Teichman, and Robert Parks ably supported my efforts. In Wilmington, Delaware, Hagley Library staff Chris Baer, Michael Nash, and Marjorie McNinch provided ready assistance, as did Joanne Hohler in Madison at the State Historical Society of Wisconsin. Erica Nordmeier and Emily Balmages at the Bancroft Library at the University of California, Berkeley, Jemal Creary of Corbis, and Gregg Plunges at the National Archives, New York City, were of great assistance in obtaining photographs. Staff at the Library of Congress Manuscript Reading Room, the National Archives Still Picture Branch, the U.S. Military History Institute in Carlisle, Pennsylvania, the Seeley Mudd Manuscript Library at Princeton University, and both the Russian State Archive of the Economy and the Russian State Archive of Social and Political History in Moscow also supported me in locating essential materials for this project. In Russia, Sergei V. Listikov of the Institute of World History of the Academy of Sciences broadened my access to and comprehension of numerous economic and party materials, as well as got me through some nerve rattling moments in a stuck archival elevator. Masha Fantalis was a most generous and kindly host in Moscow and has become a dear friend. Closer to home, the staff of the Saint Joseph's University Library, especially Chris Dixon, Mary Martinson, and Dan Cole, were always willing to help with elusive books and facts as well as balky microfilm readers.

Others from whose hand this work has benefited shall remain nameless, but not forgotten, most especially the anonymous readers of *American Communist History* and *Intelligence and National Security,* where earlier versions of this work appeared. Generous financial assistance for completing this project was furnished by the Truman Library, the Kennan Institute for Advanced Russian Studies, the Franklin D. Roosevelt Library, and Saint Joseph's University. As this book grew from proposal to completed manuscript, Michael Briggs at the University Press of Kansas remained always a most encouraging and patient editor, especially during the long months of this book's final gestation, and I am deeply grateful for his kind guidance. Larisa Martin, also at Kansas, and Jim Russo were instrumental in turning this manuscript into a publishable work. Any errors, of course, are my own.

It is doubtful that I would have survived my encounter with Soviet spies without my husband, Joe Horwitz, whose love has been a rock of support and inspiration throughout this project, and who has sustained me through the densest fogs of computer snafus and compositional snarls. My son, Jonah, whose recent arrival presented more of a challenge to this book's completion, has been a joy and a delightful distraction. Combining new motherhood with old spies would have been far more daunting without the support of many dear friends, including Marybeth Ayella, Nina Bakisian, Amy Fantalis, Fiona Harris Stoertz, Linda Hauck, Miriam Kinman, Debby Lurie, Maryanne Moore, and Sarah Starr.

When I returned from my Russian trip in 2000, my mother, Margaret M. Walsworth-Bell Sibley, had just entered the last stages of cancer. Today her spirit and her loving encouragement remain very much alive, however, and I am quite sure I would never have developed a love of history without the influence of her own bibliophilia and that of my late father, Capt. C. William Sibley. It is to them that I gratefully dedicate this book.

INTRODUCTION

"The threat of economic and industrial espionage looms over the horizon of the business world like a gray cloud threatening a placid sea," gloomily predicted Congresswoman Ileana Ros-Lehtinen (R-Fla.) in 2000. The problem was an old one, as Sheila Horan, deputy assistant director on counterintelligence for the FBI, confirmed at Ros-Lehtinen's hearing, noting that the lengthy preoccupations of the Cold War had prevented her agency from "aggressively" attacking the issue.[1] Soon, the FBI would have occasion to pursue this problem with renewed vigor. In the wake of September 11, 2001, combating espionage became the Bureau's number two priority, second only to fighting terrorism.[2]

Nevertheless, historians would largely differ with Horan's verdict that the Cold War–era FBI was insufficiently "aggressive" in responding to espionage. The government's agents may have overlooked the effects of industrial spying on American "competitiveness" (the subject of Ros-Lehtinen's hearing), yet the Bureau scarcely ignored spying, industrial or otherwise, in the preceding decades. Indeed, it was in "the early Cold War," as Ellen Schrecker writes, that "espionage . . . became central to the popular perception that Communists endangered the United States."[3] Schrecker's assessment is widely shared; for most scholars, the Cold War remains the period when Americans first seized upon the issue of espionage, especially the Communist variety, and the government used the specter of a threatening Soviet Union to create the present-day American domestic security state and counterintelligence system—a system burgeoning once again in such legislative measures as the USA-PATRIOT Act.[4]

This notion, however, has obstructed an appreciation of the work of a small but active coterie of American officials—largely in the counterintelligence community—who recognized the growing infiltration of Soviet spies *before* the Cold War and made limited, but nevertheless pioneering efforts to stop them.[5] It was Moscow's illicit wartime intelligence gathering, which centered on American military industry, that first convinced the FBI and

1

other agencies of the need for greater vigilance toward Russia—not the espionage discoveries of the Cold War. As FBI director J. Edgar Hoover well knew, "American Communists . . . made their deepest inroads upon our national life" during World War II.[6]

The war's sustained investigative campaign against Communists contributed to an important expansion in the nation's security and counterintelligence apparatus. A driving dynamic of this anti-Soviet initiative was espionage—in particular, the intelligence community's discovery of Soviet attempts to steal American military-industrial technology. Soviet intelligence gained a great deal of material from productive networks of American agents in manufacturing firms and the U.S. military, among them Jacob Golos's and Elizabeth Bentley's sources in the Pentagon, Julius Rosenberg's group of electrical engineers in defense plants, Harry Gold's contacts in the chemical industry, Igor Gouzenko's ring of radar and nuclear specialists in Canada, and, of course, the large number of sources within the Manhattan Project itself. Very few of these agents or their sources were discovered by counterintelligence at the time; the FBI remained largely unaware of the extent to which industry and the government had been penetrated by Soviet espionage. Nevertheless, the select group of industrial and military spies who were identified contributed to the emergence of a pervasive anti-Soviet outlook in the counterintelligence community. Well before the Cold War, American officials concluded that the Soviet Union and its agents posed a significant and growing threat to a vulnerable United States. Several notorious German espionage cases had already raised the profile and the budget of the FBI in the early 1940s, but the heightened secrecy surrounding the atomic bomb made the discoveries of Soviet espionage during World War II even more profoundly disturbing than the results of the German investigations. Ever more attention and resources were allocated to combating the Soviet Union's influence.[7]

Already expanding even before the Japanese attack on Pearl Harbor, the FBI would grow markedly faster after the United States entered World War II. The agency had investigated only about 35 espionage cases a year between 1933 and 1937 but handled 1,400 in the last six months of 1939.[8] In the first two months of 1941, roughly 8,500 espionage cases were initiated; the total caseload of national security cases for the year would swell to nearly 100,000.[9] Meanwhile, between 1940 and 1945, the number of FBI agents mushroomed from nine hundred to almost five thousand. Even more striking, from 1933 to 1945, the Bureau's budget expanded from $2.7 million to $45 million, having nearly doubled in the last two years of the war; at the end of the conflict it consumed almost half the Justice Department's allocation.[10]

Scholars have explored in depth such wartime FBI operations as those probing the activities of African Americans, anti-interventionist organizations, and Germans in Latin America.[11] But less attention has been paid to Washington's treatment of Communists and suspected Communists during the war, especially those in military-related industry and government facilities, or how this treatment created a precedent for the types of investigations, surveillance, harassment, and informing most typically associated with the Cold War. In an analysis of the government's 1954 security hearings on former Los Alamos Laboratory director J. Robert Oppenheimer, for example, Barton Bernstein noted that "since 1947 Oppenheimer's FBI file had swelled from frequent wire taps, some physical surveillance, occasional charges of disloyalty, and objections to his politics and attitudes." These practices and charges, however, had been extant and expanding against Oppenheimer during World War II—indeed, since 1941—because of his suspected Communist leanings.[12] Yet some historians have suggested that the wartime alliance with Russia actually *diminished* such surveillance, arguing that the threat of Soviet espionage during World War II was "secondary" to that presented by actual enemies like Germany and Japan, and therefore generated "little sense of urgency" from the FBI.[13]

Historians' perceptions of a dramatically more robust counterintelligence effort directed toward the Soviet Union after World War II perhaps stem from Cold War–era commentary suggesting that the United States regarded Russia with much less suspicion during the war years. Lauchlin Currie, an aide to FDR during the war, declared that "we were all united . . . the atmosphere of suspicion and caution only arose after I left the government" in 1945.[14] George F. Kennan recalled at Oppenheimer's hearings that "In 1943 the Soviet Union was hardly regarded by our top people in our government as an enemy . . . great masses of American materials were being prepared for shipment to the Soviet Union, many of them I assume involving the transmission of official secrets."[15] Indeed, a "wholly different atmosphere" then prevailed, as Oppenheimer's counsel Lloyd K. Garrison contended in 1954. "The whole attitude toward Russia, toward persons who were sympathetic with Russia, everything was different from what obtains today," he reckoned.[16]

But it was not entirely so different. Instead, the government's developing wartime outlook embraced a new set of assumptions about the danger the Soviet Union posed to the United States, an understanding that would influence American political culture throughout the Cold War. Indeed, this outlook had long-lasting reverberations in popular culture as well. The species of Soviet mole who features prominently in Cold War spy fiction like that of John Le Carré, haunting the dark and vulnerable interstices of Western democracy's political and military-industrial complex, had already assumed recognizable shape (with less ambiguity) in World War II, at least in the eyes of American counterintelligence officials.[17] Even FBI special agents who were not detailed to study the matter during the era recall being briefed on it: suspicion of Soviet espionage was palpable at the agency.[18]

One scholar who has noted the heightened intensity of this wartime anti-Soviet campaign nevertheless judges it a "counterintelligence failure" because the U.S. government's Venona Project (which would eventually decrypt more than two thousand Soviet cables), newly opened Soviet sources, and the testimony of defecting spies all show abundant examples of Soviet espionage that went unnoticed or unimpeded. Yet in making this argument, Athan Theoharis underestimates the importance of the FBI's and other counterintelligence agencies' discovery of Soviet spies during World War II. In contrast to the obliviousness of officials in the 1930s, the early-1940s detection of espionage galvanized counterintelligence agents to take action by launching new investigations, and helped usher in an anti-Soviet consensus that would echo throughout the remainder of the twentieth century and beyond. Nor can the wartime counterintelligence record fairly be characterized as an unambiguous failure. The FBI may have had "no formal counterintelligence program," as Hayden Peake contends, and thus no way to systematically root out spies and debrief defectors. But FBI surveillance forced such Soviet representatives as Semyon Semyonov, Gregory Kheifetz, Vassili Zarubin, and others to return to Russia, while U.S. officials effectively stymied such spies as Clarence Hiskey and Andrei Shevchenko. Moreover, FBI and Military Intelligence monitoring of agents like Arthur Adams, Steve Nelson, and Joseph Weinberg probably hindered them from conducting additional espionage.[19] Theoharis does convincingly demonstrate the government's difficulties in *prosecuting* spies successfully during the war or afterward, since its evidence, such as the Venona materials and wiretaps, was unacceptable in court. Though the revelations provided by former spies such as Bentley and by the Venona materials, among other sources, have more recently been verified in numerous Russian and American archives, such allegations, as Schrecker emphasizes, could not be proven *"at the time."* In the years since, the government itself hardly helped clarify matters; its zealous secrecy about Soviet espionage—Venona, for instance, remained secret until 1995, and FBI files have emerged generally with numerous redactions—helped enshrine a scholarly consensus that such spying largely did not exist.[20]

With Venona now open, and some scholars having obtained limited access to select KGB files, the subject of wartime Soviet espionage has recently enjoyed a huge outpouring of scholarly analyses and memoirs. As a result, in contrast to the long-held academic perspective that few, if any, American Communists engaged in spying, numerous historians now argue that Soviet espionage activity dwarfed not only what many scholars have traditionally understood of espionage levels in the 1930s and 1940s but also what most U.S. officials estimated at the time.[21] *Red Spies in America* builds on the growing body of scholarship in this area in three ways: first, as noted above, it suggests that Soviet espionage was recognized, even if only in its dimmest outlines, by American officials well before the Cold War; second, it argues that this understanding significantly influenced the mindset and actions of counterintelligence agents in World War II and left a legacy for U.S.-Russian relations that shaped the early Cold War and continues to reverberate down to the present day; and, third, the book more closely examines Soviet military-industrial espionage and its targets during and after the war, a topic that has not received focused treatment in previous scholarship.

In addition to exploring the significant cases that first alerted officials to Soviet espionage during World War II, *Red Spies in America* also considers the extensive amount of Russian spying that went undetected. Because this study investigates the consequences of officials' *awareness* of Soviet inroads in World War II, the range of espionage they knew nothing about may seem less relevant. However, a full examination of wartime Soviet intelligence gathering—including that uncovered only later—will shed light on the ways in which existing counterintelligence mechanisms fell short during the war. Here, the complicated U.S. wartime relationship with the Soviet Union is also illuminating. As U.S. Army lieutenant colonel John Lansdale well recognized, addressing Russian espionage then was "extremely difficult . . . we're dealing with an allied nation."[22]

Though the detection of espionage related to the atomic bomb was perhaps the most important development during the war years—defector Igor Gouzenko would claim that the pursuit of information regarding this weapon was "the number one objective of Soviet espionage"—American officials also became slowly aware of widespread Soviet spying in other munitions production areas.[23] These included such military and industrial targets as aircraft engines, radar and military electronics, assorted industrial formulae and techniques, such as the processes for making synthetic rubber and producing film, as well as all kinds of war plans. This effort far exceeded any previous such attempt in the United States, and American officials only dimly understood its scope. Still, though American countermeasures were, on the whole, ineffective, Soviet intelligence agents could ignore U.S. counterespionage activities only at their peril. Futile as they might often be, such efforts remained an ever-present threat, as shown in the case of Gregory Silvermaster, one of Elizabeth Bentley's main sources.

Silvermaster, a government economist, drew the attention of investigators in 1942 when he attempted to transfer to a post in the Bureau of Economic Warfare (BEW). Suspicious of his politics, especially in such a sensitive agency, both the navy and War Department objected; the House Special Committee on Un-American Activities, meanwhile, had him on a list of one hundred suspicious government employees.[24] Yet an official investigation turned up insufficient evidence to remove him from his job, and he remained on the federal payroll until 1945, turning over enormous quantities of material to the Russians. From his sources at the BEW and the Pentagon, Silvermaster provided statistics on a full range of American war production, from bombers to radar to submarines.[25] Silvermaster's Soviet superiors were concerned about the government probe, but consoled themselves by remarking in 1944, "[I]f they have not dismissed him from his present work, it means that there is no concrete information about his work for 'us' but only suspicions connected with his Communist Party membership." Moscow could not relax, however. As one agent noted, "[T]here is no guarantee that, as a result of some accident, materials he may have at his place . . . will not fall into the hands of the FBI. That would mean that 'our' sources would be compromised."[26] The government let Silvermaster slip away, but as the war continued U.S. security officials grew more sophisticated and their initiatives more successful. Such counterespionage drove Pavel Mikhailov, chief of the GRU (Soviet military intelligence) in New York, to protest in September 1943 that government shadowing was preventing agents from meeting with him.[27] In April 1944, Stepan Zakharovich Apresyan, Soviet vice consul, complained of FBI surveillance on Alexandr Semenovich Fomin, a clerk at the New York consulate.[28] Julius Rosenberg's handler, Alexander Feklisov, also felt the Bureau's presence keenly; its agents were constantly watching the exits of the Soviet consulate in New York where he worked. Indeed, the "spectacular tightening of FBI surveillance," as Feklisov put it, had sent a leading intelligence agent, Semyon Semyonov, back to Moscow.[29]

The FBI also began deploying new or newly authorized techniques in the war, including wiretapping and microphone surveillance, to investigate Soviet targets—specifically spies and "subversive activities." Alerted by such methods to Soviet espionage activities against the atomic bomb in 1943, agents launched the CINRAD (Communist Infiltration of the Radiation Laboratory, University of California, Berkeley) investigation, as well as the COMRAP (Comintern Apparatus) probe. The agency also maintained a "Security Index" of "dangerous" individuals, notwithstanding Attorney General Francis Biddle's express prohibition of such a list in 1943 as being "unpractical, unwise, and dangerous." The Bureau continued to use such tried and true practices as mail-opening and "surreptitious entry," or black bag jobs, and, of course, relied on countless informants. Through such diligent methods, by 1944 the agency had identified one million people with Communist-front associations—largely through blanket infiltration of groups like the NAACP.[30] The expanded role of the FBI was facilitated by FDR, who supported the agency's enhanced powers in return for Hoover's provision of secret intelligence on domestic radicals.[31]

These initiatives, in particular the discoveries of spying related to the A-bomb, drew a compelling picture of U.S. vulnerability to Soviet wartime espionage practices. As an FBI summary noted ominously in 1944, "Investigations have proved the continuous use of the Communists in the United States by Soviet agents and have confirmed the operation of an illegal and underground apparatus. . . . The implications of this activity in this time of vital war effort . . . and in the trying period of post-war readjustment to come warrant the closest attention and consideration."[32] No doubt with the recently revealed practice of Soviet espionage in mind, in 1944 Hoover effectively pressured Roosevelt to block a plan proposed by officials at both the NKVD (Soviet secret police) and the OSS (Office of Strategic Services) to permit a mutual exchange of intelligence agents between the two agencies.[33]

Despite the use of new (and old) techniques, American officials were hampered in grasping the full dimensions of this Soviet espionage campaign both by their nascent counterintelligence system's limitations and by strategic considerations. As Bradley F. Smith has noted, "Washington was firmly, and perhaps rather blindly, committed to making the partnership with the USSR work."[34] A significant pillar in this relationship was the lend-lease program, which facilitated the entry of numerous Soviet agents into the United States, some of whom used the opportunity to pilfer as much military-industrial information as possible. President Roosevelt saw the provision of materials as not only necessary for the war effort but as a way to gain Russian cooperation for such postwar endeavors as economic reconstruction and the United Nations.[35] Roosevelt's own naïveté about the scope of Russian intentions—or his unwillingness to consider them—is partly reflected in his refusal to entertain Whittaker Chambers's allegations about Soviet espionage in 1939 and in his limited response to J. Edgar Hoover's reports on the subject of wartime Soviet spying.[36] No doubt such wartime constraints circumscribed the activities of Bureau director Hoover and his men, but they did not stop the FBI from making tireless efforts to document Soviet espionage practices, such as its six-hundred-page COMRAP report of December 1944.[37] The very same frustrations that this situation created would lead the FBI and other counterintelligence institutions to trumpet their alarm loudly at the end of the war, when the climate of Soviet-American relations had changed drastically and the warning of espionage found more receptive ears.

Red Spies in America is based on new research in both American and Soviet archives. The author was the first to examine several long-classified Bureau case files, including those of Soviet spies Gaik Ovakimian, Steve Nelson, Arthur Adams, Boris Bykov, as well as the Amtorg Trading Corporation, the Soviet Union's purchasing agency in the United States. The pre-1945 U.S. Senate's Special Committee on Un-American Activities (Dies Committee) files, opened at this writer's request after research began on this book, are used for the first time here. While Russian archival administrators have for several years withheld from most scholars records that shed light on World War II espionage, as the author confirmed on a 2000 research trip, the Venona cables fortunately help fill in many of the remaining gaps, as do those books published by historians who had special access to KGB files. This study uses scantly touched pre–World War II Soviet archives, including party and government collections, to explore the earlier relationship between Moscow and Washington. It also takes a fresh look at some of the more familiar textual ordnance in the historiographic arsenal of Soviet espionage, including numerous congressional hearings and FBI files from the Oppenheimer, Bentley, Silvermaster, and Rosenberg cases, among many others.

Red Spies in America begins in the 1930s with an examination of some of the earliest Soviet military-industrial espionage efforts in the United States, paying close attention both to Washington's contemporary, limited conception of a Soviet threat and to the connections between these cases and later espionage episodes. Chapter 1 explores how diplomatic ties in 1933 assisted in furthering Moscow's access to American secrets, allowing scores of Soviet inspectors to visit American plants, offering regular opportunities for intelligence gathering, and facilitating the entry of numerous legal and illegal agents. These agents would groom some of Moscow's most devoted servants in the United States for years thereafter. During an era when public sentiment kept counterintelligence agents on a short leash, American officials could pay little attention to these activities. Even noisy congressional investigations, such as one conducted by the so-called Fish Committee, went nowhere. But in the years between the 1939 Nazi-Soviet Pact and the United States' entry into World War II, the country heightened its awareness of and suspicion about foreign threats, and FBI agents and other military officials took a closer look at the practices of Soviet agents. As chapter 2 details, authorities launched investigations that led to the arrests of such notorious spies as Gaik Ovakimian and Jacob Golos. Golos's espionage went largely unnoticed, however; instead, it was his position as an unregistered foreign agent that led to his detention in 1940. The chapter also closely explores the ways in which the international situation created an "emergency" at home that augmented the FBI's domestic security responsibilities and budgets in an unprecedented fashion. One result was the Bureau's extensive investigation of Amtorg, which helped convince agents of a yet only murkily imagined "Russian espionage system" at the dawn of World War II.[38]

The next two chapters closely examine the war years, 1941–45. Chapter 3 chiefly addresses Soviet military-industrial espionage, which expanded greatly during this era of Soviet-American military cooperation. It examines such cases as those of Abraham Brothman, Alfred Slack, the Silvermaster group, and the Rosenberg ring, demonstrating the breadth of Soviet penetration in American defense plants as well as the depths Moscow's agents reached in the secret files of the Pentagon's military-industrial planners. With a few notable exceptions, like the efforts of Andrei Shevchenko in the aircraft industry (which led to a successful counterespionage operation), this work went on without the faintest knowledge of American counterintelligence officials. Chapter 4 addresses Soviet intelligence infiltration of the atomic program, which, in contrast to their other espionage attempts, soon became too blatant to ignore. In March 1943, FBI surveillance uncovered a meeting in which Berkeley Radiation Laboratory scientist Joseph Woodrow Weinberg shared information with California Communist leader Steve Nelson; just two weeks later, agents recorded NKGB representative Vassili Zarubin meeting with Nelson and paying him "for . . . placing Communist Party members and Comintern agents in industries engaged in secret war production . . . so that the information could be obtained for transmittal to the Soviet Union."[39] Apparently for the first time, the FBI had recorded a party official being paid for providing classified technical information on the bomb to Russian intelligence. Agents' understanding of the threat posed by the Soviet Union expanded accordingly.[40] The issue only became more vexing when the head of research for the Manhattan Project, J. Robert Oppenheimer, told military officials that members of his staff had also been contacted by Soviet agents. Then, FBI surveillance of longtime Soviet agent Arthur Adams uncovered his meetings with Clarence Hiskey, a chemist at the Manhattan Project's Chicago Metallurgical Laboratory. A search of Adams's hotel room in September 1944 indicated that he had been gathering materials on the atomic bomb from Hiskey.[41] The defection of Igor Gouzenko, cypher clerk at the Soviet embassy in Toronto, revealed an even more alarming espionage operation a year later.[42] Gouzenko's allegations of Soviet spying on Canadian and American nuclear and radar research, substantiated by 109 documents he had secreted out of the embassy, helped to confirm the highly suspicious outlook that American officials had begun to adopt toward the Soviets and their allies in the United States.

Chapter 5 examines the implications of this deepening distrust for the developing Cold War, including loyalty programs, export controls, and heightened security. It explores as well the fruits of the Venona Project, which provided clues to infamous wartime spies including Judith Coplon, William Perl, and Klaus Fuchs. The consequences of Elizabeth Bentley's famous 1945 defection on the practices of Soviet spies in the United States is addressed, as is the increasingly intense Cold War reaction to World War II espionage as reflected in the Clifford Report of 1946 and materials documenting the trials of William Remington and William Perl, the relentless pursuit of Steve Nelson, the Rosenberg case, and the 1954 security hearings of J. Robert Oppenheimer. Only in the postwar era, as defections mounted and code-cracking grew more effective, did authorities begin to gain a more complete understanding of wartime Soviet espionage. Though Hoover and his colleagues in counterintelligence had long been convinced of the dangers of Soviet spying and subversion, other agencies, like the State Department, had held more diverse views. The new postwar atmosphere allowed Hoover's perspective to gain a much wider following in the U.S. government, thus ushering in the broad anti-Communist consensus of the Cold War.

The book concludes by briefly surveying Soviet and Russian espionage from World War II to the present. Unlike wartime spying, such recent espionage has been much more often motivated by cash than by Communism. Moreover, several contemporary spies, John Walker, Aldrich Ames, and Robert Hanssen among them, offered their services for far longer than their typical wartime counterparts, and generally did much more damage: the sheer volume of material passed by some of these notorious agents easily eclipses that of the most active World War II spies. Nevertheless, wartime military-industrial espionage practices established a template for Soviet and later Russian intelligence gathering that remains in use to this day; as long as U.S. technology maintains its preeminent global position, such espionage will likely continue, despite the attempts of congressional representatives like Ros-Lehtinen to stop it.

The American response to Soviet spies during the war years was generally unsuccessful, if judged by the number of spies caught. This was the result not only of a still-developing counterespionage capability in the U.S. government, but also the strategic interests of the wartime alliance. Still, the expanded understanding of Soviet spying that emerged in that period led the government to adopt a new approach in U.S.-Soviet relations, an approach that aggressively employed counterintelligence techniques and eventually led to an enhanced American security system. Among its postwar legacies would be a more vigilant HUAC, loyalty oaths, trade restrictions, and an enormous and powerful military-industrial-security complex. Although the uncovering of counterintelligence agencies' excesses helped end the most egregious domestic counterintelligence practices in the mid-1970s, concerns about Soviet espionage retained their currency throughout the Cold War.

These measures did not mean that spies were necessarily effectively apprehended after World War II; just as in the war years, political realities— from CIA/FBI rivalries to the priorities of global détente—often shaped the response to espionage. Perhaps it is not surprising, therefore, that the largest number of spies were captured during the Reagan administration, with its reinvigorated anti-Communist crusade. Indeed, as pundits proclaimed 1985 "the year of the spy," many grew convinced that Soviet espionage agents had never been more active. But the high number of arrests may have resulted from several new laws passed under the Carter administration, rather than from a vaster field of agents in operation. These new measures expedited both the investigation and prosecution of spies, although more recently they have been tapped to identify potential terrorists.

During the height of Reagan's renewed Cold War in 1983, the assumption of U.S. weakness in the face of Soviet danger was reemphasized by French writer Jean François Revel in a best-selling book, which noted that democracies were "easy prey to the trickery the totalitarian mind cultivates," via "psychological warfare, lies, disinformation and intimidation."[43] Two decades later, this concept of a vulnerable America remains popular with, among others, the Defense Department and Vice President Dick Cheney, who as recently as 2001 still held up Russia as the chief threat to the United States.[44] Though Russia's dangers paled after the September 11 attacks in New York and Washington—indeed, that country has become a supporter of the U.S. "war on terrorism"—its legacy of a global environment perilous to American survival seems only more vivid now, not only in the minds of U.S. leaders, but in the institutions created or expanded in reaction to the Soviet threat, such as the CIA, a more powerful FBI, and the modern spy thriller.

CHAPTER ONE

Espionage in the 1930s

In 1929, President Herbert Hoover became the fourth successive occupant of the White House to refuse to acknowledge the existence of the Soviet Union. Since the Bolshevik revolution in 1917, this official distance reflected Washington's avowed distrust of the Soviet regime for its confiscation of foreign investments, renunciation of Russia's international debt, and dissemination of pro-Communist propaganda abroad. Nevertheless, beginning in the mid-1920s, a growing commercial relationship spurred chiefly by the Amtorg Trading Corporation made up for the lack of ambassadorial ties. These economic bonds were only strengthened when Franklin D. Roosevelt decided to open diplomatic relations with Russia early in his first term, which made possible both new trade agreements and many more visits by Soviets to American plants. However, American distrust of the Soviet Union remained, as made evident in the hearings of Congressmen Hamilton Fish in 1930 and Martin Dies in 1938, both of whom investigated Communist influence in America with great zeal. Some of Roosevelt's close advisers, moreover, worried that recognition would bring "spying for trade secrets carried on by Russians 'learning' methods of production."[1]

Although counterintelligence agencies tried to limit Russian access to American defense technology, the restrictions were inconsistently applied. U.S. attachés' visits to Soviet soil revealed the ubiquitous presence of American technology in Russian military installations. The government's limited response to such espionage reflected the national mood: FBI and military staff understood well that Americans generally had little enthusiasm for a vigilant counterintelligence establishment in this era (despite such notorious episodes as Gen. Douglas McArthur's violent breakup of the 1932 Bonus March). Soviet agents like Whittaker Chambers and Harry Gold soon took advantage of the relatively lax atmosphere to begin their spying careers.

Growing Soviet-American trade had provided opportunities for industrial espionage even before official recognition of the USSR, and diplomatic ties only eased access for Soviet inspectors and spies. Despite the testimonies of espionage that former Amtorg employees offered to Congress, American counterintelligence officials were not strongly suspicious of the danger of Soviet espionage in this era, as they would be after the signing of Nazi-Soviet pact and during World War II.

Soviet-American Relations before Recognition: Trade, Espionage, and the Fish Committee

Historians have often portrayed the period before Washington established diplomatic intercourse with Moscow as a rigidly polarized standoff between the two governments.[2] Although the Roosevelt administration's recognition of the Soviet Union in 1933 appears to have been a significant shift in U.S.-Soviet relations that signaled Washington's readiness at last to do business with the Moscow regime, the change was actually less dramatic. Without diplomatic ties, certainly, none of the assistance and courtesies that an official relationship could provide existed. Despite those difficulties, however, the industrialization imperatives of the Soviet's first Five-Year Plan (1928–32), along with a growing U.S. interest in Russian trade opportunities that began as early as 1919, strongly advanced Soviet-American relations before recognition. In 1928, a triumphant Saul Bron, the chairman of Amtorg, crowed: "Beyond doubt in the future we . . . shall be able to extend our industrial relations with the United States, from whose high technical level we shall gain advantages."[3] Three years later, with still no embassy in Washington, the Soviet Union was America's seventh-biggest customer and its largest foreign purchaser of industrial machinery.[4]

These sales brought technical "advantages," just as Bron had predicted. But so too did ongoing Soviet espionage in the United States. Such intelligence collection was not consistently regarded as spying during the 1930s, either before or after recognition. At the time, the U.S. government's overall security agenda and its concerns about the threat of the Soviet Union in particular were limited, and most Russian visitors continued to be welcome to make purchases and to visit American plants. The threatening atmosphere in Europe by the end of the decade greatly increased concerns about domestic subversion of both the Communist *and* Nazi variety, but an understanding of Soviet espionage nevertheless remained indistinct.

The Amtorg operation was not without its skeptics, of course. A year after the agency opened, in 1925, an informant told the FBI that the agency was one of the key distributors of "Communist propaganda for [the] establishing of Soviet form of Government in U.S." Indeed, the informant alleged that Amtorg executive Isaiah Hoorgin was on his way back from Russia with plans and propaganda "in a false bottom of his trunk."[5] The New York Bureau office decided to ask U.S. Customs officials to search the trunk when Hoorgin arrived, only then to decide that the trunk story was probably "far fetched to say the least."[6] Regardless, the FBI continued to monitor Amtorg in the mid-1920s, noting the agency's lobbying for diplomatic recognition, its efforts to propagandize sailors in New York and Seattle, and Hoorgin's "enthusiastic" response to trade potential between his country and the United States.[7] The FBI alleged that Amtorg gave the Soviets "their first real opportunity for a broad legitimate cover for espionage agents." The purchasing agency also bought material illegally, including a secret shipment of several hundred Liberty motors in 1927. According to N. Streloff, former employee of Robert Cuse, a Brooklyn dealer who had assembled the Liberty motors for Amtorg, the Soviet trading agency had asked Cuse also to get them drawings of airplane catapults, bombsights, ships, and gun synchronizers in the 1920s.[8]

Later in the decade, Soviet Five-Year Plans were imagined by the Soviet government as a miraculous engine of industrialization, which required a steady diet of the most sophisticated equipment available. The resulting orders provided an opportunity for Soviet engineers and technicians to enter the United States in significant numbers to place and monitor contracts, staying from two to four months. New York law firm Simpson Thacher and Bartlett, which made visa arrangements for Soviet visitors, confirmed that "several thousand Russian nationals" came into the country between 1924 and 1930 under the auspices of Amtorg.[9] Amtorg president Peter Bogdanov pointed out in 1930 that "the substantial expansion of Soviet purchases here . . . would not be possible were it not for the presence of Soviet representatives in this country." Bogdanov added that American authorities had made no "specific complaints" against the visitors.[10] Indeed, Robert Kelley, one of the most hard-line anti-Soviet officials at the State Department, pragmatically declined a proposal to exclude Communist party members from joining Amtorg delegations in 1930. Kelley realized that "such an instruction would have a very ill far-reaching effect on the United States commercial relations with Russia."[11] The Soviets did not miss the significance of this, noting, "Surely the admission of . . . Communists to the USA is a favorable sign of the official American organizations who are very interested in the development of trade."[12]

By 1929, hundreds of Americans and Russians routinely traveled to each other's countries in pursuit of commercial matters. As Amtorg reported in May 1929, "During the past 16 months about 450 Americans visited the Soviet Union for business reasons while 300 Soviet executives and engineers came to this country to study American industries and to make purchases."[13] U.S. technical assistance was "creating a strong foundation for the penetration of American machinery into the Soviet Union," as Congress noted.[14] American engineers traveled to Russia from firms like International General Electric, Ford Motor, E. I. Du Pont de Nemours, Great Northern Railway, and Sperry Gyroscope. Still, they were just a fraction of the 6,800 foreign technicians in the USSR by mid-1932.[15] Among the many other Western countries that Soviet leaders looked to for assistance were Germany, Britain, and Italy.

Some of the consultants were paid "exorbitant salaries," according to the FBI, in order to provide "as much information, secret and otherwise, as possible for the plant before severing their connections."[16] Life was not always easy for these resident engineers, however. Metallurgical engineer P. A. Foren complained that he was left without a valid passport, his bags, and compensation for his travel; moreover, the agency he was working for, Gipromez, had provided him with insufficient help and facilities, including "a complete lack of blueprints."[17] Even worse was the report of William Irvine Smith, a Scottish engineer. Hired by Amtorg in 1931, he complained of having to sleep "on a table in a filthy hole overrun with rats."[18]

Such individual suffering was easily overshadowed by glowing forecasts for future business. In 1929, Dr. Joseph M. Pavloff, a Russian economist, predicted expenditures of over $7.5 billion in oil, metallurgical, coal, machine building and other industries, adding, "[I]t is only natural to assume that those markets which will be able to satisfy the demand in the most effective and quickest manner will be approached," with the United States in "first place."[19] The importance of American input was emphasized repeatedly. Amtorg's *Economic Review of the Soviet Union* noted in 1931 that "Russian engineers had already spent considerable time in America and had been impressed, as a result of numerous factory inspections, with American efficiency both in plant design and plant operation." Six months later, the same journal pointed out, "Developments under the five year plan have to a considerable extent been based on American technique."[20]

The first plan saw fifteen hundred plants constructed, and the trend showed no sign of slowing as the second one called for the construction of aircraft factories, shipyards, power plants, and foundries for the manufacture of railway, agricultural, and mining equipment, which would only require more Western expertise. As the decade progressed, Moscow was particularly interested in defense-related material. In 1937, priorities included fast planes equipped with armaments and sophisticated controls, tank engines, chemical warfare technology, high-speed battleships, submarine devices, and "telemechanics," or night vision technology.[21]

As the president of the Sullivan Machine Company noted, "They look upon the United States as their model for their industrial development, and are unquestionably doing all they can to purchase American equipment, and employing American engineers as instructors."[22] According to Robert Pitcoff, an Amtorg manager in the early 1930s, his bosses had been "very eager to obtain whatever information they possibly could from the U.S. because they consider the technique of the United States to be the superior."[23] In the mid-1930s, Commissar of Heavy Industry Anastas Mikoyan visited several American plants and declared that Europe's manufacturing infrastructure "was child's play compared with that of the United States and its industrial reserves."[24] It is telling, too, that Soviet officials trumpeted their second Five-Year Plan (1932–36) as effecting "the moment when we shall catch up with, and overtake, the United States."[25] Soviet analysts were fascinated with industrial statistics within the United States. Detailed studies were compiled about various branches of industry, including steel, automobiles, construction, and aviation.[26]

As the numbers of Soviet engineers in American factories and their American counterparts in Russia burgeoned, Soviet representatives gained increasing access to information. E. H. Hunter of the Industrial Defense Association explained in 1932: "Practically all the large industries, like the Harvester Company, Ford Motor, General Electric, A&P Stores, etcetera, are teaching technical men from Russia all the secrets of their great organizations. This is being done openly and above-board, and those people come here largely under the quota privileges."[27] Indeed, they operated not only openly, but efficiently. Chief of Naval Operations William Standley reported that at one plant thirty technicians had been replaced every three months, "thus getting four times as many trained men in one year" as authorized.[28]

While Soviet intelligence gathering in American military and industrial technology grew rapidly in the early 1930s, most branches of U.S. government devoted few resources to addressing the issue in this era, a period when "hostile public opinion" stopped even Gen. Douglas MacArthur from authorizing

Military Intelligence agents to monitor radical activities.[29] Congress was more active, although its attention chiefly concerned Communist political agitation, not espionage; in any case, its recommendations were also considered too extreme. In May 1930, Speaker of the House of Representatives Hamilton Fish Jr. (D-N.Y.) established the Special Committee to Investigate Communist Activities. Fish was incensed that "the Government . . . has practically no power to deal with the activities or the propaganda of any of the communists in the United States, and the communists, knowing that, have increased their activities within the last 6 or 7 years . . . [and] become a menace in the great industrial centers of the United States." Fish was particularly struck by the Department of Justice's weakness in this area. It had neither agents who were authorized to act nor congressional funds to support such action.[30]

Along with examining Communist propaganda, Fish's committee looked into a wide array of allegations against Amtorg, most notoriously those of New York City police commissioner Grover Whalen, who had produced documents suggesting that Amtorg was harboring thirty "undercover agents of the Communist International."[31] But Johann Ohsol, vice president and director of the Soviet agency, testified that it had "no connection with communist activities in this country."[32] After a series of exhaustive hearings and the revelation that Whalen's documentary evidence was a bad forgery, the Fish Committee agreed with Ohsol's assertion, determining that "there is not sufficient competent legal evidence in the record to prove the connection of the Amtorg Trading Corporation . . . with subversive activities."[33]

While largely focused on Communist subversives and their methods, the Fish Committee also investigated Soviet spies. Basil Delgass, former Amtorg vice president, told the committee about the agency's "espionage system" and Amtorg executive Saul Bron's connections with it. Delgass reported being approached by a Russian who "offered to me . . . a report on military activities of the United States for $500 a month," and averred that Amtorg had acquired information regarding "Army and Navy defenses."[34] Delgass told Fish that in order to collect more intelligence, a large number of Amtorg visitors had come "under false pretenses": several individuals who arrived with purchasing assignments, for instance, were hard at work in Amtorg's "cipher and secret department." And Mr. A. Petrov, who was "supposedly sent by the Metal Import Corporation to be vice president . . . of the automobile division of the export department," was instead "actually sent by the military aviation department and is engaged in espionage work." In 1929, Petrov had driven across the country "to inspect military airdromes and naval bases on the Pacific coast," with a special interest in aircraft carriers. Later, Delgass alleged, Petrov and several members of the Soviet military visited the Aberdeen Proving Ground and "made complete sketches of a 75 mm. quick-firing gun." Amtorg's technical bureaus, Delgass concluded, "represent nothing more than [an] industrial intelligence service, spying upon the industrial developments of the United States and reporting to Moscow."[35] His revelations about Amtorg's intelligence collection greatly alarmed J. V. Ogan of the Office of Naval Intelligence, who asserted that "Amtorg [is] engaged in carrying out a survey of all companies on the Government's Procurement Planning and Industrial Mobilization lists."[36]

The Fish Committee also heard about the activities of the GRU, the intelligence department of the Red Army's General Staff, in gathering military-industrial information. Yan Karlovich Berzin, GRU leader from 1924 to 1935, wanted his agents in the United States to concentrate on gathering "confidential information about the various technical improvements made in the American Army and Navy," the committee members were informed. One GRU agent, Filin, came to the United States to work through Amtorg under the cover of being a purchaser of medicinal herbs.[37]

Gregory Bessedowsky, another Amtorg veteran, augmented these espionage allegations by describing his own efforts in shaping public opinion. Telling Fish and his colleagues that he had ostensibly come to purchase tractors, Bessedowsky reported that he had also taken on the role of an "unofficial Soviet diplomatic agent" in order to press for recognition. Amtorg's "propaganda work," he pointed out, also included plans to "lay the groundwork for a revolution among the 12 million discontented Negroes and farmers of the United States."[38]

Upset by its findings, the Fish Committee recommended that alien Communists should be deported, the Justice Department's powers should be strengthened to more closely scrutinize all Communists, and party members should be prevented from using the mails. Echoing public opinion, however, newspapers responded critically to these suggestions. The *Detroit News* argued that "The Committee's recommendations show symptoms of the sort of mental stampede that should be reined in by . . . long established American ideals," while the *Baltimore Sun* decried "the hysteria and confusion of the Fish red-herring committee's recommendation."[39] Other legislators apparently agreed with the editorials, and the proposals went nowhere. Thus, despite extensive interviews and lengthy documentation, the committee's work had little legislative impact. In any case, the committee's findings could not go far, when the United States lacked relations with Russia that could facilitate such deportations.[40] Not even J. Edgar Hoover was ready at that point to have his agenda expanded into covering "Communistic inner circles," at least not if it placed the Bureau in a bad light. As he wrote Attorney General William D. Mitchell in 1932: "The Department and the Bureau would undoubtedly be subject to charges in the matter of alleged secret and undesirable methods . . . [such as] *Agents Provocateur*."[41]

Soviet observers were even more critical of the Fish findings. They thought it an "absurdity" that the Fish Committee members "are really afraid of Communists." Instead, they believed that its leaders were "reactionaries," many of whom were chiefly motivated by economic concerns, since four out of the five committee representatives were from "agrarian states" whose output competed with Soviet grain. But the committee's most important goal, the Soviet report declared, was to ensure the "creation of a Red Scare atmosphere for the coming fall campaign," designed to mitigate "the interest in Prohibition." Not to be ignored, either, was the pernicious influence of "Russian monarchist activities" on the congressmen.[42]

Counterintelligence Challenges and Limitations in the Early 1930s

Hamilton Fish's extreme response to the threat of Communism, like that of an infamous Wisconsin senator two decades hence, was more bombastic than effective, and also did little to address the real and growing practice of Soviet secret intelligence gathering. One of the earliest agents was Alfred Tilton, or Tilden, an illegal GRU representative. Soviet "illegals" like Tilton operated without benefit of diplomatic cover, using bootlegged passports obtained from purloined birth certificates and other documentation. Tilton and his wife actively spied in the United States from 1927 to 1930; prior to that, they had worked in Paris.[43] One of Tilton's key roles was obtaining false identification papers for Soviet agents, although he performed his share of espionage, including making copies of the plans for the *Royal Oak,* a British warship. Tilton also recruited Nicholas Dozenberg, one-time business manager of the Literature Department of the Workers Party of America, the precursor to the American Communist Party.[44] (Dozenberg himself helped orchestrate a counterfeit scheme that led to the arrest of his associate, Dr. Valentine Gregory Burtan, for trying to pass $100,000 in bogus money in

1932.) Later recalled to Russia to be a military commander, Tilton was rumored to have been killed in the purges.[45]

The Soviets employed other intelligence gleaning schemes in the pre-recognition era. Paul Crouch, a Communist Party member and organizer from 1925 to 1942 who had helped edit the *Daily Worker* with Whittaker Chambers, recalled that he had been instructed in Moscow in early 1928 on ways in which to penetrate the U.S. Army. "Concentration on strategic military objects was first and foremost emphasized by Marshall Tukhachevsky," he reported.[46] The American military, however, was aware of the possibility that it could be infiltrated. When Lt. Ralph Leopold Dunckel of the New York Ordnance District Reserve applied for active duty, his connections with the Amtorg Trading Corporation, where he worked as a machine tool expert, were used as grounds to reject his active role.[47] Other spies were occasionally foiled as well, despite the severely limited investigative activity in this era. In 1931, William Disch, a draftsman who designed fire control instruments for the U.S. Navy at Arma Engineering Company in Brooklyn, was introduced to "Mr. Herb," a man posing as a German spy who wanted to pay up to $2000 for seaborne military technology, including "plans for a 'stable vertical' control apparatus for fixing the aim of a gun on a target regardless of the motion of the ship." Disch told his boss, who promptly contacted the Office of Naval Intelligence (ONI), which allowed Disch to supply "Herb" with obsolete blueprints. When the navy turned over the case to the FBI, its agents soon spotted "Herb" taking documents into Amtorg.[48]

The following year, Amtorg tried to get additional military information using an agent named Fred D. Edgar, who then became a double agent for the FBI. Edgar, who had worked in the diesel engine department of the Packard Motor Company in Detroit, met in 1930 an Amtorg vice president named Markoff. In May 1932, after Edgar had been laid off from Packard, he was contacted by a friend of Markoff and asked for information. This "Mr. Dmitroff" asked him for materials regarding "the lighting of aerodromes [and] shooting and bomb throwing apparatus on aircraft." But as Edgar told the FBI in July 1932, the "most important" item he obtained for the Russians was Budd Manufacturing Company's process of making cold-rolled steel, which would assist in tractor production. Edgar, who received nearly five hundred dollars for answering Dmitroff's questions, had been turned over to the FBI thanks to the intervention of Lester P. Dodd, Budd's attorney.[49]

The Soviets had wanted more than the steel process, however, Edgar told the Bureau. Dmitroff chided him, "Edgar, you have been given small stuff until now—we believe you are trustworthy and are in a position to secure big stuff for us." Dmitroff then sent him to the New London Boat and Engineering Corporation in Connecticut. There, Edgar sought material on antiturbulence devices, as well as on the aforementioned airfield lighting and aircraft bombing equipment.[50] Edgar told the FBI in August 1932 that the Soviets also wanted diesel engine designs from the New London firm, as well as material on "air purifying apparatus, . . . torpedo tubes, [and] electric motors for submarines." While cooperating with the FBI, Edgar sought to get the information so that he could keep in touch with the Russians; he suggested that he provide "obsolete" plans to Dmitroff. Edgar declared he was ready to give up his Soviet contacts, if only he did not believe "he would be given an important assignment by the Russians in the near future which might involve . . . some other important phase of national defense."[51] Certainly, the wish list that his contacts provided showed a close knowledge of the field. Naval Intelligence officials, however, believed that Edgar was interested in staying in touch for "monetary reasons." Dmitroff was, after all, prepared to pay between $15,000 and $20,000 for the submarine-related materials.[52]

Naval Intelligence agents found Edgar's reports of "immediate interest" and expressed surprise that the FBI was "not at this time actively following up this case."[53] The navy itself would investigate Amtorg in the mid-1930s, looking for information on its budget, its employees, even its Christmas list, while also compiling a roster of "people who are friendly to the Soviet Union."[54] Naval Intelligence officials were not alone in detecting a limited response from the FBI. In the fall of 1932, U.S. Army major general Paul C. Paschal detected "less interest than had been expected" from the Justice Department and its Bureau of Investigation "in the activities of subversive groups." He conceded that a "lack of adequate legislation [existed] to curb these activities." Paschal believed the Bureau should do more, and in 1932 found an ally in a War Department colleague, Maj. Gen. Edward L. King, who also bemoaned the Justice Department's "utter lack of interest" and called for the government "to do more than observe [the] activity" of subversive groups.[55] However, as an FBI agent told Military Intelligence in 1932, "[T]he Bureau has no jurisdiction over communistic or radical activities and cannot engage in any inquiry concerning same."[56] FBI agents like Jacob Spolansky regularly observed Communist meetings, owing to the Bureau's interest in subversion, but such observation did not usually lead to action, or to discoveries of espionage.[57]

Gen. Douglas MacArthur, who had led the U.S. Army's crackdown on the

World War I bonus marchers that year, affirmed that the Department of Justice was responsible for investigations of subversives; he was unsure whether the department's inactivity "is due to inadequate legislation or to other reasons."[58] But the army itself was doing little about the issue. Its Signals Intelligence Service had recently abandoned a small-scale effort to crack Russian codes and ciphers.[59] This less-than-vigorous response, like that of the FBI, reflected American public opinion, as had the reaction to the Fish Committee recommendations. As Frank J. Rafalko has noted, the military was "severely handicapped" by "powerful influences which were constantly trying to limit activities along such lines."[60] In the early 1930s, official suspicions about Russian representatives did not translate into policy, as an undeveloped counterintelligence apparatus made effective coordination among government agencies in countering Soviet espionage well-nigh impossible.

However, the Soviet Union faced other obstacles to its acquisition of American technology. New legislation outlawing "dumping" of Russian-made goods in the United States (particularly pulpwood and matches), as well as Moscow's continuing difficulties in obtaining extended credit terms—a situation exacerbated by the Depression—led to a drastic fall in purchases by 1932.[61] The development was an unwelcome one for many American firms, naturally. As Robert Alter, vice president of American Tool Works Company of Cincinnati, noted that November, "At the present time we have not a Russian order on our books, and this winter we will have between 700 and 800 men walking the streets," men who "could have had good jobs" with Russian purchases.[62] In this bleak environment, Amtorg nonetheless attempted assiduously to influence public opinion more favorably toward Russia. Its journals were used "to correct the wrong understanding" and enhance the "image of economic ties between Russia and America."[63] The National Commissariat of Foreign Trade (NKVT) congratulated Amtorg for its actions on this matter, including the purchasing agency's articles in the *Economic Review of the Soviet Union*. But NKVT declared that Amtorg's press department was sometimes not prepared to adequately counter the anti-Soviet campaign in the United States. Its publicists needed to emphasize the link between "the problems of credits and the absence of normal relations between the countries" and make more of an effort to gain a market in America for Soviet goods.[64] Amtorg's Propaganda Bureau should further "passionately express the nonpartisan position" of Amtorg, mobilize activists like Scott Nearing, and approach sympathetic observers like John Dewey and Garrison Villard of *The Nation*.[65] It was considered essential for the agency to effectively counteract the "dumping" charges and to broadcast its ability to buy more goods through the use of an all-out propaganda effort.[66]

Of course, American recognition of the Soviet Union, which would normalize trade relations and enhance credit availability, would assist these efforts. Among other organizations, a Soviet front known as the Friends of the Soviet Union (FSU) worked hard on this issue; in the spring of 1932, the organization was attempting to raise $10,000 and gather one million signatures for the cause.[67] In light of threatening developments such as Japan's recent establishment of the puppet state of Manchukuo on the Soviet border, FSU leaders like N. H. Tallentire argued that emphasizing the danger of war in the Far East was a key element in gaining recognition for Russia.[68]

Expanding Sales and Espionage Opportunities after Recognition

Concerns about the expansion of Japan's influence in Asia did assist in ultimately bringing about diplomatic relations. As Edward M. Bennett has noted, FDR believed that ties with Russia would serve to promote peace in the region, fostering "American-Soviet cooperation against Japanese aggression."[69] Roosevelt also hoped for increased trade, since recognition would regularize commercial ties and permit a formal trade agreement between the two countries. Ironically, although trade began to rise as early as the last quarter of 1933, buoyed by greater credit accessibility, it did not approach the heights it had reached *before* recognition.[70] In 1934, the two countries signed a commercial treaty, with the Soviet Union pledging to purchase $30 to $40 million annually, an amount that it would generally exceed. The United States bought significantly less from Russia; even its record 1937 purchases, which included 400,000 tons of coal, reached only $27 million.[71] Enhanced commercial ties were hindered by the Johnson Debt Default Act, which prevented U.S. loans to Russia and placed new tariffs on Soviet anthracite coal.[72]

The Soviet Union, which required advanced technology to continue its great industrial expansion of the mid-1930s, benefited from the new access to American industry. By 1935, the Soviet Union was first in the world in tractor production, and second in total industrial output.[73] Stalin was especially proud to note in December 1934 that despite an untrained workforce, the Soviet Union had effected in less than four years what had taken Europe "decades."[74] The success, as the Socialist writer Anna Louise Strong conceded, had initially come from duplicating American methods—such as the Communar farm combine, "copied from the Caterpillar" model—but Russian output had quickly surpassed the American pattern, she declared.[75]

Diplomatic recognition thus assisted the goals of the Soviet Five-Year Plans by enhancing access to American machinery and technological expertise. In the process, this new relationship also brought a less welcome development in the United States—an expanded industrial espionage campaign. With diplomatic ties, of course, came embassies and consulates to harbor intelligence agents. For Boris Bazarov, the newly arrived station chief for the NKVD, or Internal Affairs Commissariat, the acquisition of military and technological data was a key goal in 1934.[76] Along with men like Bazarov in diplomatic posts, additional illegal agents arrived, often under the cover of business, using false passports and other documents to link up with agents in American industry.[77] Engineers were a particularly desirable target, as one informant who later defected to the FBI confirmed.[78] The Soviet Union was in a hurry to industrialize. "We want things that work," chemist and spy Harry Gold was told by his Soviet handler in the mid-1930s, so Gold obligingly stole formulae for tried-and-true manufacturing processes, including those for varnishes and lacquers, from his employer, the Pennsylvania Sugar Company, and furnished them to Amtorg.[79] As former KGB agent Vasili Mitrokhin confirms, Western technological material "was welcomed with open and unsuspicious arms by Soviet scientists." Political material, on the other hand, "was always likely to be ignored or regarded with suspicion when it disagreed with Stalin's conspiracy theories."[80]

Robert A. Kilmarx has noted that espionage was not always necessary in order to obtain American industrial technology, since "liberal United States export and security laws" allowed foreign sales anytime from six months to a year after production for the U.S. government began. And if the government were not involved in the design of a plane, for instance, sales were practically unlimited. The Soviet practice of placing inspectors in factories for long tours, where they often gathered information beyond that supplied by their vendors, also allowed Moscow's agents "to learn much about modern factory processes and technical developments" in the United States.[81] The U.S. Army noticed how much duplication was going on in Russia: "Foreign models of tanks are being copied freely, particularly fast types such as the U.S. Christie. Numerous British tanks are also used as models. . . . No original types of note have been reported."[82]

The practice of "copying" was not new and had been the expressed goal of Soviet suppliers on many previous occasions: for example, the American

Curtiss Aeroplane Company had been assisting Russia with naval aircraft technology since before World War I.[83] In the 1920s, the Soviets had garnered a good deal of information under the auspices of its secret agreements with Berlin when Germany was forbidden to build up its defenses. Both countries' militaries set up an entity called "The Company for the Encouragement of Commercial Enterprises" at the Rapallo Conference in July 1922, in clear violation of the Treaty of Versailles. This agreement facilitated Soviet bomber manufacturing and German pilot training; these airmen secretly practiced at Lipetsk, south of Moscow, from 1925 until 1933. Further, this agreement committed both countries to joint research on poison gas and artillery, as well as to the manufacture of German tanks and aircraft in Russia. One contract with Junkers, the aircraft manufacturer, provided for three hundred airplanes to be constructed in Russia, two-thirds of which were for Germany; the Soviets would benefit by acquiring new methods for constructing airplanes and their engines. Such arrangements also facilitated espionage; in 1928, Berlin police arrested an engineer from the German Experimental Institute for Aviation who "ha[d] sold quite a number of important scientific papers to a foreign power," identified as the Soviet government.[84]

In the 1930s, a key acquisition for Soviet aircraft was the American Wright-Cyclone engine, which at 630 horsepower offered 50 percent more capacity than existing Soviet designs. With the help of this engine, Soviet aircraft designer Nikolai Nikolayevich Polikarpov introduced in 1933 one of the most successful Soviet fighters, the I-16 Pursuit plane, with a top speed of 276.5 miles per hour, fifty mph faster than the leading American fighter, the Boeing P-26A (which may have inspired the Soviet plane). So great was Polikarpov's success that he was released from prison, where he had been sent in 1930 for sabotage owing to the crashes of his earlier designs, with orders to create a successful plane. The Soviets entered into an agreement with Wright Aeronautical to produce the engine, known as the Wright-Cyclone SGR-1820–F-2, or the M-25 in Russia. The Red Air Force was satisfied that "Polikarpov had provided the country with the best performing fighter in the world."[85] Soviet output continued to depend in many cases upon foreign designs in the late 1930s, and American "scientific, technical, and economic aid" was especially important.[86] In 1937, U.S. assistant military attaché Martin F. Scanlon visited a 30,000-employee plant that built Wright-Cyclone engines and observation planes and pronounced that "the factory is being set up according to the best American practice."[87]

Despite Scanlon's glowing praise of Soviet industrial infrastructure, the quality of Russian workmanship was a matter of dispute. The War Depart-ment described Russian workers as "usually heavy handed, slow witted and totally unable to appreciate the necessity for precision and rigid adherence to established standards." Productivity was estimated at perhaps one-third of the American rate.[88] Nevertheless, output increased from 860 aircraft annually in 1930 to 3,578 in 1937, contributing to a contemporary fetish with air stunts and record-breaking feats (Soviet daredevil flyers were called "Stalin's Falcons"). American officials, meanwhile, deemed the Soviet Air Force's strength to be the equal of Germany and Japan put together.[89]

Many other Soviet industries in addition to that of aircraft manufactur-ing benefited from American technology. Delegations from the Soviet auto and tractor industry, the Moscow subway trust, the rubber and asbestos industry, the all-union weak current trust, and the all-union nitrogen trust visited U.S. plants in 1933. The following year Amtorg commented favor-ably on the "increase in the number of commissions of Soviet engineers and executives arriving in this country for the purpose of studying conditions."[90] By 1936, consumer industries such as film, food, and food machinery had also joined the fray.[91] Extended Russian tours took place at manufacturers such as Wright Aeronautical, Pioneer Instrument, and RCA Camden, and shorter visits took place at firms including General Electric, Bell Telephone, Bausch and Lomb, Newport News Shipbuilding and Dry Dock Company, Bendix Products Company, and Pratt and Whitney. For one visit to Bell Tele-phone and Western Electric in 1936, for example, the Soviet inspecting team included men from the Division of Wire Communications; the Bureau of Mechanization; and the Division of Large Automatic Telephone Stations. Along with the plant visits, Soviet visitors also stopped at numerous mili-tary installations and training facilities.[92] These included the Quartermaster Corps Subsistence School in Chicago, the Command and General Staff School at Fort Leavenworth, Kansas, and the Coast Artillery School at Fort Monroe, Virginia.[93]

Soviet visitors did not always find inspections to be rewarding. In 1938, M. A. Zhuravlev traveled to Rockford, Illinois, to inspect orders for machine tools. There, he complained, the Barnes Drill Company greatly disappointed him: he had to reject his ordered tools "several times," requiring the interven-tion of the firm's president to answer "technical questions." Worse, Barnes's management "trie[d] to hide the defects from our inspectors." Zhuralev pro-nounced to his superiors: "[Y]ou must be firm. And you must prove that you know all the details and all the technical questions of this equipment."[94]

Despite their "firmness," Soviet visitors did not obtain everything they wanted, since American safeguards, such as they were, in many instances kept the inspectors away from experimental work or areas of the factory that were considered nonessential to an order under inspection. These restrictions reflected U.S. officials' growing awareness of espionage as the pace of Soviet plant inspections expanded and global tensions increased. The director of Naval Intelligence told his opposite number at the War Department, "I know that there is a great deal of espionage going on in the U.S., particularly in obtaining secret information concerning our aircraft, and I do think it is time that both the Army and the Navy exerted themselves more to neutralize this condition."[95] Thus in 1936, Amtorg representatives were welcomed at the Aviation Manufacturing Corporation's Lycoming Division in Williamsport, Pennsylvania, where they had propellers on order, but only so long as "the necessary precautions [were] taken not to reveal any information on the 0–1230 experimental engine." As "foreigners," the Soviet visitors were to be kept away from government work.[96] Sometimes, company representatives were surprised that Soviet inspectors knew as much as they did. C. I. Larsen, the president of the Marvel Carburetor Company, noted that while fuel injection technology was still new, it was no secret to E. I. Petrovsky of the United Aircraft Industries of the USSR.[97]

In March 1936, Soviet military attaché Gen. V. A. Burzin, despite being recommended by the War Department's foreign liaison officer as a "very delightful chap," was refused permission to send forty-five civilian mechanics to the Douglas Airplane Factory for training because the plant was to be placed "on the restricted list in the near future."[98] The following month, authorities also turned down his request to visit Rock Island Arsenal and Aberdeen Proving Ground—the latter of which would soon be penetrated by a different Soviet agent.[99] Similarly, in 1937, when military attaché Vladimir Begunov wanted to inspect rubber track used on caterpillar tanks at Meade Army Base, the War Department insisted that Begunov not see any "highly experimental" track.[100] Later that year, the military attaché wanted to visit the Curtiss Aeroplane and Motor Company in Buffalo, but was refused as two restricted projects were under way at the facility: the two-engine attack airplane (A-18) and the new Curtiss P-36 pursuit airplane. Begunov protested that he only wanted to see the stamping shop.[101]

As these precautions indicate, American authorities did not ignore the potential of espionage by Soviet agents before World War II. FBI agents noted the numbers of Russians arriving for visits to firms, especially where the work had "military significance." They monitored Amtorg's funds and its employees' contributions to the Communist Party, as well as the movements of its agents throughout the country. They scrutinized its officials and their political activities, including attempts to spur American recognition of Russia. They even studied the schools where Amtorg children were educated and taught "Communistic principals [sic]." But before the late 1930s, little was done other than collecting information. The Bureau's response to an inquiry from J. P. Stevens and Company regarding Amtorg's possible use of proceeds from the sale of Russian goods for propaganda was revealing: "[T]here is no federal law . . . covering communistic activities and no investigation has been conducted by this Bureau." Indeed, the reply noted, "the Bureau's files fail to reflect any information on this subject."[102] That was hard to believe; the FBI, after all, had been watching the agency for some time. Yet until 1939, when international developments led the White House to grant the FBI more extensive counterintelligence powers, the Bureau's response, like that of other investigative agencies, was to do little with its data.

The outcome of the Switz case reflected just "how little prepared were American counterespionage and the American public for the task of exposing spies," as David J. Dallin has noted. In 1934, two Americans living in France, Robert Gordon Switz and his wife, Marjorie Tilley Switz, divulged that they had photographed secret material for Russia. The Switzes had approached U.S. Army corporal Robert Osman, stationed in Panama, and paid him $400 for providing them with a copy of a secret "White Plan" that outlined army procedures in the event of domestic disturbance or revolution. Though Osman was quickly arrested and discharged from the service, he was soon acquitted of the charges on appeal.[103]

Suspicions of Soviet action were allayed, too, by the rhetoric from Moscow in the Popular Front–era of 1934–39. As Nazism grew ever more threatening, the Kremlin's message to the Western democracies changed from revolutionary antagonism to mutual assistance. At a luncheon with the American-Russian Chamber of Commerce in 1936—when Stalin's purges were reaching their peak—Amtorg chairman Ivan V. Boyeff declared that "The mood [in the USSR] is confident, cheerful and happy. There is a unanimity of mood which does not exist in other countries . . . the attitude toward the government and the Soviet system may best be gauged by the recent decision of the government establishing in the Soviet Union the equal, direct and secret ballot."[104] In 1938, Soviet ambassador to the United States Alexander Troyanovsky also addressed the chamber. "Our democracy is different from other democracies," he told assembled businessmen with a straight face. "But we prefer any democracy to fascism. And we tender our hands for collaboration and solidarity to all peace-loving countries . . . for maintaining peace and for the defense of democracy."[105]

The American-Russian Chamber of Commerce was perfectly content to swallow such tales about Soviet "democracy" in the hopes of boosting commerce. Reeve Schley, head of the chamber, triumphantly noted an increase of Soviet-American trade from $14 million in 1934 to $42 million the following year, with 900 firms filling orders, 69 of which were for contracts worth $100,000 or more.[106] Many American companies were similarly cheery about their business in the Soviet Union. In 1935, United Engineering and Foundry Company signed a $3.5 million agreement with Amtorg for construction of rolling mill equipment and sheet steel for auto bodies. The contract included the installation of equipment and workshops, the sending of nearly ninety employees to the United States for study and training, and the provision of company specialists to the USSR.[107] International General Electric vice president H. H. Dewey, who had signed a $25 million, five-year contract with the Soviets in 1929, declared that Stalin's commissars "are much less radical than they sound."[108] Such views—and the presence of other major firms on Soviet soil—helped bring around former skeptics, like Lammot Du Pont, whose family's firm sold ammonia oxidation technology and other chemical processes to the Soviet Union in the 1930s.[109]

RCA had signed its first contract with the all-union weak current trust in 1929 to assist in setting up broadcasting stations and producing radio, telephone, and telegraph apparatus.[110] Six years later, its executives initialed a $2.9 million agreement that would "comprise the entire field of manufacturing and experimental activities of the RCA and its subsidiaries, including radio and television systems and equipment, all types of tubes used in radio and television . . . all types of radio receivers, phonograph records and equipment, facsimile transmitting and receiving equipment . . . [and] motion picture systems." It would also include an exchange of Soviet engineers and RCA experts.[111] American equipment manufacturers were indeed eager for Soviet business, as a 1938 appeal from the American Radiator and Standard Sanitary Corporation shows. The company urged the People's Commissariat of Heavy Industry "to give serious consideration to our . . . numerous proposals for technical assistance in the field of heating, ventilation [and] air conditioning."[112]

Meanwhile, Soviet leaders continued to press Americans to buy more

Soviet goods. David A. Rosov of Amtorg called such orders the "best guarantee for Soviet imports from the United States." Rosov's demand for American purchases of Soviet goods as a quid pro quo for reciprocal orders was not universally accepted by his colleagues, however. As one internal report pragmatically pointed out, "[T]he threat that the Soviet Union must limit its orders would not be taken seriously because the Soviet Union shows increased military and political interest in American machines."[113]

Despite the important role that Soviet purchasing contracts played in obtaining American technology, both in legitimate and clandestine fashion, they were hardly the only means by which Moscow sought to propel its long underdeveloped industrial infrastructure into the modern age. In the 1930s, close connections forged between Soviet security agencies like the GRU and the OGPU/NKVD with the international Communist movement, or Comintern, led to greater efficiency and an expanded espionage effort. The Comintern's Department of International Relations (OMS) was an important source of agents, because "[F]oreign Communists . . . were more likely to respond to an appeal for help from the Communist International than to a direct approach from Soviet intelligence," as Christopher Andrew and Oleg Gordievsky point out. Richard Sorge, whose reports from Japan alerted an incredulous Josef Stalin to the German invasion in 1941, was one such OMS affiliate who had been recruited into the GRU.[114]

When the NKVD succeeded the OGPU in 1934, Stalin ordered it to take on military intelligence gathering under a foreign espionage section. The GRU had generated complaints from Communists abroad about the way it conducted such espionage.[115] However, the GRU hardly stopped collecting military information; in fact, it dominated Soviet espionage throughout the 1930s, drawing on the assistance of the OGPU/NKVD and the Comintern. Thus, although the OGPU/NKVD primarily gathered political intelligence and the GRU military intelligence, the two agencies' espionage work overlapped, as Bazarov's directive indicates.

The Career of an Early Industrial Spy: From Foggy Bottom to Aberdeen

Maryland pumpkin farmer Whittaker Chambers believed that the 1930s were the heyday of Soviet espionage: "To this period belongs the recruiting of the best Soviet sources. . . . The secret service rode along for almost a decade simply exploiting, and seldom seeking to amplify, this corps of sources until death, casualty and incompetence wore them away." One example was "Source 302," a staff officer in Washington who "gave the Russians practically everything on Christie tanks." Source 302 died prematurely in the spring of 1933, perhaps killed by the very payments he received from Russia: two suitcases of cognac, smuggled in by Communist sailors "every weekend during Prohibition," which the man consumed as his documents were being photographed.[116]

Chambers, then a Communist Party activist and *New Masses* editor, was a highly active source himself. He recalled that in 1932, Max Bedacht, liaison between the CPUSA and the OGPU, had recruited him to drop his open party connection in order to work secretly. He was soon introduced to GRU agent Aleksandr Ulanovsky, or Ulrich, and began providing him military and industrial intelligence.[117] He was paid from $25 per week up to $175 per month, along with expense money for train fare, rent, telephone use, and entertainment.[118] Chambers, who continued to meet with both Bedacht on party business and Ulanovsky on espionage, averred that he sometimes passed messages between the two men. Bedacht, however, would later deny meeting Chambers on a regular basis, as well as having any connections with the underground.[119] Indeed, Bedacht declared that the CP never had any thing to do with the underground as described by Chambers; if it had, he would have known about it.[120]

After Ulrich left America, telling Chambers that "the apparatus was going to disband" in late 1933 or 1934, "Bill" became Chambers's contact. An NKVD agent, Bill directed Chambers's attempts to recruit Britain-bound seamen to act as couriers. Both Chambers and Robert Gordon Switz used such seamen, and Switz noted that when the sailors complained the materials were "too bulky," he shrank the film to fit inside the back of a hand mirror. Bill also wanted Chambers to go to England to join another "Soviet apparatus"; Chambers planned to open a literary agency there as a cover. He never did go to Britain, though he obtained a false passport that he still held in 1951.[121]

Chambers is of course best known for his filching of State Department documents supplied by Alger Hiss, but when he first worked for Ulrich and the GRU he dabbled in military espionage, infiltrating installations like Picatinny Arsenal in New Jersey and the Electric Boat Company in Connecticut. At Picattiny Arsenal, he had a contact who furnished him with a clerk-typist, Muriel Smith Anderson, who traveled to New York on four occasions to type material on explosives. Isador Miller, a chemist associated with explosives at the arsenal, confirmed to the FBI that this record gathering was actually done at the behest of Dr. Philip Rosenbliett, a New York dentist and longtime Soviet agent, although Miller denied any knowledge that it was for the Soviets. Chambers disputed Miller's assertion, and averred that Miller was aware of "the plan"—to get material out of Picatinny by using the excuse that Chambers was writing a book.[122]

By 1934, Chambers was carrying out political espionage at the Agricultural Adjustment Agency and the Treasury and reporting to the head of the Comintern's American underground, J. Peters. His contacts included Julian Wadleigh at the Department of Agriculture, Ward Pigman at the Bureau of Standards, Alger Hiss, then a liaison to the Senate's Nye Committee, and Harry Dexter White at the Treasury Department. Chambers copied his documents at an apartment on Gay Street in New York.[123]

In 1936, Bill disappeared and Chambers was turned back to the GRU and agent Boris Bykov, known as Peter. Bykov was much more important than the two men who preceded him as Chambers's contacts; he was the head of Soviet military intelligence in the United States, according to Walter Krivitsky, who had worked with him in Italy.[124] Amid an increasingly threatening world situation, Bykov was more interested in what the United States knew of Far Eastern and German developments than in domestic agricultural measures, and infiltrating the State Department became a key objective. As a result of his newly expanded list of contacts, Chambers would claim to know "75 underground Communists" in the government, including Hiss, now an assistant to Assistant Secretary of State Francis Sayre.[125] Before his 1938 defection, Chambers too secured a position in the government with the aid of George Silverman, chief economist at the Railroad Retirement Board, who would himself furnish Pentagon materials to the Soviets in World War II. Chambers took a "boon-doggling job in the research department of the Railroad Retirement Board," earning $2000 a year.[126] He gave Silverman, White, and Hiss $200 Bokara rugs in January 1937 for their services to Russia.[127]

In 1937, Chambers returned to military espionage, making contact with a slender, hard-drinking mathematician named Franklin Victor Reno at the Aberdeen Proving Ground near Baltimore, Maryland. Reno was an expert in ballistics at the base. Over the course of four or five meetings, the "very nervous" Reno turned over "restricted or confidential information" on aircraft bombsights.[128] In 1948, when he was named by Chambers to the FBI,

One of the Soviet Union's most faithful industrial espionage agents, Harry Gold, never joined the organization. Among the justifications that Gold later offered Congress for having helped Russia was his "genuine sympathy" for the Soviet people. Moreover, he added, "I was cocksure. . . . [I]t seemed to me that I had the perfect right to take this authority into my hands." Gold recalled that he had "qualms," but at the time still considered himself a solid American, who did no harm to his country while helping another.[139]

Gold had grown up in a home that subscribed to the Socialist-leaning *Jewish Daily Forward* and whose inhabitants viewed leftists Eugene Debs and Norman Thomas as heroes. After he graduated from high school in 1928, he went to work at the Pennsylvania Sugar Company. Two years later, he enrolled at the University of Pennsylvania, but with his funds soon exhausted, he returned to the sugar company in April 1932 to work as an

Harry Gold

assistant chemist in the production of carbon dioxide gas. He was laid off eight months later. Desperate for a job, he leaped at the chance to work at a soap factory in Jersey City, Holbrook Manufacturing Co., when an acquaintance told him that a chemist named Thomas Black was leaving his post there. Gold and Black immediately clicked; the first night they met, they spoke until 6 A.M., mostly about Black's Communist politics.[140]

Though Gold was a keen Socialist and sympathetic to the cause of the Soviet Union, he resisted the blandishments of Black to join the Communist Party, whose members he did not hold in high regard. He despised the party meetings he attended with Black for their length, lack of direction, and for the boorishness of their members, "a shabby and shoddy lot, run through with informers and opportunists." In September 1933, Gold was able to return to Pennsylvania Sugar with the promise of setting up his own lab, relieved to be "freed of Tom's importunings to join the Communist party." He enrolled at Drexel Institute of Technology for a course in chemical engineering and received a diploma in 1936. Perhaps nothing further would have happened, except that Black continued to visit him regularly on trips to Philadelphia. By mid-1934, however, Black had stopped trumpeting the virtues of the party.[141]

Gold was unaware that Black, like Whittaker Chambers before him, had been instructed by the NKVD to drop his party affiliation and concentrate on industrial espionage. As a result, Black began pestering Gold to assist the Soviets in their attempts to obtain industrial formulae, beginning in April 1934. Black, who worked at the National Oil Products Company, wanted a job in the Soviet Union; however, he had been rebuffed by Gaik Ovakimian, the NKVD *rezident* who had recruited him, and instructed to demonstrate his abilities in gathering technical information first.[142]

Black told Gold that Amtorg wanted material such as paper fillers, vitamin D concentrates, and sulfonated oils, all useful in the making of textiles, food, soap, and other consumer goods. In addition, industrial materials were needed, and Gold could play an important role: his company made industrial solvents for varnishes and lacquers, such as butyl acetate and butylethyloxylate. Gold stalled at first, feeling guilty for betraying his boss, Dr. Gustav T. Reich. Nevertheless, he eventually agreed and took material not only from the Pennsylvania Sugar Company, but its subsidiaries, including the Franco-American Chemical Works and the Pennsylvania Alcohol Company.[143]

Gold recalled several reasons for wanting to help the Soviets, despite his distaste for party meetings. First, he remained grateful for Black's intervention on his behalf in 1932, providing him with a job that kept his family off the dole. Gold also supported the idea of helping the Soviet Union. As a Jew, he believed with Black's encouragement that Russia represented a ray of hope for his co-religionists. As he told Congress, it was "the only country in the world where anti-Semitism is a crime against the state."[144] In the United States, meanwhile, it was celebrated by popular radio journalists. This was a keen motivation for Gold, who as a child had found trips from his home on the 2500 block of South Phillip Street in South Philadelphia a traumatic ordeal, since he was forced to run a gauntlet of neighborhood youth who set out to beat him up. In winter, the children at Mt. Carmel Parochial School regularly pelted him with snow-covered rocks when he passed on his two mile walk to the library. And like all his Jewish neighbors, he was vulnerable to the Neckers, who lived in mosquito-infested squalor near his tidy neighborhood and who often came to trash the place. He knew that his father, too, was tormented at his job at the Victor Talking Machine Company, where first Italian coworkers and then Irish bosses singled him out for abuse.[145]

Gold's reports were well received in the Soviet Union, Black informed him: "They are very happy with them. They've got them in operation." But espionage in those early days was laborious. Some of the documentation was fifty to sixty pages long, and the dutiful Gold hand-copied most of it, meeting with Black every few months. The process was greatly expedited when Amtorg offered to duplicate the materials overnight.[146] The offer came in the fall of 1935 as Gold met the first of his approximately eight Russian contacts, Paul Smith (or Peterson). Among the material Gold supplied Paul for bulk copying in their dozen or more meetings were instructions on the manufacture of phosphoric acid, ethyl chloride, and synthetic butanol alcohol, a lacquer solvent with military applications. After Black introduced them, Paul told Gold never to see Black again, an order that Gold would ignore.[147]

Gold told himself he was "helping a Nation whose final aims I approved, along the road to industrial strength." Yet he worried about the potential disgrace to his family. As he became more deeply involved, he took such strains of doubt and "shoved [them] away as far back in my mind as I could." He would continue to believe the Soviets "were entitled to" the materials he provided them, especially those on the bomb during World War II.[148]

Although Gold realized that these manufacturing processes "saved the Russians time and money," he wondered why Smith's superiors didn't just buy them. Smith told him that firms set prices high out of animosity to Russia, flatly refused to deal with the Soviet purchasing agents at all, or, perhaps even worse, sent items that were misidentified, "with the deliberate intent of sabotage." Smith pronounced how much better it was to deal with Gold. "You are a chemist and a chemical engineer. . . . You tell us exactly; give us the complete details of the process as it is worked in the United States."[149] Of course, many companies were eager to sell their processes to Russia.[150] Through espionage, however, the Soviets gained far more information than they could have otherwise—some processes simply were not available for purchase.

Gold was struck by the Soviets' disinterest in experimental technology, what he termed their "lack of adventurous spirit." His contacts told him that this was not because Russia was uninterested in innovation—far from it, they were working night and day on experimental research, he was assured. Instead, what they wanted from the United States was technology that was already proving itself: profitable, productive processes, not experimental, theoretical designs.[151] Clearly, the goals of the Five Year Plans were best met with basic information that could be quickly integrated into the existing Soviet industrial structure.

In September 1936, Gold began reporting to a new contact, introduced as Steve Schwartz, whom he provided with Pennsylvania Sugar's process for making an anesthetic, as well as a formula that he was working on in Reich's lab to recover carbon dioxide from flue gases. He soon began to run out of material at Pennsylvania Sugar, however: "[W]e had looted them pretty completely." With few new materials coming, a more aggressive agent was assigned to Gold in October 1937, an Amtorg employee named Fred.[152]

Considering the difficulties Gold had with the hard-driving Fred and with his own sources over the next two and a half years, it is a wonder that he stuck with the Soviets at all. That he did says much about Gold's loyalty, a devotion that would greatly benefit Moscow's scientific research. Fred repeatedly urged Gold to find more productive employment, suggesting either Baldwin Locomotive Works or the Philadelphia Navy Yard, where "military material" would be available. But then another priority emerged and Gold was ordered to spy on Trotskyists in the Philadelphia area, including a music teacher and a pharmacist. Gold looked up Tom Black again and found him similarly engaged, having dropped industrial espionage and now insinuating himself with Trotsky's followers. Both men could discern what was brewing, and Gold said later that it made him "sick." He much preferred stealing formulae to assisting in pre-execution planning. He lamented, "We started off in a very innocuous fashion. What, after all are chemical solvents? . . . But then, step by step, they advanced the tempo." Black wrung his hands as well, Gold recalled. Indeed, "[He] despised our spying activities—he claimed that we were really not cut out for it by temperament, and that we were both happiest when left alone to work in a laboratory." Despite these issues, Gold would not stray. As his Soviet superiors recognized, his identity had become bound up in his role as Moscow's loyal servant. As he noted, "they did a superb psychological job on me." Gold's double life had its frustrations, nonetheless. In 1938, at NKVD urging, he left Pennsylvania Sugar and moved to Cincinnati to get a degree at Xavier University. His handlers thought further education would help in his work, and he could also mine the new city for more productive sources for Fred. Gold thus attempted to develop Ben Smilg, or "Lever," an engineer in Dayton whom the Soviet Union had paid to attend MIT in the early 1930s. Smilg was now to return the favor by providing information from Wright Field, but despite Gold's shoving receipts at Smilg that confirmed his past debts to the Soviets, the engineer proved singularly unhelpful.[153]

Gold coped as best he could with such setbacks. In the late 1930s, frustrated by the closemouthed Smilg and in an effort to appease Fred, he invented false recruits that he was supposedly cultivating. Fortunately, the situation changed in April 1940, when he met "Sam," or Semyon Semyonov, Fred's replacement, "the most American appearing of all the Russians." Semyonov, who came to the United States in 1938, had earned a BS from MIT in chemical engineering in June 1940. He worked first as a purchasing agent for the Soviet agency Machinoimport and then as head of the engineering department of the Soviet Purchasing Commission during World War II, with offices both at the commission and at Amtorg.[154] Semyonov would meet with Gold from July 1940 to February 1944, overseeing the most active phase of his career.

Growing Suspicion of the USSR

Even as Gold and Black burrowed into American factories and handed over numerous manufacturing formulae to their controllers, some secrets were withheld from Russia. One of the best-known examples of military restrictions on Soviet access to American technology was the U.S. Navy's foiling of Moscow's attempt to expand its navy with American components during the late 1930s. Stalin wanted to construct a state-of-the-art battle fleet, a daunting task given the age and obsolescence of Soviet shipbuilding facilities, and in November 1936 the Kremlin announced its plan to buy American parts, including large guns, armor plate, and fire-fighting equipment, to assemble a battleship in Russia. Both Roosevelt and ardent Soviet critic Robert Kelley at the State Department approved these purchases, eager to promote Russian defense in the Far East and to limit Japanese expansion there, an American priority since 1933 that would be underlined by the U.S. Navy's visit to Vladivostok in July 1937.[155] Accordingly, the Soviet government established the Carp Export & Import Corporation in New York to work with the Bethlehem Shipbuilding Corporation on the project. (Sam Carp was Soviet foreign minister Vyacheslav Molotov's brother-in-law.) However, they did not reckon with U.S. naval officials' insistent efforts to sink the deal. Rear Adm. W. R. Furlong, chief of the Bureau of Ordnance, and Rear Adm. Ralston S. Holmes, chief of the Office of Naval Intelligence (ONI), "privately warned shipbuilding firms to reject a contract with Carp because of their aversion to any assistance to a Communist government," notes historian Thomas R. Maddux, thus frightening suppliers that they might get no more U.S. Navy business if they filled the orders. Officers pointed to the Espionage Act of 1917, which forbade the divulging of secret military information and gave the navy effective veto power over the sale of items deemed strategic, while Chief of Naval Operations William D. Leahy reminded the State Department of regulations that prevented the navy from helping private contractors in business with foreign governments. Despite these points of punctilio, ideological opposition to Communism contributed most to the navy's foot-dragging. Admiral Leahy, publicly nodding to Roosevelt's request to expedite the deal, agreed with Furlong and Ralston and privately scoffed at the importance of Russia to U.S. security. He wrote in his diary that the representatives of Carp were "international villain types" and their country a "menace."[156]

In 1938, the Soviets tried one more time. They found an architectural firm, Gibbs and Cox, which designed for them a 60,000-ton ship, 25 percent bigger than any other in existence. Once the design was scaled back to 45,000 tons so as not to violate the London Naval Treaty of 1936, Moscow had every indication that FDR supported its construction. Naval officials again bristled at the project, though, so much that Gibbs and Cox, like Bethlehem, the builder, believed that the navy would "crucify them" and "would see to it that they received no Navy contracts for years to come" if they accepted the order. Thus, despite much high-level lobbying, including meetings between Stalin and U.S. ambassador to Russia Joseph Davies, as well as between

Soviet ambassador Konstantin Umanskii and Treasury secretary Henry Morgenthau Jr., the plans were scuttled.[157] The navy had clearly thwarted the president; anti-Communism had overridden American security concerns, and Roosevelt lacked the will to force the navy, to which he had historic ties, to yield.[158] Soviet lobbyists still hoped for a change in their fortunes as late as 1939, when Scott Ferris, a member of the Democratic National Committee, assured Soviet intermediary J. Z. Dalinda that "I, personally, think the war, insofar as American (*sic*) is concerned, is over for the present, therefore I rather think that congress will withdraw their very vehement attitude against this President selling arms to other nations." He could not have been more mistaken. The fate of any such sale was sealed in 1939 by both the Soviet pact with Germany and the U.S. naval buildup, which in response to an atmosphere of international "emergency" would soon consume the output of the country's shipyards.[159]

Although ideological bias had most strongly motivated the navy's obstruction in this case, military leaders also had another concern, secrecy. In the midst of a threatening global situation, officials at ONI and Military Intelligence had attempted "to insure the exclusion of foreigners from plants where confidential military construction is under way."[160] This provision, however, had hardly prevented Soviet agents from obtaining secret information, as the contributions of Gold and Black demonstrate. And in 1937, assistant U.S. military attaché Martin F. Scanlon visited a Moscow aircraft factory and reported: "I observed a wind tunnel model of a proposed American military airplane with which I am familiar (having been associated in the design of it) in the office of a Russian aviation officer. The general layout of the airplane is so distinctive that it would be practically impossible for anyone to design anything like it without first having seen the original design." Scanlon's hosts were embarrassed, but he was not completely surprised by the model's appearance in the office of a Soviet factory, because he had heard similar stories from other Americans he knew in Moscow. Scanlon pronounced that "the Russian espionage system in America has apparently been very much underrated."[161]

Soon, Congress gained detailed information about Soviet efforts to procure American technology when former Amtorg employee Robert Pitcoff testified about the real objectives of visiting purchasing/inspection delegations: "[T]he Amtorg Trading Corporation used to arrange the[ir] attendance at various American plants in order to study . . . secret trade production." At visits to glass manufacturing plants in New Jersey, for example, "they . . .

obtained more than the owners of those plants were willing to show them." The visiting commission "stayed several days, or maybe weeks . . . in order to study the process of manufacture of glass and in that way were able to obtain whatever secret methods were employed."[162]

In addition to the glass commission were others studying paper, chemicals, engines, and, most important, aircraft production. Asked if the commissions acquired military secrets, Pitcoff answered in the affirmative. Because of the visits to aeronautics plants, he claimed, "they have been able to develop—at least they have advertised it to be so—engines of equal quality to those manufactured by the United States."[163] (Of course, the quality of Russian aircraft, certainly impressive by the end of the 1930s, resulted in part from legitimate U.S. engine sales, as noted above.) Pitcoff further recalled that "There was a special attempt made to establish so-called factory nuclei, and particularly stress was laid upon the war industries," such as chemical manufacturing. He declared flatly, "It has been stated to me on several occasions by members of the commission[s] that they have obtained secrets on various production processes." Pitcoff also alleged that many agents of the secret police were working in the United States under the aegis of Amtorg. Although his memories were not exactly current in 1939, since he had not worked for Amtorg for a half-dozen years, Pitcoff's claims about the scouring powers of the inspecting missions, and the NKVD's use of Amtorg as a cover, have been widely echoed in other sources.[164]

For example, Joseph Minivitch of the Badger and Sons Company of Boston, which initiated business dealings with Amtorg in 1933, told the FBI that the man who headed Amtorg's Chemical Department "was engaged in spying on the chemical industries in the United States." Minivitch, like Pitcoff, believed that "all the representatives of the Amtorg Trading Corporation were obtaining information on American industry, either through a legitimate business channel or, if impossible to do it that way, through other sources." Amtorg was still pursuing Badger's assistance as late as January 1941, when the agency wanted the firm to build a synthetic alcohol plant in Russia and also expressed an interest in obtaining plans for a Houdry process plant. This time, the company "put them off by stating that they were too busy."[165]

Reports like Pitcoff's and Minivitch's led the FBI to conclude that Amtorg engineers' factory inspections were espionage bonanzas: "A great deal of extraneous material is gathered, related and unrelated to the subject of the visit. Blueprints, descriptive data, processes, formulae, shop routings, and sequences of steps in manufacture, output, cost, etc., are gathered by

open request, bribery, or theft; and the whole is sent to Moscow for duplication." Various espionage methods were employed—"one method is to buy
a single sample from each competing company and suggest that the order
will go to the one who is most friendly, i.e., gives most to the commission in
the line of methods, drawings, and trade secrets." Even "threats against Russian relatives" were used.[166] Such reports likely contributed to the FBI's even-
tual decision to launch an espionage investigation of Amtorg.

Effects of Domestic Politics and Culture

For most of the 1930s, American leaders' marked concern about events in
Germany also curtailed the response to Soviet espionage activities. As
Christopher Andrew points out, "With the experience of the First World War
behind him, FDR found the threat from German agents easier to understand" than a similar Soviet threat. John Earl Haynes has noted that groups
like the German-American Bund faced prosecution akin to that experienced
by Communist fellow travelers fifteen years later. Hundreds went to jail for
making speeches antithetical to the U.S. military or for accepting money
from German sources.[167] The FBI, meanwhile, received thousands of reports
of suspected fifth columnists, mostly German. A strong anti-Fascist reaction
developed in the United States, exemplified by such works as Sinclair Lewis's
It Can't Happen Here (1935), a bestseller that offered a frightening look at a
Fascist America. Such a national mood was exacerbated by the activism of
populist demagogues like Governor Huey Long (D-La.) and radio priest
Father Charles Coughlin; the work of the seemingly Nazi-controlled German-American Bund; and, of course, the *Wehrmacht*'s push into Western
Europe in 1940. After the Nazi-Soviet Nonaggression Pact of August 1939,
however, the Communist Party also came under increasing suspicion. As
Martin Dies (D-Tex.) declared with alarm, "The Communist Party's highly
synchronized and highly disciplined organization has been permitted to
entrench itself deeply into our body politic." For many, the potential fifth
column of Fascists and Communists had become an intolerable threat well
before the United States entered World War II.[168]

The U.S. Congress wrestled frequently with these competing domestic
dangers. Lawmakers had shown little interest in pursuing subversion in the
wake of the aforementioned Fish Committee hearings of 1930. But in January 1934, after the rise of Adolf Hitler, Congressman Samuel Dickstein (D-

N.Y.) had successfully pushed with John McCormack (D-Mass.) for the creation of a special committee to look into Nazi activities, the McCormack-Dickstein Committee. Although the committee lasted only one year, Dickstein's constant lobbying for its renewal, assisted by the efforts of Dies, contributed to the formation in 1938 of the more durable House Special Committee on Un-American Activities, which worked assiduously to suppress subversives, mostly of the left-wing variety, well into the 1960s (it became a standing committee in 1945). Dies was its first chairman; Dickstein, ironically, was not even on the committee. He remained closely interested in its doings, though, having recently begun a secret relationship with Soviet intelligence in which he promised to provide its agents with details on the committee's findings about American Fascists for $1,250 per month. Dickstein began public attacks on the committee as early as September 1938 for spending too much of its efforts on the Communist threat.[169]

Few worried about Communists in the mid-1930s, however, when Dickstein's own committee heard union leader William Green, president of the American Federation of Labor, explain that an "underground machine" connected the OGPU and the trading agency Amtorg. According to Green, "Moscow does not issue mere suggestions. Moscow demands obedience." He was quite right, of course, but the congressmen were not terribly moved; Dickstein's committee was then most concerned with domestic Nazis. Green further related how espionage and secret work were emphasized in Moscow's July 15, 1931, "Directions to the CPUSA," as printed in *Pravda*: "[T]he strengthening of the clever police machinery of the bourgeois governments in their fight against the Communist movement requires of th[e] latter also a more complex organization . . . [which] must inevitably be supported by a strong illegal party machinery. Today, the question of an illegal organization must occupy the center of attention of all the Communist parties of the capitalist countries, without exception."[170] The directive reflects the apocalyptic rhetoric of the party's "Third Period" (1928–34), when the Soviet Union, worried about the rise of Nazi Germany and Japanese imperialism and afflicted by war scares, took a hard stance toward the West and derided attempts to align with foreign Socialist parties.[171] Soviet Communists in this era predicted the final collapse of capitalism, as James G. Ryan notes, and at the same time called repeatedly for the construction of dual organizations abroad to parallel existing ones, including revolutionary labor unions like the Trade Union Unity League (TUUL), "capable of seizing power in the coming crisis." As Green warned Congress, Moscow had dispatched "American workmen, organized in secret units . . . [to] wreck and ruin American factory machinery." Green apparently was unaware of the parallel role of industrial espionage in Soviet intelligence operatives' work. He did recognize, though, that "United States government departments are penetrated by the OGPU subterranean organization obtaining . . . confidential information for the benefit of the Soviet regime." This practice, of course, would continue well after the war scares and hard-line rhetoric of the Third Period had ebbed.[172]

Just as Fish had, Green expressed his strong concern that "the Department of Justice has had no authority nor personnel nor funds with which to conduct, investigate, and maintain contact with revolutionary propaganda."[173] Still remembering the public's rejection of the Fish Committee's stringent recommendations, however, the McCormack-Dickstein Committee was more restrained. It concluded in 1935 that international subversive movements were alive and active in the United States, from the CPUSA on the left to William Dudley Pelley's Silver Shirts and Fritz Kuhn's American Nazi Party on the right. But rather than call for deportation of immigrants who were under suspicion, the committee recommended the registration of foreign agents, legislation that would be enacted in 1938.[174]

Like Congress, the executive branch also was affected by the increasingly volatile international environment. In January 1936, the War Department warned that a "definite indication" of espionage in the United States suggested the need for a "counterespionage service among civilians." In August, Roosevelt secretly authorized FBI director J. Edgar Hoover to launch an investigation of subversive groups, including Communist and Fascist organizations—without the oversight of Congress or, initially, even the knowledge of Hoover's superior, Attorney General Homer Cummings. The FBI director, who had already been collecting such intelligence, now had a mandate to expand this role. Among other initiatives, his agents spied upon the presidential campaign of CPUSA leader Browder and established the General Intelligence Section to collate the agency's fattening files of names and organizations, including those of left- and right-wing groups and of innocuous civic associations.[175] For the first time, the Bureau was actively collecting material on "General Activities—Communist Party and Affiliated Organizations."[176] Having been reorganized into the Federal Bureau of Investigation in 1935, the agency also initiated plans for an internal security program "which might be placed in operation in the event of a national emergency." By 1942, its special agent ranks had reached three thousand, quadrupling in less than a decade. As Roy Talbert Jr. suggests, J. Edgar

Hoover's success in fighting criminal elements gave him the power and prestige to dominate internal security by the late thirties, supplanting the traditional military agencies, Military Intelligence and Naval Intelligence, in domestic matters. Still, the Bureau remained largely unaware of Soviet espionage networks in the 1930s.[177]

Instead, a 1938 tip from British military intelligence alerted U.S. authorities to a German espionage ring. This discovery played a pivotal role in raising the FBI's profile, at the same time reversing "a decade and a half of neglect by the key government counterespionage agencies," according to Raymond Batvinis.[178] In the mid-1930s, Dr. Ignatz Griebl, a German-born Nazi sympathizer living in Manhattan, had recruited some of his German patients to spy for the fatherland; they succeeded in garnering blueprints from the Bath Iron Works, the Boston Navy Yard, and the Douglas Aircraft Corporation, among other facilities. Griebl's work was part of a larger ring associated with American-born, Austrian-educated Guenther Gustave Rumrich, a deserter from the U.S. Army who supplied the German leadership with such information as the rate of venereal disease in the American military. Unfortunately, soon after the arrest of Rumrich and his associates, fourteen of the men charged escaped, including Griebl. This botch was only one of the FBI's missteps in the disastrous prosecution of the case, which culminated in the firing of its chief investigator for signing a publicity contract with the press. Despite the bungling, the convictions of four members of the Rumrich ring, as Batvinis notes, prompted the FBI to assume a more vigorous counterespionage role.[179] The State Department, to which these duties then chiefly fell, had been largely useless in this regard. The department not only did little with leads on counterintelligence matters, but, ever conscious of keeping foreign feathers unruffled, tended to rewrite sensitive reports to avoid "awkward repercussions." FBI director J. Edgar Hoover, not surprisingly, saw many flaws with existing practice. To him, the Rumrich case was a signal that the FBI's role should expand beyond its limited domestic frontiers and take on a wide range of counterintelligence tasks. Ambitiously, he called for the FBI to include in its purview Immigration and Naturalization, Customs, plant protection, and even the Federal Communications Commission![180] Although much of Hoover's agenda was too grandiose for Roosevelt to contemplate, the FBI's profile had already increased considerably with its successes in the Lindbergh kidnapping case and several celebrated bank robberies. Now the agency would take on a new role in "counter-espionage activities," and in 1938 it was allotted $150,000 toward this effort.[181]

Meanwhile, Communists were increasingly active in the United States, swelling the party's ranks to 65,000 members in 1937. By then, too, the frosty Third Period had been replaced by the era of the Popular Front, when Earl Browder soft-pedaled his revolutionary rhetoric and even worked behind the scenes for the election of Roosevelt, discouraging votes for himself so that FDR, the Comintern's chosen candidate, would be reelected.[182] The party, encouraged by what its members viewed as Roosevelt's moves away from "isolation and neutrality," interpreted some of his rhetoric "as the expression of a mass movement of the American people striving to free itself from the oppressive domination of finance capital."[183] One sign of the party's influence was that Browder was invited to speak as part of a New York Board of Education program, "The Current Economic Crisis: Its Cause and Cure," on New York radio station WEVD. Predictably, Browder blamed "capitalists" for the crisis.[184]

As Communists worked assiduously to "mainstream" themselves, they also deftly infiltrated labor unions, as Sidney Bloomfield, a CPUSA representative, told Moscow in 1937: "On both Coasts, *guided by a central leadership,* the Party applied under two different circumstances flexible and skillful leadership . . . preventing the West Coast strike from being smashed."[185] Indeed, Los Angeles chief of police James E. Davis had earlier noted the effectiveness of the 1934 San Francisco General Strike and what he saw as the malevolent influence of the Communist-led Trade Union Unity League and the International Labor Defense among California port and agricultural workers.[186] In 1937, Bloomfield could point to the growth of the new CIO unions as an added boon for the party: "[C]ommunists play an influential and growing role" in these organizations, he noted, heading something more than "twenty-five percent of the total membership of the CIO." In the CIO, as in a number of other groups like the League of Peace and Democracy and the American Negro Congress, members tolerated "open" collaboration with Communists. Although the "Red Scare" issue was not absent, it had not affected such organizations in the era of the Popular Front. Instead, noted the party report, "Public officials deal with these organizations quite freely, accepting them more and more as authoritative spokesmen in their fields."[187]

Communists may still have appeared benign in early 1938, at least in Moscow's reading of the situation, but the rise of Nazi activity as well as Dickstein's relentless lobbying contributed to the convening of Martin Dies's Special Committee on Un-American Activities in May, which would soon turn its focus to left-wing threats. Dies, an ambitious young Texas congressman, was convinced, as his biographer notes, that he and his committee would be able to determine accurately the difference between what was an "obviously un-American" belief and what was a more palatable "honest difference of opinion." His search for subversives was no doubt heightened by the newly straitened circumstances of the American economy, with unemployment rising to nearly 20 percent in 1938 from 14.3 percent the previous year.[188]

The committee's work in the late 1930s was driven in part by the rise of the pro-Nazi movement in the United States, which included camps in New Jersey, New York, and Michigan; the FBI also publicized the potential dangers of an Axis fifth column, and the scare approached "hysterical" heights. Still, by the late 1930s the Communist threat had eclipsed the Nazi danger on the committee's agenda; indeed, as Robert Kay McDaniel asserts, "Communism . . . always received by far the majority of [the committee's] attentions." But rather than attempt to grapple with the genuine presence of Soviet agents in government and industry, committee members focused on far more spurious examples of "Communistic" groups.[189]

Thus, one of the first programs identified as a hive of Communists was the Federal Theatre Project (FTP). Dies angrily dismissed its performances of such works as W. H. Auden's *The Dance of Death:* "That and scores of other plays . . . freighted with Moscow's propaganda were what the American people spent millions of dollars to have produced all over the country."[190] The attempts of the FTP manager, Hattie Flanagan, to butter up Dies (she invited him to *Pinocchio* at Christmas in 1938) failed, as did those of ACLU leader Morris Ernst and Secretary of Labor Frances Perkins (her impeachment had instead been suggested by one member of the committee).[191] Dies axed the program.

By the end of 1938, the committee had heard one hundred witnesses, including both Communists and Nazis. Communism dominates this record, in part because some very vociferous anti-Communists, such as Walter S. Steele, publisher of the conservative *National Republic,* made it their regular practice to provide lengthy lists of individuals, organizations, and unions to the assembled congressmen. In 1938, Steele declared that 6.5 million Communists or fellow travelers were in the United States, including 75,000 party members.[192] By contrast, the committee determined that only 500,000 Nazi sympathizers were within American borders. In 1939, moreover, Dies declared that 2,850 Communists held government positions, dwarfing Senator Joseph McCarthy's later assessments.[193]

Owing to budgetary constraints, the hearings were inundated with voluntary witnesses like Steele, despite the fact that Robert Stripling, the committee's staunchly anti-Communist secretary, dubbed him a "professional patriot" of dubious credibility.[194] Left-leaning congressman Vito Marcantonio (D-N.Y.) even called Steele a "Silver Shirt," a charge the *National Republic* editor vigorously denied. No proto-Nazi, he was "straight Indiana, straight America," he declared.[195] Dies himself did not escape the Nazi slur. In 1940, David Mayne, a former agent of William Pelley, accused the congressman of also being linked with the Silver Shirts. He produced letters suggesting that Dies was "not going after fascist groups." But Mayne's evidence was forged, and he was indicted.[196]

The committee's attention to the overblown claims of "professional patriots" like Steele stands in contrast to Dies's negligent treatment of far more compelling information regarding Communist espionage—including the allegations of Whittaker Chambers, which the chairman received from Chambers's friend, the journalist Isaac Don Levine. Dies did little with these, besides announce his discovery of "far-flung Soviet secret police operations in the United States."[197] Perhaps Dies's greater focus upon cultivation of his public record, including frequent speeches and his book, *The Trojan Horse in America*, allowed Chambers's charges to fall through the cracks, as his biographer suggests. His committee launched an investigation of Hollywood that was similarly shallow; but considering the outcome of later HUAC Hollywood investigations, this was perhaps not a bad thing. Dies's hearings into Communism in the entertainment capital lasted half a day in 1940. Bewitched by the atmosphere, he returned that year with his wife and sons to collect photographs signed by Errol Flynn, Johnny Weissmuller, and others.[198]

Dies was clearly no Richard Nixon, the indefatigable unraveler of the Hiss-Chambers story, and the actions of his committee in this regard demonstrate that the U.S. security state was indeed limited in the 1930s. When genuine Soviet spies like Chambers were available, the committee chose to focus instead on the exaggerated claims of Walter Steele. As Walter Goodman writes, Dies was "an impatient fisherman" with a short attention span. He seemed much more interested in "'liberals,' gullible people, or Communist sympathizers" than in unearthing spies.[199]

Dies's focus on "public Communism" was echoed in actions taken at the local level. The Los Angeles Police Department's Red Squad anxiously expressed its concern about Communist demonstrations, which were "creating a great inconvenience upon persons going about their legitimate business." Communists, the squad contended, "are steeped in the tradition of hatred for those who have been successful in life." Worse, this police unit took pains to point out, the "character of remarks indulged in by the Communist agitators is that of vicious vilification and denunciation of the government and its institutions and casts aspersions upon the nation's leaders." Not surprisingly, the squad was attacked for attempting to deny Communist protesters their constitutional rights.[200] Its leaders also worried about the influence of Communists in American labor, and the possibility they might launch another general strike. To stay abreast of this threat, the LAPD made numerous purchases of "radical literature" and closely covered "Communist May Day Acts."[201]

Perhaps because Congress, and the LAPD, spent increasing effort exploring the threat presented by subversive protesters—even as the FBI compiled its swelling file of the party's "general activities"—the overall government response to the Soviet espionage campaign of the 1930s was limited and ineffective. With a few exceptions, until 1939 both executive-branch officials and their congressional counterparts displayed little initiative in understanding or preventing Soviet espionage in American plants. Yet, the period between U.S. recognition of Russia to the Nazi-Soviet Pact witnessed an important expansion in Soviet industrial espionage in the United States, which paralleled the growth in the number of legal and illegal Soviet agents in this country, both Russian and American, as well as the increasing battalions of inspectors visiting plants. Along with authorized sales of technology, Soviet espionage contributed to the industrial goals of the Five-Year Plans in a number of key areas, including chemicals, aircraft, and electronics. The American response to this practice was limited at best, and buffoonish at worst. Genuine spies, like Thomas Black and Harry Gold, were ignored, while long lists of suspected sympathizers were catalogued with infinite care. Lawmakers had many theories about an unverifiable, vast army of activists but seemed to have little knowledge of actual Soviet activities in the United States. Meanwhile, the FBI before 1939 was generally more interested in domestic issues, like kidnappings and bank robberies, than Communists. Although its agenda changed considerably as the worldwide "emergency" developed, the 1930s legacy of limited action would have important ramifications for the counterintelligence establishment's ability to effectively deal with Soviet espionage during World War II, when such spying grew exponentially.

During the next few years, the Dies Committee remained obsessed with suspected subversives in the media and the political arena. The FBI and other counterintelligence agencies, however, increasingly focused on Soviet spies beginning in 1939. One of the first organizations agents examined was Amtorg, which soon became the subject of an espionage investigation. Although inconclusive, that investigation and additional steps taken by the Bureau and other governmental bodies against suspected Communist representatives like Jacob Golos, Earl Browder, and Gaik Ovakimian during the era of the Nazi-Soviet Pact illustrated a shifting approach to the Soviet Union. Never again would the country be as comfortably oblivious to the activities of Russian agents.

CHAPTER TWO

Soviet Agents and the "National Emergency,"
1939–41

Europe's turn to war in August 1939 finally convinced U.S. officials of the need for an effective counterintelligence apparatus. Contributing to their decision were the Nazi-Soviet Nonaggression Pact of the same month and the resulting specter of a "Red Fascist" fifth column; Soviet representatives (and their Communist allies) thus came under increasing scrutiny in the two remaining years before the United States entered World War II. With the country now in a state of "emergency," the FBI received a new mandate from FDR to investigate domestic subversion. On September 6, the president ordered "all police officers, sheriffs, and all other law enforcement officers in the United States to promptly turn over to the nearest representative of the FBI any information obtained by them relating to espionage, counterespionage, sabotage, subversive activities, and violations of the neutrality laws."[1] The Bureau's budget expanded accordingly.

Just a month later, as if to confirm the crackdown, General Secretary of the CPUSA Earl Browder was indicted on passport fraud for using aliases to travel between the Soviet Union and the United States in the early 1930s. His indictment capped an intense law enforcement campaign against Communists who used falsified passports. Among the several people arrested was Jacob Golos.[2] Browder would later serve more than a year in Atlanta Penitentiary until FDR commuted his sentence as a wartime goodwill gesture in 1942; Golos received a fine and a suspended sentence. Although the espionage activity of Golos remained undetected during this era, as did that of veteran spies like Harry Gold, Elizabeth Bentley, and Abraham Brothman, U.S. authorities managed to apprehend longtime Soviet industrial agent Gaik Ovakimian, whose targets included the chemical industry. After war broke out between Germany and Russia, he was allowed to return to the Soviet Union in July 1941.

FBI agents also conducted an espionage investigation of the Amtorg Trading Corporation and its representatives, convinced that "Amtorg is one of the

J. Edgar Hoover in the 1930s

centers in this country from which Russian secret agents operate."[3] The international situation had undoubtedly contributed to heightened concern of
potential Soviet penetration of war industry, one of Amtorg's priorities. Con-
sequently, Soviet agents with no connection to Amtorg also were scrutinized
by the FBI. For example, Alexander Feklisov recalled that he and his colleagues were "closely watched by American counterespionage" after the signing of the Nazi-Soviet Pact until U.S. involvement in World War II. Stationed
at the Soviet consulate in New York beginning in 1941, Feklisov noted that
he was immediately "shadowed" upon his arrival. Once the United States
entered the war, however, he could breathe more easily; competing concerns
and the imperatives of the wartime alliance with Moscow distracted counterintelligence agents from pursuing suspected Soviets.[4] The FBI continued
to mishandle important opportunities for gaining a better understanding of
Soviet espionage in this era, most especially in its reception of such contem-

porary witnesses as Whittaker Chambers and Walter Krivitsky. As for the Dies Committee, its record of often misdirected meddling continued largely unabated. Nevertheless, the counterintelligence community made important transitions in the two years preceding U.S. entry into World War II, laying the groundwork for the more focused investigations that would follow the discovery of Soviet espionage during World War II.

The FBI's Enhanced Powers

The FBI's growing responsibilities in counterintelligence during this tense period built upon the agency's successful prosecution of the Rumrich spy ring in 1938, as discussed earlier. Important, too, were Hoover's own skills in packaging his agency as a bulwark against the threatening winds blowing from abroad. In order to better coordinate counterintelligence efforts against these potential dangers, in the summer of 1939 FDR established the Interdepartmental Intelligence Committee, composed of the FBI, the War Department's Military Intelligence Division (MID), and the U.S. Navy's Office of Naval Intelligence (ONI); he pronounced that "no investigation . . . into matters involving actually or potentially any espionage, counterespionage, or sabotage" could be undertaken except by those three agencies.[5] Hoover trumpeted the Bureau's cooperation with the other intelligence agencies as "a complete pooling of effort."[6] At the same time, his agency effectively gained sole jurisdiction over domestic espionage and sabotage outside the military. As "central coordinating agency," the FBI would brook no rivals. In October 1940, in fact, Hoover sent Roosevelt a four-page letter protesting that Military Intelligence efforts "have gone somewhat afield and have crossed into matters upon which this Bureau has already been conducting investigations." Such a development would only lead to "confusion," "inefficiency," and even "a chaotic condition."[7] FDR strongly supported the FBI's role, and in response to the Dies Committee's concurrent campaign against suspected fifth columnists, the president reemphasized the preeminent role of the executive branch over the legislative branch in fighting subversives. Armed with its mandate from the White House, the FBI was intent "to head the Nation's attack against foreign spies, saboteurs, and subverters," as Hoover told the American Legion in 1939. The director aimed to ensure that the FBI would control all domestic cases of espionage, sabotage, and subversion, thus sharply curtailing the role of MID and ONI.[8]

As early as April 1939 (several months before FDR's expansion of this Bureau's powers), the FBI director took advantage of his growing prestige, asking Congress for a $7 million appropriation for 1940, an almost 20 percent increase over the 1939 budget. He also wanted to expand the number of agents from 587 to 785, pointing out how the agency's responsibilities were rapidly burgeoning, with the FBI already exchanging fingerprints with eighty-three countries. At the same time, espionage cases also were growing, rising to 634 in 1938 from approximately 35 per year previously.[9]

Seven months later, in November 1939, with the world situation dramatically changed, Hoover went to Congress again to ask for an "emergency supplemental appropriation." Intending to impress his audience with news about the Bureau's "General Intelligence Division" in the nation's capital, newly established in September in response to the president's mandate, Hoover noted that the division "has now compiled extensive indices of individuals, groups, and organizations engaged in . . . subversive activities." He wanted another 150 agents, noting that espionage, sabotage, and other complaints had reached 1,651 for the year. He pointed out, too, that the Washington office was running twenty-four hours a day, with special agents working three to five hours of unpaid overtime daily.[10] Perhaps the hardest burden fell upon the fingerprint classifiers, who stood almost nine hours per day straining their eyes through magnifying glasses at tiny prints.[11]

Believing that "a distinct spy menace" plagued the United States, the FBI was on the lookout for potential subversives from Germany, Japan, Russia, France, Italy, and even Bulgaria.[12] The Bureau also began a program that deployed informants in thousands of plants to protect military secrets and avert sabotage. The work began with a priority list of 800 plants that held government contracts; by 1940, the FBI had surveyed 270 of them and planned to review 12,000 more. Hoover declared that his Bureau was "very surprised at the absolute lack of protective measures in many of our great industrial plants . . . [which] have utilized practically no measures against sabotage." At one plant, for instance, plans for a bomber were stolen. By mid-1941, the Bureau's agents had surveyed 1,536 plants.[13]

Hoover sputtered angrily about competition from private "promoters" like the Cleveland Safety Council's Industrial Safety Committee, which was offering its antisabotage and antisubversive services and "attempting to usurp the functions of accredited law enforcement agencies" like the FBI.[14] Hoover told congressional representatives that he intended to "avoid some of the hysteria of the last war" and, in words that would further gladden the hearts of civil liberties advocates, stop a "so-called vigilante surge of well-meaning citizens and patriotic groups with perfectly sincere intentions setting out to apprehend suspects." Still, the politically attuned Hoover was properly grateful for the "excellent cooperation" of the American Legion in his work. [15]

In his annual report to Congress for the fiscal year ending June 30, 1940, Hoover reported that 16,885 national defense matters had required his agents' investigative attention. [16] Later, in accordance with FDR's mandate, he would proudly report that his agency was coordinating its activities with Military and Naval Intelligence officials in weekly conferences. [17] By mid-1940, the FBI had already created a national defense division, which consumed most of the Bureau's budget. [18] To address the national defense issue, the Bureau also had opened new field offices in such cities as Honolulu, Panama, San Diego, and San Juan, making a total of fifty-two offices. [19]

Members of the Subcommittee on Appropriations, which voted on the FBI's budget each year, were only too eager to help the "vital" agency. Congressman Louis Rabaut called it "the most famous bureau. . . . [I]t is a wonderful right arm of the government. . . . Many a person, I imagine, says a prayer at night because of . . . this agency." [20] With such a welcome, Hoover was quick to raise his demands. In February 1941, he asked for 700 new agents, including 500 for national defense. [21] By then, his administrative staff was working twelve hours a day, he reported; Hoover himself was no slouch, keeping his desk warm from 9:00 A.M. until 7:30 P.M., and returning after dinner for another two and a half hours. [22]

The "emergency" had greatly increased his agency's workload, bringing an exhaustive list of new laws for agents to enforce: Public Law 418 of 1938 was designed "to prohibit the making of photographs, sketches, or maps of vital military and naval defense installations and equipment"; the more famous Hatch Act of 1939 "[made] it unlawful for any person employed by the Federal Government or paid from federal funds to be a member of any political party or organization advocating the overthrow of our constitutional form of government in the United States"; and Public Law 443 of 1940 amended the 1917 Espionage Act "to increase penalties for peacetime violations thereof." Was it any wonder that the caseload already exceeded twenty per agent in early 1941? And the work would only increase; that fiscal year included 68,368 national defense matters for the Bureau to address, quadrupling the previous year's total. [23]

To handle this burgeoning backlog, the agency wanted men (and they were always men in those days) in its special agent corps who were law school graduates, "expert accountants," or college graduates with a foreign language fluency "or extensive investigative experience." The one-in-one-thousand applicants chosen by the FBI fell within the ages of twenty-three and thirty-five.[24]

With such high standards, Hoover lashed out at the Civil Service Commission for referring unfit candidates to his agency. The commission had certified people with dementia, missing arms, cardiac enlargement, or (even worse) Communist beliefs, he complained. Moreover, he scoffed, "we have been advised with regard to Communists that unless we could find something other than their communistic beliefs or tendencies, we must accept them."[25] When Congressman Louis L. Ludlow asked if "a good many of those Communists . . . had police records," Hoover admitted that they didn't, although he quickly attempted to connect Communists with illegal activities by noting that "any person who has a criminal record is a fertile tool for any subversive element."[26]

As the numbers of cases and agents expanded in unprecedented fashion, so did the FBI's purview. After Tyler Kent, a disgruntled code clerk at the American embassy in Moscow, was arrested for espionage in the summer of 1940, undercover agent Louis Beck was posted at the embassy to spy on operations there; Beck was one of five secret FBI agents assigned to examine conditions at American diplomatic outposts. He found incredibly lax disposal of secret materials and disturbingly intimate relations between embassy staff and Russian prostitutes. The Kent case itself, by revealing the shoddy methods of the State Department in keeping sensitive materials secret (including communications between FDR and Churchill before the United States entered the war), assisted the FBI's ascension to a leading role in counterintelligence, thus eclipsing Foggy Bottom.[27]

In 1940, another German espionage effort, the Duquesne case, further assisted the department's new role, as Raymond Batvinis has shown. Assisted by defector William G. Sebold, who offered his services to the Bureau as a double agent (significantly, its agents did not find *him*), the FBI spied on an extensive ring led by Frederich Joubert Duquesne that was gathering military-industrial information in the United States and Canada between 1940 and 1941. This time the Bureau did not simply react to the ring, as it had in the earlier Rumrich case, but actually managed it, supplying fake but appetizing information that Sebold sent to his counterparts in Germany. For eighteen months, in an unusually cooperative arrangement with the U.S. Army and U.S. Navy, the Bureau fed information to the Wehrmacht through a radio station the ring had erected earlier on Long Island. The FBI operation also included some as-yet untried methods of counterespionage, including hidden cameras. When the investigation was finally cashed in by the Bureau, thirty-three participants were convicted and German spying was effectively ended in the United States. [28] Hoover made his pride evident when he mentioned the case in his congressional testimony for increased appropriations in 1942; typically, his testimony avoided direct examples of spy cases, but in this instance he provided full coverage, claiming, "It had ramifications throughout the entire world." [29] Soviet espionage would be a much harder nut to crack.

The FBI's new role in fighting espionage not only gave the agency added responsibilities, but also continued what Hoover had been doing since Attorney General Harlan Fiske Stone hired him to head the FBI in 1924. As Athan Theoharis points out, although Stone had attempted to limit the Bureau's work to investigations carried out in a "gentlemanly way" and believed it "despicable . . . to have public funds . . . used for the purpose of shadowing people," Hoover began using informants to spy on radicals from the moment he took over. (As noted previously, however, such observation did not generally lead to action in that era.) FDR's 1939 mandate, though, meant that the Bureau no longer needed a genuine allegation of criminal behavior in order to open a national security case, but was free to open cases if only "for the purpose of keeping a close check upon foreign governments." [30] A crucial development here was the FBI's use of the wiretap, first authorized by the president in May 1940, which allowed the agency to monitor more effectively such possible threats as spies and domestic subversives. [31]

If the international climate had been different, FDR probably would not have authorized wiretaps. As late as 1939, in *Nardone v. the U.S.*, the Supreme Court reversed a lower court's decision in the case of a bootlegger whose conviction was based on wiretapped evidence. The high court instead upheld a 1934 law, the Comprehensive Communications Act, that forbade the use of such evidence. The justices declared that the act applied to "federal officers as well as others." In March 1940, Attorney General Robert Jackson affirmed this stance by barring wiretap use by the FBI. At the time, Hoover dutifully denounced this method of investigation as "thoroughly unethical." However, he privately complained in a letter to Jackson that "the Bureau cannot cope without wiretaps," especially in espionage cases. He got his wish; in May, with the war heating up, FDR authorized the practice, emphasizing that the FBI in particular should use it. [32]

Hoover attempted to paint himself as a moderate on technical surveillance, however. In congressional testimony in 1941, he noted that his agency had avoided it "for many years" even before the *Nardone* decision. Donning once again his civil liberties guise, Hoover declared that Congress's current consideration of broadening the use of wiretapping for felony cases would be a "promiscuous" practice. Only more serious crimes should be subject to wiretaps, he declared, and in these cases, in which each bug would require the attorney general's approval, "civil liberties would be perfectly respected and safeguarded."[33]

Putting Amtorg under the Microscope

While the notorious German espionage cases consumed much of its attention, the FBI revealed its rising concerns about Soviet subversion by quietly opening an espionage investigation on Amtorg, the Soviet trading agency. Amtorg had already felt the squeeze of government scrutiny. In the fall of 1939, as fears grew of Nazi-Soviet cooperation, Roosevelt called for a "moral embargo" against sales of military items to the Soviet Union, including aircraft, engines, bombs, and spare parts that could be used "for attacking civilians."[34] In at least one instance, this embargo forced a shipment of aircraft engines back to port, while the Soviet government complained bitterly that firms like Wright Aeronautical had "banned our engineers from studying in their plants."[35] The aircraft industry was not the only sector affected by the embargo: the People's Commissariat of Fuel also was unable to place orders for oil equipment.[36] A $12 million aviation gasoline project was cancelled by the presidential order, as was a $3.7 million synthetic alcohol plant.[37] One firm told the FBI that owing to the moral embargo, it had actively discouraged Amtorg's patronage, making payment terms more difficult and refusing to assist in the procurement of export licenses.[38] The preparedness climate undoubtedly limited Amtorg's access. The Timken Detroit Axle Company, for example, told the FBI that it had refused a 1940 Amtorg request to visit because its factory "was engaged in too much National Defense work."[39] Nonetheless, hundreds of Amtorg inspectors remained in the United States, and the agency continued to make sizable purchases.[40]

Amtorg had offices in Detroit, Pittsburgh, Los Angeles, San Francisco, and Camden, New Jersey.[41] In April 1941, prompted by Amtorg's actual and attempted visits to numerous war-related plants such as General Electric,

RCA, Westinghouse, and Wright Aeronautical—and by its seemingly insatiable demand for information on everything from American milk output to tunnels—the FBI decided to open a "full, complete and discreet investigation" on the agency, looking into both its "trading and espionage activities."[42] The identities, locations, and objectives of Soviet inspectors were of special interest. The FBI had been informed by its New York office in January 1941 that "employees of the Amtorg Trading Corporation have been active in the theft of industrial plans, blue prints and other data." The thorough espionage investigation uncovered few episodes of successful spying, despite obvious evidence of Amtorg's frequent attempts to gather information. This very persistence, however, helped convince Bureau agents of a "Russian espionage system" in the early phase of World War II.[43]

As noted above, Amtorg had not escaped the FBI's attention before 1941. Indeed, working with Armand Labis Feldman, a Soviet spy who later turned information over to the Bureau, agents had collected the names of Amtorg's American and Russian employees in 1940.[44] A 1939 investigation of the Communist Party had also led the Bureau to Amtorg and speculation that "its extensive business activities would . . . afford a possible cover for financial transactions" benefiting the party. FBI agents learned from one informant that Amtorg employees had contributed to a $5,000 donation to the CPUSA. But the Bureau had decided not to investigate Amtorg in December 1939, even as the Dies Committee planned to do so. Nevertheless, the FBI regularly received reports from informants about the trading agency while pursuing related probes; for example, an informant in a 1940 investigation of the Communist Party supplied the Bureau with a "voluminous" report on Amtorg. This document concerned the agency's business dealings with companies like Buick, Fisher Body, Ex-Cell-O, and Firestone Tire and Rubber; it also focused on a number of Amtorg employees who had visited these plants. Soviet delegations had visited manufacturing facilities since the 1920s, but not until now did their inspections arouse suspicion at the FBI's New York field office, which declared that "the informant . . . has set forth an amazing picture of industrial espionage as it is operated in the United States by the Amtorg Trading Corporation."[45]

The FBI was not the only agency concerned about Soviet visits to American plants in the era of the Nazi-Soviet Pact. Despite the recent signing of a contract between Wright Aeronautical and the Stalin Aircraft Plant, as well as a history of frequent, long-term tours at Wright, in December 1939—the same month as FDR's "moral embargo"—Chief of Naval Operations H. R.

Stark told the inspector of naval aircraft at the firm to inform Wright executives that neither the War Department nor the U.S. Navy could "look with favor" upon the plans of Soviet visitors D. B. Oskolkov and S. A. Ivanov to be "stationed in the company's plant." The navy demanded that Russian representatives "be no longer admitted to the company's factory." The firm was making military planes for the government, not for the Soviets, whose business with the firm was "trivial," Stark explained. The Russian visitors, he charged, were

> chiefly concerned with receiving instruction in the methods employed by Wright in the manufacture, assembly, testing and servicing of certain engines, in order to manufacture these engines in the U.S.S.R., under a license agreement, [yet] no benefit to the U.S. is seen in such an arrangement, as it operates to permit needless opportunity for observation of our production and development of military engines at a time when it is particularly to the best interests of the U.S. government to exercise the utmost vigilance to prevent such observation.

Stark did assure that the Soviets would still be welcomed in the plant for inspections of products they had ordered, as well as for "casual one day visits," especially if they were "anticipatory to the placing of future foreign orders." Soviet ambassador Konstantin Umanskii reacted with displeasure to this new policy and alleged that Chinese engineers were obtaining better access. In response, State Department official Loy Henderson pressed the two navy representatives at the plant to reconsider. Navy lieutenant commander Oliver objected, however, that the Russians sent as many as twenty engineers at a time on inspections, and "apparently wanted to roam almost at will through those portions of the plant which were not regarded as strictly secret." Surrounded by signs emphasizing the perils of loose lips, the plant's workers "resented" the visitors' untrammeled access. Moreover, both Naval and War Department intelligence feared that "the Soviet engineers, after obtaining a thorough knowledge of the layout of the plant, might communicate what they had learned to certain subversive elements in the United States." Navy inspectors promised, however, to speak with U.S. Army representatives at Wright. They preferred that no more than three Russian engineers come to the plant at a time, rather than the "absurd" number of twenty.[46]

By early 1941, such analyses at last spurred momentum for a dedicated espionage investigation of Amtorg. The FBI now also believed that the trading agency, along with Intourist and Soviet consulates, harbored agents of the GPU.[47] These Soviet intelligence agents should be closely watched, a special agent urged: "Mail cover should be placed. Check toll calls. Check automobile records. Consider placing a surveillance."[48] As part of the Amtorg investigation, Bureau officials worked closely with the State Department's visa division, which provided details on Soviet visitors, and agents conducted regular surveillance on Amtorg's headquarters at 210 Madison Avenue in New York City.[49] In the process, however, the diligent special agents often got bogged down in such minutiae as the garages in which Amtorg employees parked their cars and their license plate numbers.[50] At the same time, the Bureau made an exhaustive but fruitless search of Amtorg's bank account disbursements, still looking for a connection to the CPUSA. As one informant told the FBI, while "he personally felt that it is true that the Amtorg Trading Corporation has been giving money to the CP for years," there seemed no way to prove it. The Bureau nevertheless tried to determine the connection by studying Amtorg's financial records at Chase National Bank. [51]

The agency allocated the greatest amount of its Amtorg investigation resources to a survey of plants that had received orders from the Soviet organization. Repeatedly, however, the FBI heard that the behavior of Soviet visitors was completely innocuous and that, in any case, they had been kept away from sensitive information.[52] A typical response came from J. W. Coffman, vice president of the photographic supplier Consolidated Labs in Fort Lee, New Jersey. Agents learned that "he had not noted any activity on [the Amtorg inspectors'] part which would indicate an interest other than a purely technical engineering interest and . . . he did not notice any activity which would indicate espionage or other subversive activities." Similarly, Bibb Manufacturing Works, a tire-making firm in Cleveland, assured the FBI that the Soviet representatives had not been shown work related to national defense; the only "information [they saw] was readily available from other sources." Amtorg's plant visits were generally severely circumscribed. At the Taylor Winfield Company, a maker of welders, the firm had been "particularly careful to keep them away from the engineering research laboratory where in the last two years considerable research has been done on the welding of aluminum aircraft parts."[53]

At plants ranging from Cleveland Pneumatic Tool Company to the White Motor Company, the Bureau found "no evidence of industrial espionage or subversive activities on part of subject organization." Even when Amtorg representatives "are eager to obtain all possible drawings and descriptive data" on their purchases, they were not so indulged.[54] At the Barnes Drill Company in Chicago, which made drills for gun manufacture, company president A. M. Johnson insisted to the FBI in December 1939 that Soviets inspectors did not, as a Bureau informant alleged, "lose themselves in various parts of the factory." Instead, the firm confined them to the area where their goods were being manufactured.[55] The FBI might have been further relieved to hear that not all inspectors had the talent for "espionage work." Charles Morel, secretary-treasurer of Wiches Brothers of Saginaw, Michigan, noted that many of those at his plant "did not know anything about inspecting machinery, they laid in their rooms smoking cigarettes until noon and were a general nuisance around the plant."[56] Their display of ennui was atypical, however, in the era of the purges, which placed even more weighty burdens on Soviet inspectors than did the demands of espionage. An informant at Cleveland Graphite Bronze Company recalled that the inspectors at his plant had shared their worry that their machines might not operate properly when the inspectors got back to Russia, in which case "they would be 'liquidated.'" At die maker Crosby Co. of Buffalo, inspectors protested that "if the tools were delivered in Russia and they did not work the Commission might face a firing squad."[57]

Regardless of such concerns, the FBI remained ever vigilant, and with good reason. Evidence was not lacking that Soviet visitors, despite their limited access, persistently attempted to gather industrial intelligence during plant inspections. As early as 1939, so convinced was Ford Motor Company of Russian malfeasance that it threw a group of Soviet visitors out of the plant, "on charges of attempting to bribe minor Ford officials to gain access to blueprints of new engineering developments." Forty Soviet engineers and eleven "local Communists" were evicted, a striking step at a company where representatives of both Amtorg and the Autostroy organization had "had complete run" of the plant for the preceding ten years. Unfortunately, as the FBI complained, by removing the men the firm was prevented from getting "a great deal more evidence against these Russian inspectors," such as how much information they had already taken. In emblematic Ford style, the Jewish ancestry of the Soviet personnel was singled out: "True to subversive methods . . . they cover themselves with fictitious names and are jealously protected on every step by their local Jewish friends."[58]

The FBI's own investigation revealed that Amtorg inspectors at the Electric Machinery Manufacturing Company of St. Paul "pried into every nook and corner of the plant, asking innumerable questions," leading the company to believe that "these Soviet representatives were preparing themselves ... to manufacture motors of the type which they had ordered."[59] At the Gould Storage Battery Company, where Soviet visitors spent eight months between 1939 and 1940 watching the firm build a submarine battery, a Bureau informant hazarded that their curiosity indicated "they were more interested ... in the construction of submarine batteries than they were in seeing that the batteries on order ... were built according to specifications." The company informant "stated that he had to be extra careful in the supervision of these men ... to be sure that they did not obtain any information which they should not receive."[60] At the Red Wing Motor Company in Detroit, a firm representative noticed that the Soviets asked for extra copies of drawings with their motors, and he told the FBI "that there was no doubt in his mind ... but that someone in Russia was attempting or would attempt to build a motor just like the ones they were shipping."[61] The Jones and Lamson Machine Company of Springfield, Vermont, moreover, flatly informed the Bureau that "The Amtorg officials were constantly requesting plans and specifications of everything in sight." The company strictly refused "demands that the machines be dismantled and reassembled in order that they might watch the reassembling process."[62]

Such concerns were echoed by sources like J. E. De Long, president of the Waukesha Motor Company of Waukesha, Wisconsin, whose company had sold almost a quarter million dollars' worth of automobile equipment to Russia. De Long complained that the first time Soviet inspectors came to his plant, they had "endeavored to pump the company engineers for information concerning American methods of high octane gasoline production and for information as to the results of investigations conducted in the United States on fuels." The firm had taken care to tell them nothing and keep the visitors "only in the testing rooms."[63] At Curtiss Aeroplane Company, the Bureau's source noted that "the Russians tried to pry all kinds of information out ... especially ... on plant production," and as a result the firm believed that "they were more interested in the plant than [in] airplanes."[64] Clyde A. Crowley, president and director of research at the Technical Service Bureau of Chicago, noted that his firm had been asked to complete ten chemical engineering research proposals for the Soviets, including two of possible "military significance," one on enhancement properties of octane in gasoline and another on those of cetane in diesel fuel. Moreover, the FBI learned that Amtorg agents had been trying to acquire information about other military-industrial technology, including "methods of camouflage of the oil industry and remedial steps taken in case of air bombardment," as well as "information on toluol," which went into the making of TNT.[65]

This interest in military technology was especially worrisome to Bureau investigators, who could not have been happy to hear from Ralph B. Rogers, president of the Cummins Diesel Export Corporation, that Amtorg had recently asked Morris Brenner, export manager at Cummins, "to steal the secret U.S. bombsight for Amtorg" and to acquire a "confidential Diesel submarine motor." Cummins had done significant business with Amtorg since 1938, Rogers noted, yet was eager to assist the FBI, believing that "Amtorg . . . should be investigated as a group of subversive agents." Rogers explained that Brenner's avid interest in pursuing Amtorg orders had assisted him in becoming "a personal and intimate friend as well as a business associate" of the agency's leadership; with these connections, he had learned much about "the subversive work of Amtorg." When the Soviet agency had attempted to purchase the bombsight in late 1940, Brenner stated that he could not help. Soon after, Amtorg officials requested a diesel submarine motor that was "a guarded secret of the United States government." Brenner again refused to assist. In response, Amtorg suggested that the motor could be shipped out in pieces, from different areas of the country, marked "export for parts only."[66]

Attempted espionage was one thing; actual spying was something else again. In January 1941, L. N. Rosenbaum of Rosenbaum and Son, Amtorg's financial advisers, asked Columbia Aircraft Corporation of Long Island for "blueprints and specific airplane parts vital to National Defense," as the Bureau learned from the Office of Naval Intelligence. Columbia produced army and navy planes. The firm agreed to cooperate with the Bureau and sold "altered obsolete blueprints" of an Allison Manufacturing Company drawing, doctored 297 times, to Amtorg for $50. Using some of their newly authorized techniques, agents recorded the conversation regarding the blueprint sale in June 1941 between Adrian W. Rosenbaum, representing his father's firm, and Columbia Aircraft official J. W. Kenny. Rosenbaum painted the struggle Russia faced in Washington in strikingly sexualized (and homophobic) terms; the State Department, he declared, was filled with "a lot of pansies, Back Bay boys and pantywaists, and they speak only to the Cabots, the Lowells, and God, a bunch of fairies. Very anti-Russian. And a hell of a lot of them are pro-Nazi." He insisted that the material Russia desperately needed was going instead to the Reich. When Kenny asked him about goods being sent to Germany from the Soviet Union, Rosenbaum insisted that it was the only means by which Russia could get what it needed in return.[67]

For the benefit of the listening agents, Kenny tempted Rosenbaum to make a list of parts for which Amtorg would buy blueprints. They would divide the proceeds, with Columbia getting one-third and Rosenbaum the remainder. As Kenny pointed out, "This print, and everything that goes with it is absolutely restricted. Even an airplane company . . . can't get it. So if you're going to sell it to him, boy he's got to pay for it." Rosenbaum had no problem in participating in a scheme to hoodwink his clients. He claimed to have sold them a ten cent patent for $500, and thought he would get $10,000 for the Allison drawing. He noted that his contact at Amtorg, whom he was sure would greatly desire the drawing, "loves me like a brother," largely because of the women Rosenbaum had obtained for him. Rosenbaum guffawed, "I don't know what they do with anything. I sold them a whole lot of crap. Plans, blueprints. . . . [t]hey love them." Rosenbaum, though, apparently did not completely trust Kenny, as he asked if the room they had met in had been bugged. The Columbia official assured him that it had not.[68] Despite this promising beginning to an FBI "sting," the following month Rosenbaum told Kenny the deal was off. After the Nazi invasion, he noted, "the entire attitude of the U.S. Government . . . changed toward Russia and the Amtorg Trading Corporation. . . . [T]he Russians are now able to buy any parts, plans, blueprints, materials, etc., that they desired."[69]

This was not exactly so; the defense-related nature of much of Amtorg's requirements remained a major obstacle to the agency's purchasing ability. When Nicolai Napoli, president of Artkino Pictures Inc., pressed a Du Pont Film Corporation representative—to the point of attempted bribery—to provide "information as to the . . . latest developments in nitration, emulsion cellulose, technicolor, etc," he was turned down on the grounds that this was "confidential national defense information." Dupont assured the FBI that its officials "had been exercising rigid control to protect this defense work from unauthorized sources," including the Nazis, "and that they in no way intended to relinquish this policy for the benefit of the Russian Government." Likewise, by mid-1941, RCA no longer allowed Amtorg representatives from the Chief Administration of the Electric-Weak Current Industry of the People's Commissariat of Heavy Industry to continue to "observe American industrial methods in this country," which they had been doing under an agreement since September 30, 1935.[70] While the Amtorg investigation petered out as the war commenced and Washington began sending large amounts of military-industrial matériel to the Soviets through lend-lease, it nevertheless left an important legacy for the FBI. Through its use of informants, double agents, and hidden microphones, the Amtorg probe served as a model for later Soviet espionage cases and contributed to the FBI's growing suspicions of Soviet agents, suspicions that would greatly increase during World War II.

Suspected Subversion in the Military and in War Plants

Soviet representatives were not the only spies interested in military-industrial technology, as the Duquesne espionage case reveals; nor was the FBI the only agency pursuing espionage agents. In 1940, the War Department investigated reports that an American employee at Wright Field, Irving Lee Ross, a former bombsight tester with Norden, had stolen a blueprint for stabilized bombing approach equipment, which allowed a bombsight to work more accurately. He had made a "sudden" resignation from his job, leading officials to believe he might have "ulterior motives." Ross was arrested on October 25, 1940, and charged with "unlawfully draw[ing] a map and diagram of a confidential instrument designated by the President of the United States as vital for Military and Naval equipment." Ross, who insisted he was innocent, was held on $5,000 bond.[71]

Another American, this one Russian-born and most certainly working for the Soviets, alarmed the army's Military Intelligence staff at the Bendix Corporation in early 1940. Elias Bresovitz, representing himself as working for an unnamed Soviet agent, told Bendix Radio Corporation vice president L. A. Hyland that he wanted to place large orders—up to $500,000—"dealing with certain apparatus of great importance to National Defense . . . classified as secret," including Bendix Aviation communications equipment for submarines and airplanes. Brig. Gen. George V. Strong expressed great concern that Bresovitz even knew about such devices, "which we have attempted to cover up." MID's J. M. Churchill quickly wrote to Edward Tamm at the FBI, asking "urgently" for an investigation of Bresovitz. A furniture and textile salesman, Bresovitz had long been acquainted with Hyland and previously helped him obtain many orders at Amtorg, whose purchases from Bendix ranged from $20,000 to $40,000 per year until the "moral embargo." Hyland declared he had been "incensed by the affront" of Bresovitz's request for secret information, but "thought it best . . . to string Bresovitz along in order to secure any additional information."[72]

As the Bresovitz and Ross cases suggest, the military was on the lookout for spies and subversives in 1940, in contrast to its more timid posture in the 1930s. In November, the Second Corps area, which included New York City and environs, prepared a "Special Report on [the] Subversive Situation" that encompassed Communists, Fascists, and other suspected groups. In its examination of Communists, the report concluded, "there is no doubt that these organizers are making progress. This movement might catch on at any time and assume serious proportions." Perhaps more immediate, though, was the party's "enormous capacity for harm" in the ongoing effort to assist "national defense and aid for England," the last remaining major power in Europe to remain free of Nazi control. The report went on to note a list of party "affiliates," from the National Lawyers Guild to the Veterans of the American Lincoln Brigade—and then suggested that the ACLU and Consumers Union were also "influenced" by the party.[73]

A similar "Report on Subversive Activities" from the Ninth Corps area, which included much of the western United States, stated that although there was "no evidence of any concrete organization of any subversive element within the military service" in that region, the Nazis and Communists were attempting to influence the military from the outside. The army had conducted "no real investigation" of military espionage (since there were "only a few, indefinite indications along this line"), but the existence of Nazi propaganda had been unmistakable, aimed "toward creating a defeatist attitude." As far as Nazi sabotage, the army had seen little of it, but the Ninth Corps investigation suggested that aircraft factories and power plants were most vulnerable. At the same time, the report grossly exaggerated the number of Communists in the West, estimating 85,000 in California alone, even though only 80,000 people joined the party nationwide at its height in the war years. Army officials singled out the Communists for antimilitary activity and work disruptions, including "unceasing attacks on the draft act and . . . an increase in labor disputes," especially among maritime, aircraft, and lumber workers. Moreover, the Communists were reaching out to the armed forces, whose members were "enticed to meetings . . . to be worked on." Despite this emphasis on clandestine methods, military officials believed that the party's plan was mostly an overt one, starting with "fomenting social discord and disruption," moving on to "individual acts of sabotage," then "mass sabotage," then "direct action." The Ninth Corps was convinced, all the same, that the Communists' grip on labor was loosening, and that its ability to lead successful strikes had declined, as evidenced by the recent averting of a labor action at Boeing. Yet, the report noted, "the Communist Party . . . should be evaluated as potentially the most dangerous of the subversive elements. It is very strong among the masses of unemployed and the socially submerged." The party was "more dangerous to the country in the long run" than the Nazi organization, according to U.S. Army officials.[74]

The armed forces had help from the FBI in monitoring activities at military installations. The Bureau noted that the Brooklyn Naval Yard, for instance, had a noticeable contingent of at least one suspicious element, former Lincoln Brigade members. In a vision reminiscent of the "beautiful mind" of the Nobel laureate John Nash, Hoover intimated that their coded messages were likely to appear in a "predetermined pulp magazine." Hoover also kept the army informed about Communist employees in factories, especially at firms where "sabotage would seriously affect Government activities in time of war." The FBI believed the party, to counter FDR's perceived inclinations, was gearing up for an "anti-war and anti-war preparation program" that instructed protesters "to create as much disturbance as possible." By June 1941, the Bureau and the armed services had identified more than one hundred Communist activists whom they sought to have removed from defense work.[75] Such close monitoring efforts clearly illustrate the new suspicions that Communist activism at American plants now drew from counterintelligence officials.

In November 1940, only weeks before Roosevelt would announce his program of lend-lease to aid the British, the Vultee Aircraft plant in California faced a nearly two-week strike inspired by a Communist-led union at the facility. Such an action, the MID held, was an integral part of the Communist Party's program.[76] Indeed, former party member Paul Crouch, who had headed the Alameda County (California) Council in 1941, later claimed such strikes were designed "to cripple military aid to Great Britain and secondly, to weaken the U.S. national defense."[77] The House Un-American Activities Committee, which needed little convincing that the work stoppages were rooted in the party's "determined opposition to the national-defense program," singled out such "well-known" Communists as Wyndham Mortimer at North American Aviation, whose employees went on strike in June 1941.[78] William P. Goodman, chairman of the left-leaning UAW local at North American, took exception to such allegations in an angry telegram to the committee: "We, the North American workers on the day shift, protest most vigorously the vicious and cowardly treatment of our negotiators in Washington by the Dies Commission. . . . The issue is not communism. The issue is a living wage for 10,000 North American workers." He accused the committee of promoting "a national program to break down the militance of the workers and to destroy their unions."[79]

Regardless, on June 9, acting on an executive order from FDR, Col. Charles E. Branshaw and the 15th Infantry took over the North American plant, facing down thousands of picketers who were throwing tear gas grenades. Three days later, the employees were back at work except for, as Branshaw put it, "known communists, suspended officers of the local union and all others whose presence . . . [is] inimical to the objective of speedy production of aircraft."[80] As the North American workers struck, the die casters at Alcoa's Cleveland plant also held a work stoppage. Congress of Industrial Organizations (CIO) officials believed that the strikes were "definitely of Communist origin and were following a 'pattern' apparently agreed upon by the left-wing leaders to demoralize the defense program." On the other hand, the *Washington Post* optimistically predicted, "many . . . ace organizers, working with responsible and conservative union heads, are converging on the Pacific Coast to smash the combination of radical groups, led and epitomized by Harry Bridges." The Australian-born Bridges, the founder of the International Longshoremen's and Warehousemen's Union (ILWU), felt compelled to keep his Communism closeted in order to better resist U.S. authorities' frequent attempts to deport him.[81]

The charges of Communist influence upon these strikes are convincing; certainly, the party strongly opposed U.S. assistance to the anti-Nazi forces until June 22, 1941. On June 15, the *Daily Worker* gaily pronounced: "Soviet diplomacy has triumphed. The effort of the Anglo-French group of capitalists to embroil the Soviet Union in war with Germany failed, and today it is the capitalist powers which are exhausting themselves in a devastating war."[82] Just a week later, of course, when German troops poured into the USSR, Communist workers of all nationalities would receive urgent requests to accelerate the production of war machinery for the forces fighting Hitler.

While Communist-inspired sabotage at American plants remained a pressing concern during the Nazi-Soviet Pact, so too did the possibility of Soviet sales of American products to Germany. In separate efforts, the White House, the House Un-American Activities Committee, and the FBI closely examined connections between Amtorg orders in America and subsequent USSR sales to the Reich. The Nazi-Soviet Pact resulted in several economic agreements between the two countries; in early 1941, for example, *Soviet Russia Today* reported triumphantly that a new trade agreement had been

signed between the USSR and Germany, confirming their "friendly relations." This agreement provided that "The USSR delivers to Germany industrial raw materials, oil products and food stuffs, especially cereals; Germany
delivers to the USSR industrial equipment."[83] Washington officials remained
concerned that Soviet provisions purchased from America would be used to
strengthen Germany, and in order to learn just what the Soviets were purchasing, FDR asked Winthrop Aldrich, Chase National Bank chairman, to
monitor Amtorg's account. The president was particularly troubled by Soviet
imports of American molybdenum, used in making specialty steels for the
manufacture of tanks and aircraft, as well as by aluminum purchases.[84] Raymond E. Rockefeller's analysis for the Dies Committee, "Preliminary Report
on Examination of Bank Statements of Russian Banks," suggested that the
Soviets were indeed buying from American firms and selling to the Reich.[85]
In fact, the sale of certain goods to Russia in 1940 had increased markedly
because of German war needs. For example, although Russia's own cotton
output had increased by 300,000 pounds between 1939 and 1940, the country still purchased an extra 139,000 pounds of cotton in 1940 from the
United States. Similar suspicious increases were reported in copper, oil refining equipment, and shoe leather.[86] Beginning in December 1939, the FBI also
monitored Amtorg's bank balances as another link to possible German-
related purchases. Bureau agents took note of a large shipment of gold worth
$5.6 million that arrived in San Francisco from Vladivostok in February
1940. Another shipment, worth twice that amount, came the following
October.[87] The American Council on Soviet Relations, a pro-Soviet lobby,
dismissed allegations that the Soviets were transferring goods to the Germans, quoting Ambassador Umanskii as saying that "goods which have been
or are being purchased in the U.S. by the U.S.S.R., and including oil products and industrial equipment of all categories, are destined exclusively for
the domestic needs of the U.S.S.R."[88]

Prewar Spies: Golos, Ovakimian, Brothman, Bentley, and Gold

As various offices of the federal government monitored Soviet espionage,
sabotage, trade, and banking practices, the United States also launched an
investigation of Soviet agents in the United States. One of the first to be
probed was representative Jacob Golos and his travel agency, World Tourists.
This agency, "originally set up . . . to act as an arm of Intourists . . . in pro-

moting worker tours to Russia," was also active in "furnishing fraudulent passports for Russian Agents," the FBI determined. Golos was convicted and fined $500 for failure to register as a foreign agent in March 1940, and received a prison sentence, which was suspended.[89] Throughout, he maintained a powerful grip on party affairs. By 1941, he was "chairman of the central control committee of the Communist Party," which imposed ideological conformity on the faithful—or not so faithful, as in the unfortunate Trotsky's case. Golos had arranged for his assassination in August 1940.[90]

Despite entirely overlooking Golos's parallel espionage activity, the FBI was becoming increasingly vigilant toward Soviet representatives in 1941. On May 5, officials arrested Gaik Ovakimian, an NKVD engineer who worked at the Amtorg Trading Agency. The Armenian, who first entered the United States in 1933, had already received thirteen extensions on his permit to stay in the country. Through a tip from the British, Ovakimian was apprehended by U.S. authorities and charged with being an unregistered representative of the Soviet government, thus violating the Foreign Agents Registration Act.[91] Ovakimian had also run Willy Brandes, who had entered Britain in January 1937 acting as an American cosmetics company representative and then joined a spy ring that penetrated the Woolwich Arsenal, gathering blueprints for naval guns. The British government arrested the ring in January 1938 and sent four spies to prison, though Brandes escaped.[92]

It was espionage, not his registration status, that was the most important factor leading to Ovakimian's arrest. The engineer was actually caught taking materials from an unidentified source.[93] Unbeknownst to the FBI, meanwhile, Ovakimian had also been instructed in January 1941 to investigate U.S. research into uranium at Columbia University and the University of Minnesota.[94] During his stay in the United States, Ovakimian had regularly obtained information about the industrial production of gasoline, synthetic ammonia, and various oil refining and cracking processes.[95] He was willing to pay handsomely; on one occasion, he spent $14,750 for material on oil production. Ovakimian seldom missed a chance to gain industrial intelligence. Elton R. Allison, an engineer at Hercules Powder who met Ovakimian at a speech given by Henry Wallace in February 1939, found himself quickly buttonholed by the Soviet engineer, who "made a plea for help . . . stating that the Russians were in danger of war with Germany." What kind of powder was Allison working on, Ovakimian wanted to know. Could he supply Ovakimian a layout of his plant and its materials and machines? The NKVD agent would pay him $500 to $1000 for his trouble. Allison, however, turned him down, deciding that his loyalty to Hercules outweighed his own anti-Nazi sentiments; "he could not see himself doing odd jobs for the Russians for the rest of his life."[96]

Armand Labis Feldman, who had also informed the FBI about Ovakimian, had himself collected industrial intelligence for Moscow from various American engineers from 1934–38, paying them $200 a month. He continued his relationship with Ovakimian while monitoring him and Golos for the Bureau—surveillance that the NKGB only learned about in 1945 when Judith Coplon, a Department of Justice employee who then worked for the Soviets, found the file that contained Feldman's reports. In his ongoing contacts with Ovakimian and Amtorg, Feldman recalled being pestered for information on "magnetic magnesium, fire prevention of oil pipe lines," and information on how to "camouflage the oil field flambeau," particularly important during air attacks. Feldman, indeed, continued to provide material to Ovakimian on processes such as catalytic hydroforming, even after he had assured the FBI that he would not continue to assist the Soviet agent. The money was apparently too good to pass up.[97]

As former special agent John J. Walsh recalls, the Ovakimian affair cemented the FBI's hardening outlook toward the Soviet Union, an outlook also shaped by agents' undercover attendance at antiwar meetings led by Communist groups.[98] In the Bureau, unlike in other government agencies at the time, the Soviets were considered as much an enemy as the Germans. After the German invasion of Russia, however, the State Department dropped the charges against Ovakimian, and he was allowed to return home in July 1941 in exchange for six others held in Russia.[99] He returned to Moscow to head American and British affairs in the Soviet Foreign Intelligence Directorate.[100] His work in obtaining secrets from the petroleum industry would soon be continued by another spy, Mobil oil engineer Norman J. Rees, who collected oil-related intelligence for Russia from 1942 to 1971, certainly one of the longest-serving agents on record.[101] Ovakimian was not the only Soviet spy to be repatriated in 1941. Mikhail Gorin, a former Intourist official in Los Angeles who had been sentenced to six years in jail and fined heavily in March 1939 for stealing U.S. naval intelligence about Japan from the ONI, also was allowed to return that year. Undersecretary of State Sumner Welles called for Gorin's release on March 22, 1941, arguing that "certain important considerations of an international nature make it of public interest."[102] The State Department's approach clearly differed from that of the FBI, which was busily preparing to arrest Ovakimian even as Welles worried about Moscow's sensitivities.

The FBI concluded from the Ovakimian case that "none of the actual paid agents of the Russian espionage system were American Communists." Instead, Soviet agents had been told "to disassociate themselves from any Communist activity"; thus, those who left the party now should be viewed "with considerable suspicion." Certainly, it would turn out that many Soviet spies, like Chambers and Gold, were either ex-party members or had never belonged to the organization at all. But the Bureau completely overlooked the fact that some party members were quite happy to help the "Russian espionage system" and to do so without pay.[103] American Communists like Elizabeth Bentley and Steve Nelson would assist the Soviet Union immeasurably with their connections. While it missed many Communists' ties to espionage, the Bureau kept a sharp eye on their subversive intentions. In the spring of 1940, for instance, the FBI's Boston office made ex-Communist Herbert Philbrick an informant on a suspected Communist-leaning group, the Cambridge (Mass.) Youth Council; Philbrick later joined the Young Communist League in March 1942 to aid the Bureau. Later, of course, he would be one of the FBI's most celebrated informants, testifying against Communists in several trials, writing an exposé, *I Led Three Lives* (1953), and starring in his own television show.[104]

Distracted by the pernicious plots of Boston's progressive youth, the Bureau remained completely unaware of the activities of a highly devoted spy in the United States, a man who had first come to the Bureau's attention in 1940. While pursuing Ovakimian, FBI agents had again bumped into Jacob Golos, whom the Bureau spotted with the NKVD engineer seven times in early 1941, meeting him in a "furtive manner."[105] On February 17, the FBI recorded Ovakimian picking up a package from Golos. Feldman told the agency that "Ovakimian was the bearer of instructions and funds to Golos, and . . . Golos submitted reports to Ovakimian . . . [who] utilized the diplomatic mail for dispatch of materials to Russia." Armand Feldman believed that Golos's outfit, World Tourists, also funded the *Daily Worker* and the Communist Party. Soviet intelligence archives indeed confirm the lucrative nature of World Tourists for party interests. But Golos would avoid arrest.[106]

Surveillance of Golos did lead the agency to a brief encounter with his lover and associate, Elizabeth Bentley, until she lost her pursuers in the Penn Station ladies' room.[107] Golos, meanwhile, correctly assumed the surveillance was connected with the FBI's interest in Ovakimian. Upon Ovakimian's return to Russia and the United States' establishment of a firm commitment to helping the Soviet Union with lend-lease, the FBI's surveillance of Bentley and Golos ended in September 1941.[108] Soon after, of course, the Golos operation began to peak in intensity. Just as the FBI curtailed its surveillance, World Tourists helped launch the U.S. Service and Shipping Corporation, a party- and Soviet-funded cover agency with the "ostensible business purpose" of sending packages to Russia. Bentley was soon hired at U.S. Service and Shipping, where her salary would eventually reach $800 per month. The items she most frequently sent to Russia, however, would not be business packages, but secret documents. The FBI would not learn of the extent of Golos's sophisticated espionage operation and Bentley's role in it until 1945, when she defected.[109]

Nevertheless, Golos's earlier arrest and conviction had led his own government to grow suspicious about his usefulness, as did his unusually loose style of managing agents, including his live-in paramour, Bentley. Golos had earlier evaded NKVD attempts to recall him at the height of the purge in 1939, and would instead expand his network considerably, despite a growing clamor from Moscow that he turn over his contacts to its control. Golos's continuous service represented a serious vulnerability for Moscow, as historians Weinstein and Vassiliev note. Owing to his visibility, "Golos posed to any American he contacted the threat of identification by FBI surveillance and possible exposure."[110]

Golos died in 1943, well before the FBI discovered what he was doing, and Bentley continued their espionage operation. A Vassar graduate with a (plagiarized) master's in Italian from Columbia, she had joined the Communist Party in March 1935 after she became involved with the American League against War and Fascism, a Communist front.[111] The same month she joined the party, she was introduced to Juliet Stewart Poyntz, an ill-fated GRU agent who made several fumbling attempts to recruit Bentley to underground service. Instead of joining the underground at that point, Bentley performed one of her earliest services to the party at the Amtorg Camp for Soviet children in Napanoch, New York, in the summer of 1936.[112] Two years later, she made her first foray into espionage by collecting information at the Italian Library of Information in New York City. Her attempts to interest the party in her materials eventually led to her fateful meeting with Golos, a longtime, Russian-born agent with close ties to the Comintern and the CPUSA, on October 15, 1938. At his urging, she separated herself from the open party so as to furnish intelligence more discreetly. However, her earlier anti-Fascist activism in the League had not been so subtle, and upon discovering it, the Italian Library fired her in 1939.[113] Golos would soon arrange her first assignment in industrial espionage, with engineer Abraham Brothman, whom Golos had first solicited for blueprints in 1938.[114]

Brothman, a widely published expert on thermal diffusion, had designed production facilities for aviation fuel, synthetic rubber, food processing, and saponification, or soap making.[115] Appearing before a grand jury in 1947 after Bentley's confession to the FBI had connected him to espionage, he painted himself as having innocently supplied blueprints to Golos in return for the promise of Soviet business. He claimed that as designer, the blueprints were "his own property"; what he did not tell the jury was that he met with Golos at least eight times.[116] These meetings were apparently painful for Golos, who in May 1940 gratefully turned the engineer over to Elizabeth Bentley, who collected his blueprints on perhaps ten occasions. She later recalled that Brothman provided her material on kettles, mixers, and vats for making resin and oil products.[117] The two did not operate with the most discretion. Brothman gave Bentley her documents on the street because he "did not like to be disturbed" in his office, and she then copied the documents in public print shops.[118] Bentley's lack of a technical background, however, proved to be an obstacle, and she soon stopped seeing him. In August 1941 she met Nathan Gregory Silvermaster and his wife, Helen, who were eager to help Russia after the German invasion. Silvermaster and his contacts in the Pentagon and other agencies would serve as Bentley's most important sources, and some of Moscow's as well, until 1944.[119] Meanwhile, Pennyslvania Sugar chemist Harry Gold, now armed with a Xavier University degree, took over the less-than-rewarding task of collecting Brothman's information.[120] One of the key items that Gold would receive from the engineer was the Buna-S rubber process.[121]

The Counterintelligence Response: Hoover and Dies

During the era of Nazi-Soviet Pact, the U.S. government had shown its increasing wariness of foreign influence, especially that of Soviet agents, by spying on Amtorg, arresting Golos, attempting to deport Ovakimian, and enacting several antisubversion laws. These included the Smith Act of 1940, officially known as the Alien Registration Act, which required aliens to register and criminalized membership in revolutionary groups, and the Voorhis Act of the same year, which mandated registration of "subversive organizations." Yet FBI and State Department officials' continued remarkable ineptness at detecting spies revealed a glaring structural weakness in the government's counterintelligence program. The recognition of this vulnerability during the war—following the successful uncovering of Soviet espionage targeting the atomic bomb and military-related industry—would spur an increasingly effective counterintelligence effort against Russia beginning in 1943.

The FBI had blundered most strikingly in its dealings with Walter Krivitsky, who presented officials with an unprecedented opportunity to learn more about Soviet spying. Krivitsky, a senior NKVD illegal who escaped to the United States in 1938 in the midst of Stalin's purge of the secret intelligence service, drew much public interest in his former work in a series of articles he published in the *Saturday Evening Post*, which divulged such practices as Soviet agents' use of fraudulent passports to facilitate travel into the United States. Krivitsky spoke to Loy Henderson, assistant chief of European affairs at the State Department, and Ruth Shipley of the department's passport office about these practices in January 1939. Krivitsky told Shipley that over 250 agents were active in New York City's environs alone, but since the government lacked any procedures for handling defectors, little was done to delve seriously into his allegations or to protect him. In fact, by June the INS was trying to deport him because his visa had expired.[122]

The State Department did refer Krivitsky to the FBI for interviewing, but refused to let the Bureau take over the case, which likely contributed to Hoover's lack of zeal in exploiting the defector's knowledge. When FBI agents spoke to him on July 27, rather than probe him about his extensive understanding of Soviet espionage, they focused mainly on one case, that of Moishe Stern, a Soviet spy who, as "Mark Zilbert," had worked in the United States in the early 1930s, when he also had offered his address as a drop for the Panamanian mailings in the Switz-Osman case. Krivitsky said that Stern had been killed in the purges, but the Bureau did not believe him, nor did it appreciate that Krivitsky's lawyer, Louis Waldman, had earlier gotten Robert Osman acquitted of the charge of espionage. Hoover's distrust for Krivitsky, who not only provided information that conflicted with the Bureau's own intelligence but apparently still believed "in the true Communism of Lenin," blinded the director to the significance of his story. The FBI thus lost an important chance to gather much important information about NKVD espionage practices in the United States and would not learn what Krivitsky could have told them until years later. This was so even though Krivitsky also told the Dies Committee about Soviet penetration of the government, testimony that so moved the chairman that he invited Leon Trotsky to testify in Austin, Texas, an invitation that was later withdrawn when it was feared Mexico would not take him back.[123]

The FBI's response to Krivitsky underlines the lack of an effective U.S. counterintelligence program in the 1930s. In addition to missing the opportunity to obtain Krivitsky's story on active Soviet intelligence networks, the Bureau also overlooked three other agents who defected in 1938: Whittaker Chambers, the GRU spy whose story did not emerge until after the war; Alexander Orlov, a senior NKVD officer who had visited the United States under an assumed name in 1932 and later returned to defect; and Hede Massing, who claimed to have worked with Alger Hiss in the 1930s. Chambers did talk to Assistant Secretary of State A. A. Berle in 1939, but the Bureau got the full story on him only in 1943, and did little with it, as discussed below. Orlov, meanwhile, spoke to both the attorney general and the head of INS in 1938; he was permitted to stay in the country because he claimed he would be in mortal danger at home. Adopting a pseudonym to protect himself, he told these officials to contact his lawyer if they wanted to learn more, but no one followed up. After Stalin's death, Orlov at last revealed himself to the American public in a book he published. As for Massing, she defected "quietly" and was left alone; her story seems to have first come to the FBI's attention in 1948.[124]

The British were far more alacritous in taking advantage of such sources. When Krivitsky's confidant, Isaac Don Levine, told Ambassador to the United States Lord Lothian (Philip Henry Kerr) that the NKVD agent knew of spies in the British government, including code clerks in the Foreign Office and the British League of Nations Delegation in Geneva, the British immediately looked into the matter and soon confirmed his charges. Whitehall intelligence agents were eager to interview Krivitsky extensively, and he was brought to London while his family was given safe haven in Canada. British intelligence did overlook some of the more than one hundred spies he named, including, most notably, Cambridge Five agents Donald Maclean and Kim Philby. Nevertheless, the response of MI5 and MI6, including extensive interviews and protection, differs markedly from that of the FBI, which had yet to develop a systematic response to espionage allegations. This neglect had tangible consequences: the very year that Krivitsky met with the FBI's sour reception, the NKVD stole 18,000 pages of technical documents, several hundred designs, and dozens of samples of new technology from the United States, according to Vasili Mitrokhin of the KGB's foreign intelligence division.[125] Facing a mortal threat from his own regime, then busily executing thousands of intelligence agents, and especially worried that the threat could be made good in England, where numerous NKVD agents remained at large, Krivitsky returned to the United States in December 1940—despite the best efforts of congressman and Soviet agent Samuel Dickstein to have him permanently deported. Krivitsky continued to receive a cold shoulder, however, and committed suicide on February 10, 1941.[126]

Probably better remembered is the reaction to Whittaker Chambers's 1939 allegations. When Chambers and his friend, the aforementioned Levine, visited Assistant Secretary of State Adolf Berle on September 2, 1939, to tell him about a network in the State and Treasury departments as well as other agencies involved in "Russian espionage," complete with government employees' names like Alger and Donald Hiss, Franklin Victor Reno, Julian Wadleigh, and Laurence Duggan, along with others including J. Peters, Noel Field, and Dr. Philip Rosenbliett, the assistant secretary did little with the information.[127] Though Berle later explained that he saw Chambers's allegations as requiring some response, including "organizing an effective counter-espionage group . . . developing a high state of activity in the FBI . . . getting the Foreign Agents Registration Act passed, . . . [and] strengthening the passport control," what is curious is what *he* did about them.[128] Berle did not mention Chambers to the FBI until March 1940 and did not give them a full accounting of his meeting for another three years.[129] Thus FBI official Edward Tamm, who served on the same interagency intelligence committee as did Berle, was not informed of the charges when the assistant secretary received them.[130] In the White House, Chambers's allegations went nowhere, as FDR flatly denied their veracity. The country's chief internal security agency might have been expected to show more concern, even with sketchy information, yet the FBI remained "preoccupied with Nazi spies," Sam Tanenhaus argues, and was slow to act.[131] The more pronounced anti-Soviet posture that would emerge midway through the war was only just beginning to inform the actions of agency officials.

After the FBI at last invited Chambers in 1942 to relate to them what he had told Berle three years earlier, the former spy was less than frank about his role, merely calling himself an "officer" in the Communist Party underground and denying any connection with the OGPU, the predecessor to the NKVD, or with espionage. Not surprisingly, the FBI was unimpressed with his story—Assistant Director P. E. Foxworth saw it as "history, hypothesis, or deduction"—and largely ignored Chambers for the rest of the war, interviewing him only three times, once for just five minutes. In 1945, when the Bureau began talking to him more regularly, Chambers still denied involvement with Soviet intelligence or an "espionage ring." Later, Agent D. M. Ladd attempted to explain the Bureau's actions to an irate Hoover, noting that Chambers had canceled two meetings during the war because of illness.[132]

When the Chambers case broke publicly in 1948, Berle also defended his response, noting in his diary the weaknesses in Chambers's presentation: Chambers "did not even remotely indicate that he personally had been engaged in the operation," averred Berle. Instead, "He told me that . . . a Marxist study group had been formed . . . that these would go underground and be of use to the general Russian scheme . . . his information about the Hiss boys was two years cold at least." As Berle testified to Congress, "[Y]ou don't like to file charges against a man unless you are prepared to back them up." At that point, Chambers had not produced all his evidence.[133] Indeed, Berle was never told about the existence of official correspondence that Chambers had handed over to his Soviet contacts. As Chambers recalled in 1948, "I have never discussed with anyone the producing of any documents from Government agencies for transmittal to [NKVD agent] Colonel Bykov."[134] Yet Berle had taken several pages of notes when Chambers spoke to him, and his record from the 1939 meeting, "Underground Espionage Agent," provides a detailed list of names involved in espionage and their activities.[135] Berle's lethargic response to Chambers's information, and the FBI's own mishandling of the case, only confirm the U.S. government's inconsistent and generally ineffective approach to combating Soviet espionage during the 1930s and early 1940s.

As the FBI, the State Department, and other executive agencies fumbled their chances to identify Soviet espionage after the Nazi-Soviet Pact, the House of Representatives turned up its rhetoric on the issue of Communist subversion. But Congressman Dies's Un-American Activities Committee also made little headway on this issue, despite the abundance of testimony from the garrulous Walter Steele of the *National Republic,* who continued to regale the committee with stories of Communists' sabotage in the U.S. Navy (including the blowing up of dirigibles and planes) and their spying on the U.S. Army's attempts to crush the bonus marchers in 1932.[136] In 1941, in a more ominous global environment, committee members emphasized both the need for laws that would permit "the immediate mandatory deportation

of alien spies and saboteurs" and the need "to outlaw every political organization which is shown to be under the control of a foreign government."
The committee did recognize that factory management played a part in
assisting the Communists' success, when managers allowed the existence of
working conditions that led to "real grievances."[137]

In September 1939, the committee called CPUSA leader Earl Browder to
testify about the Nazi-Soviet pact. Browder, who earlier that year had
attacked Dies for not questioning "a single authentic spokesman of the CP—
who far from being subversive or secretive are openly carrying on democratic work in behalf of the majority of the American people and can be
reached daily," came willingly. He declared the pact had aided "the national
interests of America," and also affirmed that his party took no instructions or
money from the Soviet Union. The committee members were surely skeptical of such claims, but their jaws dropped when Browder more candidly
admitted to having traveled on a fraudulent passport—until his lawyer
shushed him and he concluded the discussion by pleading the Fifth Amendment, setting an example for many later HUAC witnesses.[138] Browder would
soon be haunted by his earlier frankness.

Despite an approach that was generally superficial, hyperbolic, or both,
the committee's work yielded some results. Besides Browder's passport pre-
tenses, the committee also successfully exposed and disgraced such pro-Ger-
man fronts as the Silver Shirts.[139] Members congratulated themselves for
alerting Americans "to a far better understanding of the sinister character
and wide extent of subversive activities. We may justly claim to have been
the decisive force in shaping the present attitudes of the American people
toward the activities of the 'fifth columns' which aim at our destruction."
The committee's 1941 report claimed it had "smashed th[e] Nazi movement"
while at the same time "breaking up the People's Front." Dies Committee
hearings had aired the case of Soviet agent Nicholas Dozenberg, counter-
feiter of money and passports, leading to his sentencing. Moreover, despite
collecting hundreds of thousands of names and a vast collection of literature, the Dies Committee pronounced it had "shown that there is a way to
combat the 'fifth column' without creating a Gestapo."[140] This claim was controversial, to say the least. The White House joined the critics and called
Dies's practice of naming names "sordid," though newspapers like the *Manassas (Va.) Journal* praised him: "Chairman Dies has the majority of the people of this country with him on this issue." The committee staunchly
defended its civil liberties record, declaring that it would not recklessly chal-

lenge "those who simply hold unorthodox economic views . . . the right to individual liberties of free Americans must be preserved as zealously as the efforts of totalitarian agents are combated." Overall, despite Dies's incessant speeches and high-profile campaign, the record of his committee on protecting national security was slight.[141]

All the while, the Soviet Union's espionage agents were gearing up for their most vigorous campaign ever. In April 1941, the foreign intelligence responsibilities of the NKVD were reorganized to create new departments to promote scientific and technical (S&T) espionage practices separate from political spying, "a certain sign of their increasing priority," note Andrew and Mitrokhin.[142] As Alexander Feklisov recalled, "Soviet networks in the United States were to concentrate their efforts on securing secrets of cutting edge war technology."[143] By 1941, nearly one-quarter of the 221 NKVD agents in the United States were engineers in this line of intelligence gathering, known as "Line X" or the "XY Line." Semyon Semyonov was one: a graduate from the Leningrad Institute of Mechanical Engineering, he then attended MIT and soon tapped industrial chemists like bacteriologist Thomas Black, who sent along information on penicillin and other medicines to Russia, and Harry Gold, who worshipped the urbane Semyonov and obliged him with other industrial information.[144] The work of such agents "helped to lay the basis for the remarkable wartime expansion of S&T collection in the United States": beginning with 59 microfilm reels of materials collected in 1942, the total rose to 211 in 1943, 600 in 1944, and 1,896 in 1945.[145]

Despite this hemorrhaging of information, counterintelligence was not entirely dormant in the interwar years, as Rhodri Jeffreys-Jones has pointed out. He notes that the War Department's Military Intelligence Division (G-2) saw its budgets grow in the 1930s, while the U.S. Navy expanded its code-breaking capacity significantly—if not soon enough to prevent Pearl Harbor—and the Office of Naval Intelligence groomed Americans abroad for espionage.[146] Moreover, as Raymond Batvinis has noted, in 1940 the FBI for the first time sent a top agent, Assistant Director Hugh Clegg, to Britain to observe British counterintelligence methods from surveillance to censorship, opening up a direct line of communication between the FBI and the office of the British Security Coordinator. The visit was so successful that the FBI sent a second mission to England in 1942. That year the FBI also used its Special Intelligence Service to send agents posing as businessmen on a new mission to South and Central America.[147] These efforts were ineffective against Soviet inroads, however. As the work of Ovakimian, Brothman, Gold, Golos,

Bentley, and Chambers demonstrates, the FBI, the War Department, and the Dies Committee had only a scant understanding of the full scope of the Soviet espionage effort in the years just before World War II.

Nevertheless, this period was an important transitional one in American-Soviet relations, when authorities launched an ambitious investigation of Soviet organs like Amtorg, targeted agents such as Golos and Ovakimian for their role in suspected subversive activities, discovered Soviet spies' attempts at clandestinely purchasing documents, information, and parts and provided false documents to them, and halted both Communist-inspired strikes at war plants and war-related sales to the Soviet Union. In part, this new activity was related to counterintelligence initiatives like FDR's 1939 mandate, which assisted the FBI in greatly enhancing its forces as well as its scope of investigations. Building on these early, though often faltering anti-subversive efforts, U.S. agents would later respond to what they learned of Moscow's infiltration of the Manhattan Project, as well as what intelligence they gleaned from disgruntled or defecting Soviet agents, in a much more effective way. By the middle of the war, intelligence agents were with renewed vigor dissecting the work of Soviet representatives.[148] The discovery of Soviet espionage against the atomic project was one important motivation, but so too was a growing, if sketchy, awareness of Soviet industrial espionage, as the next chapter details.

CHAPTER THREE

Penetration of Wartime
Military-Industrial Targets

American officials had largely failed to recognize the expansion of Soviet industrial espionage before World War II. During the war, of course, Moscow made far greater inroads—and authorities missed even more. Defector Viktor Andreevich Kravchenko characterized the era as a time when "conditions in America present[ed] the most fertile soil for Soviet espionage."[1] "Had we taken the Empire State Building and put it on a ship, nobody would have cared," he declared, noting that the passing of such materials "was absolutely natural during the war." Kravchenko, an economic attaché at the Soviet Purchasing Commission from August 1943 to September 1944, had been told upon leaving the Soviet Union to "study carefully the industry in the United States, the military industry, the civilian industry, all technological and industrial processes, . . . [to] get hold of their secrets to that we can achieve similar results in our country."[2] The Purchasing Commission, which opened in Washington, D.C., in March 1942, had one thousand employees and its own NKVD installation, according to Kravchenko.[3] Indeed, the commission, the embassy, and Amtorg all worked together to obtain "secret information," he told Congress in 1950. Certainly Kravchenko would have noticed that his audience was willing, even eager, to hear the worst, and he flatly told them that "every Soviet representative . . . is a potential spy." Yet thanks to the Venona decrypts and other sources, we know that his allegations were quite credible.[4]

Despite this access, Soviet agents were hardly unmolested in the United States, especially before Pearl Harbor, as previously discussed. After the surprise Japanese attack, surveillance of Soviet agents declined sharply; yet by 1943, as Alexander Feklisov observed, he and his associates faced G-men's scrutiny once again: "American counterespionage had no doubt noticed how active we were," he pointed out.[5] Indeed, Soviet agents Semyonov, Kvasnikov, and Fomin reported that they were being "shadowed" by the FBI in 1944.[6]

Viktor Andreevich Kravchenko, January 11,
1949, at trial. Kravchenko successfully sued a
French Communist newspaper that charged his
book *I Chose Freedom: The Personal and
Political Life of a Soviet Official* (1947) was
written by American intelligence.

Developments such as the discovery of Soviet spies at the Berkeley Radiation Laboratory in 1943 would play a key role in creating a new outlook in
Soviet-American relations that envisioned Russia as a growing threat to the
United States. U.S. officials also discovered industrial intelligence-gathering
in defense plants, such as Bell Aircraft, and began to take action against it.
However, much activity continued unabated, in part because the FBI, rather
than creating counterespionage programs, typically only reacted to what it
had found.

U.S. Response to Espionage and Subversion
in the Early Years of the War

As War Department attorney John Ohly well knew, "the decisive weight of our production in the outcome of the war makes it obvious that saboteurs, spies, and other subversive elements will use every conceivable means to disrupt war production and filch military secrets."[7] Immediately after the United States joined the war, therefore, military officials declared that espionage would not be tolerated, and a joint statement pronounced that "The protection of the war effort against espionage, sabotage, and subversive activities is paramount to all other considerations."[8] The War Department created a plant security brochure that featured a segment about espionage and tactics of spies, including "making copies of documents," "questioning employees," and "infiltration"—often as an inspector or visitor.[9] The FBI, meanwhile, started a plant protection plan, surveying 2,287 plants before the War Department took over this program in early 1942; the Bureau also provided advice about countering espionage and sabotage, as well as fingerprinted millions of employees.[10] At the same time, the U.S. Army issued a strict warning to aircraft manufacturers and other defense goods suppliers: "[N]othing shall be released . . . concerning secret, confidential, or restricted projects in any plant working on defense contracts," including information on shipments that "might be used to determine troop movements and location of forces."[11]

Although the United States and Russia shared a common enemy, War Department officials remained distrustful of American Communists. Ohly insisted that "known or suspected . . . Communists or other persons likely to engage in subversive activities" should be fired from firms with "military and naval secrets." But apparently they hadn't been, since, as he noted, the FBI and military intelligence organizations had "dossiers on Communists and Nazis holding key positions in vital aircraft and other plants."[12] Ohly's position outraged Earl Browder, now freed from jail and heading up a patriotic effort among his comrades in the defense sector. The CPUSA leader wrote Roosevelt complaining that the army "had stated that Communists could not be trusted on war jobs." Deciding that "it would be impossible to deny" Browder's statement, War Department officials noted that his letter was best ignored.[13] Lee Pressman, counsel of the CIO, also "protested vigorously" about the military's removal of suspected subversives, a complaint to which the government, attentive to the threat of strikes in CIO member unions, responded with more alacrity.[14] By 1943, the unions and the army arrived at a settlement.[15]

During the war the Communist Party dominated several labor organizations (including twenty unions by 1944 and many more locals) and in a spirit of solidarity, called for "waiving time and a half on Saturdays and double on Sundays," and endorsing piecework, which its leaders had formerly rejected. As Browder declared bluntly on May 8, 1943: "[A]ny conditional form of the no-strike policy means to turn the labor movement against its own war."[16] That month, as part of the wartime solidarity message, the Comintern was dissolved, and less than a year later, Browder had changed the name of his organization to the moderate-sounding Communist Political Association. He also announced his "Teheran Thesis," calling for a union between business and labor that would transcend class conflict, ideas that astonished and outraged many of his fellow party members.[17]

Some, however, have suggested that Browder's softening of the party line was only a mask to cover a more intense form of party subversion. As Russian émigré Alexander Barmine scoffed, "[T]he 'dissolution' of the CP which set so many naïve minds at rest, marked the beginning of a Communist conspiracy . . . which is vastly more dangerous than the original party ever was to our institutions."[18] Certainly, Browder was intimately involved in clandestine activities. According to Elizabeth Bentley, he had connected her and Golos with certain sources, including Silvermaster and the Perlo group, and hoped to use the material they gathered to raise his stature with Moscow.[19] James G. Ryan notes that Bentley's allegations are consistent with Browder's self-aggrandizing and calculating character and that the allegations are confirmed by his "best friend," Philip Jaffe of *Amerasia* magazine, who suggested that Browder was quick to assist party members and others interested in spying.[20]

While American officials remained unaware of Browder's secret role, the White House sought to control potential subversion in government with the creation of the Interdepartmental Commission on Employee Investigations. The new commission would handle "the investigation and disposition of complaints of subversive activity on the part of employees of the executive branch." Those who had joined organizations favoring the overthrow of the government by force, including the CPUSA, German-American Bund, and Silver Shirts, could not keep their jobs. Yet unlike the Cold War loyalty program, which would automatically screen *all* employees, the new commission's process of investigation was not initiated unless a complaint or an FBI report had been received.[21] The commission also took a more cautious approach than would its Cold War successors. As its chairman, Herbert E. Gaston, noted in a report to the White House: "[I]nvestigations . . . need to be conducted with extreme care and wisdom lest they should have the effect of setting up bars against the employment of those who conscientiously advocate constitutional and peaceful changes." Subversives, he argued, were largely only guilty of "slovenly service."[22]

Tidy subversives could not assume they would be left alone, however, because under the Hatch Act, the FBI had a broad mandate from Congress "to investigate the employees of every department, agency, and independent establishment of the Federal Government who are members of subversive organizations." The Bureau worked from an initial list of 1,121 persons prepared by Congressman Dies; at first, the investigation could begin only with the approval of the employee's departmental head. In October 1941, a new "expedited procedure" allowed the FBI to investigate immediately any "substantive allegation[s]" against employees without having to seek such approval. By early 1942, the Bureau had handled 656 cases. After subtracting those employees who were no longer working for the government, those whose employing agencies did not respond to the FBI report, and those for whom their employers decided to take no action, a total of 11 employees were discharged.[23] Clyde Tolson, Hoover's associate, did not mention this rather unimpressive figure when he appeared in front of Congress in June 1942 asking for an additional $10 million for the Bureau, but instead testified that "a number of individuals have been discharged . . . as the result of information which we developed." He also tried to inflate the Bureau's results by intimating that "a number of persons charged with subversive activities resigned from the Government service . . . after the initiation of these investigations."[24]

Certainly, the number of cases expanded rapidly as the war continued, with 4,454 handled in 1942; by mid-1943, the FBI had completed over 5,000 investigations. Still, the total number of employees discharged, 53, remained tiny.[25] With new names constantly bubbling up from the bowels of the Dies Committee, however, Hoover had his hands full.[26] The Bureau did not act only on the Dies list, either. Various agencies had forwarded an additional 2,500 names, and at one point the Bureau had 125 special agents tied up with these investigations.[27] Hoover insisted that "the FBI was particularly alert . . . to safeguard the rights of individuals and groups" and that "there was a minimum of confusion and interference with civil rights."[28]

In addition to screening government employees, the Bureau also investigated violations of the Voorhis Act, which required "registration of subversive

Clyde Tolson (right) with J. Edgar Hoover in Florida

military or subversive political organizations in this country." Sixty such complaints had been filed by early 1942.[29] Special agents also searched the homes of enemy aliens, including Japanese, Germans, Italians, Hungarians, Romanians, and others, looking for weapons or other contraband.[30] Furthermore, the FBI investigated "the loyalty of designated aliens employed on War contracts," conducting 3,944 alien investigations during the first year of the war.[31] The Bureau was even charged with enforcing the May Act, which criminalized the practice of prostitution near army camps. The duty proved to be an annoying distraction to the Bureau, which nevertheless in 1942 dutifully sent 114 special agents to arrest a large number of venereally infected troublemakers near Camp Forrest, Tennessee.[32]

While attending to such tasks, the FBI failed at identifying many Soviet espionage agents. The Silvermaster case, discussed below, was perhaps the most blatant example of the Bureau's inability to apprehend even those Soviet spies whose names appeared on numerous "lists." But this general ineffectiveness was just part of a larger, lax security picture. As Maj. Gen. Follette Bradley of the U.S. Army Air Corps alleged, "[I]n the beginning of 1942 innumerable Russian civilian and military agents were free to move about without restraint or check and, in order to visit arsenals, depots, factories, and proving grounds, had only to make known their desires."[33] The FBI, despite having a presidential mandate to fight espionage throughout the war, overlooked most of this troubling activity.[34]

That the Bureau's resources were stretched thin did not help matters. In 1942, FBI headquarters were operating twenty-four hours a day, with no employee leave permitted.[35] At that time, 3,477 special agents were averaging nearly twenty-three cases each, more than twice their normal load.[36] By 1943, the FBI would employ 4,853 special agents, who if anything were even more overworked.[37] Meanwhile, in congressional testimony for greater Bureau funds throughout the war, Hoover and his assistant, Tolson, proudly continued to cite the Bureau's 1941 success in breaking the German Duquesne ring.[38] Indeed, the director's consistent focus on German spies, even as his agents were beginning to pick up evidence of Soviet espionage, is striking. Time and again in his appeals to Congress for additional monies, Hoover mentioned (largely insignificant) German infiltration, while never specifically referring to Soviet spies.[39] His emphasis on German agents reflected the priorities of the White House and the Department of Justice at the time; the FBI's growing interest in Soviet espionage was not matched in the executive or legislative branches, and Hoover knew well to emphasize the country's sworn enemies in his requests for additional funds.[40]

Another striking aspect of Hoover's testimony is his frequent trumpeting of his agency's success combating espionage, despite the clear evidence to the contrary, as far as Moscow's representatives were concerned. In his 1942 annual report, the director claimed that "through preventive measures . . . espionage activities have been thwarted," while Tolson emphasized that "We have investigated a large number of espionage rings and quite a large number of individual agents" and "[broken] them up before they do much damage."[41] It is true that in the first year of the war the FBI saw fifty-six people convicted for espionage or failure to register as foreign agents.[42] Yet Hoover apparently chose to ignore or remain oblivious to ongoing Soviet espionage when he claimed in 1943 that his agency was "successful . . . in carrying out its primary responsibility of protecting the home front against spies, saboteurs, and subversive agents" and that "the counterespionage program of the FBI has brought enemy espionage within the US under control."

In 1944, Hoover vaunted to Congress that "the FBI's internal security program was even more intensely pursued, with the result that no act of enemy-directed sabotage occurred during the year and enemy efforts in the field of espionage were rendered ineffective." To keep the money flowing, Hoover still hinted of "enemies . . . [who] will become even more brazen in their espionage efforts."[43] Was he at last making a cryptic reference to the Soviets?

Hoover's claims *were* accurate in regard to German espionage and sabotage, which was nearly nonexistent during the war.[44] The handful of bumbling German spies who washed ashore on the eastern seaboard in 1943 and 1944 were either executed or given long sentences. But Soviet spies remained largely unmolested during this period, and Hoover's assertion that the "paneling boards" that FBI and Military Intelligence officials had set up at the nation's borders were "a most effective barrier" against infiltration is questionable. His boast to Congress in 1945 that "we were able to quickly apprehend every subversive agent in every section of the country," moreover, is simply false.[45]

What seems clear is that while the FBI did stop German agents, and bragged of this fact quite regularly to Congress, its agents were ineffective in their fight against Soviet espionage. Perhaps the difference stems from the fact that, as Hoover told lawmakers in 1945, his counterespionage program "emphasi[zed] . . . control of Axis agents operating in the US and upon the penetration and study of the Axis intelligence system."[46] But the agency was not entirely focused on German espionage during the war. Investigations of Soviet agents like Arthur Adams, Steve Nelson, and Andrei Shevchenko were in full swing by 1944. However, because of competing priorities, and also because he lacked the men, Hoover could not pursue Soviet espionage to the extent he would have wished. By the middle of the war, as more information emerged within the agency on Soviet spies, former special agent John Walsh recalled hearing about the Adams case and the Steve Nelson affair at Bureau conferences. The concern about Soviet espionage was palpable, as was the sense of frustration as to what could be done, he recalls. Even when the FBI was given a specific mandate to find Communists, as it had been in its investigations of the Dies list, it received limited cooperation from other government departments.[47]

The Role of Lend-Lease in Industrial Espionage

As Kravchenko's comments at the beginning of this chapter reveal, the wartime alliance played no small part in the success of Soviet espionage. The

$11 billion in lend-lease aid to Russia brought a tidal wave of Soviet visitors under the auspices of new trading agencies like the Purchasing Commission and existing ones like Amtorg.[48] The Soviets took advantage of the unparalleled intelligence-gathering opportunities. Adm. William Standley, who served as ambassador to Russia during the war, recalled that the Russians "were the most avid seekers after information that I have ever seen—even more earnest and zealous than the Japanese. . . . The Russian attachés, military, naval and commercial, picked up everything—copies of all technical and trade . . . and military and naval professional magazines, blueprints of everything from nuts and bolts to washing machines."[49] An FBI informant who had worked in the heavy industry section of the Soviet Purchasing Commission later told the Bureau that Soviet engineers were making special efforts to obtain "any industrial processes which are of recent invention or discovery," which they then copied at the commission's lab.[50] Of course, much of what the Soviets wanted was not secret. As FBI director Hoover pointed out, the Soviet Purchasing Commission "copied everything" about steel plants and equipment from sources like the catalog of the Association of American Iron and Steel Engineers. They raided the Government Printing Office's publications and placed small orders at firms so that they might obtain blueprints. Moreover, from December 1944 to July 1945 the Soviets ordered over 100,000 patents.[51] Soviet engineers also resorted to copying directly the items that fell into their hands, such as some B-29 bombers that landed in the Soviet Union when they ran out of fuel. Similarly, they duplicated the designs of British Rolls-Royce engines provided to them during lend-lease.[52] Soviet technicians even obtained the blueprints for the General Electric plant in Lynn, Massachusetts, as well as its plans for the "first jet propulsion engine in the United States."[53]

The wartime alliance made intelligence sharing strategically important. The U.S. Joint Chiefs of Staff put it bluntly: "[E]ven if we get no information from the Russians it is still, on the narrowest view, to our advantage to put into the hands of the Russians the means of killing more Germans."[54] This was also the president's policy. Having lost millions of people in the war effort by 1943, the Soviets were certainly entitled to generous assistance. But the policy did not gladden the hearts of all in the military. As Maj. Gen. J. H. Burns noted, both the Military Intelligence Division of the War Department and the Office of Naval Intelligence believed there should be a quid pro quo. These agencies hoped to "use the Lend Lease supplies, which the Russians needed, as a bargaining tool in order to obtain military information from them which the U.S. military wanted." Instead, as an MID official complained,

"The Russians have exploited American help, but they do not understand our altruism . . . and completely fail to cooperate with us."[55]

According to those involved in the shipment of lend-lease materials, the Soviet Union received some rather sensitive items. George Racey Jordan, who cleared trans-Alaskan Russian lend-lease shipments at Gore Field in Great Falls, Montana, asserted after the war that the Soviets had shipped large quantities of unauthorized materials, including hundreds of pounds of uranium as well as heavy water, between 1943 and 1944. This caused one angry journalist to respond that "these samples of important A-bomb ingredients were given to the Soviet Union as part of the appeasement policy of the [Roosevelt] administration." Gen. Leslie Groves, the chief of the Manhattan Project, affirmed his opposition to the shipments of atomic matter, but pointed out, "There was a great deal of pressure being brought to bear on Lend-Lease . . . to give the Russians everything they could think of." By the time he learned of the shipments, to stop them would have only drawn attention to their importance, thus threatening the security of the atomic project. Or, as Col. Thomas T. Crenshaw, a Manhattan Project engineer, said, "[W]e didn't want to arouse [Soviet] curiosity regarding a product that had been previously commercially available." Still, Groves disputed Jordan's claim that 2,800 pounds of uranium had been shipped through Great Falls; instead, he declared, only about 1,000 pounds of uranium oxide and uranium nitrate had been sent. He was also dubious about Jordan's description of large quantities of heavy water reaching Russia, suggesting that little was being produced in the United States then.[56] All the same, the government's inability to stop such shipments in the face of Soviet demands is suggestive of the lax security climate, which continued even as the counterintelligence community became more convinced of the perils of Soviet espionage.

Many documents also were shipped out under diplomatic immunity in the war. Semen Vasilenko, a chemist at the Soviet Purchasing Commission and an expert on pipe and tube technology, traveled through Great Falls with 4,000 pounds of "diplomatic mail" in February 17, 1944—allegedly including six bags of "secret material" related to "the production of planes . . . artillery . . . [and] technological processes in metallurgy."[57] Jordan recalled that when he complained to John T. Hazard at the State Department about massive shipments of uncensored material traveling under diplomatic immunity—including blueprints of aircraft and industrial plants, industrial films, and patents—he got only a breezy affirmation that nothing left the country without Hazard's agency's consent and that "the Department knows exactly what it is doing."[58]

Jordan blamed the free flow of sensitive materials on Harry Hopkins, whose administration of lend-lease, determination to help the Russians, and personal "ardor for the Soviets" prevented anything but the most scant control of shipments.[59] Hopkins certainly wanted to assist Moscow. When H. H. ("Hap") Arnold, commanding general of the air force, refused to allow fifteen Russian engineers to visit the Wright Aeronautical Corporation plant to inspect the R-2600 engine in 1943, claiming the Army Air Force could not afford "to divert the necessary people" to fulfill the firm's contract with Russia, Hopkins intervened. He learned that the plant was also constructing the B-29 Superfortress and that "the Army Air Force is not willing that the Russians should find out very much about this engine." Hopkins urged Arnold to reconsider his stance to "help preserve the good relationships between the Russians and ourselves."[60] As Lt. Col. George F. O'Neill, a security officer at Gore Field, lamented, "All of us at Great Falls airbase knew that Russia had the ear of the White House. . . . If the Russian mission didn't like the way something was going, in no time at all they'd have the White House on the wire and then we'd be jumping."[61]

Hopkins's or the White House's predilections notwithstanding, Jordan's reports of espionage have never been fully corroborated, and some of his claims are simply unbelievable. For example, his statement that he saw reports marked "from Hiss" stretches credulity, suggesting the influence of contemporary reports of Hiss's perfidy when Jordan's book was published in 1952. Moreover, he alleged that materials authorizing uranium shipments were initialed "H. H." (Harry Hopkins), even though Hopkins did not sign his name that way.[62] As Congress's Joint Committee on Atomic Energy noted at the time, it "had been unable to locate definite evidence" that secret, Manhattan Project information had been shipped out as Jordan described. Nevertheless, with the reports of defectors Kravchenko, Gouzenko, and Bentley confirming large shipments of data, some of which occurred via the diplomatic pouch, Jordan's story cannot entirely be dismissed either.[63] A number of lower-level inspectors who monitored Soviet shipments during the war also confirmed Jordan's reports. Robert K. Califf, an officer in charge of weights and balances at Washington National Airport, noted that he was "prevented many times from examining parcels and pouches which I should have inspected . . . on the ground that they carried 'diplomatic immunity.'" Maj. Perry W. Parker, an intelligence officer at Fairbanks and Great Falls, declared that "the Russians in Montana and Alaska spent most of their time trying to worm out secret information from Americans." And Maj. John C. Starkie recalled that "a secret type of electronic equipment which was not authorized for the Russians" had been removed from a plane in Great Falls in late 1943.[64]

According to Kravchenko, all Soviet officials in the United States, as well as other countries, had two tasks to carry out: their official role (say, as an engineer), and their unofficial, more specialized task—"where in the United States he must work, which factory or chemical plant, or any kind of industry he has to watch." Purchasing Commission chairman Gen. Leonid Georgievitch Rudenko was an especially active collector of this secret information, according to Kravchenko, who noted that Rudenko maintained a safe of material on tank motors and navigation and airplane equipment. Anastas Mikoyan, head of lend-lease in the Soviet Union, had instructed Rudenko to "find out all secret information about the industrial development in the United States, and especially in the military industry." In this way, Kravchenko asserted, through lend-lease air and sea shipments, the Soviets sent home "dozens of tons" of data on everything from aircraft production to metallurgical formulae.[65]

Secret Industrial Intelligence Gathering in World War II

Information on American military industry came not only from those on legitimate technical inspection missions connected with lend-lease, but from Soviet illegals and their clandestine American contacts as well. As Lt. Gen. Pavel Mikhailovich Fitin, head of the NKVD's Foreign Directorate, noted in 1941, the Soviet government was surrounded by enemies and required "new recruitments especially in defense industries and in ministries that are impossible to penetrate through the legal station."[66] Itzhak Akhmerov became the chief illegal, or undercover agent, in the United States in December 1941. His marriage to Earl Browder's niece, Helen Lowry, demonstrated the cozy connections of Soviet agents and American Communists. Akhmerov himself always steered clear of Browder, cloaking his secret activities behind a fur shop in Baltimore.[67] Nevertheless, as the controlling agent of top spy Jacob Golos, many of whose sources were secret members of the American Communist Party, Akhmerov and his intelligence organization were never distant from party affairs.[68]

At the same time that Akhmerov was installed, Vassili Zarubin became the legal *rezident,* serving as second secretary of the Russian embassy while also heading the NKVD's U.S. station. Zarubin was a beefy man, five feet five and just over 200 pounds, a "natty" dresser with horn-rimmed glasses who was resented by his subordinates as a martinet. His chief assignment from Stalin, according to historians Christopher Andrew and Vassili Mitrokhin, was to learn as much as possible about American wartime goals and to pay particular attention to the fighting "resolve" of the United States.[69] In addition to the scientific and technical (S&T) espionage agents that Semyon Semyonov recruited, the Communist party—then reaching its peak of popularity in the United States—also provided recruits for the network of spies. Most notably, American Communist spies helped the Soviet Union infiltrate the Manhattan Project, securing information from installations in California, Illinois, and New Mexico, among other places.

Although American authorities expended huge amounts of manpower and resources on stopping what little Soviet espionage they were able to uncover on the atomic bomb, they devoted much less attention to Moscow's parallel spying in industry, an oversight replicated by historians in succeeding decades. Industrial production was not as sensitive as the atomic project, of course. Yet the material Soviet agents obtained in both industrial plants and government agencies that oversaw wartime production, like the Bureau of Economic Warfare and the War Production Board, far surpassed the information gained on the bomb.[70]

Though the FBI's investigations yielded a partial understanding of Soviet espionage during World War II, American officials would not learn the full extent of the problem until after the surrender of Germany and Japan. The decrypted Venona cables, part of a secret project that began in 1943, would provide much material about the history of wartime espionage.[71] But it was not until after the war ended that analysts gained the ability to read these now-famous Soviet messages, with master cryptanalyst Meredith Gardner of the Armed Forces Security Agency working closely with well-informed FBI agents like Robert Lamphere.[72] And it would not be until 1949 that Venona-based information led to the arrest of a Soviet agent, FBI analyst Judith Coplon.[73] As Venona would show, the Soviets had run a vast and successful industrial espionage operation during the war. In San Francisco, for example, Soviet consul Grigori Kheifetz had taken a consulate previously focused on the Japanese threat to Russia and turned it into "a center for spying on American political and technological developments," as historian

Steven Schwartz has noted.[74] Kheifetz had sources in the aircraft factories of Los Angeles, where his industry contacts included a chemist at Shell, Leo Daniel Levanas, and a group in the aircraft industry, including James Orin York, or "Needle," an engineer/designer at Northrop and Lockheed. York was mentioned in a 1943 cable as providing "five films of material" on a plane known as the XP-58. Other sources included Amadeo Sabatini of the Bohn Aluminum and Brass Company and Omnik Sergei Kapantsoff, an employee at the American Stamping and Manufacturing Company.[75] Kheifetz had a history of cultivating spies, having recruited while *rezident* in Italy an important physicist, Bruno Pontecorvo, who became a key spy for the Soviets on the Manhattan Project in Canada.[76] In 1950, York confessed to his espionage work between 1937 and 1943, listing as one of his handlers William Wiesband, an employee of the Armed Services Security Agency who later betrayed the Venona Project to the Soviets.[77]

At various points in 1944, as Venona indicates, the Soviets worried that both Sabatini and York were under surveillance, and thus curtailed some of their activities.[78] They had reason to worry. In 1943, FBI monitoring had uncovered atomic espionage at the Berkeley Radiation Laboratory, and an anonymous source identified Vice Consul Kheifetz as an important agent. These developments led the FBI to take a closer look at espionage activities in the Golden State, but they still missed a great deal—and not just in Northern California. For instance, Michael S. Leshing, superintendent of the Twentieth Century Fox lab, handed over materials on film technology to Ivan Ilych Pilipenkol, Soviet vice consul in Los Angeles. As Kheifetz noted, "From Leshing one can also get the formula . . . for developing a colored motion picture and other information on the technique of processing films." Kheifetz noted that Leshing, born in Russia, was a "serious and unselfish man," friendly with another "serious, married" colleague who might also be a good prospect.[79] The emphasis on this potential informant's sobriety and marital status suggests that the Soviets had been dissatisfied with the performance of less-stable figures.[80]

Besides those in California, the Venona cables reveal numerous industrial spies on the East Coast during the war. Eugene Franklin Coleman, an engineer at the RCA Laboratory at Princeton University, told Moscow about a new Army Signal Corps radar navigation and bombing design for B-26 planes.[81] But perhaps the greatest amount of material came from the industrial intelligence ring orchestrated by Julius Rosenberg. Rosenberg has remained most recognized for his role in atomic espionage, yet his contribu-

Morton Sobell, Julius Rosenberg, and Ethel Rosenberg

tions in that field—chiefly materials from his brother-in-law, machinist David Greenglass, who worked on the lens mould of the bomb—were minor when compared to those supplied by physicists like Klaus Fuchs and Ted Hall.[82] Rosenberg, a thin, bookish young man, first offered his services to the Soviet government in 1942 and was referred to Jacob Golos, according to Elizabeth Bentley, who herself remembered several calls for Golos in 1942 and 1943 from a man who introduced himself as "Julius."[83] When the FBI got Bentley's tentative identification in 1945, however, they did not pursue it.[84]

Following his graduation from City College of New York, Rosenberg began work at the War Department's Signal Supply Office in 1940 as a $2,000-a-year junior radio engineer. In 1941, he moved to the Signal Corps in Philadelphia and was subsequently transferred to the Newark Signal Corps Inspection District in January 1942 as an assistant inspection engineer. During most of the war, he worked at the Army Signal Corps' Engineering and Technical Division at Fort Monmouth, New Jersey, serving as an inspector at various plants under contract to the government, including

General Electric in Lynn, Massachusetts, the Radio Receptor Corporation, and RCA. In 1945, the discovery of Rosenberg's membership in the party finally led to his removal from the Signal Corps, and he went to work at Emerson Radio Company of New York. He stayed there until he started his own firms after the war, Greenglass and Rosenberg Engineering Company and Pitt Machine Products Inc.[85]

At Fort Monmouth, Rosenberg (known as "Antenna" and "Liberal" in the cables), recruited two electrical engineers, Alfred Epaminondas Sarant ("Hughes") and Joel Barr ("Metre"), both members of Branch 16B of the Industrial Division of the Communist Party.[86] Barr had been a classmate of Rosenberg's at City College, and he and Sarant became close friends in the early 1940s at the Signal Corps, where Sarant worked on a secret project designing systems for plane interception. Like Rosenberg would later, Barr lost his job early in the war at the Signal Corps owing to his Communist links; Sarant, too, was fired, for holding a secret meeting of employees and for "failing to obey orders." His dismissal was ultimately downgraded to "resignation without prejudice," which caused him little trouble in getting a post at Western Electric Company's 42nd Street Plant in September 1942 as an assistant engineer. As required for such a position, Sarant signed both the Espionage Act form and an affidavit that he had not joined the Communist Party or the German-American Bund. He was soon promoted to system engineer in the Electric Test Planning Division, which involved the design, development, construction, installation, and testing of secret ultra-high frequency radar equipment for enemy plane detection.[87] Sarant was known as a brilliant mathematician, although an FBI source reported that he was also a loner who did not always work well under pressure. According to his boss at Western Electric, Louis L. Anderson, however, this "lone wolf" also had "hundreds of girl friends" and abstained from coffee and alcohol to preserve his "sexual ability."[88] Barr, whom David Greenglass recalled as tall, handsome, and musically talented—and Alexander Feklisov described as having a "long equine face"—also transferred to Western Electric to work on radar, demonstrating how the war's need for qualified engineers clearly outdistanced security concerns.[89] His work concerned "a modulating II computer" and secret radar sets.[90] Both men continued to supply materials to Rosenberg at their new jobs. As Venona details, for example, Sarant provided the Soviets with "17 authentic drawings" of Bell's APQ-7, an airborne radar, in 1944.[91]

As Rosenberg was soon overwhelmed with documents and proved less than facile with a camera, Sarant and Barr were provided their own.[92] Feklisov recalled that Barr and Sarant produced about 500 pages of documents each month between 1943 and 1945, for a total of 9,165 pages.[93] Rosenberg also recruited Barr's good friend, aeronautics engineer William Perl of the National Advisory Committee for Aeronautics (NACA), who, like Barr, had known Rosenberg from the Steinmetz Club, a Communist discussion group at City College.[94] The connection of many of these men to City College at a particular moment in the late 1930s was one that intrigued FBI director Hoover, who in his later investigation wagered that collecting the names of all engineering graduates from that era might be fruitful.[95] Hoover would have noticed that most of the 1938 graduates were Jewish, but he probably would have thought it unremarkable that they were, to a man, men.[96]

Perl had obtained his BS in electrical engineering before he was nineteen and during the war had worked at NACA, first at Langley Field and

William Perl

then at the Lewis Flight Propulsion Lab in Cleveland. There, his tasks included directing fifteen other researchers in advanced jet propulsion projects. He had also written a dozen classified books.[97] Perl, incongruously code-named "Gnom" in the cables, was actually very tall; over six feet, he liked to eat from the top of his refrigerator. Of most importance to the Soviets, he "had access to considerable confidential information concerning the progress, experiments and development of war-time aircraft," as the FBI eventually discovered. Owing to the Venona documents, the FBI later learned that "Perl made available to the Soviets a great deal of the information" to which he had access.[98] In 1944, a cable reported that Perl's information about a Westinghouse jet engine assembly, including its configuration, dimensions, and power, was valuable enough to bring him a $500 bonus. His material "deserves exceptional attention," one of his Soviet handlers enthused.[99] According to Feklisov, in one year Perl provided "98 complete studies of secret material," half of which were "very valuable." These included 12,000 pages on the P-80 Shooting Star, a pioneering jet fighter plane. Despite the fact that the FBI overlooked Perl, as it did all the other Rosenberg engineers, the agency managed to make his provision of material somewhat treacherous. FBI men were constantly watching the exits of the Soviet consulate in New York from their spot across the street at the Pierre Hotel. Perl subsequently began providing his material to a contact in Cleveland, as it was too difficult to use the consulate for copying during his monthly visits to New York.[100]

Morton Sobell, another City College friend of Rosenberg and Perl, worked in navy ordnance before becoming an engineer at General Electric. He would be tapped for his "highly confidential work dealing with radar research for the U.S. Navy."[101] This, in any case, was what his former roommate and close friend, Max Elitcher, told the government in 1950—that Sobell had supplied information to Rosenberg on his "experimental work" in the Mechanical Radar Division at GE.[102] Sobell, however, has consistently denied any role in espionage.[103] Elitcher's source was Julius Rosenberg, who had pressed Elitcher himself for information, arguing that Sobell was already on board.[104] Elitcher had worked as an electrical engineer at the Navy Bureau of Ordnance from 1938 to 1948 after graduating from CCNY with a BS in engineering. He headed a division that worked on classified computers for anti-aircraft aiming and firing technology on heavy gun–equipped warships. In 1939, he recalled, Sobell had recruited him into the party, and he remained a member throughout his tenure at the navy. Indeed, he and Sobell were members of the same navy department Communist Party cell from 1939 to 1943.[105]

Elitcher informed the government that his old college friend Julius Rosenberg had first visited him in 1944, telling him that despite the Soviet role in the war effort, "a good deal of military information was being denied them by some interests in the United States." However, Rosenberg intimated, "many people . . . [were] providing classified information about military equipment," and Rosenberg hoped that Elitcher could use his position at the Bureau of Ordnance to join them. Rosenberg asked for blueprints and plans, noting that his Soviet contacts would screen them, and promised the documents would be promptly returned. Rosenberg hoped Elitcher could help— as, he said, Sobell was already doing.[106] Upon Rosenberg's third visit, at the end of 1945, Elitcher decided to tell him about his new assignment at the Bureau of Ordnance, including "underwater sound devices" and "anti-submarine devices concerned with offensive firing against submarines." However, he insisted that he furnished no specific information, such as blueprints, on any visit.[107] Rosenberg, who had already told his Soviet contact that Elitcher had "access to extremely valuable materials on guns," described him as "loyal, reliable, level headed and able," as well as a good photographer.[108] In the hope of developing him as a source, Rosenberg contacted Elitcher as many as eight times between 1944 and 1948, occasionally through Sobell, who asked Elitcher for "possible recruits for purposes of engaging in espionage work." Meanwhile, Sobell and Elitcher remained close friends and neighbors—close enough to share a washing machine—until Elitcher's accusations were made public. Although Elitcher insisted he had divulged nothing to the Soviets, he apparently found the frequent entreaties and their testament to his importance highly gratifying.[109]

Sobell had started working with Elitcher at the Bureau of Ordnance after college in 1939, before he entered the University of Michigan two years later. He was subsequently hired in 1942 by GE's Marine and Aeronautical Engineering Section in Schenectady and remained at the firm until 1947, when he joined Reeves Instrument Co. in New York City.[110] Sobell had a history of Communist activism that the U.S. government had been following since 1941, when he and Elitcher, his then-roommate, attended a rally of the American Peace Mobilization Committee, a Communist front that opposed American aid to the Allied Powers fighting Hitler before June 22, 1941. Sobell's name was also connected with the American Youth Congress, according to the Office of Naval Intelligence. In 1942, when Sobell was at

Michigan, he was spotted in rural Georgia photographing a flour and lumber mill, causing concern because of his reputed *German* accent.[111] Despite the suspicions, Sobell held a security clearance to work on secret military orders well into the Cold War. So valued was he to General Electric that the company asked that his draft be deferred in 1945 so that he could continue his work on air and seaborne radar. His clearance to visit top-secret military sites was renewed regularly through 1949, a sign of "laxness" in American security, note historians Haynes and Klehr, and a rather surprising one in view of the strict anti-Soviet tenor of that period, when associations like Sobell's had certainly been enough to remove others from their jobs, such as Barr.[112]

Rosenberg's responsibility for all his sources—he was the "linchpin" according to Feklisov—kept him very busy, and Soviet agent Leonid Romanovich Kvasnikov expressed his concern that "we are afraid of putting [Rosenberg] out of action with overwork." But they continued to tax him in December 1944: "We consider it necessary to organize the filming of [his] probationers' [agents'] materials by . . . himself." His hard work did not go unnoticed: in March 1945, Moscow awarded him $1,000 for his efforts.[113] In addition to the electronics information, Rosenberg also assisted the Soviets in their atomic research, as noted above.

In a most unusual step, Rosenberg himself directly supplied equipment to Moscow. As an inspector for Emerson Radio Corporation during the war, he took a ten-inch proximity fuse, which he had assembled secretly from rejected parts, and presented it to Feklisov as a Christmas present on December 24, 1944. The proximity fuse, then under a "secret" classification, was attached to bombs or warheads in order to detonate them when they approached a target. The fuse's radar technology would have been of most interest to the Soviet Union, which was following radar developments closely at the time. While Feklisov worried constantly about FBI surveillance, he recalled that the fuse-toting Rosenberg was insouciant over the course of their fifty meetings, "convinced he was doing nothing wrong."[114]

Some of the material obtained by Rosenberg may have been catalogued by E. Andriyve, a Soviet defector, who in 1956 testified to the Senate that when he was an editor and researcher at the Soviet Signal Corps Military Research Institute in Moscow twelve years earlier, he had examined "thousands" of American documents distributed to him daily by the secret police agents in his organization. Andriyve's job was "to determine how . . . they be channeled among the Soviet institutions dealing with this particular type of science or engineering." Some, for example, dealt with high-frequency tubes used in radar; others with field communications; others with "purely scientific matters." The actual materials included typed documents and enlarged microfilms and photographs of equipment. Andriyve remembered that two of the sources for these materials were Ft. Monmouth Army Base, home of the Army Signal Corps, and RCA. Many were marked "secret," "top secret," or "confidential" and appeared very new when he saw them in 1944. Andriyve learned from a friend who succeeded him that the flow continued into 1945. He was convinced that "other sections" in the Soviet military were also involved in his line of work, "translating and analyzing American confidential and classified documents."[115]

The U.S. Government Learns about Soviet Espionage

While Rosenberg's material was being transferred to Russia, American authorities, of course, remained completely in the dark. Former Soviet agent Anatoli Yakovlev, one-time vice consul in New York who was tried in absentia at the Rosenberg trial, reported that the FBI identified only half of the members of his agent network, largely only after the war.[116] Slow to catch on to Soviet espionage, the FBI did not believe as late as 1942 that American or Canadian Communists were "paid agents of the Russian espionage system." Instead, the Bureau believed they were largely assistants who obtained passports or set up commercial covers and contacts, all "necessary services for the operations of the actual agents."[117] The FBI's investigators, the State Department's Laurence Duggan noted, were "boys lost in the forest," which only helped the efforts of spies, even reluctant ones like Duggan.[118]

Still, the FBI and other intelligence agencies were following the activities of American Communists. In addition to infiltrating party gatherings on a regular basis, they also placed surveillance on certain party leaders. The FBI used its informants to search targets' rooms and to intercept their telegrams and mail, as well as to listen and report on their meetings and comings and goings.[119] One of these was California Communist leader and atomic spy Steve Nelson, and in April 1943 surveillance of him would shatter all illusions about the limited nature of Communist activities. For the first time, the FBI would record a party official in the act of obtaining secret technical information for Russia, which he then passed on to a Soviet intelligence officer, Vassily Zarubin. This episode provided indisputable confirmation for the FBI that domestic Communism and Soviet espionage were intimately connected.

The Bureau's suspicions were also fueled by its receipt of an anonymous letter that detailed the names of a number of agents, several of them under diplomatic cover, who were spying for the Soviet Union.[120] The letter's author has never been verified, but Soviet intelligence operative Pavel Sudoplatov asserts that it was Lt. Col. Vassily Mironov, an unhappy KGB officer in Washington. Mironov had taken a visceral dislike to Vassily Zarubin (also known as Zubilin) and his wife, Elizabeta Yurevna. The anonymous letter identified Zarubin as the "head of the administration of the NKVD Foreign Information Service . . . [in] charge of the illegal moving of agents into and out of the United States, organizing secret radio stations and preparing counterfeit documents," and it described his wife as having "an immense network of agents in all [U.S. government] departments."[121] The letter further accused them of being double agents; Zarubin supposedly worked for the Japanese and Elizabeta for the Germans. Since the letter was also sent home to Moscow, the author's clear intent was to get the couple into trouble. While the claims of treasonous foreign intrigue were a stretch, the letter's allegations about other spies have been verified elsewhere, suggesting that the missive came from someone knowledgeable about Soviet operations in the United States.[122]

In addition to the Zarubins, the letter also named and described Pavel Klarin, Soviet vice consul in New York, who was "bringing agents into the U.S. illegally," and Grigorii Markovich Kheifetz, Soviet vice consul in San Francisco, who was "reported to have a large network of agents in ports and war factories."[123] Others named included Amtorg engineer Leonid Romanovich Kvasnikov, Zarubin's technical assistant;[124] Semyon Semyonov, "robbing the whole of the war industry of America" with his agents in aviation and chemical plants;[125] Andrei Ivanovich Shevchenko, Purchasing Commission representative at Bell Aircraft;[126] and Leonid Tarasov, secretary of the Soviet embassy in Mexico.[127] The letter further asserted Zarubin's role in the Katyn massacre, an incident not then widely understood by American officials, who willingly accepted the Soviet version of events at Katyn in order to support the wartime alliance.[128]

The letter spurred the FBI to take a closer interest in those it named, especially Zubilin/Zarubin, Semyonov, Shevchenko, and Kheifetz.[129] The agency was not entirely unfamiliar with these characters, having begun an investigation of Semyonov in 1941.[130] Eventually crawling with government informants, Semyonov was recalled to Russia, although he managed to remain in the United States until early 1944.[131] The Soviets also quickly became aware of the new scrutiny of Kheifetz and warned the San Francisco consulate in 1944 that "intensified surveillance is being directed against you personally."[132] The FBI also monitored Soviet efforts to protect their sources. The Bureau hazarded that the April–July 1944 visit of Mikhail Milsky (or Milshtein), deputy chief of the GRU for North America, and Gregori Kossarev, an NKVD inspector, had instigated the departure of a number of agents. Owing to Milsky and Kossarev's displeasure with the security lapses they saw in America, "numerous important figures in the Apparatus of the NKVD and Red Army intelligence in the US were almost immediately recalled," the FBI asserted.[133]

By then, the accumulating evidence had led to the creation of two new investigations: the FBI's secret Comintern Apparatus (COMRAP) probe, and the Communist Infiltration of the Radiation Laboratories, University of California, Berkeley (CINRAD) investigation, both of which were launched in 1943. Separate investigations also followed employees at the University of Chicago's Development of Substitute Materials (DSM) Laboratory, which was manufacturing plutonium. In these efforts, the agency deployed new or newly authorized techniques, which included wiretapping, mail-opening, and "surreptitious entry," or black bag jobs.[134]

The Nelson surveillance and the Mironov letter would thus help cement the Bureau's growing concern about the Soviet espionage offensive and its indigenous connections and expand the Bureau's investigatory machinery during the war. While CINRAD focused chiefly on atomic espionage, COMRAP addressed espionage more broadly and examined political and propaganda efforts and the work of seamen couriers.[135] These initiatives drew a compelling picture of U.S. vulnerability to Soviet espionage practices. The FBI was now fully convinced that officials working under the cover of sanctioned Soviet agencies in the United States, along with members of the American Communist party, were conspiring "in the . . . transmission of espionage information." Moreover, through Soviet technical missions to "vital war industries," the FBI declared, Soviet agents "collect for the benefit of the USSR valuable information concerning production and commercial problems in the U.S. . . . . [W]ith very little effort and without arousing undue suspicion, they are able to learn what is going on within those industries."[136] As these assessments suggest, what had once appeared to counterintelligence officials as ad hoc intelligence collection by Soviet agents was now reconceived as a systematic espionage campaign. This new understanding, a product of World War II, would leave a prominent legacy for the Cold War era. It also led Hoover to quash the proposal of OSS director William Donovan to bring a team of seven NKVD agents, "plus the usual wives," to the United States in 1944 in exchange for establishing an equivalent OSS mission in Moscow. Ambassador Averell Harriman had written FDR in an enthusiastic endorsement of the exchange: "For the past two and a half years, we have been unsuccessfully trying to penetrate sources of Soviet information and to get on a basis of mutual exchange and confidence . . . I am certain this will be the opening wedge to far greater intimacy." But Donovan and the ambassador were rebuffed, despite Harriman's passionate declaration that "our relations with the Soviet Government in other directions will be adversely affected if we now close the door." Back at home, Hoover told the president that the proposal would create a "serious threat to the internal security of this country." Turf considerations were also likely on his mind. Thus, without mentioning spies, FDR gently informed Harriman that "the domestic political situation" required the plan "be deferred."[137] It was not taken up again.

Such preemptive strikes notwithstanding, the counterintelligence community's response to Soviet espionage developed only gradually and inconsistently. The FBI's dramatic reassessment of the role of both Soviet agents and their American assistants undoubtedly led to a level of surveillance that hounded many agents out of the country. Yet the Bureau often did not gather adequate evidence to bring espionage cases to a successful conclusion; wartime exigencies, too, put constraints on the pursuit of Soviet agents. Still, as NKVD illegal Itzhak Akhmerov told Moscow in 1942, "counterintelligence here has become very flexible and far-sighted," thus preventing him from meeting with some of his contacts.[138] Akhmerov was not alone in his concerns. The FBI's "prowling around," no matter its limitations, could not be ignored; indeed as Elizabeth Bentley learned in late 1944, Military Intelligence and other counterintelligence agents were also compromising her access to sources.[139] The FBI, moreover, succeeded in wiretapping every Soviet organization in the United States—allowing it to learn the cover names of intelligence sources and forcing Moscow to change them, as Allen Weinstein and Alexander Vassiliev point out.[140]

Espionage entailed other hazards for party members. Bernard Schuster, party functionary and Communist Political Association treasurer from 1944 to 1945, complained to Elizabeth Bentley that after underground service,

Communists "returned in an extremely anxious state."[141] Indeed, some of them "needed psychiatric treatment." Schuster told Bentley that he would—reluctantly—continue to send her people from the party "who he thought were of sufficiently strong character to stand the type of work that they would have to engage in."[142] He did so, while the FBI remained largely uninformed about the new recruits, unable to muster an effective response even as its expanded investigative campaign overwhelmingly convinced agents of the dangers of Soviet espionage.

Harry Gold's Sources

Among those whom the Bureau failed to detect was Harry Gold, who eluded the government's grasp even after Elizabeth Bentley told agents about her contacts with one of Gold's main sources, Abraham Brothman.[143] But Brothman and Gold would lie successfully to a grand jury about their wartime espionage in 1947. At that time, the government knew nothing at all about Gold's earlier espionage at the Pennsylvania Sugar Company and elsewhere.

During the war, Brothman had supplied Gold with material concerning chemical engineering, mixing equipment, and synthetic rubber from his firm, Republic Chemical Machinery. Some of this material, ironically, was also provided to the Russians through lend-lease.[144] At another of his employers, the Chemurgy Design Company, Brothman handed over information on aerosol dispensers to Gold; he also designed processes for manufacturing DDT.[145] Unfortunately for Gold and his Soviet handlers, Brothman was notoriously slow, requiring a good deal of hand-holding.[146] As a result, Gold's handler, Semyon Semyonov, felt compelled to give Brothman a "pep talk" in late 1942 or early 1943. Lauding Brothman for his work so far, he also "attempted to persuade [him] to associate himself with some large firm so that he might be able to obtain material of more value to the Soviets." Semyonov was not much interested in Brothman's own inventions.[147]

Regardless of Semyonov's wishes, Brothman preferred to work for himself (he opened his own firm, Abraham Brothman and Associates, in the summer of 1944), and he remained high maintenance.[148] To acquire the Buna-S process for synthetic rubber, Gold had to stay up all night with him, watching him type it out. Gold was gratified to hear from Semyonov later that the process was "very valuable."[149] Indeed, it was "equivalent to the efforts of at least one and possibly more Soviet Army brigades," and would help Gold earn the Order of the Red Star.[150] Brothman himself claimed later to have received a $1,000 award from Russia for his contributions.[151]

The synthetic rubber process seemed to be the end of Brothman's use to Semyonov, however. When the engineer expressed an interest in opening a laboratory to "do work on chemical processes for the Soviets," Semyonov "laughed hysterically," especially at Brothman's request for $25,000 to $50,000 in financial backing. Semyonov reiterated his view that "the best thing Brothman could do was to obtain a job with a large industrial firm in the United States." However, Brothman persisted in his requests until 1945, driving both Semyonov and his successor, Anatoli Yakovlev, to tell Gold never to see Brothman again—especially after Gold had begun gathering intelligence on the atomic bomb project.[152] Much to Yakovlev's shock, Gold actually ended up working for Brothman after the war, increasing the likelihood that their espionage on behalf of Russia would be discovered.

When Gold was arrested in 1950, numerous materials obtained from Brothman were found at his house, including information on a "Magnesium Powder Plant," several sets of blueprints prepared for the B.F. Goodrich Company on the butadiene and styrene recovery system in Buna-S, and blueprints for the Syndar Corporation of Wilmington, Delaware, on a 1,000-gallon water-cooled resin kettle. Much of the material was designed by Brothman himself. Did this constitute espionage? The FBI thought so, since the "material might be considered as classified or restricted material . . . within the purview of the Espionage Statute." But the government's key argument in the 1950 trial of Gold and Brothman was not that the material was secret, but that Brothman had provided material to Gold with the understanding that it would reach a foreign power.[153]

During the war years Gold also obtained industrial information from Alfred Slack, an "extremely competent" chemist who had been educated at Syracuse University but was "never a convinced Communist"; for that reason, unlike many wartime spies, Slack required payment. Slack had worked at Eastman Kodak before the war, when he had supplied a Soviet source named Richard Briggs with material on Kodachrome that would help Soviet engineers better understand film manufacture and development, as well as its uses in aerial photography. When Briggs died, Harry Gold replaced him in 1940 and continued to see Slack for the next four years. Paid $200 for each report, the chemist supplied information about nylon from a source at the Du Pont plant in Belle, West Virginia, and found "prospective recruits" at the Carbide and Carbon Chemicals Corporation in Charleston, West Virginia. After the war began, Slack transferred to Holston Ordnance Works in Kingsport, Tennessee, an Eastman Kodak subsidiary, where Gold found him and pressed him for information on RDX ("Research Department Explosive"), which was twice as powerful as TNT. By then, Slack had remarried and wanted out of the espionage business, but Gold's ability to blackmail him proved too potent.[154]

As for himself, Gold's allegiance to Russia made a normal personal life difficult. Before the war, he had fallen in love with a woman named Shirley Oken and wanted to marry her; his spy career, however, proved incompatible with the pleasures of a conventional life. He had instead chosen a life of "dreary, monotonous drudgery," as he put it, spending hours on corners, badgering sources, meeting with often-abusive Soviet contacts, and living a double life that his parents had not the faintest idea about, even though he lived with them.[155] To find time for his clandestine meetings, he sometimes stretched his Pennsylvania Sugar workday to seventeen hours. As he noted, "[T]he planning for a meeting with a Soviet agent; the careful preparations for obtaining data from Penn Sugar, the writing of technical reports and the filching of blueprints for spying (and then returning them); the meeting[s] . . . in New York or Cincinnati or Rochester or Buffalo . . . the difficulties I had raising money for all these trips; the cajoling of Brothman . . . and the outright blackmailing of Ben Smilg [the Dayton aircraft engineer who refused to deal with Gold] . . . [and] the many lies I had to tell at home" all took their toll on him.[156] Through it all, Gold did not neglect his mind; after finishing at Xavier University in 1940, he also managed to take courses at St. Joseph's College in Philadelphia.[157] His gratification was that he was helping the Soviet cause—no small matter for this devoted servant.

Harry Gold would have fit a later congressional report's description of spies Klaus Fuchs and Alan Nunn May: he too was "mousy" and "retiring," a "bachelor . . . with few friends and scant interests outside science and communism."[158] Although such judgments are perhaps too simplistic to adequately describe complex individuals like Gold, Fuchs, and May, these men certainly were loners whose isolation contributed both to the relative importance of this work in their lives and their willingness to perform it for little remuneration. During the war, Gold received a $100-per-month subsidy to continue his work for the Soviets, which would have only barely covered his costs for his far-flung travels and meals on the road.[159] Yet as Klaus Fuchs would remember him, Gold seemed happy, "as if he were pleased with the importance of his assignment, and, although not exactly bombastic, this word almost described his pleased countenance and demeanor."[160] By contrast, David Greenglass, who lacked the fierce devotion and sense of purpose of Gold, required more financial compensation and also turned out to be a less significant source of information.[161]

Gold's devotion was severely tested on numerous occasions. At one particularly frustrating moment in 1943, he could not reach Slack in Chattanooga while he still awaited Brothman's long-promised report on mixing equipment. Despondently waiting in New York for the train back to Philadelphia after a meeting with Semyonov, wondering about the worthiness of the whole enterprise, he was assailed by an anti-Semitic drunk who attacked him as a "kike bastard" and a "yellow draft dodger" (Gold's hypertension earned him a 4-F classification). Fearing any possible disturbance that would require explaining to authorities why he was in New York, Gold did not respond to the taunts, and the encounter only deepened his commitment to espionage. Falling back on his early motivations—Russia's supposed eradication of anti-Semitism—he recalled that "it seemed all the more necessary to fight any discouragement and to work with the most increased vigor possible to strengthen the Soviet Union, for there such incidents could not occur."[162]

Gold's work was made more bearable by the fact that he greatly admired Semyon Semyonov, his MIT-trained Soviet contact.[163] By 1943, Semyonov could report to Moscow that the Soviet Union had nearly thirty sources in strategic industries, including some coordinated by Gold and some run by Golos, such as Julius Rosenberg's group of engineers who, after Golos's death, reported directly to Semyonov.[164] This Soviet engineer was kind to Gold, furnishing him a good meal and cigars when the Philadelphian was feeling low. He even encouraged Gold to settle down and start a family: "as soon as it is possible you will once and for all close dealing in this lousy business and will completely forget it all." In the meantime, Gold invented a home life, complete with a heroically brave brother (no 4-F problem there), a wife with an objectionable mother, and twin children, Davey and Essie, in part, he reflected, to portray to his sources "the evidence of stability which a single man could not."[165]

Soon, Gold would be newly excited about his espionage work. In late 1943 or early 1944, Semyonov told him to drop his contacts with Slack and Brothman and get ready for something "big." Gold was instructed to think carefully before accepting "this most important of all jobs." With only a "vague knowledge" of nuclear fission, Gold could only imagine its importance to the Soviets and quickly accepted the job, as will be discussed in the following chapter. As cover, he planned to open a lab to address the problem of "Practical Application under Production Conditions of the Thermal Diffusion of Gases."[166] Despite such precautions, Gold's spycraft suffered from his own drinking habit, as well as packrat propensities that left a good deal of dangerous documentation in his closet. Among these effects was a Santa Fe map; its discovery would lead him to unleash a torrential confession to FBI agents who arrested him in 1950.[167]

Andrei Shevchenko: A Spy Discovered

Until that moment when Gold's double life came out of the closet, the government had completely missed his involvement in Soviet espionage, from Pennsylvania Sugar's processes to the atomic project. Yet officials occasionally learned of and successfully stymied industrial espionage while it was under way during the war, as they did with the efforts of the Soviet Purchasing Commission's Andrei Ivanovich Shevchenko (code-named "Arsenij"). Shevchenko served as liaison between his government and Bell Aircraft Corporation, where Russia had P-39 planes, also known as Airacobras, on order. Several months after he came to the United States in June 1942, Shevchenko asked Bell technical librarian Leona Franey for unclassified documents, and then pressed her for confidential information on "the first jet-propelled engine," Bell's P-59. He showered her with gifts, and although she provided him some secret material, once she had been contacted by the FBI she cooperated with them as a double agent.[168] Franey was one of over twenty thousand informants for the Bureau that year, part of a network of "reputable and responsible citizens throughout the United States" who brought the FBI "a wealth of intensely interesting and often valuable information." Shevchenko had been mentioned in the anonymous letter mailed to the FBI in 1943, which helped convince the agency of expanding Soviet infiltration.[169]

Even before being turned by the FBI, Franey was having qualms. As she noted, "I was getting to the point where I was wondering why he was asking for material, and I had to ask the other girls in the library not to issue material on jet propulsion to him."[170] With the FBI now working with her, Shevchenko got everything he asked for, including material on the P-59 and on swept-back wings (which he requested even before Bell technicians were working on the problem). All of the material was sanitized before Franey photographed it with the cameras Shevchenko had provided her. His wish list included such items as "a summary of drag results from recent Langley Full-Scale-Tunnel Tests of Army and Navy Airplanes," and the top-secret "Tests on a Partially Swept-Back Wing with Varying Dihedral."[171]

In addition to acquiring Franey's "documents," by the end of 1942, Shevchenko claimed to have successfully gained information from Bell plastics engineer George Beiser.[172] He also wined and dined another engineer at the plant, Loren G. Haas, with expertise in air and power research. Haas, too, began sharing drawings with the Soviet representative.[173] Although Haas did not see himself as a spy, he did take money from Shevchenko—up to $200 for these documents.[174] By the end of 1944, at Shevchenko's urging Haas located a position at Westinghouse Electric Company, "with still no idea of espionage in mind," he recalled. Only after the Soviet engineer had renewed contact with him at Westinghouse did Haas finally inform the FBI. From March until November 3, 1945, he supplied the Russian with documents related to "highly secret turbo jet engine data" that the FBI and the Bureau of Aeronautics previewed. In his blandishments to Haas, Shevchenko made the argument that appealed to so many who helped the Soviet Union: "I am a Russian . . . and you are an American, but we can't let nationalities interfere with progress. Scientists must be international."[175]

In July 1945, after Shevchenko moved to Amtorg to become a vice chairman, he asked Franey and her husband, Joseph, a Hooker Electro-Chemical Company rubber repairman, to microfilm more classified reports, which they did under continued FBI supervision. Although unaware of this FBI role, Soviet intelligence agents did sense the FBI's close monitoring. The Soviet consulate, where much of the material was filmed, was under "unceasing surveillance," Soviet NKVD *rezident* Stepan Apresyan told Lt. Gen. P. M. Fitin; Apresyan urged him to supply Shevchenko with a camera to film the documents at his apartment to avoid the risk of "exceptionally secret materials" being intercepted.[176]

Venona suggests that Shevchenko had a number of other contacts besides Franey, Haas, and Beiser. Assisted by two other Soviet agents, Nikolai Pavlovich Ostrovsky and Vladimir Nikolaevich Mazurin, he also developed William Plourde at Bell. He recruited a source at Curtiss-Wright named William Pinsly, and obtained material on the JB-2 Robot bomb, equivalent to the German V-1, from sources at Republic Aircraft.[177] FBI agents were surely gratified to learn later that Soviet intelligence considered the doctored material they supplied to

Shevchenko "reliable."[178] But Shevchenko also furnished material unbeknownst to the FBI. A June 1944 cable reports that he passed on information about aircraft from William Perl.[179]

After the Shevchenko story broke in the press in December 1945, he left the country with his wife and son.[180] His escape had been facilitated not only by a tip from Moscow, but also by the U.S. government's apparent reluctance to press charges. Also departing that winter was another longtime industrial spy, Arthur Adams. Following steady surveillance, Adams had attempted to escape in 1945 but was stopped by the FBI while trying to board a Soviet vessel in Portland. "Government policy" prevented his arrest and allowed his January 1946 embarkation.[181]

Joseph Franey told HUAC in 1949 that the FBI had cancelled the last trip he was to make to Shevchenko when agents "said they got orders from Washington that the State Department wanted to hold this up and appease them a little bit, and asked us if we could cooperate." Franey was still fuming about that episode, as was Loren Haas, who expostulated to the congressmen: "In good faith, you help, say, this Government of ours, with a goal of doing a good deed and helping to restrain an individual such as Shevchenko, and then . . . when you ask 'When is it going to stop, when are we going to bring this man up for trial,' you are passed off with such answers as 'Well, Mr. [James] Byrnes of the State Department says we can't touch him.'"[182] Hoover, of course, stoutly defended the dignity of his office by denying that he had been obstructed in fighting espionage. But the episode illustrates the daunting hurdles counterintelligence officials faced in apprehending even those agents for whom they had compelling evidence of spying.

The Bentley Case

Soviet spy Elizabeth Terrill Bentley's 1945 defection to the FBI was enormously significant, both for its effect on the mindset of American officials, who now redoubled their efforts in fighting the Soviet "menace," as well as for its impact on the tactics of her Soviet spymasters. Her defection had the effect of a *Titanic*-sized iceberg on Soviet operations in the United States, as the NKGB stopped all communication with a number of agents and ordered others to be circumspect in their dealings with their American contacts and to deny any dealings with Bentley. Several Soviet agents were recalled, including Akhmerov and Anatoli Borisovich Gromov, first secretary of the Soviet embassy and head of the NKGB, both of whom had extensive dealings with Bentley.[183] Agent Feklisov recalled having to cut ties with all of his agents, for which he blamed the "renewed energy of American counterespionage."[184] The FBI, which had been watching Bentley even before she defected, took her story seriously, unlike its earlier treatment of Krivitsky, and assigned twenty-five counterintelligence agents to the case. Hoover immediately launched technical and physical surveillance of those she named, believing that such surveillance would help "determine the extent of . . . activities on behalf of the Soviets and . . . [identify] espionage agents."[185]

Judged by the standard of prosecutorial effectiveness, her defection seems to have had dubious import in the United States; it led to the convictions of only two men, Edward Fitzgerald, for failing to testify, and William Remington, for perjury. The rest of those she named took the Fifth Amendment, effectively denied her charges, or avoided testifying altogether. Since the Soviet Union had been immediately alerted to her defection, the FBI's chance of catching any of her spies in flagrante evaporated.[186] Nevertheless, evidence for Bentley's statements may be found in the correspondence of

Elizabeth Bentley, testifying before the Senate, July 31, 1948

Pavel Fitin, the head of the NKVD's foreign intelligence directorate, that lists eight of the people she named, as well as in the Venona documents.[187] Bentley sometimes exaggerated her story, particularly in her later testimony to Congress during the Cold War, but the dearth of convictions does not reflect a lack of merit in her initial claims about Soviet espionage practices. It did, however, contribute to long-standing skepticism about her allegations.[188]

Bentley might never have abandoned the cause if her lover and boss, Jacob Golos, had not died in 1943 of hardening of the arteries—leaving her to the tender mercies of Moscow's top intelligence men. Akhmerov, who had long been concerned about Golos's methods of doing business and his vulnerability as a target of FBI surveillance, now wanted Bentley to turn all her contacts over to him, including her prize source, the Red Banner–winning Nathan Gregory Silvermaster, with links to the Pentagon and other agencies. An angry Bentley resisted Akhmerov for over a year.[189] Earlier, Golos had faced similar pressure from the NKGB to hand over Bentley and his other sources directly to Soviet intelligence and to separate his people from the party; he too had refused to do so.[190] Bentley meanwhile got little help from CPUSA head Earl Browder; at Moscow's insistence, the party leader acquiesced in June 1944 to the transfer of Silvermaster and his group to Russian intelligence. Bentley became thoroughly disillusioned with the party leader and with Communism.[191] As her biographer writes, she was by then depressed, drinking excessively, and pursuing lovers of both sexes. Akhmerov still maintained that "her life is connected with us," but that would not be the case for long.[192]

Under pressure from Moscow, Bentley at last ended her contact with Silvermaster in September 1944.[193] That month, she received a new boss, "Al," Anatoli Borisovich Gromov or Gorsky, first secretary of the Soviet embassy and head of the NKVD in Washington, who demanded in December that she turn her remaining sources in the Perlo group—who were connected with the Treasury and the War Production Board—directly over to him. These efforts were all part of a larger push by the Soviet Union to take greater control of their sources.[194] Bentley was told she must "go 'on ice'" for six months; as she noted in a mix of metaphors, "[T]he whole set up of [Golos's] was full of holes, and they were afraid of leaks, I might be what they called 'quite hot.'"[195]

To mollify her, Gromov told her she had received the Order of the Red Star from the government of the USSR for her "distinguished service" and tempted her with promises of money, air conditioners, and fur coats.[196] At the same time, he once more "insisted that [she] make arrangements to turn over all of [her] Washington contacts." Bentley told the FBI later: "I became thoroughly disgusted with Al because of his obnoxious behavior."[197] With little choice, she did stop acting as a courier, gathering her last information in Washington in December 1944. Meanwhile, her nervous Soviet superiors believed that she would be more stable with another lover—like Golos.[198] However, Akhmerov and Gromov were not comfortable with the man she soon picked up at her hotel, Peter Heller, who professed to be a lieutenant in the New York National Guard; they believed, as Bentley did, that he was a government investigator. But Heller, it turned out, was nothing but a "bag of wind," according to the FBI—he worked in textiles and was married.[199] Convinced of the worst, however, Gromov ordered her to drop Heller and then recommended to his Soviet superiors that it would be best if Bentley left the United States. Even though she was no longer acting as a courier, she was a "serious and dangerous burden," he noted. If only there was a "legal" way to send her to Russia![200]

To entice her to leave, Al told her that her "position was extremely dangerous" and she should abandon her shipping business, go to Mexico or Canada, and from there, be "smuggled . . . to Moscow." She would get a "monthly salary" in Russia, "special training" for new work in Latin America, Canada, or the United States under a new name, as well as an apartment and free transportation and vacations. Bentley knew what a trip to Moscow might mean. In August 1945 she was asked again to leave her firm, U.S. Service and Shipping, a request she once again refused. At that time, Bentley remained vice president and secretary of the company, and the NKGB had long been concerned that her public connections there would lead to discovery of her secret work. In November 1944, Allen Wardwell, honorary chairman of the Russian War Relief organization in the United States, wanted to know whom to contact in order to ship packages to the Soviet Union, and Soviet intelligence wanted to make sure that Bentley had absolutely nothing to do with it. "In as much as [his] plan directly threatens the existence of MYRNA's [Bentley's] cover, we think it necessary . . . to advise Wardwell to approach Comrade [Anastas] Mikoyan direct," advised Pavel Ivanovich Fedosimov.[201]

Indeed, the FBI had been following World Tourists and U.S. Service and Shipping for some time already.[202] In November 1944, the Bureau was also looking into World Tourists' "fraudulent handling" of packages. The following July, agents had investigated the organization's balance sheet.[203] Gromov warned Bentley that the grim financial picture of World Tourists—to which Bentley also was still connected—could mean that "The FBI might come to believe that the concern was not strictly legitimate but rather, a front for Russian activity"—which, of course, it was.[204]

Believing, then, that the U.S. government was after her (using Heller as the vehicle) and feeling most oppressed by the agents of the Soviet intelligence service, Bentley became increasingly restless and uncomfortable. At a meeting in September 1945, Al once again tried to get her out of U.S. Service, telling her she should busy herself with a dress shop or some other small business for six months, after which she "would be given some important government officials to contact . . . in the same way as formerly."[205] Bentley was incredulous; she recalled, "I became so angered with him that I told him in plain words what I thought of him and the rest of the Russians and . . . that I was an American and could not be kicked around." Al retorted, correctly, that she was drunk.[206] He also reported back to Moscow that it might be best to have her killed, and even Akhmerov, while less inclined to pursue this violent option, began to believe her "unbalanced." But NKVD official Vsevolod Merkulov dismissed the likelihood of Bentley's defection, and urged Gromov to continue to be "friendly" with her and offer her money, which he did—telling her she could go back to her shipping business and offering $2,000 for her own use on October 7. Meanwhile, as Weinstein and Vassiliev point out, Soviet authorities could not have failed to note the August defection of *Daily Worker* editor Louis Budenz, who knew of Bentley's role and emerged as another risk for exposing her activities.[207]

As Bentley professed, by the time she went to the Bureau, a combination of "the effect of Mr. Golos wearing off, the effect of the Russians brutally showing their hand to me . . . and suddenly coming in contact with high functionaries of the Communist Party, like Browder, and discovering that they were just cheap little men pulled by strings from Moscow" all made her decide to go "back to being a good American."[208] Golos had protected her from the realities of the Soviet operation; she saw him as "working for the . . . betterment of the world." His Russian bosses, though, "made no bones of the fact that they had contempt for American Communists with their vague idealism."[209] Bentley had joined the party as a young idealist herself; she had been convinced that Communism would end discrimination. But now she believed that "a Communist is a very unscrupulous and clever psychologist who takes advantage of a person who is pretty confused and manages to sell him [a] program." As Kathryn Olmsted points out, the immediate precipitant for her defection seems to have been a threat made against her life by a party official, who demanded a refund of the party's $15,000 investment in her company, U.S. Service.[210]

She first went to the FBI on August 23, 1945, even as she was still meeting with "Al." Bentley traveled to the New Haven FBI office because it was less "conspicuous" than Washington or New York, places where she was convinced she might run into party agents.[211] At this first meeting, she only discussed Peter Heller. The FBI representative she spoke to, Special Agent Edward J. Coady, knew nothing about Heller, and wondered if Bentley were completely sane. Other than determining that her boyfriend was a nonentity, the agency did not follow up on her. Two months later, she returned not only to talk about Heller, but also about herself—they were both "involved in Soviet espionage," she claimed. Still clueless but finally concerned, the FBI called her back for her third and fateful interview on November 7. On that day, the FBI interrogated her for eight hours and Bentley signed a 31-page statement.[212] Her espionage confession went on for weeks afterward, resulting in a 107-page final report naming more than eighty individuals.[213] As Bentley explained, "[American] Communists . . . felt very strongly that we were allies with Russia, that Russia was bearing the brunt of the war, that she must have every assistance, because the people from within the Government . . . were not giving her things that we should give her . . . that we were giving to Britain and not to her. And they felt . . . it was their duty, actually, to get this stuff to Russia."[214] Some of her sources believed, too, that their material was going to the Communist Party and not to the Soviet Union. They also did not know what she did with the materials; Pentagon source George Silverman, for example, thought Silvermaster would memorize his documents and bring them to Earl Browder; he did not know they were being photographed.[215] Browder certainly kept a close eye on her espionage activities, Bentley confirmed.[216]

The FBI was impressed with Bentley's claims, noting she "has reported with a high degree of accuracy . . . [policy issues] which were only known within the Government itself."[217] From her varied sources, the Bureau learned, the Soviets were apprised of German battle plans, official American assessments of the Soviet-German front, secret policy discussions on Lend-Lease, trade, and currency issues, and even "the approximate scheduled date of D-Day."[218] Her allegations of Soviet espionage in the government and industry confirmed—and greatly expanded upon—the previous reports of ex-spy Whittaker Chambers, who had spoken in detail to the FBI in May

1945. And when officials considered Bentley's confession in conjunction with Russian defector Igor Gouzenko's reports from Canada of a major case of atomic espionage in September, they became convinced that Soviet intelligence collection was an explosive and growing danger. Hoover told Truman about Bentley (known as "Gregory") the next day, but the public would not learn of her charges until 1948, when news of her allegations began to leak in the wake of a 1947 grand jury investigation.[219]

As Bentley told it, Golos's poor health was what first brought her in touch with his Washington sources in the summer of 1941. At his behest, Bentley went in August to meet Helen Silvermaster at her home at 5515 Thirtieth Street, N.W., but the visit did not go well. Mrs. Silvermaster, suspicious that Bentley was an FBI agent, responded to her in "a very careful, cagey manner." According to Bentley, the Silvermasters had been eager to help Russia since the Nazi attack, when Gregory Silvermaster asked Earl Browder "to put him in contact with someone who might transmit information he obtained to Russia."[220] Golos had chided Bentley for not being more trustworthy in appearance on this visit. Despite the bad impression, Bentley returned to the Silvermaster home two weeks later; this time, she received an envelope with a dozen typewritten sheets inside, along with party dues.[221] She dropped off Communist literature in return, continuing this practice every two weeks thereafter. As far as Bentley knew, initially only Silvermaster and his friend, Army Air Force captain William Ludwig Ullmann, a Pentagon employee who lived with the Silvermasters, were supplying her with information. The material "steadily increased," however, and she soon realized that more people were involved, especially after Golos told her to start reading the material herself as he became increasingly enfeebled. Bentley's knitting bag stretched with the load. At first, Silvermaster traveled to New York quite frequently to meet Golos and learn from him exactly what interested the Russians the most. By the end of 1942, however, Golos was giving such instructions directly to Bentley herself to pass on to Silvermaster.[222]

Gregory Silvermaster, a Russian émigré (née Zielbernelster) who was raised in China, reached a leading post in the war bureaucracy, despite widespread official suspicions regarding his loyalty. A Communist activist as an undergraduate at the University of Washington, Silvermaster received a PhD at Berkeley in 1932 (his dissertation was titled "Lenin's Contribution to Economic Thought prior to the Bolshevik Revolution") and provided refuge to Earl Browder when the party leader was being hunted down during the 1934 longshoremen's strike in California. Eventually, he became a senior labor economist at the Resettlement Administration.[223] In 1940, Silvermaster joined the Department of Agriculture's Farm Security Administration as its principal labor economist. At the same time, both he and his wife, Helen Witte Silvermaster, were active in groups considered "subversive," and in 1942, Silvermaster's involvement in such organizations led to a government investigation under the auspices of the Hatch Act. In particular, his membership in the American League for Peace and Democracy and the Washington Committee for Democratic Action had drawn scrutiny, as had his wife's involvement in the League of Women Shoppers, a suspected subversive organization. Silvermaster's name, moreover, had also appeared on the Dies Committee list of suspected government employees.[224] Though Silvermaster had always denied his Communist affiliation as well as any connection with the NKVD, in considering his application for the position of head economist at the Board of Economic Warfare in 1942, the Civil Service Commission acted on a complaint from the Office of Naval Intelligence to recommend that "the applicant be declared ineligible."[225] According to FBI investigator Louis J. Russell, Civil Service produced evidence that since 1920 "the applicant [Silvermaster] was an underground agent for the Communist Party . . . he has been everything from a fellow traveler to an agent for the OGPU." On July 16, 1942, Civil Service representative R. E. Greenfield recommended Silvermaster be removed from government service "for the duration of the national emergency." The head of Army Intelligence, too, called on Silvermaster to resign, providing further evidence of the government's widening concern about Soviet agents in government.[226]

During that tense time, Bentley followed Moscow's orders and stayed away from Silvermaster. But after interviews with his colleagues inside and outside the Roosevelt administration, government investigators determined that there was not "evidence sufficient to warrant charges that Silvermaster was a member of an organization which directed the overthrow of the Government of the United States."[227] Harry Dexter White and Lauchlin Currie had both provided favorable reports on the economist to Undersecretary of War Robert P. Patterson, who was investigating the matter for the BEW, and Patterson cleared Silvermaster in November 1942.[228] Silvermaster then became head of the BEW's Middle East division, gaining access to confidential economic data and military intelligence.[229] The Department of Agriculture, which still officially employed Silvermaster, launched a separate investigation of him in 1943. However, this operation went nowhere when the FBI proved unable to access adequately other counterintelligence agencies' reports on the economist, demonstrating a crippling lack of coordination in the intelligence community. Golos, of course, had told his Soviet superiors about the investigations, in which they were naturally closely interested; a Venona cable passed on the information that the FBI had asked Lauchlin Currie about Silvermaster.[230]

As Bentley's haul from the Silvermasters continued to increase, it was no longer possible to use typing as a means of copying the information. By the fall of 1942, Golos began providing microfilm, and Ullman acquired a camera and began photographing the documents in Silvermaster's basement. Although Bentley witnessed this process only once, she "knew from their conversations and remarks that such was carried on in the basement." The illicit material was supplemented by items that the two men dictated to Bentley from "small pieces of paper they would take out of their various pockets"; she transcribed her dictated notes later.[231] At the peak of the Silvermaster operation, Bentley noted, she brought forty rolls of microfilm at a time to Golos, although her usual collection was less than a half-dozen rolls.[232] Ullman also gave Bentley an enlarging machine and a viewer, which she set up in her apartment so that she and Golos could view the microfilm. By the spring of 1943, the rolls were taken to be developed in the Soviet embassy's laboratory.[233] Soviet cables confirm this mass quantity; the heavy stream of incoming material detailed planes, munitions, and manpower.[234]

Ullmann was a true member of the Silvermaster household, helping to mow the lawn and paint, driving with Silvermaster to work each morning, and later becoming a lover of Gregory's wife, Helen. She, too, photographed some documents and sometimes worked as courier when Bentley was unavailable.[235] Ullman, whose wealthy Missouri family had sent him to Phillips Exeter Academy and Harvard, where he received an MBA, had like Silvermaster come to Washington in 1935 to work for a New Deal agency, the National Recovery Administration's Consumers Advisory Board. Similarly, too, Ullman also joined the Agricultural Department's New Deal Resettlement Administration. By 1939, however, he had become principal economic analyst at the Treasury, working under Harry Dexter White. During the war, he received a commission to work at the Pentagon, where he had access to highly coveted aircraft production statistics thanks to the intervention of the sympathetic George Silverman, who worked as a chief production specialist in the Army Air Force Matériel Division. Outside the Pentagon, the Silvermaster group collected information from such sources as the Treasury Department's White and Lauchlin Currie, FDR's administrative assistant.[236]

White, like Silvermaster, had been the subject of a 1942 Hatch Act investigation for belonging to the Washington Union for Democratic Action. He, however, vociferously denied any Communist connections and attacked the investigation and the Dies Committee that had spawned it.[237] Yet as Bruce Craig and Kathryn Olmsted both note, White and Currie did pass information to Silvermaster, knowing it would go on to the Soviets. They did so believing they were not harming the United States, but rather spurring Soviet-American good will. Ironically, as Olmsted writes, they were "ultimately providing ammunition to men who would work to destroy [their] liberal ideas after the war."[238]

Bentley's contacts were highly productive. Despite near exhaustion—Silvermaster was afflicted with asthma—and often poor-quality film, recalled Bentley, "the Silvermaster group managed to collect a fabulous amount of confidential material [for] . . . the Russian Secret Police. Our most fruitful source of material . . . [became] the Pentagon. . . . Through Silverman and especially through Ullman came every conceivable piece of data on aircraft." This included, for example, "results of testing of aircraft . . . personal data concerning important Air Force officers, opinions of aircraft personnel on other nations, Army gossip," as well as "reports on the efficiency of particular types of airplanes, technological developments in aircraft manufacture, statistics regarding high octane aviation gasoline . . . all pertinent developments concerning the planning, construction, and completion of the B-29, and proposed movements of these planes when they were completed."[239]

In recognition of the importance of his material, the Soviet Union gave Silvermaster a handsome reward in 1944. Stepan Apresyan reported that the economist was "overjoyed" by the recognition and had confided that "his work for us is the one good thing he has done in his life."[240] By then, Silvermaster's personal life was growing more complicated: he, his wife, and their live-in guest were in a ménage à trois. In 1945 a combination of FBI pressure, the defection of Bentley, and the recall of several key Soviet agents all adversely affected Silvermaster's intelligence collection, and the group disintegrated.[241]

Along with Silvermaster's network, Bentley also collected material from the Perlo group, whose members she had first met at the New York apartment of John Abt, general counsel for the Amalgamated Clothing Workers, in early 1944. The group included Victor Perlo, Harry Magdoff, and Edward J. Fitzgerald of the War Production Board (WPB), Harold Glasser of the Treasury Department (an "incredibly valuable" source, according to Weinstein and Vassiliev), Charles Kramer of the office of Senator Harley Kilgore, and Donald Wheeler of the OSS.[242] Perlo himself furnished extensive information on aviation from his position in the aircraft division of the WPB, including material on the P-80, an experimental jet engine that the United States was developing to augment its existing P-47 and P-51 Mustang fighters, as well as the entire production plans for military aircraft at the board for 1945 and 1946.[243]

Another wartime entity with ties to the WPB, the Resources Production Board (RPB), gave Perlo access to "secret data on aircraft production, location of plant-making engines, wings, struts, aircraft armament, B-29 synchronized turrets, and automatic computing aircraft gunsights." Indeed, the RPB "drew in secret information from all phases of the war program" and "focused this data to show at a glance the most strategic and vulnerable and key points" of the program, according to a congressional analysis. As Senator Karl Mundt noted in 1948, the RPB had full information on such important war needs as aviation gasoline, covering everything from the cracking process needed to make its chemical components to how much gasoline each plant produced. Much of the material concerned scheduling of output at war plants, as well as updates on vulnerable transportation points such as bridges and railroads. Despite the variety of material, Bentley described the Perlo organization as "floundering" in its efforts "to secure desirable information."[244] Though Bentley eventually named more than one hundred people with Soviet links, only twenty-seven of those identified still worked for the government in November 1945. The Bureau, which had already investigated a number of them, dismissed many as "minor figures in whatever espionage activity may still exist today of the groups with which [she] worked in 1944."[245]

Some of the characters may have been minor, but the case was major. Within two weeks of Bentley's November 7 meeting with the FBI, the Bureau's Washington field office had 37 agents assigned to the investigation, most of whom were instructed to conduct either physical or technical surveillance of those she named.[246] Employees targeted within the government included Silvermaster, Victor Perlo, Harry Dexter White, George Silverman, Ludwig Ullman, and Helen Tenney; others outside it included William Remington, Abraham Brothman, and Alger Hiss. The World Tourists agency also was investigated.[247] By December the number of assigned agents at the New York and Washington offices had ballooned to 227 as the Bureau undertook its most ambitious espionage investigation yet. In pleading for an expanded

George Silverman testifying before HUAC,
August 18, 1948

budget for the increased Bureau payroll, Hoover explained that the hundreds
of new agents hired "during this emergency investigation" were not available for the handling of regular criminal and civil work at the FBI.[248]

As the Bureau geared up to investigate Bentley's accusations, she was
instructed to proceed with an already scheduled meeting with Gromov at
Bickford's Restaurant in Manhattan on November 21, 1945. As the Bureau
knew, she would now tell "Al" that she wanted to work again for the Russians: she was prepared to be a double agent, unbeknownst to Gromov.[249]
The two agents who watched the meeting, Floyd L. Jones and John Almon
of the Washington field office, reported an "innocuous" conversation

between Bentley and Gromov. When Bentley broached the idea of resuming her former espionage work, Gromov was "wholly unresponsive," as of course he had been for some time. He told her she should be happy to have "a normal, peaceful, settled life," for which she had once expressed a desire.[250]

Neither of them knew that this would be their last chance to hash over the issue. Gromov did notice the two G-men attempting to tail him after he left the restaurant, but this would not have surprised him.[251] More important was Kim Philby's informing Soviet intelligence the previous day about Bentley's defection. Philby's message cut short Bentley's potential masquerade as a double agent. Most important, it prevented the FBI from catching in the act any of the spies she named.[252] Following normal procedure, Hoover had immediately informed William Stephenson, head of British intelligence in the United States, about Bentley's defection, whereupon Philby quickly learned of it. Gromov himself returned to Russia on February 22, 1946.[253]

After her FBI confession, Bentley also went to visit another former contact, Earl Browder, who had been disowned by the party the previous April. Browder was now "extremely glad to see her" and "talked more freely with her" than he had previously done.[254] The only Soviet agent who apparently had not been alerted of Bentley's defection was Helen Tenney of the OSS; she continued to meet with Bentley until 1947, even though the Soviet Union was already well aware of Bentley's true allegiance.[255]

Following Bentley's confession, the FBI put in place "technical surveillances, mail covers and physical surveillances" on government employees that Bentley identified. This included twenty wiretaps.[256] In addition, the FBI planned "a 'black bag' job on Bentley" herself: while she was being interviewed, agents would search for evidence in her hotel room. As far as physical surveillance of those she named, the director wanted only "the best and most experienced men on tail jobs" and urged that the agents be extremely careful not to elicit suspicion. But this was apparently impossible; the "extreme surveillance consciousness" of suspects soon made physical surveillance impracticable.[257] The agency then proposed to cut off the physical surveillances, replacing them with "spot checks" and "physical cover of important meetings correlated with data from technical surveillances." Ending this surveillance also would allow 156 agents to pursue other work at their home offices, which turned out to be an appropriate response given the limited results of the agency's investigation. Meanwhile, technical surveillance continued on those for whom physical surveillance could no longer be justified.[258]

The Bentley case was an enormous endeavor with very little payoff. As Hoover knew, Bentley's testimony as an uncorroborated witness would have very little value by itself in court, and thus pursuing the case to prosecution could only embarrass the FBI because of its likely failure. Not only did the case rest on her word against those she had named, but proving that her sources had intended to harm the United States and assist another country, as required in espionage cases, also would be extremely difficult for the government. As a result, Bentley's allegations remained largely unproven, contributing to a pattern of academic as well as popular skepticism regarding her claims that continues to haunt her reputation years later.[259]

The FBI nevertheless hoped to find a witness who would corroborate her story, which proved extremely difficult. In 1947, a grand jury explored her findings—with most of those called taking the Fifth—and in 1948, House and Senate committees heard her testimony (as will be discussed further in chapter 5). Meanwhile, Hoover worked to deny job opportunities in the administration to those named by Bentley; when Silvermaster wanted to take a job at the labor relations branch of the National Housing Administration, Hoover wrote to George E. Allen, director of the Reconstruction Finance Corporation, to stop the transfer, declaring that Silvermaster "is reliably reported to be a Soviet espionage agent."[260]

Of all those she named in government, only two served jail sentences: WPB employee Edward Fitzgerald, for refusing to testify despite being granted immunity, and William Walter Remington, also of the WPB, for falsely claiming he had never been a Communist. Remington's response to Bentley's allegations against him was unusual in that instead of issuing a blanket denial of his conversations with her—she accused him of providing her with material on airplane production, high-octane fuel, and synthetic rubber—he tried to frame them as the innocent discussions of a government employee with a journalist. A bright young Columbia ABD, Remington had been watched by the FBI as early as 1941, when he had worked with the American Peace Mobilization.[261] Considering his party background, which dated to his undergraduate days at Dartmouth and was not difficult to discover, his insistence that he had not known that Bentley was a Communist convinced few.

The puniness of prosecutorial results, coupled with Bentley's dearth of documentation, led scholars to dismiss her allegations of spies in the U.S. government as the "imaginings of a neurotic spinster."[262] In the last decade, however, many of Bentley's claims have been amply corroborated by Soviet archives and the Venona cables.[263] Moreover, one scholar has recently highlighted how Bentley's supporters and detractors alike used her gender to minimize her. To those who put some faith in her claims, Kathryn Olmsted suggests, Bentley was still caricatured as a stock femme fatale, the "blond spy queen"; her opponents, meanwhile, dismissed her as an "old biddy." Both sides were uncomfortable with a strong, albeit unexceptional-looking woman who claimed to spy through her own "agency."[264] Some historians continue to shrug her off: Ellen Schrecker declares that Bentley was "melo-dramatic, unstable, and alcoholic," as well as "slightly hysterical." But like DNA testing in criminal convictions, Venona's long locked-up version of events presents a challenge to such old certainties.[265]

The Dies Committee's Wartime Work

During the war, the Dies Committee, despite (or because of) its diligent list-making, remained a controversial target. Along with the tongue-lashing Dies got from Harry Dexter White during the investigation of the latter under the Hatch Act, the committee chairman also was sued for mistakenly malign-ing David B. Vaughan, chief of the administrative management division of the Board of Economic Welfare. Vaughan sued for $75,000, and Dies, after apologizing, asked the government to pay Vaughan's legal costs.[266]

White and Vaughan were hardly alone in attacking the committee dur-ing the war. *The Nation* scoffed that Dies was even ready to put the vice pres-ident on the stand: "Whether the Dies committee has found anything in [Henry] Wallace's writing which could be twisted for its purposes has not yet been learned. . . . [I]t remains to be seen whether Dies will have the courage for a direct attack."[267] And groups sympathetic to Russia, not sur-prisingly, were apoplectic about the committee. The National Federation for Constitutional Liberties, believing that Dies and his fellow members were conspiring against the Soviet Union, blasted the committee for "fraterniz-ing with fascists."[268] The federation called for the committee's termination, claiming that "by continued and repeated attacks on our great ally, the Soviet Union, [it] has utilized its resources to obstruct the cooperation of the United Nations[,] which is a prerequisite to victory."[269] The group also lam-basted Dies's antipathy to the labor movement, for which the congressman indeed reserved a special animus. His last major study before he left Con-gress in 1945 was a compilation of thousands of names and organizations with links to the National Citizens Political Action Committee, the CIO's

PAC, which the House Special Committee on Un-American Activities argued was a Communist front. Many CIO leaders were indeed Communists, but most of those named in connection with the group's PAC were not (indeed, the committee destroyed the list in 1945). The report resulted from Dies's long history of distrust of labor unions and his particular pique at the Communists' success within the CIO.[270]

Although the Texas Democrat continued to investigate Nazis in the United States during the height of the war, his committee focused most of its attention on suspected Communist activity, as noted earlier.[271] Organizations like the Union for Democratic Action, for example, complained that its "leading members . . . have been attacked as Communists by the House Committee on Un-American Activities." The UDA, a pro–New Deal organization that included Reinhold Niebuhr among its founders, had provoked Dies by stating that his committee was "acting in the best interests of the Axis Governments."[272]

Sometimes it seemed that Dies was more concerned with suspected enemies of the committee than with those who threatened the country itself. The popular radio journalist Walter Winchell, for example, had his scripts and his producer subpoenaed, in what seemed mainly to be a spiteful reaction to the producer's refusal to give Dies an entire slot on Winchell's show. The journalist struck back, slashing Dies for focusing on the Communist proclivities of a prepubescent Shirley Temple. "How long will America stand for this person from Texas? Look at him! Who is he?" railed Winchell.[273] The Dies Committee's trigger-happy pursuit of suspected subversives compares quite strikingly with the caution exercised in the White House, where genuine reports of Communists in government were given little credence. It also represents an interesting contrast to the Supreme Court's approach. In its verdict on party leader William Schneiderman's citizenship case in 1943, the high court reversed a decision by the U.S. Circuit Court of Appeals, which had confirmed a district court's decision to deny Schneiderman his naturalization and citizenship rights. But the high court justices declared that Schneiderman's advocating the overthrow of the government fell into a vague category: "mere doctrinal justification or prediction of the use of force under hypothetical conditions at some indefinite future time." It was not, therefore, "agitation and exhortation calling for present violent action which creates a clear and present danger of public disorder or other substantive evil." Schneiderman's status as a naturalized citizen for seventeen years was also taken into account.[274]

As the Supreme Court prepared to give Schneiderman the benefit of the doubt, the U.S. Army also grew less apprehensive of Communists. Army adjutant general James A. Ulio announced a more liberalized policy on suspected Communist officers in February 1945, noting, "[P]ersons in the Army suspected of, but not proven to be, Communists [a sort of early "don't ask, don't tell"] had not proved to be a source of any difficulty and were loyally supporting the war effort." Ulio added, "There seemed little justification . . . not to use the services of such persons to the fullest in all capacities for which they were qualified." The War Department's new instructions of January 31, 1945, noted that "no action . . . will be taken that is predicated on membership in or adherence to the doctrines of the Communist Party unless there is a specific finding that the individual has a loyalty to the Communist Party . . . which overrides his loyalty to the U.S."[275] Although the army eased up on Communists, relations on the diplomatic front seemed less promising in this last year of the war. In April, Secretary of State Edward Stettinius wrote the new president, Harry Truman, that the Soviet Union "has taken a firm and uncompromising position on nearly every major question." Its leaders, for example, had refused to allow "contact teams" to help liberated prisoners in Poland, and they were delaying "an agreement providing for orderly liquidation of Lend Lease aid."[276] Future relations looked tenuous.

The Dies Committee's focused pursuit of innocuous characters, such as those in Hollywood and in the CIO's rank and file, typically blinded it from identifying real hazards to the country. The committee did call Jack Bradley Fahy, a government employee with ties to agencies including the Office of the Coordinator of Inter-American Affairs and the BEW, who was also a spy for the naval GRU (cover name "Maxwell"), to testify in 1943. He refused, and American counterintelligence sent him into the army instead. A Soviet cable reflected upon this decision: "We assume that: 1. The Greens (American intelligence) considered it was inopportune to make the case public. 2. They did not get documentary evidence of our activity." The cable confirmed that "Maxwell really was chosen by us." So well-connected was Fahy that he had been granted a "special payment" for each piece of key information he provided.[277]

Dies, of course, was not alone in letting Fahy slip through his fingers. The counterintelligence community missed him as well, just as they overlooked Bentley, Gold, Silvermaster, Slack, and so many others. But, as shown, the FBI also began to grasp the shadowy outlines of Soviet espionage in World War II, through its monitoring of such cases as Shevchenko's, and by its regular surveillance of Soviet agents in America. Still, the discovery of spying on the atomic bomb would be the most significant factor in solidifying a growing anti-Soviet outlook of American counterintelligence officials, even as some in other branches of government proved more welcoming to Moscow. That such a top-secret weapons project—unknown even to the FBI—would have been infiltrated by Soviet-supporting scientists appalled American investigators, spurring them to more vigorous action in the remaining years of the war. Beyond that period, of course, this increasingly vigilant approach would have the most serious repercussions.

CHAPTER FOUR

Soviet Spies, the Atomic Bomb, and the Emerging Soviet Threat

To the FBI, "the most striking example of Comintern operations in this country" during World War II was not Soviet spying on military-related industries like aircraft engineering, electronics, weaponry, petroleum, and synthetic rubber, most of which the Bureau had missed anyway, but "the Soviet-directed espionage attempts against military research projects dealing with atomic explosives."[1] The Bureau's detection of Soviet espionage on the bomb would significantly affect the American counterintelligence apparatus during the war. Despite the imperatives of the alliance against Hitler, atomic espionage had a galvanizing effect on American officials' approach to the Soviet Union and its agents and greatly increased their suspicions of that country and its potential dangers well before the Cold War.

At the Quebec Conference in the summer of 1943, Franklin D. Roosevelt and Winston Churchill had agreed that their nations would share atomic information with each other but with no one else, in seeming violation of earlier British-Soviet agreements.[2] Secrecy was vital, as FDR told Manhattan Project leader J. Robert Oppenheimer: "[T]he fact that the outcome of your labors is of such great significance to the Nation requires that this program be even more drastically guarded than other highly secret war developments."[3] Yet because of the efforts of clandestine sources like Klaus Fuchs, the Soviet Union was already well aware of the Western nuclear effort, a development that the FBI and other agencies were only just starting to comprehend.

Soviet intelligence agents had "heard rumors" of atomic research as early as 1940 and pressed their agents, including Gaik Ovakimian, to learn more about work at American universities in early 1941. The Soviets gained their "first reliable" information about the atomic project that September in England, where John Cairncross, a member of the Cambridge Five spy ring, was private secretary to Lord Hankey, an intelligence expert in Churchill's War Cabinet and chairman of the government's scientific advisory committee.

With this access, Cairncross first supplied material on gaseous diffusion of uranium from the British Uranium Committee to Anatoli Borisovich Gorsky—later Elizabeth Bentley's contact in the United States. That same month, Morris and Lona Cohen, an idealistic young Communist couple who were already supplying Moscow with material on aircraft machine guns, learned of the American atomic project and informed their Soviet handler. After Morris was drafted in 1942, his wife served as a Soviet courier, gathering material from Los Alamos throughout the war, attending to young physicist Ted Hall and another unidentified physicist code-named "Perseus." But the most important contributions would be made by Klaus Fuchs and delivered by his courier, Harry Gold.[4]

Ignorant of Fuchs's and the other above-mentioned agents' roles throughout the war, U.S. counterintelligence forces were nevertheless quite alert to Moscow's interest in the bomb; as Lt. Col. John Lansdale of the War Department told Oppenheimer in September 1943, "[W]e have known since February that sev-

Klaus Fuchs

eral people were transmitting information . . . to the Soviet Government."[5] James B. Conant, the Harvard University president who served on the National Defense Research Committee, had actually recruited Lansdale a year earlier "to infiltrate Berkeley undercover and snoop on the physicists there." In 1942, the Berkeley Radiation Laboratory, which had experimented with a cyclotron to split atoms, was the site of Ernest O. Lawrence and J. Robert Oppenheimer's construction of a prototype machine to separate fissionable uranium-235 from uranium-238 for possible explosive use, under the purview of the War Department. Lansdale, pretending to be a law student, listened in on lunch conversations in the cafeteria and soon learned that "atomic research on campus was common knowledge." When Conant got wind of the lack of secrecy, Lansdale was sent back to Berkeley in military dress to impress discretion upon the scientists.[6]

Lansdale told Oppenheimer of the "great weight the government attached to maintaining this operation secure against Russian espionage or Russian intelligence."[7] As project leader Gen. Leslie Groves would assert in 1954—hardly an auspicious time for expressing any subtlety on the matter—"there was never . . . any illusion on my part but that Russia was our enemy." He averred, "I always had suspicions and the project was conducted on that basis." Yet Groves also recalled that wartime security "was a secondary consideration . . . the major objective was to get the bomb perfected as soon as possible in order to end the war and save American soldiers."[8] Indeed, Groves himself had insisted that Oppenheimer must remain head of the program when it moved to its new lab at Los Alamos, New Mexico, regardless of counterintelligence officials' suspicions about his left-wing politics. Yet the general did try to keep the atomic scientists from talking to each other, a tactic that Oppenheimer quickly dismissed as counterproductive to the aims of the project. As Lansdale noted, compartmentalization was minimized at Los Alamos, "at least so far as the important people on the project were concerned."[9] Indeed, Oppenheimer strongly criticized the practice as leaving people in "isolation" with "almost no sense of hope or direction." Thus, by early 1944, despite Groves's strictures, "there was no part of the American plan to construct the plant at Oak Ridge for the manufacture of atomic bombs that was not known to the British group," as Albert I. Baker, vice president of project contractor Kellex, observed.[10] The lax security would allow a range of secrets to leak out of Los Alamos.

Although Lansdale and Groves considered the Soviets to be the chief espionage threat, early in the war the Germans were thought to be making the most progress on the bomb. The Nazi effort, however, soon lost steam, while the Soviets pushed steadily on, targeting American sources for their

J. Robert Oppenheimer during World War II

research assistance.[11] In March 1942, the NKVD chief in the United States, Vassili Zarubin, had been instructed by his bosses in Moscow "to obtain information . . . [on] the problem of uranium," as well as on radar and other weapons. And by 1943, Igor Kurchatov, the head of the Soviet atomic project, had identified the Berkeley Radiation Laboratory as the most promising site for NKVD information on a plutonium bomb.[12]

Two FBI Targets: J. Robert Oppenheimer and Steve Nelson

One scientist the Russians regarded as a most likely recruit was Robert Oppenheimer. In December 1941 Soviet consul Gregori Kheifetz (who also happened to be an NKVD *rezident)* met Oppenheimer at a party to raise money for Spanish civil war victims at the San Francisco home of left-wing socialite Louise Rosenberg Bransten. The two set a lunch date for the following day.[13] Kheifetz had a history of cultivating atomic spies; as noted previously, he had also recruited Bruno Pontecorvo while *rezident* in Italy. Working for the British, Pontecorvo would spy for Russia while stationed in Canada at the Chalk River atomic pile during the war. He continued to be an agent until 1950, when he moved to Russia in the wake of the Fuchs case.[14] As evidence that Kheifetz successfully cultivated Oppenheimer as well, Jerrold and Leona Schecter point to a document in which the consul told his superiors that in the months following their luncheon, the scientist "informed us about the beginning of work"—ostensibly, the atomic project, which was only just being launched in 1942. However, as Gregg Herken has argued, the lack of other evidence makes it difficult to determine whether Kheifetz was not simply boasting about the conversation's results to assist his own career.[15] In any case, Kheifetz was recalled to Moscow in September 1944 "because of his failure to bring any of 'Enormoz's' scientists into the field," according to Weinstein and Vassiliev—suggesting he actually failed with Oppenheimer.[16] The physicist does not seem to have had the personality of an informer; just as he was slow to tell American authorities later about his Communist friends' attempts to obtain more information, so he apparently resisted the entreaties of Communists to divulge materials as well.

Still, Oppenheimer was responsible for organizing at the Radiation Laboratory a branch of the Federation of Architects, Engineers, Chemists, and Technicians (FAECT), which the FBI alleged "was under Communist domination." Positioning itself in critical war industries, the union was a "potential menace to national safety," the Bureau thundered.[17] Indeed, FAECT activist Giovanni Rossi Lomanitz, one of Oppenheimer's graduate students at the lab, held conversations with Communist Party leader Steve Nelson that first alerted the U.S. government that the research facility was the site of "a studied effort by the Party to place its qualified members . . . for the purpose of gaining knowledge of the experiments being conducted."[18]

Nelson's home at 3720 Grove Street in Oakland, California, was already under surveillance when Lomanitz arrived on October 10, 1942, to tell the party leader about his secret work. Unlike the FBI informant who was secretly listening, Nelson seemed well aware of Lomanitz's research, and he alluded to other Communists "who considered this project even more important than Party work." Nelson told Lomanitz to stay "on this extremely important project." The scientist was now "considered an undercover member of the CP"; not only should he quiet his party activity, but he must also behave most discreetly and abstain from alcohol. Nelson impressed upon Lomanitz: "[I]t [is] important for [the party] to have knowledge of these discoveries and research developments."[19]

Uninformed about the "important project," the FBI had nevertheless been watching Nelson since 1940. The Office of Naval Intelligence had followed him beginning in 1939, when agents recorded him discussing the Nazi-Soviet Pact and the potential U.S. entry into war and noted his attendance at Communist Party meetings.[20] In May 1941, FBI Special Agent in Charge N. J. L. Pieper had recommended that Nelson be considered for "custodial detention" if the United States entered a national emergency. In October, Hoover asked the attorney general to approve the installation of telephone surveillance on Nelson, in light of his position as chairman of the Alameda County party organization as well as his work in furthering the party's program, "including [issues] pertinent to national defense."[21] Nelson's interest in

Steve Nelson (left) confers with his attorney, Emmanuel H. Bloch, before testifying at a closed HUAC session, September 14, 1948. (Corbis)

defense issues rang alarm bells for American officials in such agencies as the army's Military Intelligence Division, which was already investigating Communist influence in munitions plants.[22] But Hoover's request was rejected. He asked for reconsideration in February 1942, noting that "a technical surveillance on Steve Nelson offers a very likely source of information concerning the policies of the Communist Party." This time, he was granted permission, and Nelson became the target of technical surveillance, as did California Communist Oleta O'Connor Yates, the party headquarters in Oakland, and the International Labor Defense organization. A confidential informant also watched Nelson's movements.[23]

The FBI later contended that Nelson's espionage activities had been spurred by "instructions from Moscow" delivered through a Comintern agent.[24] Yet the Bureau's investigation developed only slowly, typical of its often scattershot approach in this era. On February 16, 1943, Assistant Attorney General Wendell Berge wrote to J. Edgar Hoover that his last report on Nelson was over one year old, and Berge wondered if the investigation was still under way. Hoover quickly contacted the San Francisco office and ordered a formal investigative report, as he knew that "office has an abundance of information concerning this subject."[25] Soon the Bureau would gather much more significant evidence that Nelson was involved in spying at the Radiation Laboratory, and SAC Pieper believed his involvement was part of a much larger espionage case.[26]

Nelson, born Steve Mesarosh, had come to the United States from Yugoslavia in 1920 on a false passport with his mother and two sisters.[27] The Bureau was somewhat unsure about his ethnic origins. One report noted he was a "Polish Jew" even as it acknowledged his birth in the Balkans, while another referred to him as a Hungarian Catholic.[28] The FBI was more clear on his limited English-speaking abilities, his sartorial challenges, and his "Jewish" features.[29] Nelson, whose education had ended in the eighth grade, had first been exposed to Communist ideas in Philadelphia as a teenager and become a member of the party in 1925, on the anniversary of Lenin's death. Working as a carpenter, he began taking on increasingly important positions in the party. He set up councils for the unemployed in Chicago in 1930 and was a party secretary in Pittsburgh in 1931.[30] Then, claiming to be the American-born son of a Swedish immigrant named Otto Nelson, he traveled throughout Europe and China between 1931 and 1933 on a fraudulent passport. He attended the Lenin Institute in Moscow, which provided training in revolutionary methods, and aided the Comintern in Shanghai.[31] After he returned to the United States in 1934, Nelson became an organizer in the anthracite coal region of Wilkes-Barre, Pennsylvania. The Pennsylvania State Police summed him up as someone who "specializes in creating unrest among relief recipients," but he also was arrested for picketing in front of the German consulate in Philadelphia.[32] In 1936, Nelson ran as the Communist Party's state representative for the Seventh Legislative District of Pennsylvania, but received only nineteen votes.[33] The following year, this hard-core devotee of the Communist cause served in Spain as a lieutenant colonel in the Loyalist Army and as a political commissar, enforcing ideological correctness among the troops in the International Anti-Fascist Volunteers. Because Loyalists held a wide range of opinions, the political commissars had their work cut out for them. They were "the watchdogs of the People's Front," according to *Daily Worker* columnist Joseph North.[34] Nelson soon assumed leadership of his battalion, where he proved a brave fighter—"the best commander the Americans had ever had," according to one observer—only to be seriously injured at Belchite in August 1937.[35]

While many wounded members of the Abraham Lincoln Brigade stayed on to fight in Spain, Nelson had important work elsewhere. Three months after his injury, he returned to the United States on a passport made out for Joseph Fleischinger (who actually *was* a relative) and resumed his party activism.[36] Earl Browder appointed him to the Central Committee of the CPUSA, and Nelson also became membership chairman of the American League for Peace and Democracy, a Communist front.[37] In May 1939, he moved to the West Coast, where he organized strike-training schools and became especially interested in the U.S. military's organization. In 1940 he instructed 1,500 specially chosen party members on how best to infiltrate the army. That June he became one of seventeen selected by Earl Browder to serve on the party's National Committee, a post that eventually led him to San Francisco where he became secretary of the Alameda County Communist Party and a member of the California State Politburo assigned to cover matters of national defense. There, Nelson proceeded to assist in the development of a cell at the Berkeley Radiation Laboratory.[38]

Work at the lab in the earliest months of the war was not necessarily "secret." Not until the fall of 1942 did the research officially fall under that category, according to one of the physicists at the lab, Irving Fox, who recalled, "I was informed that the work was secret; that I would be told only what I had to know for my work. I understood at the time there was some kind of competition going on with Germany; that we were in a race with them and there would be possible espionage." Even insiders were not to be conversed with "too much."[39]

J. Robert Oppenheimer and Nelson had a personal connection: the scientist's wife, Kitty, had been married to Nelson's late friend, Joseph Dallet, a casualty of the Spanish civil war. Nelson visited Oppenheimer perhaps five times in 1941. Although Oppenheimer knew that he was a party functionary, he did not believe that Nelson held a leading position, and he told the FBI that he was not aware Nelson had contacted anyone at the laboratory. Oppenheimer claimed that "Nelson never approached him directly or indirectly to obtain information regarding the experimentation . . . at the Radiation Laboratory, and . . . never visited him or otherwise contacted him at the University." [40]

The FBI closely monitored Oppenheimer beginning in 1941, looking for substantiation of his Communist connections. Agents monitored his conversations, magazine subscriptions, activities, and sleeping partners, as well as his involvement in the party.[41] They learned that Oppenheimer had attended party meetings at the home of Berkeley French professor Haakon Chevalier in 1940 and given $100 to the party in 1941. Bureau and Military Intelligence officials also watched Oppenheimer's wife, brother, and former girlfriend, all of whom had ties to the party.[42] The FBI's reports noted that he belonged to such "Communist front organizations" as the Consumers Union, the Committee to Aid China, and the American Federation of Teachers. Moreover, he had made a large donation for the purchase of an ambulance for Spanish Loyalists in 1938.[43] The Bureau examined his contacts with other professors at Berkeley, including meetings that FBI agent Pieper decided were not work related. But Hoover initially refrained from technical surveillance.[44]

The Bureau learned that prior to 1942 Oppenheimer was regarded as a Communist by party members in Berkeley. The scientist, while acknowledging membership in "practically every known front group," always denied any Communist affiliation.[45] He admitted to only "an academic interest" in the party.[46] He also recalled that he had become disillusioned with Soviet Russia after the Nazi-Soviet Pact.[47] However, as newly unearthed documents reveal, Oppenheimer's relationship with the party was more than theoretical: he donated $150 monthly as late as 1942, which indicates that he was almost certainly a member.[48] The FBI linked him with party leaders such as the secretary of the California Communist Party, William Schneiderman; the financial adviser to the party, Isaac Folkoff (who had collected his "generous" donations); and, of course, Nelson.[49] None of his affiliations prevented Oppenheimer from assuming directorship of the Los Alamos Laboratory in 1943. Although his background made him a "calculated risk," his scientific expertise also made him the top choice to head the new weapons facility.[50] The Manhattan Engineering District trusted Oppenheimer, the FBI noted, because "it was felt that he was above all things a scientist first."[51]

At the same time, Lansdale, too, worried about Oppenheimer. Yet he agreed with General Groves's assertions that Oppenheimer was "essential" to the project, as well as loyal, even as "virtually" all the security men in the army opposed Oppenheimer's clearance. Lt. Col. Boris T. Pash, for example, who headed the Manhattan Project's investigative arm as chief of Ninth Corps Area counterintelligence, believed that Oppenheimer "is not to be fully trusted and that his loyalty to the Nation is divided." Because of such "considerable doubts," noted Lansdale, "we continued to the best of our ability to investigate him. We kept him under surveillance whenever he left the project. We opened his mail. We did all sorts of nasty things that we do or did on the project."[52] As Lansdale's comments confirm, the heightened importance of the atomic program led to an expansion of the instruments of the security state in order to assure the program's secrecy. Mail censorship, for instance, was applied not just to Oppenheimer but to all the most important scientists on the project, along with those having "derogatory information" in their files. Their phone calls also were monitored. Oppenheimer was never told he was such a target, but the army "believed that he was aware of it."[53]

Relying on FBI information, Pash filed an investigative report on Oppenheimer on June 29, 1943, in which he concluded that the "subject may still be connected with the Communist party." His material came from party official Bernadette Doyle, who had mentioned Oppenheimer and his brother, Frank, as being members. Robert Oppenheimer's visits with Jean Tatlock, and another party member, David Hawkins, also were considered to demonstrate his party ties. Pash made a rather harsh recommendation, given the secondhand nature of his source; he called for Oppenheimer to be replaced (after the scientist had trained a suitable substitute), to be assigned bodyguards (ostensibly to protect him from German spies but in reality to keep him under surveillance), and for him to be thoroughly investigated and interviewed. Pash's party informants had indicated to him that their organization was "making a definite effort to officially divorce subject's affiliation with the party," but that Oppenheimer could nevertheless be providing material to persons who, in Pash's estimation, "may be furnishing . . . [it] to the Communist Party for transmission to the USSR." However, Pash was later dispatched to Europe to hunt for German spies, and though bodyguards were assigned to Oppenheimer, he was not replaced.[54]

The FBI had been unaware of the atomic project at the time of the Lomanitz meeting—when indeed the project was only just beginning—but soon the implications of Nelson's information gathering would become all too obvious. On the night of March 29, 1943, the Communist leader was overheard at his home securing "some highly confidential data regarding the nuclear experiments" at the Radiation Laboratory from a young physicist named Joe, later identified as Joseph Woodrow Weinberg.[55] Weinberg, who was hired by the lab on April 14, 1943, had been previously associated with the lab as a research fellow, thus learning "many of the secret details of the Project." A former Regent's scholar at CCNY, Weinberg had come to Berkeley in 1939 to pursue his PhD, which he completed in 1943. One of his references described him as a "genius."[56] The Nelson-Weinberg conversation was recorded by an informant stationed outside, although the subjects' whispering made surveillance a challenge.[57] In their discussion, "Joe" told Nelson of his long devotion to Communism, his training, and his reliability. Yet he pointed out that he worked on only one part of the project, and thus could not supply full information. Nelson assured him that whatever he provided would be "very valuable."[58]

Nelson told Weinberg that because the party was well supplied with people in American factories "who are always sending information on industrial processes to the Soviet Union," no one should assume they could define what that country needed or what its laboratories could or couldn't do. With its "outstanding authorities" on technical matters like explosives, anything could be useful.[59] Soviet scientists "have been pretty damn ingenious in many ways," Nelson asserted.[60] He reassured "Joe" that in the early 1930s he himself had done "this discreet work" for Moscow.[61] Nelson further told Weinberg to gather all the information he could from "trustworthy Communists" at the lab, since "collectively the Communist scientists working on the project could assemble all the information regarding the manufacture of the atomic bomb."[62] How Nelson knew this is not clear.

Informing the party secretary that the separation process for uranium was the lab's chief problem at the moment, Weinberg said that another six to eighteen months could be required before experimentation would begin in earnest. Despite his candor in discussing the processes under way, Weinberg noted that he was "a little bit scared" to hand over a published document on the project. Nelson, however, pressed him for concrete information, dismissing Weinberg's worry that Nelson might make a mistake in carrying back the information. He did not, however, attempt to assuage Weinberg's fear that his espionage could result in an investigation. He declared that the young physicist would undoubtedly be both surveilled and "thoroughly investigated."[63] Then, just as with Lomanitz, Nelson lectured the nervous Weinberg about the need to be extremely circumspect, telling him that those who were involved in sharing information should meet only in twos, and that they should avoid alcohol, throw out their party membership cards, and discuss lab matters only while outside walking or swimming.[64] Nelson was nothing if not discreet; upon hearing that some of the Communists at the lab had "expressed a desire to come out more into the open and affiliate themselves more closely with CP activity," he advised against it, since "they would then be of no use."[65]

With some trepidation, then, Weinberg provided Nelson a formula of about 150 to 200 words concerning the "calutron," a separator for enriching uranium. The Bureau's listeners found most of the conversation unintelligible.[66] Weinberg also told Nelson that two Communists had left the lab for Los Alamos.[67] He noted as well that the project had a production facility in Tennessee, which Weinberg guessed employed two to three thousand people, including five hundred physicists and a far larger number of machinists.[68]

Nelson and Weinberg also discussed Robert Oppenheimer at their meeting. Contrary to Oppenheimer's recollection, Nelson told his visitor that he had talked to the scientist about the project, but had not pressed him, since "I didn't want to put him in an unfriendly position. I didn't want to put him on the spot, you know." Weinberg agreed, noting that Oppenheimer would not think Nelson the "proper party" for gaining these materials.[69] Nelson acknowledged that he and the party made the physicist "uncomfortable," even "jittery." Weinberg complained that as for himself, Oppenheimer had "deliberately kept" him from the project, in part because of Weinberg's political stance, which, according to Weinberg, was "a strange thing for him to fear. But he's changed a bit." Both men agreed that Oppenheimer was "just not a Marxist" and that while he "would like to be on the right track," he was being pushed away by his wife, who was "influencing him in the wrong direction." Her tenure in the party had been brief, and her ambitions for him, as well as his own, were leading him away from his old associations.[70]

Soon after the meeting with Weinberg, as the FBI would discover, Nelson tried to reach Soviet vice consul Peter Petrovich Ivanov, a Soviet military intelligence agent, by telephone. On the night of April 6, Nelson was seen passing information to Ivanov on the grounds of nearby Saint Joseph Hospital.[71] FBI agents could not get close enough to see what was being exchanged without being recognized.[72] But two days after the Nelson-Weinberg meeting, SAC Pieper circulated a memo asserting that "with proper handling of the matter an espionage case may be developed involving the Communist Party itself." Pieper fantasized about planting an FBI-run physicist on the project, one who could join the party and even supply doctored information to Nelson. But such an investigation could not be effected without the cooperation of the War Department's Military Intelligence Division, which had "exclusive jurisdiction" over the laboratory.[73]

According to an agreement dated April 5, 1943, the War Department controlled all investigations of Manhattan Engineering Project personnel. The Bureau could launch no independent investigations of "persons connected with the Atomic Bomb Project."[74] The FBI, therefore, had to call off its two-year-old investigation of Oppenheimer, not officially resuming it until March 13, 1946, when the Bureau immediately reinstated technical surveillance on him.[75] The agency was instead authorized to "conduct all necessary investigation regarding Communist activities and the activities of individuals interesting themselves in the project" who worked elsewhere.[76] Candidates for FBI observation included any labor unions whose members' employers supplied materials to the project, particularly left-wing ones like FAECT and the United Electrical, Radio, and Machine Workers of America.[77] Despite these careful delineations of turf, the FBI quickly launched its own secret investigation at the lab, complete with extensive surveillance, code-named CINRAD (Communist Infiltration of Radiation Laboratory). Soon, as Gregg Herken has noted, both the FBI and army intelligence were stumbling over each other in their zeal to uncover new spies at the Berkeley lab.[78]

Their zeal in part explains why Weinberg, despite his evident espionage, was allowed to stay at the lab until March 31, 1944, when he left to become associate professor of physics at Berkeley. Authorities hoped his continued employment at the lab would lead them to more spies.[79] Meanwhile, his friends there came under scrutiny, including Rossi Lomanitz, Max Friedman, David Bohm, and Irving David Fox. On August 12, 1943, FBI surveillance discovered a meeting of Lomanitz, Bohm, Fox, and Friedman at Weinberg's apartment, also attended by Nelson and his assistant, Bernadette Doyle.[80] Despite their acquaintance with Nelson, these young men apparently knew nothing of Weinberg's espionage, and the extensive surveillance yielded little. Unlike the more fortunate Weinberg, though, they all lost their jobs. Friedman, who later changed his name to Ken Max Manfred, was pushed out of the lab in August 1943 and ended up at the College of Mechanical Arts in Mayaguez, Puerto Rico. Bohm and Fox also were fired and prevented from going to Los Alamos as they had planned.[81]

Lomanitz, meanwhile, was drafted into the army in September 1943 with no explanation. He asserted that "unnamed charges are being pressed against me. . . . I was questioned for a long time on my interest in unions in general and the FAECT in particular. I was then told that some unknown person had instigated the charge that I am connected with 'communistic organizations.' . . . I brushed this aside as ridiculous." Lomanitz, involved in highly specialized work at the lab, reported that Radiation Laboratory director Ernest O. Lawrence "was quite taken aback" at the army's move. Lomanitz tried to defer his military posting first by getting a job teaching math to aviation cadets at Berkeley and then by taking a position at a radar tube manufacturer. He was unsuccessful on both counts. Neither Oppenheimer nor his union were able to help him; indeed, "the union soon collapsed," which Lomanitz believed had been a "chief intent of this affair."[82] Oppenheimer acknowledged later that he should have revealed more about Lomanitz's political leanings to his superiors, because he knew the young scientist to be rather vocal and "extremely Red," but claimed he had tried to persuade Lomanitz to focus less on politics and more on science.[83] Oppenheimer's decision to allow Lomanitz to remain on the project is suggestive of his tolerance for these views, an outlook grounded in his own personal history. However, he later told Groves that he "was sorry that he had ever had anything to do with him."[84] Lomanitz would spend September 1943 until April 1946 in the army. He subsequently returned to Berkeley to finish his degree.[85]

Although the FBI would find no more evidence of espionage by the Radiation Laboratory scientists, the extent of Soviet infiltration of the atomic program was revealed even more starkly just two weeks after the Weinberg-Nelson meeting. On April 10, the man who headed NKVD activities in the United States stopped to visit Nelson, setting the FBI's recorders in motion.[86] Vassili Zarubin (aka Zubilin), whose day job was second secretary in the Soviet embassy, had compiled a secret career that included service in Germany in the early years of Hitler's rule, followed by roles in the Red Army purge in Russia and in the Katyn massacre in Poland.[87] In his demeanor, he showed every indication of being Nelson's "Soviet superior."[88] Zarubin forked over "10 bills of unknown denominations," payment to Nelson, as the FBI put it, "for . . . placing Communist Party members and Comintern agents in industries engaged in secret war production . . . so that the information could be obtained for transmittal to the Soviet Union."[89] Their meeting also included a rambling discussion of American Communist Party politics, West Coast activists, the cooperation of members (or lack thereof), and the suspected reasons why the British and Americans had not opened a second front. The FBI declared that "it was obvious that Zubilin was in control of the intelligence organization." Indeed, as he told Nelson, "I'm about five heads up over people you know nothing about."[90] Nelson, in turn, proudly informed Zarubin that he had gotten his assignment, "which he distinguished from his regular Communist Party duties," from Moscow and that the national party, including Browder, "approved" of it. However, not all Communists supported Nelson's role; State Party Secretary Schneiderman and Los Angeles party leader Carl Winter were both nervous about it being "dangerous" to the party.[91] As Nelson told Zubilin: "[W]hen you see the old man [Browder] you can tell him that the fellows out here right now don't believe that the Center [New York Headquarters] is approving this . . . the Russian angle. . . . [T]hey feel that we are running a dangerous political—I mean, taking a chance."[92] But the suggestion that some party members were reluctant to embrace the agenda of Soviet intelligence did not impress the FBI; instead, Nelson and Browder's enthusiasm did. Nelson, indeed, had met with Browder the previous January while he was in San Francisco, further illustrating the links between the party and Soviet intelligence.[93]

The Nelson-Zubilin meeting apparently marked the first time that the FBI recorded a party official being paid by Moscow for providing secret technical information on the bomb.[94] The meeting "establishes the fact that the Government of the USSR is using Nelson and other high officers of the American Communist Party as part of an espionage network in this country," the FBI declared. The Bureau brought the matter to the attention of Harry Hopkins, Roosevelt's aide, although with little apparent effect.[95]

The 1943 Nelson surveillance, which kindled the Bureau's growing wartime concerns about the Soviet espionage offensive and its indigenous connections, led to an expansion of the FBI's investigatory apparatus.[96] American counterintelligence authorities' attempts to monitor and obstruct Nelson and his scientific sources became part of a major probe into the Soviet penetration of the bomb project that covered both the Radiation Laboratory at Berkeley and the University of Chicago's Development of Substitute Materials (DSM) Laboratory, which was manufacturing plutonium.

CINRAD, the FBI's special unit studying Communist infiltration at the Radiation Laboratory, included a listening post in Oakland—a furnished room rented out for a dummy company called "Universal Distributors." Ideally situated near the Communist Party Headquarters at 1723 Webster Street, the post would facilitate watching and filming Nelson and another spot he frequented, the Twentieth Century Bookshop. The U.S. Army, meanwhile, established both its own outfit for conducting and collecting electronic surveillance in Berkeley and an office in San Francisco for its bogus "Universal Adjustment Company," which conducted physical surveillance.[97] The FBI duly investigated the individuals referred to in Nelson and Zarubin's conversation. Agents followed Zarubin in New York, Washington, and Los Angeles; continued trailing Nelson and Ivanov in San Francisco; and tried to identify the Comintern head in New York.[98] They searched suspects' rooms and intercepted their correspondence and used informants to listen and report on their meetings and movements.[99] But watching Communists was not always easy, as Pash, who headed the Manhattan Project's investigative arm, pointed out: "[T]hey avoided fixed positions."[100]

As all this activity suggests, the CINRAD operation and other investigations spurred significant increases in the number of Bureau personnel. Although in 1940 only one man, Robert King, was assigned to counterintelligence (or the "commie squad") at the FBI's San Francisco field office, in 1943 the discovery of Soviet espionage at the Berkeley Radiation Laboratory brought 125 new agents to the Bay Area.[101] Nelson was a favorite target for these men: FBI special agents compiled no less than sixty-seven reports on him from March 1941 to May 1948, the bulk of them falling between 1943 and 1947.[102] As the FBI learned, Zarubin began to harangue Nelson to leave his post for this very reason, but the American Communist refused.[103] Nelson was identified as an "espionage suspect," but the United States could do little to apprehend him, unless he wished to cooperate with authorities. Wiretapped evidence was not sufficient ammunition for a successful prosecution.[104]

The FBI, G2 (military intelligence), and other law-enforcement authorities maintained a tight watch over the lab and its employees, as well as Nelson, but no further evidence of espionage emerged in this quarter during the war. Nevertheless, "there have been several instances of neglect on the part of the employees . . . relating to the security of the Laboratory," the FBI reported in 1943. Moreover, the Bureau passed on an alarmist "rumor" it had received from an unnamed source, which professed that "slowly but surely an alien control is creeping through the Laboratory unseen and unsuspected by the true scientists there." An equally excitable FBI informant declared, "[T]here is no doubt of any sort that Soviet Russia is in possession of every discovery developed at this Cyclotron Laboratory." Whether the agency itself believed that, it nevertheless entertained the notion of "an espionage effort of major proportions which may develop into a national catastrophe."[105]

Such hyperbole aside, the Soviet Union was certainly interested in developments in the lab, as Robert Oppenheimer had already learned. At the end of 1942, Peter Ivanov of the Soviet consulate, who would later be seen accepting materials from Nelson, contacted George C. Eltenton, a sympathetic chemist at Shell in Emeryville, and complained to him that "the Russians . . . needed certain information and that for political reasons there were no authorized channels through which they could obtain such."[106] Eltenton contacted left-leaning Berkeley professor Haakon Chevalier, knowing he was a friend of J. Robert Oppenheimer. Eltenton recalled he then "requested him to find out what was being done at the radiation laboratory, particularly information regarding the highly destructive weapon which was being developed." He even offered Chevalier money. Eltenton told Chevalier that since "Russia and the United States were allies, Soviet Russia should be entitled to any technical data which might be of assistance to that nation."[107] The British-born Eltenton had worked in Leningrad for the Institute of Chemical Physics for five years before joining Shell in 1938, where he had organized the FAECT union. The FBI noted he "had a Communistic background."[108]

In Chevalier's telling, Oppenheimer would be "horrified" to hear of the "preposterous" suggestion. Yet he decided to inform the physicist, whom he considered his "most intimate and steadfast friend," owing to his professed concern that Eltenton's attempt might be only the first to get more information about the secret project.[109] Chevalier claimed that when he told Oppenheimer about the matter in early 1943, the physicist labeled the entreaties "treason."[110] Still, Oppenheimer did not tell army security about the episode until some six months later. As he later recalled, it was Lansdale's suspicions about members of FAECT that finally led him to tell the army about Chevalier and Eltenton, though only in a convoluted way.[111] But Chevalier's account would also turn out to be bogus!

On August 26, Oppenheimer provided *his* fictional account to his U.S. Army interviewers, Lt. Col. Boris T. Pash and Lt. Lyall Johnson, security officer at the lab. As Pash recorded, Oppenheimer related that sometime in the winter of 1942–43 he "had learned from three different employees of the

Haakon Chevalier (Bancroft Library)

atomic bomb project . . . that they had been solicited to furnish information, ultimately to be delivered to the USSR. . . . All of these employees had been bewildered by the proposition and had asked Oppenheimer for advice." None of the men had cooperated, according to Oppenheimer, so he refused to name them. Two were now at Los Alamos, and one at Oak Ridge. However, he did identify Eltenton as the man who had requested that a certain other person act as intermediary for the Soviet consulate in order to obtain this information from the three scientists. Oppenheimer refused to name this go-between, not only as a friend but "because he considered the intermediary as innocent."[112] He did say that while he did not personally object to offering information to the Russians, as long as it was a shared exchange, "I don't like the idea of having it moved out the back door." He suggested that Pash watch Eltenton.[113]

The unnamed intermediary had contacted the three scientists, according to Oppenheimer, "explain[ing] to them that the United States was failing to discharge its obligation to its ally, Russia, by its failure to furnish scientific data to that country. . . . The employees were reminded that Russia was entitled to, and badly needed the information for its war effort." The intermediary allegedly wanted each employee to meet with a contact who would transfer their findings to the Soviet consulate official "who was said to have had a great deal of experience with microfilm and who was in a position to transmit the material to Russia without danger of a leak or scandal."[114] But Oppenheimer had made up this entire story.[115]

Oppenheimer's allegations led to much fruitless, "tedious" work for Pash, who attempted to find the three men who had been contacted by the then-anonymous Berkeley professor. His effort was made more urgent by the fact that authorities "already knew definitely that there were espionage activities conducted in favor of the Soviets in that area," a veiled allusion to the Nelson matter. His reaction illustrates how the espionage revelations built on each other to amplify the government's response.[116]

At his interview with Pash, Oppenheimer also brought up Lomanitz, noting that he had learned from Lansdale a few weeks before that Lomanitz had been "indiscreet about information."[117] This appraisal of Lomanitz's "discretion" (or lack thereof), he claimed, had contributed to his coming forward; he now saw that Eltenton's scheme "might very well be serious."[118] What was worse, Oppenheimer noted, was that Lomanitz was in a position to be approached by those sympathetic to the Soviet Union for information. "I feel quite strongly that association with the Communist movement is not compatible with a job on a secret war project. It is just that the two loyalties cannot go."[119] Pash was immediately suspicious of Oppenheimer's introduction of Lomanitz's name: "It was my opinion that Dr. Oppenheimer wanted to present this information to us for the purpose of relieving any pressure that may be brought on him for further investigation of his personal situation."[120] And to Los Alamos security officer Peer de Silva, Oppenheimer's testimony about the Eltenton overture did not indicate his loyalty; not at all. De Silva was sure that it was Lomanitz's losing his draft deferment, and the resulting implications as to his radical tendencies, that had indicated to Oppenheimer that "some sort of a general investigation, more extensive than a routine security check" was in process and thus his most "obvious and natural move" was to come forward. Oppenheimer, de Silva imputed, had waited with his information until "it became obvious to him that an investigation was being conducted," when he could be in "the favorable position of having offered the information."[121] De Silva was convinced that the physicist had "allowed a tight clique of known Communists or Communist sympathizers to grow up about him within the project." As a result, he declared, "J. Robert Oppenheimer is playing a key part in the attempts of the Soviet Union to secure, by espionage, highly secret information which is vital to the security of the United States."[122]

Although de Silva's view was extreme, and Oppenheimer's position as research director was never seriously threatened, it suggests not only the government's sharpening focus on a Soviet espionage threat, but also the extent to which army intelligence officers distrusted Oppenheimer's ability to maintain the security of the project. Their distrust was unfair, as Oppenheimer had faced some stiff resistance for his active involvement in enforcing secrecy at Los Alamos.[123] More charitably, Lansdale himself speculated that Oppenheimer came forward when he did because Lansdale had told him about the army's wish not to transfer to Los Alamos those "who figured prominently in the attempted or actual espionage incident on the west coast."[124]

Two weeks later, in a follow-up interview with Lansdale in Washington, Oppenheimer downplayed the importance of the still-unnamed intermediary as merely a "cocktail party channel." Lansdale protested, noting that such a casual communication wouldn't have had the endorsement of the Soviet consulate. But Oppenheimer continued to resist: "I would just bet dollars to doughnuts that he isn't still operating." An exasperated Lansdale responded, "I don't see how you can have any hesitancy in disclosing the name of the man who has actually been engaged in an attempt at espionage for a foreign power in time of war." To which Oppenheimer replied, "I know, it's a tough problem, and I've worried about it a lot." Unimpressed, Lansdale asked him what would make him speak the man's name. Oppenheimer said only if he discovered that "something was transmitted." Testing him, Lansdale retorted, "Well I'm telling you it is. . . . I think it was about a week ago." He then asked slyly, "Is part of your feeling based on the fact . . . that you don't consider that it would be such a catastrophe anyway for us if they did find it out?" To this, Oppenheimer disagreed strenuously: "I think it would be a catastrophe."[125]

Continuing in this vein, Lansdale asked the physicist very frankly, "What are we to do" with someone like Oppenheimer, married to a former Communist, with many Communist and front associations, who sat on a report of espionage for six months? Exasperated, he noted, "We know that information is streaming out from this place every day. We know about some of it. How much of it is there that we don't know about?"[126] Although Oppenheimer kept mum about Chevalier, in an interview with Groves the same month, he was all too willing to identify another professor, A. Flannagan, as "a real Red," and named Los Alamos technical librarian Charlotte Serber as "probably" having been a Communist.[127]

That Oppenheimer did not get in more trouble over this incident may be related to his having "benefited from exceptional treatment," as Barton Bernstein puts it. Despite his well-known left-wing past, not until 1954 would Oppenheimer find himself "a victim of the loyalty-security standards that had quietly wrecked the careers and lives of less notable people."[128] Indeed, Lt. Col. Lansdale had gushed to him in the opening moments of their September 1943 interview, "[Y]ou're probably the most intelligent man I've ever met." This buttering up was certainly part of an attempt to disarm Oppenheimer, so that Lansdale could get to the true story of who had approached whom for information at the lab. But it is also suggestive of the way that some security officials saw Oppenheimer.[129]

Lansdale offered a revealing observation during the scientist's 1954 hearings. In seeming confirmation that political circumstances had changed greatly since the war, he noted that applying standards from 1954 to "associations in 1940"—an allusion to Oppenheimer's earlier party links—was "hysteria" and "extremely dangerous." He added, however, that in the war "another dangerous attitude" was prevalent: "I was being subjected to pressure . . . because I dared to stop the commissioning of a group of 15 or 20 undoubted Communists. I was being vilified . . . because of my efforts to get Communists out of the Army and being frustrated by the blind, naïve attitude of Mrs. Roosevelt and those around her in the White House."[130] At the same time, General Groves defended himself at the hearings for not letting go of *more* suspected scientists, noting how difficult in practice the process was, because "men would become violently excited about the most minor thing" and the stresses of the work meant that the scientists "were tense and nervous and they had to be soothed all the time."[131] But it was more than that, as Col. Lansdale noted; the pressing need for people made winnowing out subversives a lower priority. In the beginning, for example, "the Germans were far ahead of us in the development of an atomic bomb. . . . We were under, believe me, a very terrible feeling of pressure." When suspected Communists were doing "useful work and . . . important work," he noted, "good judgment required that we keep them," even if they had to be "insulated." Moreover, he added, in a refreshing contrast with the prevailing mood of 1954, "it would be a terrible mistake to assume that, once having had sinister associations, a man was forever thereafter damned."[132]

In December 1943, Oppenheimer at last revealed to General Groves that his intermediary was Haakon Chevalier.[133] At the same time, as Gregg Herken has recently shown, Oppenheimer told the general—after swearing him to secrecy—that the professor had contacted not three people but only one: his younger brother, Frank. Robert apparently gave his earlier complicated story to authorities in order to protect Frank, like him a physicist with a Communist past; Frank had told his brother about the contact some months before.[134] Thanks to Groves's discretion, this more accurate story remained almost completely unknown until 1954, and during the war officials continued their wide-scale, futile effort to find the three people described by Oppenheimer.[135]

In 1946, Oppenheimer admitted he "concocted a completely fabricated story" about the three contacts. Moreover, he did not think Chevalier knew anything about the project, except that it was something experimental and related to the war, and averred that he had certainly told the French professor nothing. Oppenheimer explained that it had taken him six months to report the incident to a security officer at the lab because he dismissed Chevalier's knowledge of the situation and thus "failed to recognize the potential threat to the nation's security which was present in the incident." FBI agent William Branigan snarled later that Oppenheimer "was a master at innuendo and evasive answers . . . [and] can evade a question by talking around it."[136]

Well before 1946, stories like the one Oppenheimer had told in 1943—as well as Nelson's inroads—had steered American counterintelligence agents away from actively pursuing German spies who might have been tracking the atomic project. Instead, "the Bureau's interest in the DSM Project has been in the identification of Communist activists and Soviet agents." Such counterespionage was a high priority, the Bureau claimed, because "successful completion of the DSM project . . . is not *alone a matter of winning the war but of surviving in the world thereafter.*" If the Russians got the technology first instead, it "would place the United States at the mercy of the Soviet Union."[137]

Atomic Espionage Continued: From the Fish Grotto to the Yukon Territory

Oppenheimer's stories helped consolidate the official view that Soviet spying was a growing danger, but so too did other wartime discoveries of potential espionage. In early July 1944 at the San Francisco restaurant Bernstein's Fish Grotto, army and FBI officials taped a conversation whose participants included chemistry professor Martin David Kamen of the Radiation Laboratory's cyclotron department, Soviet vice-consul Grigorii Markovich Kheifetz, and Kheifetz's successor, Grigori Kasparov. The event was ostensibly a farewell dinner for Kheifetz, who left for Russia three days after the meeting, as well as an appreciative gesture to Kamen, who had met Kheifetz earlier that year at a Russian-related charity event at the home of the vice-consul's lover, Louise Rosenberg Bransten; Bransten's leftish cocktails had earlier provided an opportunity for Kheifetz and Oppenheimer to meet. At the 1944 party, the vice-consul had asked Kamen for information about the lab's research on radiation treatments for cancer, and Kamen had connected him with John Lawrence, lab director Ernest Lawrence's brother and an expert on medical radiation at the facility. Kamen, who had joined the Radiation Laboratory in August 1942, worked on "highly confidential experimentation at the DSM Project" himself. He had earned his PhD in chemistry at the University of Chicago six years earlier, when he was just twenty-three years old. Investigative authorities had already targeted Kamen before this dinner, in part because he was known to be quite "voluble" on the subject of his research; once, he was overheard talking about it in the university's faculty club.[138]

As a lab employee, Kamen recalled later, he was tailed "continually." Agents watched his house, bugged his phone, and even rifled his apartment. He scoffed, "[W]e paid no attention to them because we were keeping the security to our knowledge quite adequately." However, Kamen did notice the two Manhattan Engineering District (MED) intelligence agents, Wagener and Zindle, who appeared at the Grotto that July 1944 evening. They had asked for a booth next to Kamen, but deferred to FBI men whom they saw entering the restaurant with "special equipment," as HUAC was later told. The MED agents then sat by the door, "taking notes and attempting to overhear the conversation." Kamen somehow missed seeing the nearby FBI representatives.[139]

They, however, were listening closely, and they reported that he "dominated the conversation." More important was what he was alleged to have said; General Groves later testified that "certain of the statements made by Kamen to Kheifetz and Kasparov constituted highly confidential information," including that concerning work at Oak Ridge, Tennessee.[140] Ten days later, Kamen's superiors informed him that he "had committed an indiscretion and . . .

[must] resign." He heard nothing about the nature of his security violation; his notice of termination referred not to the dinner, but to his earlier indiscreet remarks at the faculty club.[141]

When Kamen was grilled about his Grotto garrulity by HUAC in 1948, he told Congress he had merely discussed "cultural matters" with the consuls (Kamen, an expert viola player, and Kheifetz were both interested in music), as well as the aforementioned use of radiation to treat leukemia. This was unclassified information and of great interest to Kheifetz and Kasparov, Kamen said, because another Russian official in the United States was suffering from the disease and hoped to get some of the radioactive phosphorous being developed at the lab. The topic of atomic energy had arisen during the two-hour conversation, but more as a matter of general interest, the chemist reported, as something the "Sunday supplements" were addressing at that moment. When the Russians asked him if radioactivity could be a power source, and not simply a cancer cure, Kamen recalled telling them "there is nothing to that; nothing at all." He also remembered being asked "whether the Army was interested in atomic energy sufficiently to put any large effort into it. I said I doubted it very much." Evidently, when judged by Kamen's recollection of a two and a half hour conversation, the Soviets knew something about atomic energy themselves.[142]

According to MED agent Wagener, who also testified at the HUAC hearings, Kamen had used the words "Oak Ridge" and described some of the dangers of his job; he had also mentioned scientists Nils Bohr and Ernest Lawrence. Kamen denied Wagener's allegations, but later noted that because a number of people were being sent to Oak Ridge, many Berkeleyites were mentioning the facility "in the streets," and thus it was not surprising that Kheifetz had also brought it up. He flatly dismissed the FBI's version of the conversation as "entirely mistaken." Committee investigator Robert Stripling, however, retorted that "The FBI was sitting in the next booth from you with recording equipment, sound equipment . . . [and] they took down 25 pages." Stripling added that a scientist had gone through the transcript and his report indicated that "[Kamen] was telling about the [uranium] pile . . . as well as the work at Berkeley . . . the health hazards connected with the pile . . . he was telling definite security information, classified information, which he had no business doing."[143]

In retrospect, Kamen admitted that the dinner conversation might have been indiscreet. Still, he vigorously defended himself against the allegations of the listening agents. He pointed out that the Grotto was very loud, and that his rapid speaking pace would have been difficult to understand. Not very convincingly, he argued, "There was no security violation because I was conscious all the time that there was a possibility of a leak." Yes, he admitted, he had associated with left-wing friends like Bransten, but "I never took any personal part in any demonstrations or . . . politics." Indeed, while Kamen was a member of the suspected FAECT, he had not been active in the organization, and despite his many connections with Communists in the Bay Area, only rumors existed of his own leanings.[144]

The congressmen would not be assuaged. Why did Kheifetz meet with Kamen at the last minute before leaving for Russia—unless it was for "cultivating" him? Kamen disagreed; the Russians were simply grateful for his tips on health-related radiation studies. The chemist declared it was actually he who was cultivating Kheifetz, and not the reverse. "I envisioned some day I would get to Europe on a scientific matter and there would be an occasion where we would be asked if we cared to go to Russia and have conferences there."[145]

In 1948 HUAC was still unsure if Kamen had merely committed a "gross indiscretion" or something more "willful and deliberate." In any case, its members concluded that "There is no evidence connecting Kamen otherwise than casually with members of the Communist espionage apparatus that was operating on the Pacific coast."[146] Indeed, when Kamen was fired in 1944 he had not been charged as a spy, and he stayed involved in the war effort; after leaving Berkeley, he became a test engineer at Richmond Shipyard in the East Bay. In a move that would have surely gratified Kheifetz and Kasparov, Kamen subsequently became involved in cancer research at the Washington University cyclotron in Saint Louis.[147]

Although Kamen's role in passing information remains unclear, such is certainly not the case with another chemist, Clarence Hiskey, who was successfully cultivated by Soviet agents, as the FBI learned in 1944. Hiskey worked at two atomic research sites during the war, the Substitute Alloy Material Lab (SAM) at Columbia and the University of Chicago's DSM Laboratory.[148] Born Clarence Szczechowski in Milwaukee, Wisconsin, Hiskey earned a PhD in chemistry from the University of Wisconsin in 1939. After his graduation, he became director of the Rhenium Research Project at the University of Tennessee, where he was remembered as an outspoken supporter of Communism.[149] Two sources, including former Communist Party organizer Paul Crouch, also remembered seeing Hiskey at party gatherings in the San Francisco Bay Area.[150]

Soon after he had become an instructor at Columbia in September 1941, Hiskey met veteran Soviet spy Arthur Adams at a left-wing music store.[151] The following year, he joined Columbia's SAM lab, which housed a program to develop the gaseous diffusion process for separating uranium-235.[152] In 1942 Hiskey had blurted out to an undercover NKVD agent—posing as a prospective postdoctoral student named Franklin Zelman—that he was working on a "radio-active bomb" that could destroy the city of New York. Hiskey, who did not know Zelman was an agent, begged him to keep quiet, yet paradoxically also expressed his hopes that the Soviets knew about his project. Zelman maintained contact with the Columbia chemist, passing reports to Zarubin and thus providing among the earliest materials that Moscow received on the bomb.[153]

In October 1943, Hiskey moved his group to the University of Chicago's metallurgical lab. According to the Smyth Report on atomic technology, this lab's "ultimate objective . . . was to prepare plans for the large-scale production of plutonium . . . for its use in bombs."[154] He and Adams reconnected and met five or six more times before Hiskey was drafted in May 1944. The chemist would claim that he had not "given any information of value concerning the DSM project" to Adams.[155] But the army, assuming correctly that Hiskey *was* a source of information for the Soviet agent, closely watched the two men's meetings.[156] The FBI, meanwhile, kept Adams "under daily surveillance" from the summer of 1944 until he disappeared in January 1946. Adams found the surveillance oppressive and complained about the presence of "five or six men" who followed him extensively in this period, putting both him and his associates, including his girlfriend Victoria Stone, under a microscope.[157]

An FBI break-in to Adams's dwelling on September 29, 1944, showed plainly the presence of notes about the nuclear project, including mention of the progress of the Oak Ridge plant, material on isotope separation and Norway's production of heavy water, and speculations about uranium salt and sources of radium and uranium in Czechoslovakia, Germany, and Sweden. His jottings, the FBI declared, "reflect an intimate knowledge concerning highly secret phases" of the DSM project. A technically proficient informant told the FBI that "careful examination of the notes revealed they were comparative questions which probed the progress and methods of the DSM Project in this country with similar projects abroad." The materials delved deeply into "one of the most closely guarded secrets of any nation." As a result, agents believed that Adams was "the most dangerous espionage agent yet discovered in the Comintern Apparatus."[158]

Adams's early history is murky. Records revealed that he entered the United States from Toronto in 1915, and he claimed at various times to have been born in either Toronto or Sweden. More clear is that he graduated from Kronstadt Naval Engineering School in Russia as a mechanical engineer in 1909, and after the Tsarist regime sent him to Siberia for subversive activity, he fled Russia for Canada. In the 1910s, he worked at a New York machinery concern where he was known as "a radical Socialist."[159] He then became technical director at the short-lived Soviet Commercial Bureau in New York City, leaving when its director, Ludwig C. A. K. Martens, was deported in 1921. Back in Russia, he held a series of prominent posts at automobile and aircraft factories, including a job as chief engineer of the aircraft engine department of the Obuchow Works in Leningrad. The Communist writer Anna Louise Strong remembered him as part of "a group of Russian-Americans who had returned to Russia . . . with the aim of rebuilding the Soviet industry setup."[160]

Adams, who continued to visit the United States in the 1920s, "usually sought employment in the aeronautical industry where he assimilated information on the latest developments . . . which he took back to Russia," according to an FBI informant.[161] In 1932, he represented the Soviet Aviation Trust at the Curtiss-Wright Corporation; six years later, he returned for an extended stay, assisted by Samuel Novick of the Wholesale Radio Service Company Inc., who claimed Adams as his Canadian agent and consultant.[162] Adams did open a consulting business, Technological Laboratories Inc., which seems to have been a cover for clandestine activities.[163] In 1941, his Soviet superiors twice tried to recall him—perhaps because of his independence as an agent, as well as his background as an old Bolshevik. He evaded what might have been a very unpleasant fate by insisting that he had made important connections that were of "great potential value to the Soviet Union."[164] During the war Adams developed another cover for himself, though hardly an inconspicuous one, at the Keynote Recording Company, "the outstanding Communist music store in New York City," according to the FBI. Owner Eric Bernay, former advertising manager of the *New Masses,* produced such leftist hits as the Abraham Lincoln Brigade's "Six Songs for Democracy" and Paul Robeson's recording of the Russian national anthem. Paid a salary of $75 per week, Adams worked for Keynote from June 1943 until June 1945.[165]

Adams's meetings with Hiskey, as well as Hiskey's own history in the party as a young man, made MED security chief James Sterling Murray "highly suspicious" of the chemist, and he had Hiskey drafted on April 28,

1944. This kind of reassignment was no easy matter, as a military informant told Congress: "We had trouble with scientists when we tried to move one." But because Hiskey had been in ROTC in college and had not dropped his commission, the army could simply call him to active duty. Hiskey received the rather undesirable assignment of going to the Yukon Territory to serve as property survey master, or, as an army official put it, to "count underwear." It was during his remote posting, actually at Mineral Wells near the Arctic Circle, that "seven pages of notes" on DSM were discovered in his effects.[166] His belongings also contained a notebook of secret information on the SAM lab—information that the army and the FBI believed that Hiskey was going to supply to another Soviet agent.[167]

At the same time Hiskey was sent into the army, his mistress, Miriam Rebecca Sherwood, got a divorce from her husband. These events seem to have made Hiskey's wife, Marcia, increasingly dependent on Adams. He provided monetary support to her on at least one occasion, and she stayed in frequent contact with him, which he discouraged because of the FBI's surveillance. In March 1945, Adams was overheard by an FBI informant to say that "he had told her fifteen times never to call him at his hotel," warning her, "It's not good for you either." When Marcia shrugged that off, Adams retorted, "I give a damn about Hiskey, so you better shut up."[168]

The day after he was assigned to duty, Hiskey donned his fatigues and flew to Cleveland to visit chemist John Hitchcock Chapin, who would soon join the Chicago metallurgical lab.[169] Hiskey first asked him what he thought about the "aggressive" use of atomic power. When Chapin indicated his alarm, Hiskey asked him "if he would be willing to do something which would alleviate [our] fears as to the possibility of atomic power being misused," and Chapin agreed, giving Hiskey a key to give to Adams. When he was later asked why he thought Hiskey had approached him to meet Adams, Chapin told the FBI that his "liberal views," as well as his openness to sharing information on the atomic project, may have played a role. Nevertheless, he insisted, his sentiments did not reach "the extent of taking extra-legal means to disseminate such information." Asked, too, why he had agreed to meet with Adams, Chapin stammered that it all "depend[ed] on the definition of 'sympathetic' . . . I must have been somewhat so or I would have come trotting around to the FBI, I suppose." Indeed, he conceded, "I must have considered the possibility of cooperating with Adams."[170]

On September 25, 1944, by which time Chapin had moved to Chicago, Adams stopped by Chapin's apartment and produced his key, the previously agreed upon signal. A few days later, Chapin came to Adams's hotel room, where, as the chemist would tell the FBI, Adams asked him for "information on the work in which he was engaged." Adams did not say what he wanted, and Chapin assumed he would be happy with anything in his desk. Adams then offered Chapin a camera for the purposes of gathering information for him, but Chapin, apparently uncomfortable with the idea, put him off. Adams never contacted him again.[171]

Hiskey also introduced SAM scientist Edward Tiers Manning to Adams. Manning and Adams first met for lunch at a conference of the American Chemical Society in New York in July 1944. When a HUAC member wondered why he was not more suspicious of Adams, Manning noted that while some in the lab believed that Hiskey's ouster might have been due to his connections with the Soviet agent, no one was sure.[172]

Manning met Adams on several occasions, prompted by the hope of work in Russia, yet during those visits, as he told Congress later, he "had no idea [Adams] was connected with any [intelligence] apparatus of the Soviet Union." They did not discuss the SAM work, he averred, until their last meeting when "Adams made direct references" to it.[173] Despite his disclaimers, in a letter to a close associate Manning expressed his distrust for Adams, whom he believed was a "Commie," and his impression that Hiskey and Adams were too close: they "took to each other like a duck takes to water." Although he continued to maintain that "Clarence was properly evasive . . . with Adams," he also thought that "somehow Arthur knew what was going on at Columbia—generally—and what was going on at Chicago." Adams and Manning, meanwhile, had "long chats" during which the subject of "atomics" would arise. "I got a definite impression he was after information," said Manning.[174] He recalled Adams asking him, "Don't you feel that this thing you are working on belongs to humanity?" But the SAM scientist refused to cooperate.[175]

Nevertheless, Manning lost his job in September 1944. "By that time I had been subject to a great deal of surveillance," he noted. Intelligence officials had contacted his friends, and Manning became convinced that his firing was—like Hiskey's—"connected somehow with Arthur Adams." He subsequently told the Russian he was "pretty bitter" about the dismissals of himself and Hiskey, but Adams told him that this was an inappropriate response because it was "all for the good of the general world." Adams continued by asking if Manning did not think that the work at the Chicago lab "should be made available to all mankind," but Manning asserted that he had responded in the negative—unless "the world were well ordered." For the present, "I was committed to security and secrecy," he insisted.[176] A month later, Manning wrote Adams that "I've left Chicago for good. Events indicate that I am suspected of being a Communist."[177]

James Perlowin, a military filmmaker, cooperated more readily with Adams, providing him much information about his work beginning in 1940, "regardless of whether it was secret or not." The FBI noted that Perlowin had passed on material at "every place that he worked," from the Training Film Production Laboratory at Wright Field to the Laucks and Knorling Company, where he continued to make films, to Sperry Gyroscope, where Perlowin wrote manuals for the assembly of instruments in the field and worked on the Mark XIV 37mm gunsight. The FBI first espied Adams at Perlowin's home in 1944, but he recalled meeting Adams much earlier, perhaps in 1938. Perlowin declared in 1946 that "he never suspected any illegal motives on Adams's part . . . [but] he now believed Adams had let [sic] him on."[178]

In March 1945, a federal grand jury charged Adams with "making false and fraudulent statements in registering under the Selective Service Act" as well as under the Alien Registration Act.[179] But the imperatives of the Russian-American alliance allowed Adams to disappear quietly to Russia in January 1946, his departure eased, as HUAC delicately put it, by "government policy in existence at that time."[180] The following year, Anna Louise Strong visited him in Moscow, and agreed to forward his dues for a three-year membership in the American Society of Automotive Engineers after she returned from Russia. Adams also asked her to take back a note to Victoria Stone: "Please tell her that I love her." Strong recalled her "surprise" at the message, since she knew that Adams had a Russian wife. Stone, however, was "pleased to hear that Adams was alive."[181]

As Adams's story reveals, the ease with which he and "Franklin Zelman" contacted and cultivated Hiskey, and felt free to attempt to recruit others, demonstrates that the FBI and other counterintelligence agencies faced a daunting struggle to keep the atomic bomb secret from the Russians during the war. Afterward, the difficulty became demonstrating that espionage had actually occurred. On October 24, 1946, the FBI sent its transcripts on the case of Hiskey and Chapin to the criminal division of the Department of Justice for prosecution. However, as with so many wartime espionage cases, insufficient evidence existed to make a case. Released from his arctic purgatory, Hiskey, to no one's surprise, claimed he had provided no secret information.[182] Joseph Weinberg, who was also interviewed by the FBI in 1946, similarly denied his involvement in espionage, insisting he had never met Nelson nor discussed the bomb with him and even attesting that he did not enter the lab until well after the recorded meeting with Nelson.[183] In both cases, the wiretapped evidence so prized by the FBI would not hold up in court without outside corroboration. As a result, this chapter of Soviet atomic espionage has remained obscure.

Atomic Espionage at Los Alamos

Although the government at least developed an inkling of Soviet inroads at Berkeley, Chicago, and Columbia during World War II, its agents failed completely to detect Moscow's penetration of a site that was of much more importance to the development of the Soviet bomb, J. Robert Oppenheimer's camp in Los Alamos. The most significant source there for the Soviets was physicist Klaus Emil Fuchs, an émigré from Nazi Germany and a loyal Communist who had been involved in the anti-Fascist movement in his homeland. As Stephen Spender writes, Fuchs "made a religion out of communism," as it seemed the only reliable and potent countering force to Nazism. Robert Chadwell Williams suggests too that Fuchs was very much influenced by the idealism of his father, a Lutheran activist who converted to Quakerism in the 1920s and became the first minister to join the Social Democratic Party. He later became a devout Communist and moved to East Germany after the war.[184]

In 1933, the younger Fuchs came to Paris and London as a student and Communist activist. When the Nazi government refused to renew his passport in 1934, his status as a student allowed him to stay in Britain, where he took a PhD at the University of Bristol in 1936. He then went to work with renowned physicist Max Born at Edinburgh University. After hostilities broke out between Germany and Britain, however, he was interned as an enemy alien in Quebec in May 1940. Born's efforts won his release six months later.[185] Back in England, Fuchs accepted Rudolph Peierls's offer to come to Birmingham University to work under contract with the Ministry of Aircraft Production on atomic research—specifically, the gaseous diffusion process—despite several suspicious items in his record, his party membership among them. It was at Birmingham in 1941 that Fuchs "decided to furnish information . . . to the Soviet Union" on his work, owing both to his desire to assist that nation as well as his conviction that the West cared little if Germany and the Soviet Union destroyed each other. He contacted Jurgen Kuczynski, a German Communist in London, who connected Fuchs with Simon Davidovitch Kremer, secretary to the military attaché's office at the Soviet embassy, whom Fuchs supplied with notes on his research for approximately six months in 1942. Fuchs's second contact would be Kuczynski's sister, Sonia, whom he worked with until he left for the United States in November 1943 as part of the British Diffusion Mission (BDM) to the Manhattan Project. [186]

Fuchs planned to hand over only the work he himself had done, but even when he was still at Birmingham, as his colleague Michael Perrin reported, this included a great deal: the gaseous diffusion process for separating isotopes, as well as "mathematical methods for evaluating the critical size and efficiency of an atomic bomb." [187] Fuchs had signed an oath committing him to the provisions of the Official Secrets Act, and he became a British citizen in July 1942, after the Birmingham Police Department determined he had refrained from political activity. [188] With the blessing of British security, then, Fuchs gained "unlimited access to secret files," and one result was that the United States never ran a check on him. [189] Later, the FBI learned that it had Fuchs's name and his "relatively important" associations with Communism on file in 1945, in captured German documents that were buried in a five-thousand-name indexing project. [190] Fuchs's simultaneous cooperation with Russia and pledge of secrecy to the British authorities were part of what he liked to call his "controlled schizophrenia," or, as the FBI put it, "the two compartments in Fuchs' mind." [191]

Fuchs stayed on at the BDM in New York until August 1944, working as a consultant for the Kellex Corporation, a nuclear contractor, even after many of his compatriots had returned home. During this period, the physicist apparently dropped his reticence to share others' material, and he passed over "all the reports prepared in the New York Office of the BDM." [192] In February 1944, Harry Gold met him for the first time, beginning a process of regularly collecting material from Fuchs that he then handed off to a Russian contact. A Soviet cable described their meeting: "REST (Fuchs) greeted him pleasantly, but was rather cautious at first . . . [in] the discussion GUS (Gold) satisfied himself that REST was aware of whom he was working with. . . . The whole operation amounts to the working out of the process for the separation of isotopes of ENORMOUS [the atomic bomb project]." [193] Gold, who called himself "Raymond," met Fuchs three more times that summer in New York. [194] The Philadelphia chemist was always properly obsequious to him, the international physicist, Fuchs remembered. He also recalled that Gold and his other Soviet contacts initially asked him only "general" questions that gave no hint of Russian "progress" on the bomb. Instead, he got questions about people, especially the "outstanding scientists."[195] Fuchs's assistance would certainly accelerate Soviet progress; in this period he wrote thirteen highly secret scientific papers, all of which he passed on to Gold.[196] In addition to these, Fuchs supplied his courier with other information on the project, including the explosive properties of fissionable material and details about the plans for the Oak Ridge facility.[197] Such a trove of materials led Soviet intelligence officials to authorize a $500 payment to Fuchs for his work—Gold remembered offering as much as $1,500—but Fuchs "turned it down cold"; Gold returned the money to his handler, Semyon Semyonov.[198]

Semyonov would not receive Fuchs's important material much longer. By 1944, the FBI had made the handler a regular target of surveillance, thus greatly limiting his usefulness and eventually leading to his removal from American soil. On September 30, 1944, Semyonov was recalled to Russia and replaced by "John," Anatoli Antonovich Yakovlev (or Yatskov), the Soviet's vice consul in New York.[199] Gold, who never spoke of Yakovlev in the same glowing terms he used in referring to Semyonov, described his new contact as about five feet nine inches, twenty-eight to thirty years of age, and slim, with a long nose and dark eyes. Yakovlev ran Gold from March 1944 until December 1946, although their meetings became infrequent as time wore on.[200]

Fuchs was transferred to Los Alamos on August 12, 1944, but the Soviets did not learn where he had gone until three months later, and even after that were unsure about his new work.[201] They would soon find out. From Los Alamos Laboratory's Theoretical Physics Division, Fuchs would provide Moscow with unparalleled information about the bomb project. For example, according to Karl Cohen, who had worked at the SAM lab in 1943–44, "[Fuchs] had intimate and detailed knowledge of all phases of the design of the K-25 (Oak Ridge) plant." Added Manson Benedict of Kellex: "[H]e was in possession of information which, if transmitted to the Russians, would have saved them years of development effort."[202] Indeed it did.

Gold and Fuchs next met when Fuchs was on leave at his sister's house in Cambridge, Massachusetts, in February 1945. There, Fuchs gave instructions to Gold about their next rendezvous in Santa Fe, as well as extensive information on such topics as atomic bomb construction, detonation principles, the lens system of the bomb, implosion, and the fission rates of certain types of plutonium.[203] According to Michael Perrin, Fuchs now "realized

Anatoli Yakovlev

for the first time . . . the importance of plutonium as an alternative to U-235" and that a plutonium pile would be built to accompany Oak Ridge's U-235 plant.[204] Gold, who met with Yakovlev the same day, gave him a report a week later.[205]

In May, Gold and Yakovlev planned Gold's upcoming trip to New Mexico, where he would meet not only Fuchs but also Los Alamos machinist David Greenglass.[206] Gold was instructed to bring five hundred dollars to Greenglass.[207] Because the young machinist wouldn't know him, Gold also was told to produce half a Jell-O box top that would match the half that Greenglass had and say, "I come from Julius"—a reference to Greenglass's brother-in-law, Julius Rosenberg. Gold was very nervous about this extra contact at Los Alamos, but Yakovlev would hear no protests. Gold's fears proved correct. This additional connection helped make the link that would expose the Rosenberg ring once Fuchs was discovered.[208] Soviet intelligence

David and Ruth Greenglass and their children

agents had hesitated about putting all their atomic eggs in Gold's basket; it would be "too risky." But they had done so anyway.[209]

In his court testimony in 1951, Greenglass testified that the first person he gave information to was his wife, Ruth, in November 1944; she presumably passed it on to Rosenberg. Greenglass also furnished more information on the bomb's lens mold directly to his brother-in-law when he was on furlough two months later. He claimed that his willingness to serve the Soviet Union was based upon years of indoctrination from Julius, who had visited their house frequently while dating Greenglass's sister and who began talking to him about the merits of Communism when Greenglass was an impressionable fifteen-year-old.[210]

When Gold came to Santa Fe in June, Fuchs gave him materials including a plutonium bomb sketch "with important dimensions indicated," as well as information about the bomb's imploding and ignition, calculations of the weapon's efficiency, comparisons of its power with TNT, and information about the plans to use it against Japan.[211] Afterward, Gold traveled to Albuquerque to see Greenglass, who provided him with sketches and several pages of handwritten notes on the lens mold. The young man also was eager to describe other recruits he had identified at Los Alamos. Gold told Greenglass to cut out such activity; to even think about recruiting people for the Soviet Union was dangerous for him. Back in New York on June 5, Gold handed over both Greenglass's and Fuchs's materials in a hasty meeting with Yakovlev. Two weeks later, Yakovlev told Gold how "extremely excellent" the material had been, and Gold provided full details of his conversations with the two men.[212]

At his final meeting with Fuchs in September 1945, Gold obtained information about the Trinity tests, production of U-235, blast waves, and other technical details.[213] Fuchs mentioned to Gold that a Los Alamos security officer had told him that "Army Intelligence realized there were hundreds of Soviet agents in the United States and England."[214] If so, U.S. officials remained ignorant of what many of them were doing, including Fuchs and other spies at Los Alamos like Ted Hall. Still, with the war over, Fuchs already saw that "there as no longer free and easy cooperation between the British and the Americans at Los Alamos," preventing him from gaining access to certain areas, and leading him to believe he would soon be sent back to Britain. Fuchs and Gold then discussed a plan by which Fuchs could reconnect with Soviet intelligence once he returned to England, as well as the possibility of the two getting together in Cambridge later in the year.[215]

Soviet archives have confirmed that the material Fuchs supplied to Gold was used by Igor Kurchatov, head of the Soviet nuclear project, and physicist Iulii Khariton "as the design of the first Soviet bomb." David Holloway argues that Fuchs was "by far the most important informant in the Manhattan project." Thanks to Fuchs, notes Alexander Feklisov, the first three bombs made in the Soviet Union were "replicas" of American models, smaller and more accurate than existing Soviet types.[216] Of course, Fuchs was hardly the only source the Soviets had on the Manhattan Project; others included the aforementioned Hall, as well as still-unidentified sources including "Fogel/Pers," a source at Oak Ridge, and "Quantum," who provided materials on isotope separation. Still, the Atomic Energy Commission, upon studying Fuchs's later confessions, declared that the Russian process was "probably advanced by two years" because of the information he had provided. Especially damaging were his materials on the plutonium implosion bomb (Trinity), as well as projectile-type nuclear weapons.[217] Fuchs later expressed surprise that the Soviets had detonated a bomb as quickly as they had, since he had not imagined they had the required engineering and construction expertise for rapid production.[218]

The Canadian Link: Gouzenko

While Fuchs's intelligence gathering at Los Alamos remained a mystery until 1950, the government had been aware of Soviet atomic espionage since 1943, with its monitoring of events at the Berkeley Radiation Laboratory. The discoveries at Berkeley, however, paled in comparison to the revelations of Igor Gouzenko less than a month after the war ended. A cipher clerk for military attaché Col. Nikolai Zabotin at the Russian embassy in Ottawa, Gouzenko defected on September 5, taking 109 documents that illuminated Soviet successes in obtaining atomic, radar, and other military-industrial secrets from contacts on both sides of the border. The case's potential embarrassment to the U.S. government loomed large, and Canadian prime minister McKenzie King had to assure Truman that "he would hold up for two weeks on the Corby [Gouzenko] case" just to address such discomfiture.[219] By December, Washington "no longer requested delay."[220] Still, because of official reticence in both the Canadian and the U.S. governments, the revelations were not made public. Only in February 1946, acting on a tip, did Washington journalist Drew Pearson scoop the story. The sensitive nature of the allegations was clear in his report: "Serious secret differences inside the U.S. Government have resulted from these revelations, with the State Department anxious not to disrupt Russian relations, but the Justice Department anxious to arrest and prosecute."[221] It was an old refrain. The Justice Department—indeed perhaps the FBI—may well have been Pearson's source; clearly, Truman was in no hurry to publicize the matter.[222] At any rate, Gouzenko's story revealed a large and successful Soviet espionage effort orchestrated by Zabotin, then head of Red Army intelligence in Canada.[223] Zabotin himself was most interested in military information, including, not surprisingly, the atomic bomb, as well as aerial photography, locations of army divisions, and personnel issues. Meanwhile, the NKVD section at the embassy was most concerned with political and economic intelligence.[224]

FBI director Hoover professed his deepest alarm regarding this latest Soviet spy scandal: "[T]hey are so well entrenched . . . that they are able to obtain documents from the Minister of External Affairs of Canada and from the United Kingdom High Commissioner's Office . . . with ease." As the FBI noted in a 1946 intelligence report, seventeen men at the Soviet embassy had been "actively and continuously engaged in directing and supervising these espionage activities," including Zabotin, assistant military attachés Vassili Rogov and Petr Motinov, and Second Secretary Vitali G. Pavlov, the leading Soviet intelligence representative at the outpost; moreover, these men "were in the closest communication with the headquarters of the Red Army intelligence and the headquarters of the NKVD in Moscow." Hoover asserted that Moscow's top military priority was to obtain "complete construction plans of the atomic bomb itself by the end of this year."[225] Indeed, the weapon *was* "the number one objective of Soviet espionage," Gouzenko told the FBI.[226] Like the Bentley case that same autumn, this investigation spurred an expansive counterintelligence response in the Bureau and, of course, commensurate increases in the agency's budget. Hoover would cite the Gouzenko case—"another international espionage case involving the protection of the atomic bomb," and one to which seventy-five special agents were already "exclusively assigned"—as justification for higher FBI allocations in 1945.[227]

The Ottawa embassy served as a conduit for information coming from a range of outside sources, described by the FBI as "fourteen Canadian public officials in positions of trust . . . [who] were identified as active Soviet espionage agents furnishing the most highly secret and important information . . . to Zabotin and his assistants." Some of them had been recruited by Canadian Communist leaders Sam Carr and Fred Rose.[228] Agencies with active sources included the Departments of External Affairs and Munitions and Supply, the Canadian Army, Navy, and Air Force, the National Research Council, the Bank of Canada, the U.K. High Commissioner's Office, and the Canadian National Film Board.[229] The quantity of material they provided was so great that the embassy duplication equipment could not keep up, Gouzenko alleged. Much of the information was microfilmed and sent on by courier. In January 1945, for example, Moscow received two pouches with over two hundred items, mostly secret or classified government documents.[230]

The Soviet government reacted to the unfavorable publicity by downplaying the importance of the information its agents had collected in North America and blaming the furor on an anti-Soviet campaign. In a radio statement, Soviet officials acknowledged that military attaché Nikolai

Zabotin had "received from acquaintances among Canadian citizens certain information of a secret character," but pointed out that this material was not of "special interest" to Russia, where "higher technical achievements are in existence." The Soviet statement declared that the notion that such information presented a threat to Canada's security was "ridiculous."[231]

Justices R. L. Kellock and Robert Taschereau of the Canadian Supreme Court formed a royal commission to investigate the Gouzenko case and concluded that the Soviet embassy had indeed sought information about the weapons industry and defense plans of Canada, the United Kingdom, and the United States, as well as those countries' political and economic policies.[232] The War Department responded to the findings by noting, "[P]erhaps the most startling single aspect of the entire fifth column Soviet network is the uncanny success with which the Soviet agents were able to find Canadians who were willing to betray their country and to supply agents of a foreign Power with secret information."[233] Yet one of the most important sources was not a Canadian but a Briton: Allan Nunn May, or "Alek," a prominent Cambridge-trained nuclear physicist who worked for the Department of Scientific and Industrial Research (or Tube Alloys Research, as it was commonly called). In late 1944 Col. Zabotin first tapped "Alek," who had earlier agreed to assist because, like so many others, he "thought this was a contribution [he] could make for the safety of mankind."[234] May gave the Soviets "a survey of the entire atomic bomb project" as he was aware of it, largely concerning the atom-splitting process, because he did not know how the bomb was assembled.[235] To obtain this information, he traveled twice to Chalk River, three hours north of Ottawa, where a "heavy-water-moderated natural-uranium reactor" operated. In return, he received token amounts of money, along with liquor.[236] He also made three trips to the Chicago Metallurgical Laboratory, from which he transferred uranium-233 and -235 samples to Soviet military intelligence in Canada in 1944. At Chicago, he "had almost unrestricted access to a large amount of highly valuable technical and scientific information concerning nuclear fission." It was no wonder that, as Gouzenko reported, the embassy considered May a "prize catch" and Zabotin was beside himself with joy. May also provided general information about the Anglo-American atomic research project, especially on its Hanford, Washington, plutonium plant and the Harwell atomic research facility in Britain. In the process of gathering his materials, he became more familiar than any other British scientist with the graphite pile for constructing plutonium, and this so bothered Gen. Leslie Groves that he forbade May from making a fourth visit to Chicago in 1944. The Manhattan Project chief confessed no reason for suspecting May, but noted simply "I did not like to have him acquire such a wide knowledge." After the bombing of Hiroshima, May passed on more information, including "production figures" and uranium-233 samples. The physicist also furnished material on an electronic detonator that used radar to explode a shell in the proximity of an airplane; the technology was being used against Japanese kamikaze pilots.[237]

May returned to England in September 1945. But he did not reconnect with a Soviet agent there as planned; ironically, his view was that such a meeting would be unnecessary, since U.S. officials were then considering international control of atomic energy. His was a vain hope.[238] British authorities questioned May on February 15, 1946, just as Gouzenko's story appeared in the press. He confessed and was sentenced to ten years of penal servitude.[239] Still, officials reassured themselves that May could not have told the Soviets how to make a bomb, even if he knew a great deal about the Chicago plutonium pile, something about the technical problems at Hanford, and somewhat less about production of uranium. Of course, a more knowledgeable source was still working for Russia: Klaus Fuchs.[240]

Eleven men received a guilty verdict in the Gouzenko case.[241] They included Harold Samuel Gerson, a geologist code-named "Gray" who worked during the war at the Department of Munitions and Supply and, since 1942, furnished Moscow such material as the "complete technical information and listings of locations for the storing of guns, ammunition, chemical warfare equipment, fire control instruments and the like across Canada." Some of his technical reports were 150 pages long. A mathematician and physicist named Durnford Smith, meanwhile, supplied information on field-artillery radio locators and other radar devices from his post at the radio laboratory of the National Research Council, where he was assistant research engineer, as did his colleague, electrical engineer Edward Mazerall.[242]

The Soviets also received material from Raymond Boyer, a chemist at McGill University, on the RDX explosive—for which Harry Gold had also sought information. Journalist David Gordon Lunan, who worked at the Wartime Information Board, had provided a wide range of information, including material on uranium, bombs, and explosives. Physicist David Sugar of the navy's electrical supply department had also assisted the Soviets with specifications on such advanced devices as a range-detecting recorder and a depth-finding oscillator from his work at the Sagamo Lab Company of Springfield, Illinois, in 1944. The investigatory commission alleged that using his extensive naval contacts, "he would have the occasion to obtain information covering subjects much beyond the duties entrusted to him." At a time when radar development was "highly secret," Gouzenko noted, this material was greatly valued.[243]

The Supreme Court of Canada's royal commission was particularly alarmed about espionage on radar, then "perhaps the most vital work accomplished by the English-speaking Democracies in the technical field." Research on antisubmarine devices, explosives, and propellants had also been "compromised," the commission noted. In short, "much vital technical information, which should still be secret to the authorities of Canada, Great Britain, and the United States, has been made known to the Russians," concluded the justices.[244]

As a result of the Gouzenko case, the FBI began to develop a more complete picture of Soviet espionage in the United States, about which it still knew little. The Gouzenko revelations alerted officials not just to the targets of Soviet technical espionage, but also to the methods by which they obtained the information.[245] For example, the affair had demonstrated high concentrations of Soviet spies in Russian posts abroad; the army reckoned they constituted from 30 to 60 percent of embassy staff.[246] As Hoover deduced, "The Soviet intelligence services in the United States are organized on a basis closely paralleling that revealed . . . in Canada," only with "a far greater number of espionage agents."[247] The Gouzenko case also would furnish American and British investigators with the code names of scientists who had been of interest to Russia and, in conjunction with Venona later, would allow for identification of key sources. American officials were particularly distressed that *"persons with an unusually high degree of education"* had been over-represented among the identified spies.[248]

A congressional committee, meanwhile, concluded that May's personality, like Fuchs's, lent itself to espionage—both men were described as "shy, retiring" and "mousy, little." Indeed, noted Congress's report, "such individuals can perhaps be imagined as relishing the secret knowledge that they, despite the seemingly prosaic pattern of their lives, were actually trafficking in information which affected the destiny of nations." Harry Gold seems cut out of the same cloth. The report went on to note, less persuasively, that Fuchs's and Pontecorvo's escape from Fascism made them "naïve and irrational" in their politics—as if an allegiance to Fascism was somehow more rational—and that they, like May and Greenglass (and the report might have added, Gold), had received an education with "an unusual lack of contact with the liberal arts disciplines." The congressmen claimed that scientific work and its "orderly and rationally satisfying" nature explained their fondness for Communism's "regulated order."[249] Leaving aside the likelihood that German Fascism was, if anything, even more orderly, at least in theory, Fuchs's own attorney, Derek Curtis-Bennett, went so far as to say that "scientists do not have flexible minds." But it is hard to imagine a more elastic mind than Gold's, with its inventions of family and its management of a double life.[250]

Although the work of Gold and Fuchs remained undetected in 1945 and 1946, Gouzenko's allegations at the end of World War II helped solidify the perception among members of the U.S. counterintelligence community that the Soviet Union and its espionage practices were a serious threat. Building on the evidence of Steve Nelson's work and J. Robert Oppenheimer's reports from Berkeley, Arthur Adams's and Clarence Hiskey's spying at the Chicago and Columbia labs, Gregori Kheifetz's intrigues at the San Francisco consulate, not to mention the industrial espionage of Andrei Shevchenko and others mentioned in the previous chapter, the Gouzenko investigation suggested a wide-ranging scope of Soviet industrial intelligence activity. Elizabeth Bentley's reports, of course, soon added even more to the picture. The FBI and other counterintelligence agencies were now well aware that the Soviet government had used wartime cooperation and a large presence in the United States (they did not know yet how large) to pursue its interests in obtaining the ultimate secret of the war, the atomic bomb. The discovery of atomic espionage at the Radiation Laboratory in 1943 had been the crucial turning point in creating this new understanding, an outlook that was cemented by the subsequent wartime revelations and probes outlined here. The changed perception would have disastrous implications for Soviet-American relations in the postwar era.

CHAPTER FIVE

Cold War Consequences of
World War II Espionage

In the aftermath of World War II and the discovery of the Soviet Union's military-industrial espionage, American counterintelligence officials became even more distrustful of their former partner as further evidence of perfidy arose from such sources as "Venona," the U.S. government's secret project to decode wartime Soviet cables.[1] Here were not only records that confirmed the role of well-known spies like Steve Nelson, but also new material that by 1950 had implicated many hitherto unknown Soviet agents—from Judith Coplon to Klaus Fuchs to William Perl. The postwar discovery of a vast Soviet wartime espionage operation that emerged both from signals intelligence, like Venona, and human sources, such as Elizabeth Bentley, Igor Gouzenko, and Harry Gold, stiffened the American intelligence community's already hostile stance toward the Soviet Union and quickly heightened suspicions in other government agencies as well. Building upon a growing diplomatic standoff in Europe, Asia, and the Middle East, these cases helped consolidate a permafrost in Soviet-American relations for the next four and a half decades.

Although the FBI and the War Department had embraced this wary view of Soviet dangers by 1945, the State Department had not, and lingering U.S.-Soviet wartime solidarity might well have continued to prevent widespread distrust from establishing itself throughout Washington. Indeed, wholesale adoption of a suspicious outlook was not inevitable. In June 1945, the Soviets presented Gen. Dwight D. Eisenhower with the Order of Victory and invited him to attend their country's victory parade, which he did in August. Later that year, Eisenhower invited Marshal Zhukov to the United States, but because of illness and scheduling problems, the marshal was unable to visit.[2] At the same time, a delegation of congressmen, including such later fire-breathers as Karl Mundt (R-S.Dak.), traveled to Russia and called for a meeting of the "Big Two"—Stalin and Truman—"to determine . . . what policies and purposes can be implemented which will tend to bring Russia and the United States closer together." Such a meeting would "dispel Soviet suspicions of American purpose and intent," as the congressmen noted with optimism.[3]

Despite such hopes, Moscow had already detected an unfriendly shift in U.S. policy by the end of the European war in May 1945. Vladimir Pravdin, a journalist for TASS who was also an undercover KGB agent, told Moscow that "the reactionaries (Senators [Robert] Taft, [Burton K.] Wheeler, [Alben W.] Barkley) are setting particular hopes on the possibility of getting direction of [U.S.] foreign policy wholly into their own hands, partly because [Truman] is notoriously untried and ill-informed on these matters." In addition, Pravdin named Gen. George C. Marshall, Senator Arthur Vandenberg, and Admiral Leahy as "carrying on a systematic anti-Soviet campaign."[4] Pravdin's hunch of a chill in relations emanating from U.S. military officials at this time was not inaccurate. As Mark Stoler has pointed out, in the wake of Moscow's push into Eastern Europe during the summer and fall of 1944, Secretary of the Navy James Forrestal and other members of the Joint Chiefs grew increasingly distrustful of Soviet plans. Although they did not express these sentiments publicly and American policy remained tied to cooperation with the Soviet Union, the top brass were already contemplating the kinds of changes in U.S. military posture that might be needed to meet this "very formidable potential enemy." The failure of the Yalta agreements only strengthened this view, as Stoler notes, and once Germany was defeated, the Joint Chiefs embraced a "new paradigm based on an unlimited, global view of both U.S. national security and Soviet goals . . . [and] a fundamental clash of interests between the two superpowers."[5] Stoler connects this "new paradigm" to the armed forces' recognition of a shifting and increasingly threatening Soviet military position in 1944–45, and he links it as well with the rise of "the national security state" in the early Cold War; however, as this book has shown, the FBI and other counterintelligence officials had adopted the view that the Soviet Union was more of an enemy than an ally as early as 1943. Moreover, the discovery of Soviet espionage had already launched an extensive security apparatus, including continuous surveillance of suspected Soviet agents, Russian representatives and American Communists alike, among other measures.[6]

By early 1946, worries over the Soviet threat would proliferate throughout Washington. Notwithstanding the hopes still cherished by Secretary of Commerce Henry Wallace and some others, the spirit of wartime cooperation had largely disappeared. The Cold War outlook was most prominently signaled in the bellwether blasts of George F. Kennan's "Long Telegram" of February 22 and Winston Churchill's Iron Curtain speech on March 5. With its Manichean tones, Kennan's telegram declared that the Soviets were "committed fanatically to the belief that with U.S. there can be no permanent *modus vivendi.*" Still, he remained optimistic, since "communism is like a malignant parasite that feeds only on diseased tissue." If the United States showed "strong resistance," the Soviets would "easily withdraw."[7] Churchill's oration in Fulton, Missouri, which he originally titled "the Sinews of Peace," also addressed the dangers of "weakness" in the face of Soviet aggression. The former prime minister called for the "Western democracies [to] stand together."[8] Delivered on the same day as Truman's demand that Soviet troops pull out of Iran, Churchill's timing was suggestive of a coordinated Anglo-American effort. As Fraser Harbutt has argued, the speech provided the opportunity for a now "eager" Truman to publicly harden his anti-Soviet line.[9]

Unbeknownst to the public, that same March 5 the FBI prepared a summary report of wartime espionage, addressing "Communist infiltration" of the Berkeley Radiation Laboratory, the University of Chicago's Metallurgical Laboratory, and the Soviet embassy in Canada. Not unexpectedly, the FBI's view of the continued dangers of Soviet spying in 1946 was based on what its agents knew of wartime practices. Thus, the Bureau continued to maintain that the Soviet Union was still making efforts to obtain further information on the bomb, the "No. 1 priority objective of Soviet espionage," and alleged it was doing so by means of the United Nations, through sympathetic scientists, and "with outright operational espionage by the Soviet intelligence services."[10] As it happened, though, Moscow had put the brakes on "virtually all intelligence activities by the NKGB in North America" after the Gouzenko and Bentley defections. Most operations remained dormant until the end of 1947, when, as the FBI had correctly surmised, the priority would be atomic espionage once again. At that point, Moscow resumed contact with such sources as Harry Gold, David Greenglass, Morris and Lona Cohen, Ted Hall, Klaus Fuchs, and Julius Rosenberg (who actually had never stopped gathering industrial intelligence for them). Soviet agents had recognized what they saw as Americans' "firm intentions to maintain a complete monopoly on 'Enormoz' and to use [it] for aggressive purposes against us."[11]

Though its analyses derived chiefly from the patterns of wartime spying, the FBI also made attempts to check current espionage practices. On March 26, 1946, agents arrested Lt. Nikolai Grigorevich Redin of the Soviet Purchasing Commission in Portland, Oregon. Redin had bought plans for a destroyer tender, the *Yellowstone*. Initially, both the Department of Justice and the State Department were reluctant to arrest Redin, but the FBI director convinced them that the lieutenant was guilty of "considerable Soviet intelligence activity." In fact, as Daniel J. Leab notes, "the FBI did not have a very strong case at all."[12] The evidence largely drew from the reports of engineer Herbert Kennedy, who had provided material to Redin, but it was not entirely clear the Russians could not have procured the same information through lend-lease arrangements. Following an extensive wiretap and physical surveillance operation, Redin was charged with attempting to procure material for the Soviet Union, as well as with contravening the Espionage Act, which could have resulted in the death penalty.[13] But at his trial, the government was unable to make a compelling case that his material was secret; its wiretaps, moreover, yielded almost nothing of substance. Leab argues that the case was further weakened by "the absence of anti-red hysteria" in 1946, even if the prosecution's arguments revealed "increasing tension between the U.S. and the U.S.S.R." Hysteria was as yet embryonic, but when compared to the fate of Adams and Shevchenko, bona fide spies who returned to Russia in early 1946 untroubled by the American legal system, the arrest and trial of Redin suggests increasingly contentious U.S.-Soviet relations.[14]

As if to confirm the United States' tougher stance, in the summer of 1946 George Elsey, assistant to Truman's counsel Clark Clifford, prepared his boss's secret and later infamous report, "Summary of U.S. Relations with the Soviet Union," more commonly known as the Clifford report. The report was based on a set of responses to Clifford's requests for information from various government departments about Russia—requests that were slanted, largely to preclude a sanguine reply. For instance, Joint Chiefs of Staff chairman Adm. Leahy was asked for a "statement of violations of a military nature of political agreements of the United States and the Soviet Union" and "recent activities of the Soviet Union which affect the security of the United States."[15] Accordingly, the Joint Chiefs responded with a letter outlining the ways in which Moscow had violated treaties, including overstaying their welcome in Iran and not repatriating Japanese soldiers. Moscow was, moreover, consolidating its "military technological position." The Soviet Union, too, had used the American Communist Party as a means to promote its "control of American labor" and conduct sabotage and espionage; "Soviet espionage nets are far-reaching, well organized and the personnel well trained," according to the Joint Chiefs.[16]

Secretary of War Robert P. Patterson replied in similar fashion, lashing out at Soviet moves in Iran and other areas, lamenting their attempts to "discredit U.S. intentions in securing bases necessary to our national security," and lambasting Moscow for "avoiding fair compromise" in areas governed together with the United States, such as Germany. No doubt with some remorse for having earlier supported the promotion of Elizabeth Bentley's best source, Nathan Gregory Silvermaster, he called for Washington to adopt "an adequate intelligence service" to stop "infiltration" through the Communist Party.[17] George F. Kennan, meanwhile, doubted that "high level conversations or negotiations with Russian figures" would be effective. "The Russians have always been difficult to deal with . . . [they] work best with us when the coat fits snugly, doesn't give at the seams."[18]

Attorney General Tom Clark responded to Clifford's request for "a description of any Soviet subversive activities known to the Department of Justice" with a lengthy inventory of Soviet transgressions, including espionage cases, mostly from World War II.[19] Here, he drew chiefly from the reports of his more famous deputy, J. Edgar Hoover. Hoover, of course, had been sounding the alarm for months about the existence of "an enormous Soviet espionage ring," the aims of which were "obtaining all information possible with reference to atomic energy, its specific use as an instrument of war, and the commercial aspects of the energy in peacetime."[20] As a result of such input, the Clifford Report concluded that the Soviets had "thousands of invaluable sources of information in various industrial establishments as well as in . . . the Government." Indeed, it declared, "every American Communist is potentially an espionage agent of the Soviet Government."[21]

The fact that the report's scorecard of *current* "subversive activities" derived from wartime information was hardly surprising, even though the material was in some cases several years old. The notorious nature of the wartime examples made them especially appropriate for a White House eager to tabulate "violations." Counterintelligence agents who had been unable to catch in action those named by Bentley should perhaps have realized that numerous Soviet operations had in fact been suspended in the wake of her and Gouzenko's defections. With the exception of such spies as Julius Rosenberg and Judith Coplon—still secretly meeting with their contacts—the heyday of Soviet espionage in the United States had ended.[22]

Yet as the responses to Elsey show, wartime espionage remained very much alive in the minds of U.S. counterintelligence officials and distinctly framed their postwar approach to Russia. Examining the responses in conjunction with the armed forces' reports regarding Soviet territorial aggrandizement and military expansion, Elsey could only draw one conclusion: "The ultimate aim of Soviet policy is world domination."[23] Such a drastic threat required an equally extreme response, and the final Clifford Report trumpeted: "It must be made apparent to the Soviet Government that our strength will be sufficient to repel any attack ... the US must be prepared to wage atomic and biological warfare. ... A war with the USSR would be 'total' in a more horrible sense than any previous war." And in case anyone had the temerity to suggest bilateral negotiations in this environment, Clifford intoned, "the U.S. ... should entertain no proposal for disarmament or limitation of armament as long as the possibility of Soviet aggression exists."[24] In September 1946, Truman fired the most prominent dove in his administration, Commerce Secretary Wallace, for publicly expressing views critical of the new hard-line approach to the Soviet Union. As Truman fulminated in his diary, "He is a pacifist 100 percent ... the Reds, phonies, and 'parlor pinks' seem to be banded together and are becoming a national danger."[25] Less than a week later the finished contents of the Clifford report landed on Truman's desk and showed how out of step Wallace was.[26]

Early Cold War Espionage and Investigations

Just as they would for the FBI, the patterns of World War II remained vivid in the minds of U.S. Army intelligence officials in the early Cold War. An army study published in June 1947 pointed out that "during the past six years official Soviet representatives and special missions have been granted relatively unrestricted access to many industrial, technical and military establishments and installations ... the intelligence overtones of which appear obvious." At the same time, the study alleged, such "open, technically legal" operations were enhanced by "clandestine intelligence parallels."[27] Soviet espionage objectives were vast, believed army officials, who by 1947 nevertheless were also aware that the wartime defections had had an impact: "[T]here has been a definite slackening off of direct contacts between important Soviet intelligence officials in the United States and sub-agents of the Soviet Intelligence Services."[28] Outside the country, however, the army detected high levels of activity by Soviet espionage agents.

In 1946, for example, the army's Military Intelligence Division identified eighteen Japanese spies who had been recruited to obtain information for

Moscow. Teams were being "smuggled" into the Hokkaido region "for the purpose of reporting on U.S. military installations" there, according to Brig. Gen. C. A. Willoughby of General Headquarters, Far East Command. They were looking for information about the location, number, and supplies of U.S. troops, as well as the attitudes of Japanese toward the Soviet Union, he reported. Hokkaido, near the Russian Far East and possessing an ample coastline, had proved a useful staging area. When interrogated by Military Intelligence, the Japanese agents said their efforts had been forced "through threats and intimidations, with families held as hostages." Those caught had yen that had been issued by the U.S. military to the Soviet mission in Moscow.[29]

Even as Russia sent Japanese agents to spy on the American occupying forces, Soviet agents appropriated German technology by forcibly uprooting specialists from that country. At the BMW plant near Magdeburg, which was producing turbine-powered fighter planes, technicians were removed from their homes and forced to sign a statement committing them to five years' work in Russia. Indicative of the scale of the exodus was that the supreme Soviet commander of Russian-occupied Germany felt compelled to state in late 1946 that "no more deportations would be made." Yet many German plant officials and American authorities believed such promises of little worth, largely because "Russians do not have nearly enough German technicians to carry out their future plans for the reconstruction of Russia." One worker, Edward Schoen, said he had been offered fifty thousand marks to come to a factory in Soviet-controlled Leipzig to make V-2 weapons for Russia. He had no choice in the matter, nor did a German rocket specialist seized from his Berlin home at 4 o'clock in the morning on October 23, 1946.[30]

The nocturnal visit took place in a week of wholesale removal of German factory equipment and employees to the USSR, including 1,500 men from the Junkers Aircraft Works of Dessau, 560 at the Carl Ziess Optical Works of Jena, and 37 chemists at I. G. Farben plants in Wolfen and Bitterfield.[31] The United States, meanwhile, was importing its own German scientists, albeit voluntarily, under the aegis of the famous Operation Paperclip.[32] But as Russia took technicians and dismantled cement factories, V-2 works, and other industrial plants, Americans worried that this wholesale plucking of German technology could lead to an unwanted technological advantage to the Soviet Union.[33] They had reason to worry. Col. Grigorii A. Tokaev, former chief of the aerodynamic laboratory at the Moscow Military Air Academy as well as an officer of the Soviet military administration in Germany, recalled his excitement when he and his fellow Russian occupiers discovered the Sanger-Bredt Project, which was researching a "piloted rocket plane capable of flying vast distances at enormous speed and altitude." Tokaev, who urged his superiors at the Ministry of Aviation Industry to use the German scientists, found a receptive audience in the higher reaches of the Kremlin, where Georgi Malenkov and N. A. Voznesensky insisted he come and tell them more. As Tokaev reported, "[W]e were far behind other nations in the sphere of reactive and rocket technology. . . . If we did not do something about it swiftly, we were going to fall even further behind."[34] Tokaev also recalled being told: "We were too hasty in defeating Germany. . . . We should have allowed them to complete their work on the V-10 . . . then we could have taken it over ready-made. How much trouble that would have saved us!" Based on such talk, Tokaev became convinced that Stalin "desired nothing so much as rocket aircraft capable of dropping bombs on the people of the U.S.A.," or as Molotov described them, "degenerate riff-raff."[35] American officials may not have known about such fantasies, but they were already concerned about the expansion of "basic research activity" in Russia, which had "continue[d] during the war to an extent not duplicated in any other country." The 1946 budget, for instance, included a 240 percent increase in appropriations for scientific research.[36]

Back in the United States, Soviet agents slowly emerged from their defector-induced torpor in the early postwar period. Harry Gold, for instance, made an unsuccessful attempt to find his former Los Alamos contact Klaus Fuchs at Fuchs's sister's apartment in Cambridge, Massachusetts, in January 1946. He did locate his handler Anatoli Yakovlev that month, who complained that one of his sources "had been trailed by Intelligence men continually."[37] They made two subsequent appointments, but Yakovlev missed both and Gold did not see him again until December.[38] The Soviet agent then expressed his regret that he had had to "lie low" for so long; he now had a new plan for Gold, to go to Paris to meet with a physicist. But Gold had already compromised himself dangerously—he had taken a job with his old contact Abe Brothman. This outraged Yakovlev, who knew that Elizabeth Bentley's defection in 1945 had made Brothman, also one of her previous sources, a target for counterintelligence surveillance. Previously, Yakovlev had been confident that Brothman did not know Gold's real name; now, Brothman clearly did. Yakovlev stormed away from their meeting and soon left the United States altogether.[39]

He need not have been so worried; called to testify in front of a grand jury the following year, Gold and Brothman successfully denied any role in espionage. They portrayed Brothman's delivery of drawings to both Bentley and Gold as simply an attempt to garner Soviet business from Jacob Golos.[40] Not until October 1949 would a Soviet contact again visit Gold, then working as senior biochemist in the cardiac ward of a Philadelphia hospital. The agent, who was unfamiliar to Gold, wanted to learn exactly what he had told the grand jury and its possible relationship to Fuchs. The men made plans to meet again on a regular basis, but Gold failed to keep the next appointment.[41] Six months later, he would tell all to the FBI.

Over at the G&R Engineering Company, established after the war by David Greenglass, his brother Bernard, Julius Rosenberg, and neighbor Isidore Goldstein, Rosenberg was still looking for electronic devices for Russia, including valves, tubes, capacitors, transformers, and tube manuals, among them top-secret ones, Greenglass later told HUAC.[42] He claimed that Rosenberg had shared with him information from Joel Barr about a top-secret "thinking machine" that would send out surface-to-air missiles to hit incoming weapons. Greenglass also noticed that Rosenberg made frequent trips to Philadelphia to visit "espionage contacts." When Greenglass worked at Arma Corporation in 1949 and 1950, he reported, his brother-in-law contacted him for information on a "fire control gyroscopic and radar apparatus" that Greenglass was working on.[43] As Soviet archives reveal, Rosenberg continued to meet with his Soviet contact until the eve of his arrest in July 1950.[44]

During the same time period, Klaus Fuchs had returned to the British nuclear program at Harwell, England, where he became head of the theoretical physics division in July 1946. Although he had been primed by Gold to set up a meeting with a Soviet contact once back in England and had even planned what he would carry to this rendezvous (a copy of *Life*), the Gouzenko spy case made him hesitate. Instead, as he had done in 1941, he made discreet inquiries through the German Communists in London, who soon connected him with Soviet intelligence. He met his contact in early 1947: Alexander Feklisov, Rosenberg's former handler who was now in the British capital as second secretary in the Moscow embassy. From then until May 1949, Fuchs would provide Feklisov with numerous documents, including information on plutonium's blast calculations, radiation intensity from the Bikini Test, and material on a "mixed" bomb, composed of plutonium and uranium. He did not, however, pass on anything about the planning meetings on the "super" (hydrogen) bomb he had attended with Edward Teller.[45] From the detailed questions he received, Fuchs quickly gathered that the Soviets had other sources. Donald Maclean of Britain's MI5 was just one of those who kept Moscow posted about American nuclear policies and developments.[46] Another was Rudolf Abel. Born William Fischer in New-castle-upon-Tyne, England, the son of an anti-Tsarist revolutionary, Abel's family had re-emigrated to Russia in 1921. He began his connection with the OGPU in 1927; during and immediately after World War II, he worked under Pavel Sudoplatov in radio deception and other intelligence "special tasks." In 1948, Abel entered the United States through Canada, with the intention of reinvigorating the Soviet espionage organization after the Bent-ley "shocks." Although it is unclear if he obtained much new information, he was soon in contact with atomic spy Ted Hall and the tireless couriers Morris and Lona Cohen before the Rosenberg case put a damper on such activities. (Hall and the Cohens departed for Britain and the Soviet Union, respectively.) Abel allegedly also set up a sabotage network in the United States, which included the placement of explosives on ships heading to Asia.[47] The same year that Abel entered the United States, the American public first learned of the espionage allegations of Whittaker Chambers and Elizabeth Bentley. Chambers named several former government employees as his sources in the 1930s, including Assistant Secretary of the Treasury Harry Dexter White, State Department officials Alger Hiss and Henry Julian Wadleigh, Pentagon economist George Silverman, Bureau of Standards chemist William Ward Pigman, and U.S. Army ballistics expert Franklin Vic-tor Reno. Reno admitted to assisting Chambers; Pigman denied the charges; and Wadleigh took the Fifth Amendment but admitted his espionage when interrogated by the FBI.[48] White dismissed any connection with Chambers's apparatus in front of HUAC in 1948, lashed out at the committee's hearings (once again), and died of a heart attack three days later.[49] Alger Hiss, the most infamous target of Chambers's allegations, at first claimed never to have known Chambers. When this proved unconvincing, he refuted the charge that he had transmitted forty-seven documents to the former Soviet agent in 1937–38. Although former undersecretary of state Sumner Welles agreed that the papers Chambers claimed to have gotten from Hiss were a security risk, President Truman refused to believe that the case was anything but a "red her-ring," championed by Congress to "divert the public's attention from infla-tion."[50] Truman's stance enabled congressmen like Richard Nixon (R-Calif.) to quickly disgrace the administration as insufficiently vigilant against Com-munism, and diligent forensic work on the part of the FBI helped convince a jury to convict Hiss of perjury in January 1950.[51]

Truman's staff also dismissed the reports of former spy Elizabeth Bentley and Whittaker Chambers when they finally became public in 1948. Rather unlike his treatment of wartime espionage in his famous cowritten report of the year before, George Elsey now put a priority on shelving the issue and saving the administration from embarrassment. He thus queried Clifford as to "the desirability of referring the question of Soviet espionage . . . to a bipartisan commission." Elsey also urged that Chambers's mental history be studied and that the exact nature of Bentley's materials be examined "to make it clear that Miss Bentley was not successful in transmitting secret material to the Russians that they did not already have."[52] The secret nature of Venona enabled the administration to affirm this skeptical posture, one which only confused the issue for decades thereafter. It is difficult to imagine a more striking contrast to the FBI's continued obsession with Bentley and her sources. Unfortunately for the administration, Bentley was not going away. Well into the early 1950s, she would be much in demand in front of HUAC as an "expert witness." Her notoriety, in fact, prevented her from keeping a job, and because the Bureau's agents valued her testimony in support of their goals, the FBI found it necessary to keep her on its payroll.[53]

As with Chambers, those Bentley named, such as Gregory Silvermaster of the BEW, William Ullman of the Pentagon, Robert Miller of the Office of the Coordinator of Inter-American Affairs in the State Department, and Duncan Lee of the OSS, either denied her charges or took the Fifth Amendment—or sometimes did both. Only former War Production Board staffer William Walter Remington was willing to testify that he had given information to Bentley. Remington's willingness to come forward, however, was not matched by candor about what he had provided her. He told Congress that he thought Bentley was merely a reporter and minimized the importance of what he had passed along.[54]

Although the FBI had watched Remington since his days at the National Resources Planning Board in 1941, when agents discovered he had worked with the left-leaning American Peace Mobilization, it was only in December 1945, after Bentley had informed them, that the Bureau became aware of their meetings. She reported that when the young economist had worked at the WPB between 1942 and 1944, he had supplied information about aircraft production to her "at least 10 times" while giving her his Communist Party dues. The aircraft information was not necessarily new, but it provided "an added check" to what her superiors already possessed, Bentley claimed. In addition, she asserted, Remington gave her a somewhat questionable formula for the production of synthetic rubber from garbage. Over the course of their meetings, Bentley had noticed that Remington became increasingly uncomfortable, and she thought that he "did not like what he was doing." Remington's wife, Ann, later confirmed that the couple was then growing distant from the party. After Remington moved from the WPB, his job was no longer a source of interest to the Soviets and their meetings stopped.[55]

Even as the FBI nipped at his heels, Remington had ascended to ever more prestigious heights in the Washington establishment. After the war, he served as an economist with the Council of Economic Advisers from 1947 to 1948 and then as director of the export program staff at the Department of Commerce's Office of International Trade. In 1948 as one of the only figures named by Bentley who still worked in the government, he thus remained a tempting target for investigation. Using its newly expanded security apparatus, in May 1948 the government at last launched a loyalty investigation of him, which found grounds for his disloyalty based on his past political associations and led to his suspension from his position at Commerce. Remington appealed the decision to the Loyalty Review Board. When Elizabeth Bentley refused to show up and testify against him, the board cleared him in 1949. Moreover, its members flatly declared (despite the clearly conflicting contemporary assessments of the FBI and other counterintelligence agencies) that during the war "giving the Russians information with respect to the progress of our war effort wouldn't necessarily spell disloyalty."[56]

Remington's troubles were not over, however. Despite a favorable profile in the *New Yorker* and a successful settlement of his suit against Elizabeth Bentley, whom he alleged had libeled him as a Communist on *Meet the Press*, the FBI was still investigating, and so was HUAC. The issue became his membership in the Communist Party, which he had denied; nevertheless, a grand jury investigation indicted him in June 1950 for perjury on this score.[57] Remington's innocence was significantly undermined by the testimony of his estranged wife. Browbeaten into testifying at the grand jury proceedings by the foreman, John Brunini—who was being paid at the same time by publisher Devin-Adair to help Bentley write her tell-all book—Ann Moos Remington declared that both she and her former husband had wanted to send information to Russia and had been introduced to Golos and Bentley by Joseph North, editor of the *New Masses*, in 1942.[58] Remington did not deny her account but argued that he did not know that Golos and Bentley were Communists. He later tried to have a doctor declare his wife "not a competent witness."[59] Remington soon would also suffer from increasingly damaging charges by Bentley, who expanded upon her previous allegations

William Walter Remington (right) shakes hands with his attorney, Joseph Rauh, February 11, 1949, after being cleared of disloyalty and reporting back to the Commerce Department.

against him in his 1951 perjury trial. Thus, his "'worthless'" reports to her were now transformed into "'super-secret'" materials.[60]

But Remington did the most damage to himself. He not only denied any Communist associations in his past—or blamed them on his mother-in-law—but also insisted that the monies he paid Bentley were not dues at all, but "contributions to a refugee fund." His Communist past was easily demonstrated by people who had known him in his youth.[61] Insisting that he had only produced unimportant scraps of information for Bentley, Remington then tried to defend himself by appealing to the wartime zeitgeist: writing to his supporters that even if Bentley was "extremely New Dealish . . . 1943 was a period when the US was trying to charm the USSR . . . and pro-Soviet views were not subversive AT THAT TIME." Of course, the counterintelligence community hotly contested this view.[62]

Throughout, as his biographer Gary May notes, Remington lied and omitted details.[63] He was found guilty of perjury for his statements about membership in the party and sentenced to five years in prison and a $2,000 fine. After the sentence was thrown out on a technicality, the beleaguered Remington was put on trial again the following year, although this time his evasions about his party membership were no longer the central issue. He was convicted instead for having "denied that he had ever given confidential information to Elizabeth Bentley" and for insisting on his ignorance of the Young Communist League chapter at Dartmouth, where he was a student in the 1930s. This time, he was sentenced to three years. Remington paid a high price for his conviction; a fellow inmate murdered him at Lewisburg Penitentiary on November 22, 1954.[64]

Espionage, Venona, and Wiretapping: The Case of Judith Coplon

Just five days after Remington's death, on November 27, 1954, a more fortunate Alger Hiss walked out of the same Pennsylvania prison, having himself served three and a half years for falsely denying he knew Whittaker Chambers. In Hiss's case, the statute of limitations on his earlier espionage had expired by the time Chambers first named him publicly in 1948; he was thus tried for perjury instead. Indeed, as the Hiss, Remington, and William Perl perjury convictions all demonstrate, proof of espionage was exceedingly difficult to establish in the early years of the Cold War. Even as suspicions of Soviet treachery spread among American officials, with investigations quickly swamping the wartime tally, a combination of insufficient and unacceptable evidence consistently limited the government's ability to prosecute these probes successfully. Signals intelligence—most notably the Venona decryption project—was perhaps the most tantalizing of the unusable evidence. Certainly, investigators found Venona crucial in providing much new information about wartime and even postwar espionage: by February 1951, the cables had assisted the government in making 108 identifications. Although only 44 of these were corroborated by other sources, intelligence agencies learned the identities of 64 additional spies who would have otherwise remained unknown.[65]

In the investigation of Judith Coplon, the decrypted cables actually alerted officials to an espionage case in progress. Coplon would be the first to be arrested based on a Venona link after her cover name ("Sima") was found in a cable that FBI agents analyzed in December 1948.[66] But as a highly guarded government secret, Venona would be compromised if introduced in court proceedings against suspected spies like Coplon. Moreover, Venona identifications, as secondhand information, required corroboration. Wiretapped evidence, also a key element in the Coplon investigation, was similarly problematic. A favorite FBI technique that had flourished in the war, wiretapping, like Venona, could assist in finding perpetrators but not necessarily in prosecuting them.[67]

Coplon, a political analyst in the Foreign Agents Registration Section (FARS) at the Justice Department, had access to sensitive FBI monitoring records on suspected individuals and groups.[68] Recruited by her friend Flora Don Wovschin of the Office of War Information, Coplon first met Soviet NKGB representative Stepan Apresyan on January 4, 1945. Though she always denied she was an espionage agent, Venona makes a highly compelling case against her, given that she and "Sima" started working at FARS on the same day. Coplon was the only female political analyst there.[69]

Once the Bureau discovered her, agents launched extensive surveillance, including bugging her phones, a decision that would almost derail the government's case. She was arrested in March 1949 as she was supplying material to her Soviet handler, Valentin Gubitchev, who worked at the United Nations.[70] The documents included profiles of possible spy recruits, as well as "a statement of . . . [her] efforts to obtain access to a top secret report of the FBI."[71] In addition she had summary slips that the FBI had purposely circulated to her desk to entice her, one of which concerned a supposed American agent at Amtorg. Coplon would face two trials: one alone, in Washington, based on her lifting of documents, and a second in New York with Gubitchev, related to her transmittal of the FBI materials to him.[72]

Coplon claimed that she and the married Gubitchev were lovers, and that this explained their surreptitious rendezvous, but the jury wasn't buying it, especially when the FBI produced evidence of her trysts with a coworker, Harold Shapiro.[73] Coplon then claimed that her FBI materials were gleaned in support of a novel she was writing, a work about "this whole espionage hysteria." She also suggested she used them to prepare for her civil service examination![74] But the Bureau had its own troubles in the case, beginning with its agents' arrest and search of Coplon without a warrant. Worse, the agency's methods were exposed in the first trial. Coplon's attorney, Archibald Palmer, first asked whether wiretaps had been used, eliciting a denial from FBI agents, who of course perjured themselves.[75] Palmer further demanded that the full files behind the slips she had been carrying the night she was arrested be included in the evidence. To the FBI's shock, Judge Albert L. Reeves backed up Palmer. Bureau agents were embarrassed by the sensitive, hearsay nature of the documents, which included many unsubstantiated allegations, including some that suggested the Communist leanings of the actors Frederic March and Helen Hayes.[76] Coplon also appeared to have been a victim of entrapment. Regardless, she was found guilty of intent to commit espionage and of stealing government documents and sentenced to ten years.[77]

Liberal groups were apoplectic. Attorney General J. Howard McGrath told Truman that the National Lawyers Guild was "preparing a report attacking the Administration." As McGrath noted, the guild planned to "recommend that you issue immediately a directive ordering the FBI to cease wiretapping, mail opening, and illegal searches in which . . . the FBI engages." McGrath was not worried. He stalwartly defended the FBI's electronic surveillance as being used "only in cases involving espionage, sabotage, grave risks to the internal security of the nation, or cases in which human lives are in jeopardy."[78] As noted earlier, FDR had authorized wiretaps in 1940 on "persons suspected of subversive activities." Truman himself had recently had political operator Tommy "the Cork" Corcoran bugged. Although the subversive nature of the lobbyist's doings was dubious, the president believed that Corcoran's machinations with other former FDR administration members could hurt him.[79]

In Coplon's second trial, with Gubitchev, her lawyer made the FBI's wiretapping practices even more central. The agents who previously had declared they had "no personal knowledge" of wiretapping now had to admit they did. Judge Sylvester Ryan wanted all the wiretap logs and independent corroboration of any material in the taps, which could not legally serve as the basis of the charges against Coplon. The FBI found itself in even more trouble when it became apparent that agents had listened in on Coplon's conversations with her attorney. Just as troubling, some of the transcripts had been destroyed, and other recordings were downright unintelligible, leading to questions about what the Bureau had done to them. Judge Ryan, not surprisingly, declared the wiretap evidence "tainted."[80]

Nevertheless, the judge determined that the government had sufficient uncontaminated evidence to make its case. Coplon and Gubitchev had been charged with conspiracy to commit espionage; she alone was also charged with making an "attempt to communicate and transmit" U.S. intelligence documents to an unauthorized source despite having "reason to believe they would be used to the injury of the U.S."[81] She and Gubitchev were found guilty and sentenced to fifteen years in prison (bringing her total sentence to twenty-five years). But her conviction was overturned on appeal in 1952 by Judge Learned Hand, largely based on the reason that her arrest had been illegal, both because there had been no warrant and because she was denied the knowledge that some of the evidence against her came from illegal wiretapping.[82] Under State Department pressure, Gubitchev was allowed to return to the Soviet Union. Coplon, however, remained confined to a limited area of New York State until 1967, when the government finally dismissed the case against her.[83]

The arrest of Coplon would have been impossible without Venona, but the government's heavy reliance on the weak reed of wiretaps in her case shows that the cables remained of little use as evidence.[84] As FBI official Alan Belmont knew, the decrypts could be considered "hearsay"; they were "fragmentary" in nature and full of code names; and perhaps most important, their use risked "exposure of Government techniques and practices in the cryptograph field," including the "disadvantage [to] NSA" that would result if the Soviets learned about the successful code cracking. Worse for the FBI, any thought of releasing the information in the highly partisan atmosphere of the early 1950s would "place the Bureau right in the middle of a violent political war," as each party would seek to use the documents to its own advantage. Rather surprisingly in the Cold War climate, the Bureau was even concerned that the Soviet "propaganda machine would work overtime proving that [Venona] was evidence that the U.S. never acted in good faith during the war" when the two countries were allies.[85] But this sensitivity was misplaced. Thanks to Kim Philby, the Soviets obtained the actual Venona translations directly from Washington beginning in the fall of 1949.[86]

Klaus Fuchs, Harry Gold, and Julius Rosenberg's Ring

Although the first spy unmasked by Venona, Coplon was hardly the most important. Her gleanings at FARS were of limited concern in comparison to what Klaus Fuchs, Harry Gold, and Julius Rosenberg's contacts had supplied on atomic and military-industrial information. Early in the Cold War, their extensive wartime intelligence gathering practices were at last uncovered by officials through the decrypted cables. Still unknown to U.S. or British officials, Fuchs's work had resumed in the early Cold War, as noted above, but he soon began to harbor growing doubts about his espionage. As he would tell his old friend and fellow scientist Michael Perrin, "[H]e did not give [the Soviets] all the information that he could have given and . . . did not always answer questions that were put to him." For example, he did not divulge the American rate of production nor its atomic stockpiles, despite repeated queries.[87] Further, Fuchs began to realize that he "disapproved of a great many actions of the Russian Government." Deciding he could no longer "continue handing over information without being sure in my own mind whether I was doing right," he stopped serving as a spy in May 1949.[88] Later that year, analysts in Washington decoded a World War II cable on "Fluctuations and the Efficiency of a Diffusion Plant, Part III," which was identified as a Fuchs-authored document. Confronted by British intelligence, the scientist denied his role in espionage when first questioned on December 21, 1949. But at his third meeting with investigator William James Skardon on January 31, 1950, Fuchs finally confessed, not only to spying at Los Alamos and Harwell, but at Birmingham University and the British Diffusion Mission in New York before that.[89]

Fuchs was arrested on February 2, but the FBI was not allowed to interview him until his trial was completed at the end of March.[90] The delay infuriated Hoover, who sneered, "The sly British are gradually getting around to having unearthed Fuchs themselves."[91] The Bureau desperately wanted to talk to the physicist, who they hoped would help them in finding his American contact named in Venona.[92] In February 1950, the FBI had thought that "Goose," as he was called in the cables, was a Brothman partner named Gerhard (Gus) Wollan, an associate professor of mathematics at North Georgia State University.[93] Venona had identified "Goose" as a close associate of Brothman who was familiar with his work on aerosol and DDT as well as his difficulties with colleagues.[94]

When Robert Lamphere, then a young FBI supervisor, and Hugh H. Clegg finally visited with Fuchs in London, they met a thin, sallow, and balding man who blinked nervously. Fuchs also smoked and "swallow[ed] hard, frequently, and audibly'" throughout the interview. His own family history was not a happy one. One of his sisters, Elizabeth, killed herself in 1938; his only brother, Gerhard, was in a sanitarium in Davos for tuberculosis; and Kristel, the sister that Gold had met, was now in Westborough State Hospital in Massachusetts as a "schizophrenic-melancholic."[95] Fuchs reflected on the ways in which he too had manifested "controlled schizophrenia": "I used my Marxist philosophy to establish in my mind two separate compartments.

One compartment in which I allowed myself to make friendships . . . to be . . . the kind of man I wanted to be . . . [where] I could be free and easy and happy with other people without fear of disclosing myself because I knew that the other compartment would step in if I approached the danger point." Like so many in his family, Fuchs too would be institutionalized; he received a fourteen-year jail sentence.[96]

The FBI turned to finding the elusive "Goose" in a manhunt that ranged from hotels in Albuquerque to Fuchs's New York apartment building. Once identified, Harry Gold initially refused to cooperate. For instance, he once again told the story that his wartime visits to Brothman—numbering at least fourteen—were only innocent gatherings of blueprints. Other New York trips, he asserted, were related to his work with Siboney Distillery Company, a Penn Sugar subsidiary. The agents interviewing him noted that it was "entirely illogical" for him to have continued to collect blueprints if he had

Harry Gold

not been giving them to Golos, whom he claimed only to have met once. Gold responded by emphatically stating he had no Communist connections.[97] However, when agents fished out a map of Santa Fe from his closet (picked up at a museum in the city while on a visit to Fuchs), Gold broke down. Although he initially refrained from identifying his sources, soon from "the seething maelstrom" of his mind "I amazedly found myself irresistibly revealing more and more of the true facts."[98] On May 23, 1950, Gold would be charged with "conspiracy to commit espionage on behalf of the USSR"; Fuchs helped provide the final identification of him.[99]

Once Gold opened his mouth, he could not stop. As he said later, "I have tried to make the greatest possible amends by disclosing every phase of my espionage activities, by identifying all of the persons involved, and by revealing every last scrap, shred, and particle of evidence."[100] His volubility contributed to a thirty-year sentence for himself and a fifteen-year sentence for his contact Alfred Slack.[101] He implicated Abraham Brothman, confirming Elizabeth Bentley's earlier allegations and those of Venona. He also named machinist David Greenglass as another contact at Los Alamos; Greenglass, too, would soon talk with authorities, divulging his brother and sister-in-law's involvement in espionage activities. The Rosenbergs, of course, never cooperated.

In 1951, a joint congressional committee declared that the espionage of Fuchs, Greenglass, and others had "advanced the Soviet atomic energy program by 18 months as a minimum. In other words, if war should come, Russia's ability to mount an atomic offensive against the West will be greatly increased." Such an outlook certainly helps explain the extraordinary severity of the Rosenbergs' sentence.[102] At their trial, Judge Irving Saypol bombastically described Julius and Ethel Rosenberg's orchestration "of an elaborate scheme which enabled them to steal through David Greenglass this one weapon, that might well hold the key to the survival of this nation," as if the couple had been the sole perpetrators of wartime Soviet atomic espionage rather than small players in a much larger effort.[103] Physicist Theodore Hall (code named "Youngster"), a much more important source who had also spied at Los Alamos, was far luckier. Like Rosenberg, he too denied his involvement, but he escaped arrest because corroborating evidence outside of the classified Venona intercepts was not available.[104] Hall, a nineteen-year-old graduate of Harvard University with "an exceptionally keen mind" and a "politically developed" outlook, according to his Soviet contact, had volunteered himself as a source of information in 1944. The FBI believed that he and his friend Saville Sax had provided material to Sergei N. Kournakoff, a military analyst at the *New Masses* and *Daily Worker*.[105] Hall escaped to England, where he lived nearly another fifty years before succumbing to complications from cancer and Parkinson's disease in 1999; he had publicly admitted his espionage role only the year before.[106]

Just a month after Gold came forward, implicating Greenglass, cryptanalysts had discovered Julius Rosenberg's identity in Venona and began to develop information about his ring of engineers (see chapter 3). As Venona revealed, the "brilliant" Barr had provided materials to Rosenberg during the war when he worked at Western Electric. After the war, Barr became a project engineer in long-range radar at Sperry's Radio Engineering Division, where he furnished Rosenberg with information about an antimissile device, according to David Greenglass. Sperry fired Barr as a "security risk" when officials at the firm became aware of his past political activity; among other things, he had signed a petition sponsored by the Communist Party for a five-cent subway fare in New York.[107] Barr next went to Paris to pursue music studies with composer Olivier Messiaen, his program paid for by Soviet intelligence.[108] As soon as Gold and Greenglass were apprehended, Barr escaped to Czechoslovakia.[109]

Joel Barr, Vivian Glassman, and Louise and Alfred Sarant

Venona showed that Barr's good friend Alfred Sarant had also supplied radar material from Western Electric during the war. In October 1945, he moved to Bell Telephone's Radio Transmitter Group and then went to Cornell University's Laboratory of Nuclear Studies from May 1947 to June 1948. There, he worked on wiring the lab's cyclotron, but was later deemed not "sufficiently qualified" to handle this task. With his hopes of attending graduate school fading, Sarant decided to open a painting business in Ithaca.[110] Then, in August 1950, the Rosenbergs' arrest also compelled Sarant to flee to Czechoslovakia, via Mexico. Leaving his wife behind, he took with him his neighbor Carol Dayton, a "very attractive" young woman who herself abandoned two children, including an infant, as well as her husband. For the FBI, this departure suggested a license to stop Sarant's escape on the grounds of "immoral behavior."[111] The Bureau had no basis for a warrant, "no substantial information" by which to charge Sarant, but hoped to subpoena him anyway.[112] Meanwhile, Carol Dayton's husband, Bruce, fully expected her to return, noting sympathetically that "he was sure her trip was taken with considerable conflict on her part . . . and that her reasons deserved respect and patience." She never came back. Sarant's and Barr's families paid a stiff price for their disappearance: extensive FBI surveillance and regular questioning.[113]

When the FBI searched Sarant's house, they found an old letter from engineer William Perl and his wife to Barr, proposing a vacation in the summer of 1945. Perl and Barr were good friends; they had taken a two-week canoe trip in Upstate New York in 1944 with Barr's then girlfriend, Vivian Glassman. Agents seized upon the letter as evidence linking the three men, who had also shared a Greenwich Village apartment under Sarant's name in the late 1940s—an apartment that the FBI believed was used for photography purposes. Officials guessed that puttied-up holes in the apartment's bedroom door were designed to hold a lamp for photo shoots, especially since the building superintendent had told them the apartment was furnished only with cots and work benches.[114]

Perl, another college friend of Rosenberg's, had indeed been of immense assistance to the Soviets, as previously detailed. He would spend the years after the war working on his PhD at Columbia University (his classified dissertation was titled "Calculations of Trans-Sonic Flows Past Thin Airfoils by an Integral Method") and then return to the National Advisory Center for Aeronautics (NACA) in Cleveland in June 1948. Two years later, he was appointed to a position teaching physics at Columbia.[115] The FBI, apprised by Venona of Perl's wartime espionage, was not convinced it had ended.

Agents learned that in mid-1948, when he was living in the apartment sub-let from Sarant, Perl had checked out some two thousand pages of documents from the office of Theodore von Karman, his adviser at Columbia, including test reports of advanced aircraft and helicopters such as the D-558 research airplane and the NACA 66–006 airfoil. A source of "unknown reliability"—Jerome Tartakow, the jailhouse informant who became Julius Rosenberg's chess partner and close confidant in prison—informed the Bureau that Perl, Rosenberg, Michael Sidorovich, and an unknown individual had gathered at Rosenberg's home with von Karman's documents over the Fourth of July holiday weekend and "photographed for 17 hours without interruption."[116] In addition to Tartakow's tattlings, the FBI also relied on a defrocked priest serving as a prison liaison with Perl, Father William Gordon, a lecturer at Catholic University. His information, however, was of little value.[117]

Unlike Barr and Sarant, Perl did not flee. But the FBI knew that allegations from Tartakow and Gordon—sources of "unknown reliability"—would not stand up in court. And because officials were even more reluctant to introduce the wartime Venona materials, Perl could not be charged as a spy.[118] Instead, he was charged with perjury, for denying he knew Julius Rosenberg and Morton Sobell. Perl had argued that since "he was not intimately acquainted with Rosenberg . . . he had not associated with Rosenberg," and therefore had not known him.[119] But his refusal to admit knowing the two engineers was easily challenged, as the CCNY's registrar's records revealed that Perl had joined Sobell and Rosenberg in many of the same small, upper-level classes at the college. Members of the Communist Steinmetz Club also remembered Perl attending meetings where Rosenberg and Sobell were present, and Sobell had used him as a reference when he applied to General Electric.[120] Perl next tried to defend himself by pointing to his family's history of mental illness, which had claimed two of his sisters. He alleged that the FBI agents who interviewed him said that "Rosenberg and Sobell are going to fry," which deeply rattled him. The agents insisted that they had said no such thing.[121]

Perl then admitted, to no one's surprise, that "he had played down" some of his friendships "because of CP associations." He also acknowledged that Vivian Glassman had visited him on July 22, 1950, after Rosenberg's arrest, and offered him two thousand dollars to flee to Mexico. He sent her away, refusing the money, and "in an impulse to erase out memory of her visit," threw away the piece of paper she had given him with Rosenberg's name on it. His defense attorney, Raymond Wise, told the jury that Perl "is still a mystery, a young Einstein, a genius with a mind of unusual complexities. . . . [H]is subconscious mind has actually blocked out all these incidents . . . genius and insanity (in his family) is separated only by a thin line."[122]

The jury was apparently affected by these arguments; its members, finding Perl guilty of perjury, asked the judge for clemency. But Judge Sylvester Ryan, a veteran of the Coplon case, had received additional information about Perl's espionage activity, information "which cannot be made public"—and for this reason gave him the "maximum sentence" on May 22, 1953.[123] Venona had covertly worked its way into a court proceeding, and Perl received two concurrent five-year terms that were almost certainly connected more closely with his alleged espionage activity than his perjury. The chief assistant U.S. attorney, Lloyd MacMahon, told Judge Ryan that if Perl had been forthcoming, he could have been "of great help in putting an end to Soviet espionage in this country.'" Instead, the "country's security" had been harmed by his obfuscations.[124]

MacMahon's allegations are revealing, suggesting as they do that Perl's knowledge would have exposed *existing* Soviet espionage practices. Indeed, two months after Perl was sentenced, a U.S. Air Force aerodynamics expert claimed publicly that the engineer's information had been used in the development of the USSR's new MiG fighter, and alleged that "the unusual tail of the MiG was specifically a NACA development as was another anti-turbulence design feature."[125] This allegation, however, remains controversial, and recent accounts have dismissed American provenance in the Soviet MiG, instead attributing features of the aircraft to British technology.[126]

Perl's trial was significant in strengthening the FBI's stature in the government's national security program, and agents who had been involved in the Perl case were warmly commended. W. A. Branigan congratulated the New York office in particular for its sleuthing into Perl's background. "It should be pointed out that the conviction of Perl, a known Soviet agent, is a signal victory for the Bureau in discharging its responsibilities in the internal security field," he noted.[127] Still, Perl had only been convicted of perjury, a fact that rankled Hoover. A month after Perl's sentencing, Julius Rosenberg was executed for espionage; had he chosen to talk about his connections, Perl too might have faced an espionage conviction. Hoover could take cold comfort in Perl's treatment at the New York Federal House of Detention, where the brilliant engineer was now relegated to cleaning toilets. The Bureau, meanwhile, continued to monitor Perl's activity as late as 1970.[128]

Although he was never mentioned in Venona, Morton Sobell also became the target of an espionage investigation thanks to the testimony of Max Elitcher, whose name did appear in the cables. Close friends since college, Elitcher and Sobell had stayed in touch through the war, when Sobell worked at General Electric in Schenectady, and later at Reeves Instrument in New York City, where Sobell got Elitcher a job in 1948. Elitcher testified that Sobell had asked him whether he knew any "progressive" engineering students or graduates who might want to help the Soviet Union by providing information. Elitcher also recalled that Sobell had told him in August 1948 that "he had some 'good material' for Julius Rosenberg." That year, Elitcher claimed to have followed Sobell to a meeting with Rosenberg to drop off a roll of film, but he insisted he never become a source himself.[129]

On June 22, 1950, the day of David Greenglass's arrest, Sobell left the United States for Mexico.[130] The FBI quickly launched a manhunt for him as a key player in the Rosenberg ring. Seized by the Mexican police, Sobell resisted arrest by fighting and biting, but eventually "was subdued by a blow on the head with a .38 caliber pistol butt." Agents found airline and steamship brochures in his apartment, with information about Poland-bound ships. Sobell and his family were driven to Laredo, Texas, where he was held for $100,000 bail on August 18.[131] At his trial with the Rosenbergs, he received a thirty-year sentence; he served eighteen years, five of them at Alcatraz.[132] His penalty was certainly an unusually harsh one for industrial espionage; Sobell paid a high price for his refusal to talk with authorities, just as Julius and Ethel Rosenberg would. Sobell, who is still alive, has always denied his role in Rosenberg's ring.[133]

Other Wartime Legacies:
J. Robert Oppenheimer and the Chevalier Case

Nothing in Venona connected Robert Oppenheimer with an espionage organization. However, after the war the government continued to investigate him, as it had since 1941. Doubts about his loyalty spread beyond the counterintelligence community; eventually, the president suspected him as well. Although Oppenheimer's growing reluctance to developing a hydrogen bomb contributed to his downfall, it was his previous political ties—his wartime sympathies with Communism and his obfuscations about Soviet contacts while at the Berkeley Radiation Laboratory—that launched the government's case against him. General Groves had downplayed the renowned physicist's politics during World War II because of his important role in meeting the war's objectives, but the issue would reemerge in the Cold War, finally coming to a head in 1954 when Oppenheimer, then a consultant to the Atomic Energy Commission, lost his security clearance.

In 1946, when permitted once again to investigate Oppenheimer directly, the FBI reinstated technical surveillance on him, as the scientist soon realized.[134] Investigative agents continued to attempt to demonstrate Oppenheimer's party membership, explore his potential espionage links, and study his positions on international control of atomic armaments and, later, the H-bomb.[135] As a consultant to the government's weapons program after the war, he still "had access to practically all the secret information concerning its progress," which included such developments as the March 1946 atomic tests held in the South Pacific.[136] Oppenheimer, who became director of the Institute of Advanced Study in Princeton in 1947, maintained a security clearance for his position as chairman of the Atomic Energy Commission's General Advisory Committee, which was consulted on scientific and technical matters.[137] Meanwhile, his brother Frank, a former Radiation Laboratory physicist who had just taken a job at the University of Minnesota, was also wiretapped by the FBI. The FBI reported both men's alleged Communist connections to Truman in 1947.[138] At that time, the case against Robert Oppenheimer was weak, as even the FBI acknowledged, noting "there is no substantial information of a pro-Communist nature concerning Oppenheimer subsequent to 1943."[139] In fact, the FBI's most compelling evidence on Oppenheimer's party membership showed that his last monthly payment of $150 was made in April 1942.[140] As a result, the Bureau focused on such tenuous links with Communism as his wartime relationship with Jean Tatlock, a former Berkeley student and Communist who later committed suicide.[141]

The FBI's allegations largely drew from their "confidential sources"— wiretaps and informants. Party meetings could yield juicy information, though often of dubious reliability. At a November 1945 meeting of the North Oakland club of the Alameda County Communist Party, for example, Jack Manley declared that "Oppenheimer told Steve Nelson several years ago that the Army was working on the bomb." Allusions that Nelson wanted "to keep in touch with Oppenheimer" were also duly noted by FBI informants.[142] But these reports and allegations of espionage were simply unconfirmed gossip, as the Bureau knew, and its agents were driven to more aggressive measures to find additional evidence. Just as it had with Perl, the Bureau recruited an

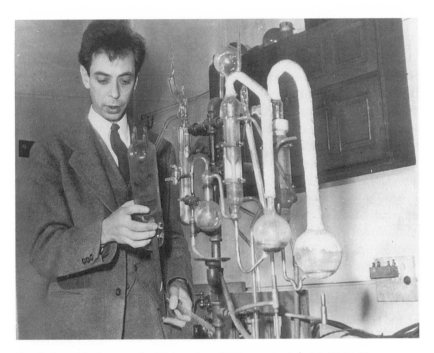

Frank Oppenheimer at the University of Minnesota, July 14, 1947. He long denied the government's allegations that he belonged to the Communist Party.

obliging priest. Father John O'Brien attempted to influence Oppenheimer's secretary, whom the Bureau hoped "on the basis of her religious convictions and patriotism" might become a source for the Bureau. However, when Father O'Brien requested "derogatory information" to conduct a successful "pep talk" with the secretary, agents balked: this was "not a safe tactic."[143]

Oppenheimer's security clearance was renewed for the last time in 1950, the same year that Senator Joseph McCarthy (R-Wis.) made his accusations about 205 Communists in the government (later changed to 57, and subsequently to 81), introducing a new chill in the political environment that was only exacerbated by the outbreak of the Korean War that June. By 1953, when the Rosenbergs were executed by electric chair, the old story of Oppenheimer's less-than-candid reports of Chevalier and his entreaties for atomic information on behalf of the Soviets had acquired newly sinister significance. President Eisenhower, now convinced that "Oppenheimer is a liar," followed the recommendation of Atomic Energy Commission chairman Adm. Lewis Strauss to suspend the physicist's clearance and create a "blank wall between Oppenheimer and any secret data" in December 1953. Gen. Kenneth D. Nichols of the AEC sent Oppenheimer a letter containing the government's brief against him, which, in addition to raising his obfuscations about Chevalier, also charged Oppenheimer with delaying development of the H-bomb, as if his opposition to the new weapon in his professional capacity as a consultant were somehow a crime. Rather than accept the suspension, Oppenheimer decided to defend himself in hearings the following April.[144]

The hearings, recorded in lengthy proceedings titled *In the Matter of J. Robert Oppenheimer,* focused in detail on the physicist's having told several different stories about Chevalier, evasions and untruths that he did not deny. Although his inability to satisfactorily explain his inaccuracies ("I was an idiot," he noted) cost him his security clearance, the government never demonstrated that he was a Communist, at least not after 1942.[145] Yet A. H. Belmont believed that the Bureau's old surveillance tapes of San Francisco party members, at least, would be useful in a "possible perjury proceeding"; Oppenheimer had always denied party membership, and the recordings featured other party members who thought differently. However, these phone logs were insufficient as evidence, as the Bureau well knew, and the San Francisco office was urged to find more information "which might corroborate the information set forth in the logs." Unfortunately for the FBI, though, "many communists and ex-communists have been interviewed but none have furnished admissible corroborating data." At the AEC's request, the FBI had contacted a host of people who knew Oppenheimer, from his colleagues to his wife. But all of those reached responded "favorably concerning his loyalty and character," even when acknowledging his earlier history and "unfavorable associates." And when one former Communist, Paul Crouch, professed that he'd met Oppenheimer at a party meeting in July 1941, the physicist was able to show he had been out of California during the period mentioned. The Bureau did manage to enter California Communist Party leader Bernadette Doyle's allegations that both Oppenheimer brothers were members of the party into the hearings; agents did not disclose that Doyle's material came from a wiretap.[146]

Oppenheimer's new status in 1954 as a security risk led the Bureau to resume technical surveillance on him after a seven-year hiatus. In January, Belmont had defended the wiretapping as a way to detect "any indication that Oppenheimer might flee"—despite the scientist's professed plans to defend himself at the hearings three months later. This technical surveillance revealed "absolutely no information of security interest," W. A. Branigan admitted in April.[147]

The hearings, which concluded the first week of May, were a defeat for Oppenheimer, ratifying the AEC's decision on his clearance. The physicist returned to private life, where surveillance at his home continued. Six men watched Oppenheimer in his "exclusive" Princeton neighborhood each night, including a posse half a mile away on Mercer Road with a three-way radio, whose members were on the alert for possible train trips to New York. Another FBI vehicle monitored automobile travel half a mile north of the residence. The FBI even entertained a rumor that Soviet intelligence "had reportedly contacted Oppenheimer to arrange his disappearance behind the Iron Curtain." Such fears were excited by a lengthy vacation Oppenheimer took in the Virgin Islands, which prevented surveillance. Yet during the periods that the Bureau had wiretapped him (May 1946 to June 1947 and January to July 1954) "no information was developed by this method indicating his contacts with espionage agents or Soviet officials." By then, his past Communist associations were as much as seventeen years cold.[148]

The lack of results did not stop the FBI from doggedly applying to the Justice Department for another authorization to wiretap Oppenheimer, which was approved in August 1954; the department, meanwhile, was considering the Bureau's reports for possible action. Alas, sighed Belmont, "Oppenheimer suspects that his telephone conversations have been monitored," thus eliminating much chance for interesting information. Moreover, "the residential nature" of his neighborhood hindered effective surveillance, and monitoring Oppenheimer on Princeton's campus was no easy trick either. Belmont noted that "it has been necessary for Newark [field office] to expend considerable manpower in maintaining the surveillance." At last, he conceded, "[T]he Bureau cannot anticipate any great results from either the technical or physical surveillance." The FBI finally discontinued surveillance in October 1954.[149]

Fort Monmouth and the Legacy of the Rosenberg Case

Just as the long shadow of World War II fueled the Oppenheimer investigation at Princeton, so too did it drive a government investigation further up the New Jersey Turnpike at Ft. Monmouth in the early 1950s. As the Rosenberg case had revealed, the Signal Corps facility there had provided a sanctuary for a major spy operation throughout the war years, suggesting that the base might still be a hotbed of spies. Accordingly, the U.S. Army asked the Bureau to conduct a "mass espionage investigation." But the FBI, reluctant to embarrass itself on an unwarranted fishing expedition, refrained from such a wholesale probe. In careful passive voice, D. M. Ladd informed Hoover that "it was not believed desirable to institute a mass investigation of civilian employees of the Army to determine if espionage violations existed, as alleged by the Army." Ladd, indeed, took sharp exception to the army's fears. Just mentioning Rosenberg as a reference, or even providing a reference for someone who had also given his name, did not make an applicant a possible spy. He scoffed, "CIC [the army's Counterintelligence Corps] has apparently drawn the conclusion that the person himself must be an espionage agent or suspected espionage agent because of his association with such people as ROSENBERG, SARANT, et al." [150]

Yet the Bureau quickly fell into the same trap in its scaled back Monmouth investigation; one of the first places its agents looked for spies at the Signal Corps was in Alfred Sarant's address book. Solomon Greenberg was one such unfortunate individual who appeared in these pages. As it happened, the FBI would also find classified documents from the Federal Telecommunications Laboratories at his home in August 1952. Although the Bureau did not prove that he had any intention of spying, he was fired. Rosenbergian connections also seemed to be important in the Bureau's fingering of longtime Signal Corps employee Aaron Hyman Coleman, chief of the systems section of the radar branch at Evans Signal Laboratory. Coleman had led a secret program at the Signal Corps involving "the development of the radar network on the eastern North American coast," from Canada to the Gulf of Mexico. He had become a target because his views "were closely allied with Communist trend of thought," although the Bureau could not verify his party membership. What they did have was his unsavory associations: he was a former classmate and friend of Morton Sobell, and Julius Rosenberg allegedly had tried to bring him into the Young Communist League at CCNY. Coleman further was accused of obtaining confidential information on experimental radar from another Signal Corps employee, Fred Joseph Kitty, in 1944. It was not clear that Coleman had passed on this information; moreover, the statute of limitations for an espionage conviction had expired. In September 1946, the Ft. Monmouth Security and Intelligence Division had uncovered forty-eight documents in Coleman's home, ranging from confidential to secret in designation. He was suspended for ten days. Kitty, meanwhile, had defended himself against the charge of "wrongful" intent in sharing information, denying he had ever been a spy, but admitting that he had left out his earlier membership in the International Workers Order and the Young Communist League in three security questionnaires, for which he was indicted in May 1953. The government forbade him to work on classified material ever again.[151]

Though the FBI had scoffed at the army's paranoia about spies at Monmouth, the Bureau was apoplectic at the security lapses that had allowed the Kitty-Coleman exchange to take place. The case was "a typical example of the Army's failure to take action after having been advised by the FBI through submission of Investigative reports ... of a dangerous security situation existing at Fort Monmouth," the Bureau averred.[152] Still, the FBI eventually determined that no espionage ring was in operation at the base.

Employee Loyalty

As the Fort Monmouth investigation shows, the loyalty of government employees remained a key barometer of national security, just as it had, if less intensely, since early in World War II. The Cold War heightened an emphasis on employee loyalty in all branches of government, both reflecting and contributing to the overwrought domestic environment of the era. As it had earlier, the FBI responded to the Soviet threat by continuing to monitor suspected individuals and compiling their records in its infamous Security Index, which grew to include 26,000 people during the first Eisenhower administration. Despite the prevailing political currents, the Communist Party was actually gaining members in the immediate aftermath of the war; according to CPUSA chairman William Z. Foster, the party had recruited 15,000 new members between March and July 1946 and "doubled its membership in the South."[153] Concerned about such developments, FBI director Hoover took a leading role in the formation of the Truman Administration's Temporary Commission on Employee Loyalty by choosing its chairman, Assistant Attorney General A. Devitt Vanech, and later subverting Truman's plans by convincing Congress to give the FBI a larger role than the president had intended.[154]

The close connection authorities established in this period between the Soviet foreign threat and American domestic security created an anxious mindset among government officials.[155] Because even trustworthy staff could be instruments of the disloyal legions thought to have bored their way in, the government's security apparatus undertook a wholesale screening of all on the federal payroll. The War Department's S. J. Chamberlin told Vanech: "The espionage agent of the foreign power who has been able to infiltrate government employment and secure for himself a position of trust and responsibility, can press into his service many perfectly loyal employees, who, at his request . . . feed him information which he, in turn, can pass on to his foreign government."[156] His suspicions mounting, Chamberlin added: "With regard to espionage, great care is taken by the agent to thoroughly establish for himself a reputation for loyalty and efficiency . . . this being a prerequisite to the successful accomplishment to his mission."[157] The most diligent employees, then, were apparently among the most dangerous.

Shortly after the midterm elections of 1946, which relegated his party to minority status in Congress, Truman had created the President's Temporary Commission on Employee Loyalty to address what was becoming a most explosive political issue. In its first report that November, the commission pronounced that "the presence within the government of *any* disloyal or subversive persons, or the attempt by *any* such persons to obtain government employment, presents a problem of such importance that it must be dealt with vigorously and effectively."[158] More mildly, however, the commission concluded that "it is unable, based on the facts presented to it, to state with any degree of certainty how far reaching [employment of disloyal or subversive persons] is," although cases such as Gouzenko's, among others, "provide sufficient evidence to convince a fair minded person that a threat exists."[159] This rather temperate message reflected the range of views on the commission as to the extent of the danger posed by the Communist "menace." Yet with defectors' revelations still fresh, the group concluded, "It would be unreasonable to assume that foreign powers are not maintaining intelligence networks in this country."[160]

Chairman Vanech wrote to fifty departments, agencies, and commissions in December for their input, asking for recommendations of "corrective measures," methods to determine loyalty, and investigation and dismissal procedures.[161] Hoover, in turn, urged the commission to create a loyalty review board that would be more powerful than individual departments in determining loyalty, but he was unsuccessful. Instead, Truman's executive order of March 22, 1947, created a loyalty program whose board reviewed cases rather than dictated firings to agency heads. The order also required the Civil Service Commission to share responsibility with the FBI for screening employees: the Bureau would continue to investigate existing staff, while the commission would focus on new hires.[162] The program also created a mechanism by which organizations were designated as "Totalitarian, fascist, communist, or subversive." A large number of groups, from the left-wing American League against War and Fascism to the right-wing Ku Klux Klan, fell into these categories.[163]

Hoover was ready, grudgingly, to share the reins with the Civil Service.[164] But he was furious. Though he was reluctant to speak in front of HUAC on this issue—he told the attorney general in March 1947 that the ensuing discussion "would bring about the disastrous consequence of a drying-up of our sources of information"—he nevertheless did testify that month in order to attack the president's program, pouncing on such founts of Communism as the Federal Council of Churches in the process. His appearance in front of Congress was unprecedented and effective, as Richard Gid Powers has noted. The program as implemented by Congress gave a much greater role (and more funds) to the FBI, including the screening of new employees (such as those of the new Atomic Energy Administration) as well as existing ones, and by 1952 the Bureau had conducted 20,000 investigations.[165] At the same time, the FBI's secret "Responsibility Program" sent out anonymous letters to employers regarding suspected subversives on their payroll, most of them school teachers and professors, without the accused knowing the source of this information. Attorney General Tom Clark defended the Bureau's right to maintain "sole discretion (to) refuse to disclose the names of confidential informants," since the FBI argued it would lose its sources "if proper secrecy and confidence cannot at all times be maintained." In that case, the Bureau argued, it might as well jettison the whole program.[166] The *New York Times*, lamenting that those charged with disloyalty could not confront their accusers and had only fifteen days to convince investigators of their loyalty, deemed it a "thoroughly bad bill." But a *Washington Post* editorial argued that "an extremely dangerous world situation" made the "lenience" of earlier decades no longer appropriate.[167]

The FBI's phased-in investigation of the two million U.S. employees in the executive branch (Congress and the courts were exempt) began in August. Agencies were to turn over the names of their staff to the FBI, which would check them against Bureau files. Hoover, moreover, wanted fingerprints, in case employees changed their names. He insisted, too, that his agency was not conducting in-depth probes of all federal employees; it was simply running background checks.[168] Only something "derogatory" would trigger "a full investigation."[169] One such unfortunate was Morton Friedman of the War Manpower Commission, who had earlier belonged to the American Peace Mobilization. Two federal courts upheld his firing, and the Supreme Court refused to review his case. Another was State Department employee Carl A. Marzani, accused of lying about his Communist affiliation. Marzani actually was a Soviet agent, although it is unclear that the government then knew of the extent of his connections.[170] In the wake of such firings, the American Civil Liberties Union blasted the loyalty process and its consequences as violations of civil rights, ruing the "sharply unfavorable change" that had occurred since the war years when "freedom of public debate and minority dissent functioned with few restraints." Attorney General Clark, however, pronounced that "the presence within the Government service of any disloyal or subversive person constitutes a threat to our democratic processes."[171]

During the war, certainly, existing screening procedures did not typically bring dismissal of Communist employees from government jobs. In 1941, for instance, federal judge Guy L. Fake vacated an indictment against a former WPA worker charged "with falsely swearing he was not a Communist." He pointed out that since some held that even "those who believe in government ownership of irrigation projects and government dams . . . could reasonably be classified as Communist," the term was meaningless.[172] But the war years did not preclude persecution of government workers for their views, either. In 1939, Congress passed the Hatch Act to prevent political activity by employees. Two years later, as discussed previously, the FBI began investigating employees following complaints about their loyalty, referring its information to their departments. In February 1943, FDR created the Interdepartmental Committee on Employee Investigations to advise departments as to the FBI's role and provide "an advisory opinion" on specific cases. Its chairman, Herbert E. Gaston, offered a New Dealish report on the committee's work that emphasized the importance of civil liberties. His view was that "persons who have been found to be members of organizations judged to be subversive have never presented any substantial danger to our government."[173] The legislative branch saw things a bit differently; Congressman Martin Dies compiled an ever expanding list of subversives for the FBI to follow up. As a result, between 1942 and 1947 the FBI's investigations of federal employees "who might be affiliated with 'subversive' organizations or advocate the overthrow of the US Government" produced more than

6,000 cases, with a total of 101 leaving the government, including 21 resignations and 75 who were not dismissed but experienced other "administrative action."[174] Fake's and Gaston's views notwithstanding, such investigations show the strong links between counterintelligence efforts of World War II and those of the Cold War era.

Indeed, the legacy of World War II espionage remained clear in Truman's executive order, which specifically emphasized the activity of spies, targeting any organization that "permits or encourages its membership or other persons to obtain or transmit information to any foreign country to the detriment of the security of the United States."[175] At the same time, existing laws, which dated from World War I, were deemed highly inadequate. For example, stealing a document or blueprint "connected with the National Defense" still wasn't illegal unless the government could prove that the pilferer had "intent or reason to believe that the information to be obtained is to be used to the injury of the United States or to the advantage of a foreign power." Because, as Bentley had reported, many of her sources thought they were giving information to the American Communist Party, this legal loophole let them off the hook. The Justice Department began drafting a new law in 1948 that would take out the "intent" clause from the law, make the holding of secret material itself a felony, broaden the definition of secret material, and remove the statute of limitations on espionage. The proposal, which drew opposition because of its provision to allow wiretapping in espionage cases, was compared to Britain's stringent "official secrets" act.[176] But the "intent" clause remained (as it does to this day), causing the FBI to complain in 1950 that poachers of documents, such as those belonging to the Atomic Energy Commission, were only charged with theft of government property.[177]

Export Restrictions

One way to stop the theft of technology was to make procurement of it more difficult in the first place. Thus early in the Cold War, Congress passed legislation to prevent advanced American technology from reaching the Soviet Union through commercial transactions.[178] As Philip J. Funigiello has argued, "[E]xport controls would become the economic equivalent of political containment," as for the first time the United States sought to shrink rather than expand its global market, at least with one set of customers. In 1947, a red-baiting senator, Karl Mundt, wanted to go so far as to publicize the names of all individuals and firms that were dealing with the Soviet Union in any goods whatsoever, essentially creating an embargo on trade. The Truman administration countered this extreme solution (which would prevent the United States from obtaining items it needed from Russia, like manganese) by instead extending wartime export controls to limit the sales of sensitive items to the Soviet Union. The National Security Council contended that American security needs would best be met by "the immediate termination, for an indefinite period, of shipments from the U.S. to the USSR and its satellites of all commodities which are critically short in the U.S. *or* which would contribute to Soviet military potential." This step appeared vital to legislators who were apprised that lend-lease had facilitated the gleaning of "secret information about the industrial development in the United States . . . especially in the military industry."[179]

Soviet policymakers were naturally upset by these measures: "[T]he Soviet Union needs American industrial material," longtime Soviet attorney Charles Recht complained. They also were baffled by provisions that "eliminate shipments of materials to the Soviet Union that are . . . available . . . through western European countries."[180] To address just this problem, the Truman administration pressured its Marshall Plan allies to keep "strategic goods" out of Russian hands, while also attempting to maintain more limited Russian trade with Western Europe. The final list of prohibited goods included metal-working machinery, oil and chemical equipment, power-generating devices, electronics, computers, and synthetic rubber.[181]

Efforts for keeping strategic goods from the Soviet bloc culminated in the 1949 Export Control Act and the establishment of the international Coordinating Committee on Multilateral Export Controls (COCOM) the same year, which was charged with establishing common rules on exports between the United States, Europe, and, later, Japan. But the efforts were often ineffective, as the Soviet Union received products both through intermediary nations and in the form of resold goods. U.S. trade with Russia, meanwhile, fell from $236 million in 1946 to $10 million four years later and only $2 million in 1953. Not until 1972 would Russian imports of American goods reach the levels they had twenty-six years earlier. The issue of European exports to Russia did not disappear. In 1951, Congress enacted the Mutual Defense Assistance Control Act, often called the Battle Act after its sponsor Laurie C. Battle (D-Ala.), which prevented war matériel and strategic goods from reaching the Soviet Union but gave Truman "discretionary authority" to deal with countries that violated the act's terms.[182] Numerous loopholes remained, of course. The policies continue today, in amended form, under the Export Administration Act.

Steve Nelson: A Wartime Spy Continues His Party Activism

As the export regulations suggest, in the early years of the Cold War the safety of military secrets was a particularly sensitive issue, just as it had been ever since the FBI first discovered the Soviet theft of nuclear research during Steve Nelson's conversations with Berkeley Radiation Laboratory scientists and Soviet NKVD agents in 1943. In early 1950, after several sessions of HUAC hearings in which Nelson had refused to answer most of the questions put to him, journalist Donald Robinson fulminated in *American Legion Magazine* that Nelson "single-handed . . . had run a Communist espionage ring which stole some of America's most precious atomic secrets. . . . Fantastically, there are no charges pending against him." Robinson declared that the FBI had determined that "Nelson was obviously 100 percent guilty. He can and should be convicted of espionage." However, the State Department had earlier halted any such prosecution, Robinson alleged, because of wartime diplomatic considerations.[183] Unmentioned was the weakness of wiretapped evidence in a courtroom.

The article prompted a frustrated Hoover to ask his close associate D. M. Ladd, "Is there any action that can be taken in this case?" Hoover would have known all about his staff's tireless pursuit of Nelson, but Ladd dutifully described how the Bureau had forwarded the CINRAD case—which concerned the leaks at the Berkeley Radiation Laboratory—to the Justice Department in June 1947, asking for "an opinion as to prosecutive action." However, the following December, as Ladd reported, department officials "advised that no action was contemplated relative to the Cinrad subjects." Reckoning that a focus on Nelson's party activities might go further than one based on his espionage, the Bureau had passed on additional information in September 1948 to the Justice Department "as to whether the activities of Nelson would come within the purview of . . . advocating overthrow of the government." Hoover provided the same materials to the Immigration and Naturalization Service a month later. In April 1949, the Justice Department responded that indeed, "a review of all file information concerning Nelson revealed that Nelson's activities violate Title 18, Section 2385,

U.S. Code," activities related to the overthrow of the government. Yet, the department declared, "no decision regarding a prosecution is being made at this time." As Robinson's article appeared, the FBI was planning in early 1950 to produce for the Justice Department another summary report on Nelson in Pittsburgh, where he was then party leader. Ladd noted that this time he would "request a more specific statement as to a decision relative to prosecutive action." To which Hoover handwrote a hearty amen: "I would definitely recommend to Dept his case be considered for prosecution and denaturalization." But despite repeated nudges from the FBI between 1947 and 1949, the Justice Department made no plans to prosecute Nelson or any of the "CINRAD subjects," either for spying or for Communist activism.[184]

While pestering the department for action, the Bureau also had been closely following Nelson's work through phone and physical surveillance, and by using informants. At the end of the war, its agents watched him emerge unscathed after the famous attack by French Communist Jacques Duclos brought down his patron, Earl Browder.[185] Nelson had moved on October 10, 1945, from Berkeley to South Nyack, New York, to be close to his new activities on the National Board of the CPUSA; the following year, he became chairman of the National Groups Commission, which was responsible for foreign language affiliates in the organization.[186] He supervised "all mass work being done by the Party," including the efforts of such groups as the International Workers Order and the American Slav Congress.[187] He remained a militant: addressing Pennsylvania coal miners during the 1946 steel strike, he declared, "[The Communist Party] won't overthrow the United States Government by force and violence, but we will oust that Government by mass pressure." Nelson believed that the party was on the move worldwide, except in the United States, where it was retracting. For this he blamed Browder.[188] In an address to the Lenin Memorial Meeting of the Communist Party in Milwaukee, he condemned American foreign policy, especially toward Poland, Greece, and Spain. As the FBI knew, Nelson also met frequently with Rudy Baker, alias "Al," head of the American Comintern apparatus.[189]

In February 1947, Hoover had demanded that the special agent in charge in New York quickly produce a report "setting forth legally admissible evidence that [Nelson] is a member of the Communist Party and has knowledge of revolutionary aims and purposes of party." The New York office complied in early April. However, in October the director wrote back to New York, complaining that he'd heard nothing for the past three months.[190] Hoover took a personal interest in the case, ordering his lieutenants to be ever more vigilant in watching Nelson and his whereabouts, as well as his work in the "underground apparatus."[191] The FBI director, no doubt with Nelson's wartime activities in mind, contended that the Communist leader's role went beyond open party involvement to something more sinister. He asserted in December 1947 that the "activities of Nelson indicate he may be going 'underground' and it seems a logical possibility he may be attempting to reactivate the illegal apparatus of the party." But if he was doing so, it was from rather inauspicious surroundings. In 1948, Nelson was working with the foreign language groups from a "grimy little office in downtown Pittsburgh," living in nearby Cheswick, Pennsylvania, and serving as district organizer and chairman in the Steel City.[192]

In May 1948, Hoover had chastised his special agent in New York for "incomplete coverage" of Nelson's doings. "Steve Nelson is most certainly a principal suspect . . . in organizing the Communist Party underground," declared Hoover. If he wasn't "completely covered," the director thundered, "we are materially cutting down on our coverage of Communist Party activities as a whole." To Hoover, Nelson's role in a national "emergency" was key; he believed, in fact, that such a state of emergency was under way.[193]

At the time, a Bureau informant described Nelson as "a typical party bureaucrat with moderate ability. Fairly good speaker. Friendly in nature, good personality. Absolutely subservient to party line and leadership; ruthless and unprincipled in carrying out any party directive."[194] Thus, when Josip Broz Tito broke with Stalin in 1948, Nelson was quick to "condemn" the Yugoslav leader, though as an émigré from Yugoslavia, he delicately cautioned his fellow Slavic Americans not to "slam the Communist Party of Yugoslavia as a whole." In 1948, the card-carrying Nelson attempted to effect change in the United States by working for Henry Wallace's presidential campaign and against Congress's Mundt-Nixon Bill, which called for all Communists to register with the government.[195]

His activity was curtailed that fall, however, when he was interrogated by the House Un-American Activities Committee. Nelson took the Fifth Amendment in his appearances in front of HUAC in 1948 and 1949. He refused to say that he had been a member of the party, though many written records, such as articles in the *Daily Worker* and *People's World*, discussed his progress in the ranks of the organization and numerous informants' reports confirmed his attendance at party gatherings.[196] He even refused to answer a query as to whether he'd been in a car belonging to the Soviet consulate. And he flatly denied any role in espionage, and continued to do so for the rest of his life:

"There may have been a Soviet espionage network operating in this country," Nelson wrote in 1981, "but common sense would dictate against recruiting prominent Party officials."[197] Nelson declared that since 1919, "[T]here has not been a single conviction of a Communist on the charge of espionage or of using or advocating 'force and violence' against the United States. That is so, because the CP opposes and will fight against the use of espionage or of force and violence for purposes of overthrowing American democratic institutions." His statements, of course, are belied by many Venona cables, including one that confirms that a Communist agent had penetrated the Berkeley laboratory.[198]

Congressman Parnell Thomas was eager to charge Nelson with contempt of Congress in 1948 after he spurned questions and was "uncooperative." Eventually, HUAC issued thirty-three contempt citations for his refusal to answer questions on April 26 and June 8, 1949.[199] The FBI itself prepared for an extensive check of Nelson's background, necessitating the review of 5,700 references and requiring the employment "full time of 3 supervisors for approximately one month."[200]

Nelson would not be charged with contempt of Congress until December 5, 1950.[201] In the meantime, however, he had already been apprehended in Pittsburgh the previous August, with two other Communist Party members, Andy Onda and Jim Dolsen, and charged with violating a 1919 state sedition law. The three were indicted on October 16.[202] The obscure edict made sedition against Pennsylvania a felony, subject to as much as a twenty-year prison term.[203] Unfortunately for Nelson, several members of Pittsburgh's judicial hierarchy were part of a crusading new organization, Americans Battling Communism Inc., and it was ABC member and common pleas court judge Michael A. Musmanno who had engineered and carried out a raid on party headquarters, with the help of former FBI informant Matt Cvetic. Musmanno was running for lieutenant governor that fall and no doubt benefited from the publicity.[204] Among the items seized in the raid, including copies of the *Communist Manifesto* from the party's bookshop, were "an outline of future communist strategy in warring against the Federal Bureau of Investigation." Party documents, understandably, "assailed FBI operatives as 'enemy agents' and gave methods for detecting and removing 'spies' within the Communist ranks."[205] The Communist Party was indeed riddled with FBI informants at that time, as revealed by Cvetic's own career, which was later featured in the 1951 movie *I Was a Communist for the FBI*.

In his trial in April 1951, Nelson and his fellow party members faced another ABC judge, Harry M. Montgomery, along with "prosecuting witness[es]" Musmanno and Cvetic. Injured in a car accident soon after the trial began, Nelson had to stand for a second trial that began the following December and ran for seven months. Acting as his own lawyer, Nelson defended himself ably, as even Musmanno had to acknowledge.[206] Nevertheless, he would be sentenced to twenty years in the ancient Blawnox Workhouse, alternating between being shoeless and "cold on the wet stone floor" and experiencing "long months of sweat," and facing a fine of $20,000. From jail, Nelson was unrepentant: "I stand by our party's position . . . the struggle for world peace and the right of the Korean people to establish their own independent unity are in the best interests of the American people."[207]

He quickly appealed his sentence, but the state Superior Court supported the county court's decision, so the Communist leader next approached the Pennsylvania Supreme Court. There, he won his appeal in 1954, on the notion that the Smith Act "pre-empted" sedition charges on the state level; only the federal government had the right to prosecute such offenses. Pennsylvania's attorney general then appealed to the U.S. Supreme Court, where a large number of the forty-two other states with sedition laws filed supporting briefs. The nation's highest court, however, upheld the lower court's decision, and Chief Justice Earl Warren got in a good swipe at the (now) illegal and incoherent maze of state sedition laws. Separately, Nelson had also been convicted for sedition against the United States under the Smith Act, but the Supreme Court dismissed that too on the basis of trial irregularities. Five years later, ironically, disgusted with Khrushchev's 1956 revelations about Stalin, Nelson would abandon the Communist Party.[208]

During his Pittsburgh trial, FBI agents declined to testify against Nelson, explaining "they did not participate in the investigation launched by the local authorities." Pittsburgh detectives wanted to know if they could use FBI wiretap information in the proceedings all the same, but the Bureau wanted to "keep itself divorced entirely" from the arrest.[209] The FBI pronounced that its files were "confidential" and thus not available.[210] But Hoover and his agents were gratified—or possibly jealous—at Pennsylvania's success in nabbing Nelson after their own department had failed to take action for so long. Nelson's arrest capped a broad and multipronged investigation of the Communist leader that dated from the late 1930s, an investigation that would likely have been far less ambitious—even at the height of the Cold War— had Nelson not been connected with espionage, as the Pennsylvania authorities' attempts to secure those earlier wiretaps indicate.

HUAC: A Wartime Committee Continues

Hoover's wiretapped evidence on Nelson was not only eagerly sought by Pittsburgh's anti-Communists, but by members of the House Un-American Activities Committee as well. Here, Hoover was more helpful, secretly passing congressional staffers many of his best recordings from surveillance operations on a wide range of targets.[211] A "special committee" associated with Martin Dies from its birth in 1938, HUAC had been made a standing committee in January 1945 after Dies retired. The early Cold War was its heyday, of course, with investigations of screenwriters, scientists, and spies, for starters. Armed with its Hooverian bugs, in 1949 the committee members went after alleged atomic espionage agents like Nelson, Joseph Woodrow Weinberg, and Clarence Hiskey.[212] These investigations were generally unsuccessful. Nelson, as discussed above, repeatedly took the Fifth Amendment. Weinberg denied knowing Nelson or delivering any secrets to him; although subsequently charged with perjury, he was acquitted. Clarence Hiskey also refused to tell HUAC whether he was a Communist Party member, though he acknowledged that he had belonged to progressive groups such as the League against War and Fascism while at the University of Wisconsin.[213] Considering the large number of people who refused to answer queries about their party affiliation, it is perhaps surprising that HUAC continued to insist on "the necessity and propriety of the committee's use of the question, 'Are you a member of the Communist Party?'"[214] Regardless of the lack of admitted spies at its hearings, the committee trumpeted in 1949 its conclusion that "espionage is one of the most deadly weapons in the hands of the American Communists at the present time." As Frank S. Tavenner, HUAC counsel, explained, "the committee's investigation of Soviet espionage has reflected that there are a great many Soviet espionage agents who operated in the U.S. and who may be still operating because of the fact that they have never been publicly identified."[215] HUAC's bombast, and its lack of proof, would later leave a legacy of distrust in the government's espionage claims, as well as a stubbornly limited perception of Communists' connections with spying that persisted for decades.

In 1949, HUAC issued a brochure, "Spotlight on Spies," that asserted rather simplistically that "the aim of the rulers of Russia is to take over the United States along with the rest of the world" and alleged that to support this aim, Soviet spies were actively at work in the United States. HUAC called for vigilance and new laws: "[S]pying is a never-ending business with the

Russians. New secrets are being born every day as American science and industry progress." Fortunately, as the brochure informed its readers, "Your committee is doing everything it can to run down the Communist spy rings in this country and has already succeeded in exposing many of the spies."[216] The claim was a stretch; most of those who spoke in front of HUAC, like Hiss, Nelson, Weinberg, Lomanitz, Silvermaster, and Ullman, never admitted anything; Chambers and Bentley exposed *themselves.*

When the pamphlet's first run of nine thousand disappeared quickly, HUAC issued a second, larger publication, "100 Things You Should Know About Communism."[217] Sadly, this report noted, the American people had shown "indifference to the realities of Communism" during the war and thus agencies did not vigorously pursue suspected subversives, just as they had not during the New Deal when "Communist-corrupted" artwork and plays had flourished at government expense (until Dies stopped them, of course). To HUAC, though, the literary pursuits were all a "side job" to the party's main concern: "the same as it remains today. Espionage."[218] Indeed, there were spies working in the government "RIGHT NOW," the committee alleged, because "Russia wants the industrial capacity of the United States," including technology from atomic research, aviation, munitions, transportation, steel, chemicals, communications, oil, and mining.[219] HUAC went on to assert that "It's every Communist's duty . . . to pick up any information around the plant he can lay hands on." Citing the various departments that had been Bentley's bailiwick, the pamphlet conveyed the impression that the entire apparatus was still at work in 1949. The United States was the "NUMBER ONE target of Russia's spy effort," HUAC declared. Moreover, behind every party member stood ten supporters, a potential fifth column of 825,000 that threatened the United States.[220]

The inflated rhetoric fit well the times, in which McCarthy's ever-shifting tally of Communists in the government also impressed many. In 1949, the diligent archivists of HUAC had added 300,000 items to the committee's collections, including mimeographed Communist circulars, "crudely lettered handbills" of subversive groups, and FBI documents. Much of this voluminous evidence had been provided by the 1,100 witnesses who had appeared before HUAC, which kept track of its fattening inventory on 470,000 index cards to individuals and their affiliations and maintained a record of 363,119 signatures, including those who had endorsed Communist candidates and causes. The committee's holdings filled two hundred filing cabinets.[221]

HUAC hype notwithstanding, Soviet spies were not completely inactive in this period. They were on the whole quite useless, however. Against all odds, as Weinstein and Vassiliev point out, Sergei Savchenko, the head of NKGB intelligence, was eager to establish a new intelligence organization in the United States in 1950. He wanted "devoted" and "brave" souls, ready to face the climate of supreme anti-Soviet hysteria in the United States. Alexander Panyushkin, NKGB station chief in Washington, scoffed at such recruitment ambitions; he insisted that there was no way to "acquire people working in the State Department and other governmental institutions in the current fascist atmosphere in the U.S. . . . . [W]e work here in the period of unfinished investigations of cases involving almost 50 agents exposed long before us." Indeed, only one Soviet agent remained active in Washington a year later, an acknowledged party member who spent his time putting out innocuous anti-imperialist tracts.[222]

An investigation that was concluded in this era culminated in the CPUSA's Smith Act trial of 1949. A federal grand jury had indicted the party's leaders in 1948 for violating the Smith Act, a 1940 law prohibiting the teaching and advocacy of overthrowing the government by force, even though the CPUSA had not been "actively contemplating overthrow of government in near future," as prosecuting attorney John F. X. McGohey conceded. The party members had, however, "unlawfully, willfully, and knowingly conspired with each other."[223] Defector Louis Budenz provided immense help to the government's case at the ensuing trial. The former editor of the *Daily Worker* had an extensive knowledge of Marxism-Leninism that assisted him in undercutting the arguments of the party's general secretary, Eugene Dennis, who used the trial to proselytize the precepts of Communism rather than defend his right to his political beliefs based on the First Amendment. The courtroom atmosphere became quite raucous; seven of the defendants were sent to prison, as were five of their lawyers, who failed to keep them in order. The Supreme Court upheld the decision in *Dennis et al. v. United States* in 1951, basing its brief on the continuing danger presented by Soviet Communism to the United States.[224] The party did not take all of this lying down. As Dennis wrote Truman in 1949, "The Communist Party is a legal political party and its members are patriotic and loyal citizens. . . . [W]e shall continue to combat the forces of reaction and fascism which are organizing the current attacks on democracy, equality and peace."[225]

Not content with the Smith Act trial's verdict, legislators also sought to find other methods by which to make Communists disappear. In 1948, the House had approved the Mundt-Nixon bill, which would have forced all

Communist and front groups to register, presenting the prospect of jail time to any organizations that did so. Some members of the Senate considered it too extreme, however, and prevented its passage. Nevertheless, in 1950 both houses of Congress endorsed the Internal Security Act, which required the CPUSA to register with a Subversive Activities Control Board (SACB). Doing so, however, meant members would face job restrictions and possible internment. When the party refused to register with the SACB, the attorney general's office filed a legal brief, most of which was devoted to detailing the CPUSA's secret actions. In words right out of J. Edgar Hoover's mouth, the brief alleged that "Extensive preparations for taking the CPUSA underground were commenced in 1948," and, continuing for the next four years, "a large number of Party members have been . . . transferred. . . . in order to assist in underground planning and to receive instructions in underground activities." The party was conducting "extensive secret practices," the government contended, to further the "objectives . . . of the world Communist movement, and for concealing its direction, domination and control by the Soviet Union."[226] But in a 1953 suit brought by the SACB, party witness John Gates maintained that "the leaders of the Party do not recognize and do not consider themselves subject to the disciplinary power of the Soviet government, the Communist Party of the Soviet Union, the Comintern, the Cominform or any agencies of these organizations."[227] Few were so convinced. The case eventually reached the Supreme Court in 1961, which declared registration constitutional and the party guilty for its failure to comply; a 1963 appeal addressing the Fifth Amendment implications of the registration requirement reversed this decision. The SACB finally died during the Nixon administration, never having registered a single Communist.

Developments in the early Cold War, as this chapter has shown, only hardened suspicions toward the Soviet Union's "underground" activities that had first developed in World War II. As wartime Communist spies ranging from Remington to Rosenberg emerged in the glare of investigative light, U.S. agencies and lawmakers monitored more closely government employees, conducted numerous hearings and trials, and also enacted tighter controls on exports. After the first successful Soviet atomic test in August 1949, the National Security Council issued NSC-68, which called for systematic economic and military measures to frustrate the Kremlin "by the strategy of the cold war." It based such a response on bombastic allegations that "the Soviet Union, unlike previous aspirants to hegemony, is animated by a new fanatic faith . . . and seeks to impose its absolute authority over the rest of the world." Historians as diverse in their views as Bruce Cumings and John Lewis Gaddis have cited NSC-68 as highlighting a new and more aggressive American policy that was confirmed in the Korean War, when Dean Acheson told congressional leaders and the cabinet that " there was only one possible step open to us and that was the greatest possible buildup of our own military strength and the military strength of our allies. Nothing else could stop the drive of the Soviet Union for world domination." Other scholars, like Gregory Mitrovich, have argued that the developments of 1950 only confirmed an existing policy that was first articulated in 1948 with NSC 20/4, which proposed that the United States should "compel" the Soviet Union to change its "conduct of international relations . . . to conform with the purposes and principles set forth in the UN charter" and limit Soviet "power and influence" by deploying "all methods short of war."[228]

These pronouncements doubtless each exemplify an important shift to a tougher line in Soviet-American relations, but what has often been forgotten in discussions of Cold War policies are their important connections with the hardening outlook toward Moscow during World War II. Although U.S. counterintelligence officials did not speak in terms of Soviet "hegemony" during the war, they were nevertheless closely focused on limiting threatening manifestations of Soviet influence. As noted in the previous chapter, the FBI believed in 1944 that the United States would be at Moscow's "mercy" if Russian scientists developed the bomb first.[229] Espionage, of course, assisted the Soviet Union's successful atomic weapons development within a few years of the war's end. Moreover, subsequent spying would play an important role throughout the Cold War and beyond in assisting Soviet economic development, countering American military advantages, and convincing counterintelligence officials and the public of the need for vigilance against an ever-present Russian threat.

CHAPTER SIX

Soviet and Russian Spies since World War II

The most notorious chapter of Soviet espionage in the United States—that of World War II—ended with the sentencing of Gold, Fuchs, Greenglass, and Sobell and the execution of the Rosenbergs. Although the events of that period have often seemed the acme of Soviet espionage in America, they were hardly the end of the story. Since the second half of the last century and continuing up to the present, the Soviet Union and its successor, the Russian Federation, have never ceased attempting to gain military and industrial intelligence in the United States.[1] In the past decade alone, the shocking successes of Aldrich Ames and Robert Hanssen have reminded Americans that the post-Soviet Russian Foreign Intelligence Service (SVRR) has a highly effective espionage apparatus. Most of these recent spies, unlike their World War II predecessors, have been motivated by financial incentives more than ideological ones; even when psychology and personality have contributed to their espionage, monetary compensation has rarely been absent.[2]

Military and economic intelligence gathering in the postwar era has extended the prominent role of espionage in U.S.-Russian relations not only through the Cold War but even beyond the life of the Soviet Union; Russia's still awesome military arsenal and its history as a fount of spies against the United States bestows a special significance upon its modern espionage activity. As recently as 2001, Vice President Dick Cheney and the Defense Department still held up Russia as the chief menace to America. Though that status changed on September 11, and Russia has lent support to the U.S. "war on terrorism," if not the war in Iraq, President Vladimir Putin's "authoritarianism" and "backward looking . . . national security establishment"—still dominated by "alumni of the intelligence services"—continued to raise concerns in Congress in 2004.[3]

Over the last half century, agents assigned to diplomatic offices, first Soviet and then Russian, have continued to work with recruits and volunteers at American firms and government agencies. These spies were highly active even at the height of the *glasnost* era, when their industrial espionage targets included such militarily sensitive items as semiconductors, computer-aided design systems, fiber optics, and nuclear energy. Indeed, as a Defense Department study ruefully concluded at the height of Mikhail Gorbachev's openness campaign in 1988, "[T]he damage to national security from espionage, technology theft, and electronic surveillance amounts to a staggering loss of S&T [scientific and technological] information." As in earlier decades, Moscow used legal means to obtain these new technologies: visits to trade conferences, subscriptions to such journals as *Aviation Week and Space Technology* (which had 146 subscribers with Soviet addresses), and materials from the U.S. Patent Office, as well as illegal methods. For both their industrial and military needs, they relied on both HUMINT (human intelligence), or the recruitment of actual agents inside industrial plants, universities, and government agencies, as well as SIGINT (signals intelligence), through which Soviet technicians could eavesdrop on telephone messages, break into computer networks, and use telemetry techniques to monitor weapons tests or read radar signals either from aboard ship or through satellite imaging systems. Indeed, these satellites and other reconnaissance methods themselves became a coveted asset in the race for technology. The Soviets, just like the Americans, were keen to gain an edge in monitoring their enemies' military readiness; such an edge would lead to further advantages should any conflict arise.[4]

Before the existence of satellite technology, however, the Soviets, just like their American counterparts, relied on humans to do the heavy lifting. Because of the risks associated with recruitment inside the United States in the highly security-conscious aftermath of the Rosenberg case, Russian agents focused increasingly on cultivating American spies overseas, especially men in uniform. Of thirty-three U.S. espionage cases prosecuted between 1950 and 1975, fully twenty-three were either soldiers or civilians connected with the military abroad.[5] Soviet agents also infiltrated military bases in the United States; former U.S. Army Counter Intelligence Corps agent Charles Whittaker, for example, remembers identifying "sleeper agents" in the armed services in the mid- to late 1950s.[6] Although numerous spies in the military sector were apprehended and convicted, American intelligence agency operatives who spied for Russia were seldom publicly revealed in this era. The CIA and the Justice Department had a secret agreement, first signed in 1954, that allowed the CIA to decide whether to send any of its agents suspected of illegal activities to Justice for prosecution. Not surprisingly, the agency preferred not to subject its soiled laundry to the attorney general's scouring cycle, and suspected personnel remained known only to the CIA for reasons of "national security." Both the CIA and the Justice Department supported this policy as one that reduced the risk of both provoking Soviet retaliation against American agents abroad and embarrassing the U.S. government.[7]

Washington had no such concerns about retaliation when its agents arrested KGB illegal Rudolf Ivanovich Abel in Manhattan in 1957. After all, the United States did not regularly place its spies inside the Soviet Union—or so the public believed. With the shock of Sputnik still fresh, Abel, who had been in the United States for almost ten years, was found guilty of conspiracy to obtain and transmit defense-related material to the Soviet Union, and of being an unregistered foreign agent. He was sentenced to serve thirty years in prison; after an appeal, the Supreme Court upheld his conviction in 1960. Two years later, however, after U-2 pilot Francis Gary Powers was caught red-handed after a crash in a Russian field—a humiliating reminder to Khrushchev of how the United States was regularly infiltrating his country's airspace if not its actual territory—the United States let Abel go in exchange for the downed flyer.[8] Another spy arrested in this era was Jack Soble, a KGB agent whose ring had been infiltrated for the FBI by Boris Morros, himself a longtime Soviet spy, back in 1947; ten years later, Soble, his wife, and two others were convicted of espionage.[9]

Not all spies were Soviet plants. In 1960, Powers's exposure led two disgusted Americans, National Security Agency mathematicians Bernon F. Mitchell and William H. Martin, to defect to Russia, providing the Soviets with a gold mine of cryptographic information. In a public attack on the United States from Moscow's House of Journalists, Mitchell and Martin angrily vilified American secret missions over Soviet airspace. HUAC, however, blamed the men's supposed "homosexuality" for their betrayal.[10] Another NSA employee who also spied in the early 1960s, Jack Dunlap, was never caught. After failing a polygraph test in 1963, he made several attempts to kill himself; he completed the deed before authorities could unearth what he had stolen from the NSA, but James Bamford argues that it was far more than Mitchell and Martin pillaged. The same year, a U.S. Air Force employee, John Butenko, was successfully apprehended for furnishing the KGB the secrets of the Strategic Air Command's communications technology; he received a thirty-year sentence.[11] Unfortunately for the United States, efforts to recruit its own moles to penetrate Moscow's intelligence agencies in this era remained stillborn owing to the paranoia of James Angleton, head of the CIA's Special Operations Group, who became convinced that working with Soviet double agents would only involve the CIA in a deceptive KGB "monster plot."[12]

The FBI, not laboring under such handicaps, launched a risky deception plan in 1963 using army sergeant Joseph Cassidy to supply inaccurate information on U.S. chemical weapons development to the Soviets. Cassidy was posted at Edgewood Arsenal, a facility that researched top-secret nerve gases. In this scheme, as David Wise writes, the government hoped "to cause the Soviets to conduct extensive research . . . to replicate or defend against a chemical agent that the United States had not actually produced." In the formula that Cassidy gave his Soviet handlers, the nerve gas was not only unstable, but had no antidote, making it presumably useless owing to the risks it presented to the troops deploying it. Cassidy's dangerous deception operation continued for over two decades.[13]

Meanwhile, the CIA-Justice "gag" rule would run into withering scrutiny in the mid-1970s from the Rockefeller Commission and Frank Church's (D-Ida.) Senate Select Committee to Study Government Operations with Respect to Intelligence Activities, both of which were investigating intelligence agencies' abuses in the post-Watergate era. President Gerald Ford soon axed the rule, but counterintelligence officials did not entirely drop their resistance to prosecution. When William Kampiles, a disgruntled CIA trainee, stole a top-secret manual for a KH-11 military surveillance satellite in 1977 and sold it to the Soviets for just $3,000, both the CIA and the Defense Department opposed his going on trial. The CIA was embarrassed by the laxity demonstrated by Kampiles's espionage, while the Pentagon worried about maintaining the secrecy of the satellite. As a result, the trial included closed sessions and limits on access to the material in question. Similar measures were employed in the prosecution of Christopher Boyce, a TRW employee who sold defense secrets from his firm to Moscow in 1977. Such provisions were enshrined in the Classified Information Procedures Act of 1980.[14]

Thus, at the same time that Congress made it more difficult for the CIA and other intelligence agencies to refuse to admit the existence of suspected spies under the cloak of national security, lawmakers also enabled the prosecution of spies without jeopardizing secrets. They also permitted the use of controversial methods to catch even more spies. The Foreign Intelligence Surveillance Act (FISA) in 1978 allowed investigators to wiretap suspected terrorists and espionage agents without worrying about violating the Fourth Amendment's protection of criminal defendants from unlawful search and seizure. Under this act, a panel of judges reviews the government's requests for surveillance, and almost always accepts them: in 2002, for example, the panel approved all 1,228 requests put before it. This law was also designed to protect secrets that might be uncovered in the course of identifying suspected spies or terrorists, by limiting access of information only to the judges and other specially screened Justice Department lawyers. As these new measures provided for much more effective pursuit of spies, the number of espionage agents apprehended ballooned to sixty-two in the 1980s.[15]

Despite the notoriety of the 1980s as the "decade of the spy," it was really in the 1970s that intelligence agencies first became effective in finding clandestine intelligence agents.[16] Perhaps this was a result of Congress's unmasking of CIA abuses like Operation CHAOS, in which the agency spied on thousands of American antiwar activists, or the FBI's COINTELPRO initiatives, through which Bureau agents infiltrated "extremist" groups. Once these operations had been exposed and discredited during the Ford administration, counterintelligence operatives were freed to focus on more appropriate goals, like catching and putting on trial espionage agents who worked for foreign governments. As the U.S. Defense Security Service (DSS) pointed out, it was in 1975 that "the government decided to resume an aggressive prosecution of arrested spies." After a decade with almost no successful espionage cases, the Justice Department oversaw thirty-one prosecutions from 1975 to 1985.[17]

One reason for the earlier inactivity, as Nigel West notes, was the diplomatic environment of détente. In this context, the story of Valery I. Markelov is revealing. Markelov, a UN translator and KGB operative, met an unidentified Grumman engineer at a party in 1970 and mentioned to him that he was very interested in the Grumman F-14 fighter jet and its wing-sweep mechanism for his "doctoral dissertation." Markelov cultivated the American engineer, who mentioned that he had financial problems; the engineer then contacted the FBI, and the Bureau monitored the two men's meetings over the next two years. Markelov gave the Grumman employee a photocopying machine, a special camera, and monthly payments of $250. At their last meeting, in February 1972, the FBI arrested Markelov with confidential documents in his hands. Soon indicted for espionage and violating the Foreign Agents Registration Act, Markelov saw his indictment dismissed by the Nixon administration, which claimed such a step "would best serve the national and foreign policy interests of the United States." Markelov returned to Russia.[18]

By 1975, however, with the United States' ignominious rout from Vietnam and the Helsinki Accords' seeming legitimization of the Soviet sphere, the bloom had decidedly faded from the détente rose. That June, the FBI arrested Sarkis O. Paskalian, one-time director of performing arts at the Armenian General Benevolent Union in New York City and a longtime KGB agent, along with his cousin, Sadag K. Dedeyian, a former mathematician at the Johns Hopkins Applied Physics Laboratory. In 1973 Dedeyian had provided Paskalian a file from his lab with the enticing title "Vulnerability Analysis: U.S. Reinforcement of NATO," which Paskalian had then copied and provided to the Soviet UN mission. Paskalian received a twenty-two-year sentence, and Dedeyian a three-year term. The arrests prompted FBI director Clarence Kelley to declare that the United States was a "prime target" for Soviet intelligence collection.[19]

Increasingly, as the Markelov case suggests, the government had begun to use double agents to catch these spies. Norman Rees, mentioned earlier, began working as a double agent for the FBI in the early 1970s after a thirty-year career spying on the oil industry for the Soviet Union; his FBI tenure abruptly ended, however, in 1976 when he committed suicide after his spy career was "outed" in the media.[20] In the same period, Paul Nekrasov, an engineer at the RCA Space Center who was also working under Bureau direction, provided Ivan N. Rogalsky materials on communications satellites that Rogalsky passed on to the Soviet UN mission. Authorities arrested Rogalsky in January 1977, but he avoided a trial on the basis of insanity: he claimed to hear voices.[21]

In the summer of 1977, in another successful effort, the FBI used a so-called "dangle operation" to send retiring U.S. Navy lieutenant commander Art Lindberg on a Bermuda cruise aboard the Soviet tourist vessel *Kazakhstan*. The craft was a floating nest of spies, according to U.S. officials. Although aware that others had drowned on this pleasure boat, Lindberg was game, and his "dangling" spy bait soon got a nibble. Following the cruise, Lindberg began furnishing Valdik A. Enger, Rudolf P. Chernyayev, and Vladimir P. Zinyakin—all of the Soviet UN mission—with navy-screened materials on antisubmarine warfare and an advanced helicopter system, collecting almost $30,000 until the FBI arrested the three Soviet agents at a drop site in May 1978. Zinyakin had diplomatic immunity as an attaché, but the other two lacked such protection and were tried for espionage. The case created much controversy inside the government, in some ways mirroring World War II–era debates over diplomatic sensitivities. The State Department, hoping for continued détente, strongly opposed the prosecution, while the Pentagon worried about secrets emerging during the trial. But former navy man Jimmy Carter approved prosecution of the case. Over strong Soviet protest, Enger and Chernyayev were sentenced to fifty years in prison, although they were later exchanged for five Soviet dissidents.[22]

As such cases show, the Soviets remained highly interested in defense technology during the nadir of Soviet-American relations in the late 1970s and early 1980s, just as they had been in World War II. One defector from Soviet intelligence indicated that their "number one target" in the U.S. then was General Electric, but numerous other defense firms, from Lockheed to Rockwell, also were desired sites for infiltration.[23] So alarming was the leakage from Silicon Valley, in fact, that the State Department, suspecting the San Francisco Soviet consulate was the conduit for this illicit information, moved to ban all those "suspected of wrongful use" from this diplomatic outpost.[24]

A more famous spy arrested in this era was the aforementioned Christopher J. Boyce, a TRW employee who stole top-secret material on CIA satellites for the Russians, including cryptological information, in 1975 and 1976. His boyhood friend, Andrew Daulton Lee, passed the materials to agents at the Soviet embassy in Mexico City. Ironically, Boyce, who secreted rolls of film out in potted plants, was the son of a security chief at another defense contractor, McDonnell Douglas. Because he worked in the top-secret "black vault" of TRW, where he handled coded messages between the firm and the CIA concerning not only spy satellites but also the routes of submarines, Boyce was an especially valued source.[25] Soviet intelligence agents were thrilled to gain material on the top-secret Rhyolite surveillance system, designed to capture communications transmissions from Russia and China, as well as the Pyramider, a satellite program by which the agency could keep in touch with its agents in remote locales. Although he earned $20,000 for his work (a good deal less than Lee did), Boyce seems to have been motivated most by a strong disagreement with American foreign policy. He was particularly upset with what he saw as duplicity in the U.S. relationship with Australia, a country that provided bases to support satellite intelligence collection without being furnished with the full information drawn from these satellites. Boyce claimed later that he merely wanted this issue to become public, but his friend Lee had already passed material to the Russians and had blackmailed Boyce to provide more.[26]

Lee was a less-than-reliable courier, however; he actively sold drugs and at one point asked his Soviet handlers to import cocaine for him. The Mexican police, which twenty-seven years earlier had stopped Morton Sobell for American authorities, nabbed Lee with top-secret information on his person in January 1977. He soon implicated his old friend and the two received hefty sentences; life for Lee, forty years for Boyce. Three years later, Boyce escaped from jail—some believed he had been rescued by the KGB—and survived outside prison for almost two years, helped by a sympathetic woman from Idaho. During that time, he also participated in sixteen bank robberies. Upon his capture, another twenty-eight years were added to his prison term. Boyce initially showed little remorse for his actions, telling an Australian television audience in 1983: "I think that eventually the United States Government is going to involve the world in the next world war. And being a traitor to that, I have absolutely no problems with that whatsoever."[27]

Boyce was beaten by members of the Aryan Brotherhood at Leavenworth Prison but avoided William Remington's fate when authorities transferred him to solitary confinement in the penitentiary at Marion, Illinois, the federal system's most secure lock-up, where he spent six years. This experience seems to have sobered him, for in 1985 he told the Senate Select Committee on Intelligence that espionage was "pretty dirty business . . . it is not what you see on television." Spies, he noted, are "bringing down upon themselves heartache more heavy than a mountain. There is no exit from it."[28] Boyce was released from prison in March 2003.

In 1981, U.S. intelligence uncovered another defense industry source in Southern California, William Holden Bell of Hughes Aircraft in El Segundo. Bell had provided Marian Zacharski, a neighbor and a Polish intelligence agent posing as president of the Polish American Machinery Corporation, with an amazing trove of top-secret information including radar related to the F-15, the B-1, and the Stealth bombers, as well as missile-related materials. Bell was in need of money, and the espionage earned him $150,000. After they were found out, Zacharski received a life sentence and Bell, who had cooperated with the FBI, got eight years. Zacharski was later returned to Poland in an exchange for several East bloc refugees.[29]

In 1983, another industrial spy, this time from Northern California, was also arrested for passing defense information to the Poles and their KGB partners. James Durward Harper sold materials on the Minuteman Missile from Systems Control Inc.(SCI) for $250,000. His documents were so sensitive in their description of NATO's defense capacity that a U.S. Army representative declared their value "beyond calculation." Harper had obtained them thanks to his wife, Ruby Schuler, a secretary at SCI, who let him snoop around the plant after closing time. He then brought the materials to his handlers in various European capitals. In 1981, after two years of espionage, Harper anonymously approached the CIA, hoping to be a double agent in return for immunity, but got a life sentence instead. His wife, meanwhile, died of alcoholism.[30]

Continuing the string of defense-related espionage discoveries during the era of the Reagan defense buildup was the December 1984 arrest of Northrop engineer Thomas Patrick Cavanaugh, who had attempted to sell material on radar-impervious Stealth airplane technology to the Soviet Union. Cavanaugh, broke and going through a divorce, was caught in the act of providing documents to FBI agents posing as Soviet contacts, from whom he accepted $25,000. He received two concurrent life terms. After Cavanaugh's arrest, FBI director William Webster declared: "We have more people charged with espionage right now than ever before in our history," an assessment echoed on the front page of the *New York Times*.[31]

Although Cavanaugh, like Bell and Harper, seems to have been motivated mainly by money, one would-be spy from the early 1980s claimed his in-progress novel, "Operation Heartbreak," motivated his espionage. Second-class PO Brian P. Horton wanted "to learn their M.O.," according to his lawyer, so the young naval nuclear analyst made contacts with the Soviet embassy to sell the highly classified Single Integrated Operation Plan, or SIOP, for just $3,000. His efforts were intercepted, and Horton was court-martialed and sentenced to six years of hard labor.[32] Even the hallowed halls of Congress were not immune from espionage in the "decade of the spy." Randy Miles Jeffries, a stenographic messenger with a history of heroin abuse, twice supplied top-secret materials from closed hearings of the House Armed Services Committee to Soviet military officials. He was arrested in a sting operation in 1985, on his third effort to deliver documents, and sentenced to serve from three to nine years.[33]

Jeffries, in fact, was the twelfth person charged with espionage in 1985, "the year of the spy."[34] Among those apprehended that year were Richard Miller, an FBI agent in Los Angeles who started an affair with a KGB operative he was monitoring, and Jonathan J. Pollard, a naval analyst who spied for Israel.[35] Ronald Pelton was yet another. An NSA communications specialist for fourteen years, he furnished information about a top-secret navy program, "Operation Ivy Bells," in which U.S. submarines placed bugging devices on Soviet undersea cables between Vladivostok and Petropavlovsk; before Pelton revealed the operation, it had netted a wealth of unencrypted messages and operations information.[36] Interestingly, Pelton did not contact Soviet intelligence until 1980, well after he had left the NSA, when financial difficulties sent him through the door of the Soviet embassy. He thus provided information from memory. Famed KGB defector Vitaly Yurchenko identified Pelton in 1985, and he received three life sentences.[37]

Yurchenko also identified CIA agent Edward Lee Howard, whom the agency, now freed from Angleton's anxieties, had hired in 1981 for the delicate task of managing Russians cooperating with the CIA inside the Soviet Union. Howard, like Jeffries, had a history of substance abuse. Fired in 1983 for his problem, the disgruntled employee soon told CIA staffers that he was considering becoming a Soviet source. In line with the agency's long history of cloaking its agents' lapses from the prying eyes of the FBI, the Justice Department was not informed until much too late. Meanwhile, Howard began passing important information to the KGB, resulting in the death of at least one American agent. Then, he averted arrest by escaping to the Soviet Union, the first member of the CIA to do so.[38] He died in Russia in 2002.

The most significant spy arrest in 1985, of course, was that of John A. Walker Jr. Walker had first betrayed highly sensitive Navy codes in 1967, when he was a debt-ridden watch officer aboard a U.S. submarine. The Soviets paid the unhappily married man with four children to support $4,000 a month, a princely sum compared to his $725 monthly navy salary. Walker picked up work for the Soviets where U.S. Army warrant officer Joseph Helmich had left off the year before; between 1963 and 1966, Helmich had provided materials on navy cipher machines.[39] Walker, considered "intensely loyal" by his superiors, left the service before his divorce was final in 1976, realizing he would not pass a background check if his ex-wife, who knew of his espionage, were interviewed. By then, Walker had established his network by recruiting his close friend Jerry Whitworth, a naval communications specialist, telling Whitworth that he was working for "our friends the Jews." Whitworth spied with Walker off and on for ten years, supplying generous amounts of cryptographic and other information from the navy's communication center in Diego Garcia, from positions on the USS *Constellation* and the USS *Niagara Falls*, and from the Naval Telecommunications Center in Alameda, California. Some of Whitworth's material revealed U.S. war plans. Whitworth grew increasingly skittish about the spy business and began sending anonymous messages to the FBI hinting he would tell all, but fearing arrest, refused to reveal himself.[40] Whitworth's cryptological espionage was extremely damaging; as former NSA director Earl Clark claimed: "If I can get access to your codes . . . I have access to all your critical secrets." Indeed, according to John Barron, the material that Whitworth and Walker provided "contributed significantly to the development of the modern Soviet navy and the diminution of the U.S. technological lead."[41]

As Whitworth's yield became intermittent, Walker decided to enhance his Soviet payments by recruiting even more sources and turned to his family. His daughter Laura, who had served in the army, dithered. His half-brother turned him down. He had more luck with his brother Arthur, who in 1980 began to furnish him documents, although in limited quantities, from his position at defense contractor VSE Corporation. John Walker was most successful with his son Michael, who as a sailor on the USS *Nimitz* had access to many secret documents, despite not having proper clearance. With responsibility for numerous burn bags of classified information, Michael had a field day for his father.[42] Walker's arrest was also a family affair: his ex-wife did indeed turn him in.

Before being rolled up, the Walker ring had provided a vast amount of information, including the authentication codes needed to start nuclear weapons in war, keylists that allowed the Soviets to read messages sent between American naval ships, and the navy's plans for possible war in Central America. Walker provided enough information for Soviet cryptanalysts to decipher over one million messages. His case officer was made a general, and Walker himself was named an "honorary admiral" in the Soviet Navy.[43] Yurchenko contended that Walker's ring represented "the most important operation in KGB history," even more so than the World War II efforts to acquire nuclear secrets in the United States.[44] The accolade probably would not have surprised Walker, whose ego was not small. After he was arrested, he remained "totally bewildered" that the FBI did not take advantage of him as a double agent; after all, he declared, "I know more about espionage than the FBI and the Central Intelligence Agency combined!"[45]

Although the enormity of the Walker episode may have squashed most other spy cases of 1985 into insignificance, the sheer number of other spies uncovered in this period was nevertheless impressive. The Justice Department convicted twenty-five espionage agents in 1985 and 1986. The Defense Department responded by creating a blue-ribbon panel under Gen. Richard Stilwell, which made recommendations that led to tighter security regulations and the formation of the Defense Personnel Security Research Center for screening employees and conducting "research on espionage."[46]

Even so, some notable new espionage operations began in 1985, which happened to be the year that Aldrich Ames of the CIA's Soviet counterintelligence branch launched his nine-year career in Soviet service. At the same time, another extremely damaging spy, Robert Hanssen, changed masters from the GRU to the KGB and greatly accelerated his espionage work. In 1979, FBI special agent Hanssen had first walked into the Amtorg Trading Agency, volunteering to assist the GRU. He subsequently revealed the identity of one of the United States' most important agents inside the Soviet secret service: Dmitri Fedorovich Polyakov, or "Tophat."[47] By the mid-1980s, Hanssen's job as FBI squad supervisor in New York was to monitor Amtorg, a Bureau surveillance target since before World War II. Although the trade operation was by then considered a backwater of Soviet activity, the presence of intelligence agents there could not be overlooked, as Hanssen's own history confirms. Indeed, it was while spying on Amtorg in 1985 that Hanssen first contacted the KGB, offering the names of three American moles in Russian intelligence, as well as documents, and requesting $100,000. He thus entered the most active period of his spy career.[48]

Hanssen and Ames provided highly valued secrets about U.S. intelligence and counterintelligence activities, but the Soviets also maintained their strong interest in scientific and technical information with military applications, which was so vital during the 1980s arms race. As the CIA observed in 1982, because of "assimilation" of Western industrial and scientific developments in Russia, the West was "subsidizing the Soviet military buildup." This buildup was of no little concern to then-president Ronald Reagan, who was pushing hard for a bigger American stockpile. The Soviet Military Industrial Commission's Directorate T (for "technology") included numerous KGB and other intelligence agents overseas, whose job was to buy over $1 billion annually in military materials from a secret list that included computers, radar, nuclear submarines, and thousands of other items, as Soviet double agent Vladimir Vetrov, aka "Farewell," revealed in the 1980s. Specifically, this espionage assisted the Soviets in developing copies of the F-18 fighter, the B-1 bomber, and the AWACS radar system. In the mid-1970s Directorate T included over one hundred agents and "trusted contacts" in the United States. "Farewell," who had worked most closely with French intelligence sources (France had expelled forty-three agents thanks to his information), helped expose the Soviets' penetration of American industrial technology as well, from universities like MIT and Caltech to corporations such as Boeing and General Electric. So too did defector Vasili Mitrokhin, who named thirty-two agents at McDonnell Douglas and the U.S. Army's Material Development and Readiness Command, among numerous others.[49] The Soviets also gathered American technology secondhand in Japan; fully half of the KGB's residents in Tokyo were involved in "high-tech intelligence."[50] Such efforts continued well into the glasnost era, as the previous career of current Russian president Vladimir Putin demonstrates. In the mid- to late 1980s as a KGB officer in East Germany, Putin worked diligently to steal Western technology, using traveling East German technicians and academicians to link up with agents in the West. His office was particularly interested in "wireless communications," no doubt imagining the efficiencies of cell phone–toting KGB legions.[51] Mikhail Gorbachev's tenure thus in no way lessened Soviet S&T espionage. Indeed, he saw this practice "as an important part of economic *perestroika*," as Christopher Andrew and Vasili Mitrokhin note.[52]

In 1989, Congressman Henry Hyde (R-Ill.) charged that "virtually every major Soviet weapons system incorporates US, Japanese, German, French and British technology to various degrees—in many cases, decisively." He estimated the cost of "technology loss" to be in the tens of billions of dollars. Hyde cited the problem of espionage, but also chastised companies whose dealings with Russia skirted long-established export regulations: "A small core of business interests scattered throughout the industrial West have maintained close (and presumably profitable) dealings with the Soviets irrespective of the East-West political temperature—in some cases to the detriment of Western security."[53] Three years later, after the fall of the Soviet Union, defector Stanislav Levchenko told Congress that "high-tech, industrial and economic intelligence" had replaced political information as the "number one priority" of the new Russian intelligence service, whose efforts ranged from espionage on foreign corporations that had entered into joint ventures in Russia to the longstanding use of agents working undercover in Russian diplomatic posts abroad. This work was coordinated by analysts who compiled a "shopping list" of desired items. According to Brian Freemantle, this "list" was actually a twenty-seven-chapter book titled *Coordinated Requests for Technological Information.*[54]

Western security suffered even more damage from the activities of Aldrich Ames, whose 1994 arrest elicited shock in the intelligence community as well as in the wider public. As head of the CIA's counterintelligence service in Europe, Ames closely scrutinized Soviet activities and thus was an extremely valuable source for the Kremlin. He is reputed to have broken more than one hundred anti-Soviet operations, as well as contributed to the deaths of ten agents, including Valery Martynov (who himself had told the FBI about at least fifty agents in the Soviet embassy), Sergei Motorin, and

Dmitri Polyakov. Unlike Walker, Ames's material was not related to U.S. military capabilities, but to individual agents and their operations. The CIA also was privy to double agents run by the military outside the United States, and Ames provided those names too.[55]

The agents' deaths were not hard to miss, and the CIA began a major effort to find their mole, soliciting the FBI's help for the first time.[56] For too long, however, Ames's grandiose lifestyle, supported by the $2.7 million he received from the Soviets, went unsuspected; the CIA's leadership remained closed to the concept that their spy could be a top agency official, even one with a serious drinking problem who was often indiscreet in his discussion of agency operations.[57] CIA spy hunters also were distracted by such scandals as that of U.S. Marine Clayton Lonetree, a guard at the American embassy in Moscow. CIA Soviet division deputy chief Milt Bearden was not the only officer to believe that Lonetree, an alcoholic who had had an affair with a Soviet woman in 1986, was chiefly responsible for the compromise of so many operations. The KGB, meanwhile, capitalized on this mistaken belief.[58]

While the CIA fumbled, the FBI, too, had taken "hundreds" of agents out of counterintelligence operations in the late- and post-Cold War era, deploying them instead in the fight against newly perceived threats such as drug-inspired violence.[59] As Glenn A. Fine, the Justice Department's inspector general, recently commented: "[T]here was essentially no deterrence to espionage at the F.B.I. during the 1979 to 2001 time period," which coincided with the span of Hanssen's spying.[60] Besides the CIA and the FBI, the army had its own issues with moles in this era, as well; U.S. Army Reserve colonel George Trofimoff, arrested in 2000, had supplied defense secrets to the Soviet Union while stationed in Germany from 1969 to 1994. Trofimoff supervised the U.S. Joint Interrogation Center in Nuremberg, where the army interviewed Warsaw Pact defectors, and had access to information on U.S. intelligence and strategic aims, as well as "documents which detailed the U.S. current state of knowledge of Soviet and Warsaw Pact military organizations and capabilities," including their "chemical and biological" potential. Trofimoff provided his materials to Igor Vladimirovich Susemihl, a Russian Orthodox priest whom he had known as a child, and Susemihl took them to the Soviet Union. Paid a total of $250,000, Trofimoff was the highest-ranking army officer ever to be charged with espionage. Evidence of his guilt was provided by former KGB general Oleg Kalugin, who testified at Trofimoff's 2001 trial.[61]

Ames, who netted far more cash, was not only convicted on espionage charges but also for tax evasion on his earnings from spying. He received a life sentence with no chance for parole. His wife, Rosario, got five years for collaborating with him. Although Ames was certainly chiefly culpable, some have argued that he got into the spy business in order to please Rosario; she was reportedly disappointed with the standard of living his CIA salary afforded. Significantly, the Ames case led to the appointment of an FBI agent, Edward J. Curran, to head counterespionage at CIA Headquarters. Another important development was President Bill Clinton's signing of the Violent Crime Control and Law Enforcement Act, which restored the death penalty for spying under certain conditions, including passing materials that resulted in the death of a U.S. agent. The act effectively removed the ten-year statute of limitations on espionage, which was enacted with the passage of the Internal Security Act of 1950. Because espionage is now an offense that may be "punishable by death," an indictment can be filed at any time.[62] The Rosenbergs still remain the only convicted U.S. spies to be executed, however. Prosecutors know that dead spies don't talk, and they have been loath to give up the opportunity to extract more details from them. Moreover, in capital cases the prosecution is required to produce more evidence, thus jeopardizing the secrecy of documents or sources.[63]

Two years after Ames's arrest, three more Russian spies were apprehended in the United States. In February 1996, the FBI arrested Robert Stephan Lipka at his home in Millersville, Pennsylvania, acting on a tip from his ex-wife. As a nineteen-year-old NSA clerk thirty years earlier, Lipka had provided documents on communications intelligence to the Soviet Union in packages wrapped around his legs in exchange for $27,000. Such a leak at the height of the Vietnam War was probably quite damaging. With the statute of limitations no longer an obstacle to prosecution, Lipka received an eighteen-year sentence.[64] In December, Earl Pitts also was arrested for spying. An FBI agent in charge of finding Russian spies in New York, he had earned over $220,000 for providing documents to Soviet and then Russian intelligence from 1987 to 1992; the materials included the names of FBI informants in Russia as well as American estimates of Soviet intelligence capabilities. Pitts was identified by his handler, Alexander Karpov, after Karpov defected. Pitts's main motivation seemed to have been his disgruntlement with the FBI. He was enticed to return to espionage in 1996 in an FBI sting operation and was sentenced to twenty-seven years in prison in June 1997.[65]

More important than Pitts's or Lipka's arrests was that of Harold James Nicholson in November 1996. Nicholson, the branch chief of the CIA's Counter-Terrorism Center, is still the highest ranked CIA operative to be arrested. In his short span of spying, which authorities tracked back to 1994, Nicholson was indefatigable. Not only did he provide identities of CIA agents and sources, including businessmen, as well as counterintelligence information (including an interview with Aldrich Ames), he stole everything he could from the CIA's secret computers. He also tried to obtain information about Chechnya that the Russians wanted. Nicholson received $120,000 from the SVRR. A combined FBI-CIA investigation tracked him down, in part based on his bank deposits, and his arrest was trumpeted as confirming a new era of intelligence community collaboration in counterespionage. The 1995 Intelligence Authorization Act had mandated immediate notification of the FBI "whenever there are indications that classified information may have been disclosed without authorization to a foreign power." No longer could the CIA go it alone. As Director of Central Intelligence John Deutch declared, "The arrest of Nicholson is the direct result of an unprecedented level of cooperation between the CIA and the FBI. We are now able to demonstrate quite conclusively that the post-Ames reforms work." Nicholson agreed to cooperate with officials, and his jail term was reduced to twenty-three and a half years.[66] The last major arrest of the Clinton era was that of NSA analyst David Sheldon Boone in 1998. Boone was arrested for providing material on reconnaissance and Soviet nuclear targets to the USSR from 1988 to 1991. He had walked into the Soviet embassy in the wake of an expensive divorce, desperate for money. The Soviets paid him $60,000.[67]

Of course, Americans weren't the only ones spying for Russia inside the United States. Just as in World War II, Russian nationals also assisted in this task. In December 1999, the FBI arrested Stanislav Gusev while he dawdled in front of the State Department. Gusev, an attaché at the Russian embassy, was in fact remotely controlling a listening device that had been secretly installed in a seventh-floor conference room down the hall from the offices of Secretary of State Madeleine Albright! Agents found the bug through a sophisticated "sweep" of the building, then arrested Gusev the next time they saw him wandering below. The U.S. government sent him back to Russia. Paul Redmond, former head of counterintelligence at the CIA, was surprised by the Soviet's evident interest in State Department meetings, even though the United States and Russia were no longer enemies. He thought that technology would be a better target for them: "If I were in Moscow, what I'd want to know is what's Microsoft going to do? What's Sun going to do?"[68]

The well-publicized arrest of Robert Hanssen in 2001 capped a fifteen-year hunt for an agent who was responsible for the deaths of numerous U.S.

sources in Russia, and who had sent more than six thousand pages of documents to that country over a twenty-two-year career in espionage, earning $600,000 in cash. Hanssen supervised the FBI's intelligence division—a perfect position in which to avoid detection.[69] After his stint at Amtorg, as described above, he returned to FBI headquarters in Washington in 1987, where he could be more helpful to the KGB. He provided them information about U.S. intelligence agencies' internal electronic communications, as well as materials about the Strategic Defense Initiative. In 1989, he informed them about a tunnel the United States was building under the new Soviet embassy in Washington.[70] He handed over extensive U.S. analyses of Soviet capabilities, including Soviet nuclear strength and the American ability to withstand a nuclear attack, the U.S. understanding of Soviet intelligence operatives and operations, and top-secret documents describing U.S. intelligence activity, from satellites to radar. He also supplied Moscow with the identities of fifty sources, including Soviet double agents and defectors, several of whom were executed because of his betrayal.[71] The Bureau had remained acutely aware after arresting Ames in 1994 that he could not have caused certain recent intelligence disasters—someone else was surely responsible. Working with a former KGB officer who had secretly obtained Hanssen's Soviet file and was willing to cooperate for a fee ($7 million), the FBI eventually obtained not only a list of all the materials that Hanssen had supplied, but, even better, actual evidence of his role including a tape recording of his voice and fingerprints on a plastic garbage bag in which he had enclosed documents.[72] The FBI's generous remuneration of this defector in order to capture a key spy was a far cry from the agency's treatment of Krivitsky sixty years earlier, or even Bentley in the 1950s.

Hanssen's motivations have puzzled his biographers. Certainly he was motivated by money, but not to the extent that others were, like Ames. His psychiatrist, David L. Charney, suggested that he wanted to "keep up his reputation" with his wife as a good provider. Moreover, Hanssen resented the FBI, where he felt perpetually passed over and had few friends, and he seems also to have spent his life getting over an abusive father who reveled in humiliating him. He was fascinated, too, with the life of the spy. Milt Bearden and James Risen suggest he had an "addictive personality" that was only satisfied by his espionage binges.[73] Hanssen was sentenced to life without parole in 2002.

Russia was hardly the only nation interested in American military technology. In the 1990s, the Chinese obtained information about a highly advanced atomic weapon, a miniaturized warhead called the W-88. Suspicion fell on a Los Alamos physicist, Wen Ho Lee, whose saving of classified documents onto his own computer tapes—including forty thousand pages of secret nuclear information—and associations with suspected spies drew the concern of officials. Worse, some of his tapes were missing. Lee, however, claimed he was innocent. He was nevertheless placed in solitary confinement in December 1999 for nearly a year, in part based on false information supplied by an FBI agent. After the judge assigned to his case began to question the government's allegations, Lee's lawyers and the United States agreed to a plea bargain in which Lee was freed in return for agreeing to a lesser charge (essentially, mishandling classified materials) rather than espionage. The Bureau's embarrassment, along with the Hanssen debacle, contributed to the resignation of FBI director Louis Freeh.[74]

The events of September 11, 2001, also significantly affected the fate of accused spies. Caught earlier in 2001, Hanssen's case never went to trial; his lawyers, like Ames's, plea bargained for his sentence. By contrast, Brian P. Regan, a National Reconnaissance Office employee who was arrested in August 2001 for offering to sell information to Iraq, China, and Libya, *did* go on trial, where he faced the very real possibility of the death penalty. The countries he was said to have assisted, especially Iraq and Libya, were considered "sponsors of terrorism," making his espionage particularly damaging in the eyes of the government after September 11. As legal analyst John Parry noted at the time, "There is a belief that this is worse espionage because of who is getting the material. . . . Giving things to the Russians is bad, but not threatening in the same way as giving things to irrational terrorists or those who support them." Defense lawyers, however, argued that a letter to Saddam Hussein found on Regan's computer was part of his "fantasy" of espionage rather than evidence of genuine spying. At his trial, Regan would be acquitted of the charge of spying for Libya; the Chinese espionage charges, moreover, did not carry the death penalty. That left only the Iraq espionage, largely based on his letter to Hussein, and a jury decided in February 2003 that the case did not warrant such a sentence. Regan bargained for life in prison to spare his wife from being charged with obstruction of justice in his case. Five months later, Regan's effort seemed less of a fantasy when shovel-wielding FBI employees unearthed twenty thousand pages of documents, as well as CD-ROMs and videotapes, that he had buried in nineteen different holes in Pocahontas State Park in Virginia and the Patapsco

Valley State Park in Maryland. The interred documents included materials on spy satellites, early-warning systems, and weapons of mass destruction.[75]

Another case affected by the post-September 11 environment demonstrates, too, that ideology has not died as a motive in espionage. That very September, authorities apprehended Ana Belen Montes, a Defense Intelligence Agency Cuban analyst identified as "Cuba's top spy," in an arrest accelerated by new security priorities. Montes had spied for Cuba since 1985, and thus some of her materials had presumably reached the Soviet Union. She had most recently turned over information to Castro's government on U.S. defense plans and on the identities of four intelligence agents assigned to Cuba. She pled guilty to espionage in March 2002, her work based not on a desire for money, her lawyer claimed, but inspired by her beliefs "that U.S. policy does not afford Cubans respect, tolerance and understanding." At her sentencing, she professed, "I obeyed my conscience rather than the law." Like spies of old, she also used short-wave radios, pay phones, and encrypted transmissions. Montes was sentenced to twenty-five years in prison in return for providing full information to counterintelligence officials.[76]

Though many of these recent cases have involved espionage against the U.S. government and its intelligence secrets, industrial espionage has continued to be a pressing problem. A Computer Security Institute/FBI survey in 2002 conservatively estimated theft of "proprietary property" from firms at $170 million. Other sources estimate the losses as being in the billions.[77] Many of the countries that spy on the United States are allies, including Japan, Israel, South Korea, Germany, France, and Taiwan.[78] In response to private and public assessments that theft of trade secrets was soaring at an alarming rate, and that the existing Interstate Transportation of Stolen Property Act of 1934—which said nothing about computer data and other kinds of intellectual property—was an ineffective instrument to stop the problem, Congress passed the Economic Espionage Act of 1996. Initially, the act was only supposed to apply to foreign espionage on American trade secrets, but it was later expanded to cover domestic theft as well. Individuals found guilty under the law may be fined up to $500,000 and jailed for up to fifteen years, while corporations may be fined for up to $5 million. Foreign corporations' and governments' fines range as high as $10 million. As of April 2003, thirty-four prosecutions had taken place under this legislation.[79]

One of the first cases tried under the act involved a Taiwanese firm, the Yuen Foong Paper Manufacturing Company, and its attempt to gain the technology

for producing Taxol, a plant derivative used in the treatment of ovarian cancer, from Bristol-Myers Squibb in 1997. Developing the technology had cost
the drug firm $15 million. In a second case, also in 1997, another Taiwanese
company, Four Pillars Enterprises, was discovered to have paid an employee
of office products maker Avery Dennison for adhesive technology over the
course of a decade, costing the company $50 million.[80] Not only was Avery
Dennison awarded $5 million from the Taiwanese company, but it also
received an additional $80 million judgment in a civil case.[81] This new
emphasis on fighting economic espionage was handicapped by the shrinking number of counterespionage agents in the FBI, as noted earlier; their
numbers plummeted by roughly 30 percent after the fall of the Soviet Union.
By 1998, however, the Bureau began changing its focus in accordance with
Congress's mandate and had seven hundred economic espionage investigations in process. FBI director Freeh declared this problem "the biggest threat
to our national security since the Cold War." Meanwhile, Russian president
Boris Yeltsin was urging the SVRR to make efforts "to close the technology
gap with the West by more efficiently using industrial intelligence." Yeltsin
was concerned that not even one-quarter of the material Russian spies
acquired overseas had been used, even though it "derived directly from foreign blueprints." The Soviet's inability to put new technologies into practice
was an old problem: in the 1930s, Harry Gold's Soviet handlers insisted they
wanted not experimental designs, but "things that work."[82]

Today, of course, the FBI no longer regards espionage as the country's
"biggest threat." Since 1998, new and more pressing hazards have emerged.
Nevertheless, the Bureau's Web site currently lists fighting espionage as the
agency's second priority, after terrorism. At the same time, as evidence continues to accumulate regarding the technological pillaging carried out by
such countries as China and Russia, the FBI has added 167 counterintelligence agents and established a counterespionage operation in each of its
fifty-six field offices. While no doubt only more diverse challenges and crises
await America's chief law-enforcement agency, the government's concerns
about industrial espionage, especially in defense-related fields, are unlikely
to disappear. And although Russian espionage may no longer be as "bad" as
spying for countries that fall under President George W. Bush's so-called
"axis of evil," the contributions of Soviet-era espionage to the notion of an
America vulnerable to foreign infiltration and subversion seem very vivid
nonetheless.[83]

CONCLUSION

From the earliest days of the Republic, when Citizen Genet's intrigues against the Washington administration caused a scandal, to September 11, 2001, when terrorist attacks on New York's World Trade Center and the Pentagon stunned Americans and created a crisis that is still unfolding, national anxiety over the domestic influence of foreign conspirators and spies has seldom disappeared from American political culture. Even in the context of this long history, however, the suspicions that freighted U.S. relations with the Soviet Union beginning in World War II were of a most unusual duration and intensity. As late as 1971, Morton Sobell, released on probation from jail after nearly two decades and legally vindicated in his attempts to travel to antiwar protests, nevertheless remained under the FBI's watchful eye and in its security index, in part because of his "sympathy [for] the world communist movement." His peace activism no doubt appeared to underline such sympathies. "In time of national emergency," the Bureau declared, "he would represent a threat to the security of the U.S."[1] And as late as the Carter administration, with J. Edgar Hoover five years in his grave, his former agency also maintained the name of missing spy Joel Barr in the same security index, with an order at U.S. Customs to interdict him if he were to return to America. As FBI officials alleged, "Because of his previous work on behalf of the Soviets, it is believed he has the willingness and capability to engage in espionage."[2]

Although the danger posed to the United States by Sobell and Barr lived on in the minds of officials through the 1970s, new examples of Soviet espionage also abounded, as detailed in the previous chapter. In 1985, the arrest of the Walker ring of spies, whose longstanding and intergenerational practice of cryptographic espionage was said to be "the most important operation in the KGB's history," only confirmed the continued need for vigilance. And after the fall of the Soviet Union, the 1994 arrest of superspy Aldrich Ames provided further evidence of the enduring and dangerous phenomenon of the Soviet mole that had first surfaced fifty years earlier. So too did the detention of FBI agent and spy Robert Hanssen in 2001, a full decade after the collapse of Communist Russia.[3]

More than half a century before, in 1946, with revelations of espionage pouring in from sources like Gouzenko, Bentley, Chambers, and the Venona intercepts, FBI veterans of the COMRAP and CINRAD investigations had hardly needed additional evidence that Soviet spying, long a threat, had become an explosive and growing danger. Suspicions about the Soviet Union that had emerged among stalwarts of the counterintelligence community like J. Edgar Hoover were spreading even to "conciliatory" members of the State Department like Undersecretary Dean Acheson. Over at the White House, President Harry Truman, too, was fed up with "babying the Soviets." The Cold War had begun.[4]

The beginning of the Cold War is most often identified with the launching of an unparalleled anti-Communist crusade in America, but as this work has shown, such a crusade had its roots in the discovery of Soviet espionage during World War II. Few in the early years of the Cold War, however, recognized that counterintelligence agents had been pursuing Soviet spies— and even catching some—during wartime. The legal difficulties in effectively prosecuting these spies had the effect of convincing many that the issue had been ignored, or worse, suppressed, perhaps by the machinations of a duplicitous President Roosevelt. Kellis Dibrell told a newspaper in 1948 that when the FBI apprehended Steve Nelson with materials in his hands that "had to do with uranium," the Bureau's attempts to arrest the Communist agent were stopped when "the pussy-footing administration felt that it would create an unfriendly diplomatic incident if this Red agent were stopped in his tracks."[5] Dibrell, a former FBI agent, was not inaccurate about the delicacy of Soviet-American relations during the war. Yet as he should have known, the FBI had made no attempt to arrest Nelson in 1943 because it had no admissible evidence to do so. Similarly, two years later, in the wake of Elizabeth Bentley's accusations, Hoover "quietly" attempted to have those government employees she named fired rather than launch prosecutions that might go down in flames. Such secrecy meant that Bentley's charges were not heard publicly for three years. Indeed, the lack of evidence sufficient to meet the "high thresholds of the American criminal justice system," as John Earl Haynes and Harvey Klehr put it, contributed to a vitriolic debate in the country, with anti-Communists like Dibrell and Senator Joseph McCarthy charging that the government had ignored a clear menace, and skeptical academics continuing to see the lack of prosecutorial success as evidence that espionage allegations like Bentley's were unreliable and that little if any spying had occurred at all.[6]

The gist of Dibrell's accusations—a courageous FBI that was stymied by the pro-Soviet ethos of the war years and thwarted by mushy New Dealers in the White House—was itself a characteristic Cold War distortion of the government's wartime counterintelligence efforts against Russia. *Newsweek* epitomized this outlook by claiming in 1953, "The Communists had roamed the Federal precincts with ease until the Cold War began. Are they still at work?"[7] While the FDR administration certainly did not make the capture of Soviet spies a priority in the war, counterintelligence agents nevertheless monitored, harassed, and otherwise interfered with numerous Soviet spies. Lacking a comprehensive counterintelligence program, or evidence sufficient to prosecute those spies it did capture, the FBI was prevented at first from fully grasping, and then from adequately demonstrating, the extensive scope of Soviet infiltration in the war years and the early phase of the Cold War. Nevertheless, such initiatives as the Nelson, Adams, and Shevchenko surveillances and sting operations cemented the Bureau's growing concern about Soviet espionage and its indigenous connections and expanded the Bureau's investigatory apparatus after 1942.[8]

Perceptions of a lax wartime approach, however, were pervasive, and not just in the media. In the polarized environment of the Cold War, officials became increasingly strident in their criticism of the government's earlier counterintelligence response to the Soviet Union. Gen. John R. Deane, a former member of the American military mission in the USSR, pointed to FDR's March 1942 directive to supply the Soviet Union weapons of war above all other allies as "the beginning of a policy of appeasement of Russia from which we have never recovered."[9] A 1960 U.S. Army intelligence study, moreover, traced the problem back to the 1930s, and attributed the War Department's inability to counter Soviet espionage then to agents' preoccupation with competing Japanese and German espionage threats, while "communists continued their systematic infiltration and penetration of countless critical positions in industry and government—many of which would not pay off for another five years or more." During "these dismal years of American security," the document noted with anguish, "the FBI still lacked the authority to halt Communists as it had halted major crime."[10] Gen. Dwight D. Eisenhower, too, admonished his interwar predecessors for "a shocking deficiency that impeded all constructive planning . . . in the field of intelligence." The president blamed the problem on domestic culture: "The American public has always viewed with repugnance everything that smacks of the spy."[11]

Like the 1930s, counterintelligence during World War II was also "deficient," according to another Cold War observer, Richard Hirsch, author of *The Soviet Spies: The Story of Russian Espionage in North America* (1947). He informed members of the Truman administration's Psychological Strategy Board in 1952 that during the war "no action was taken on data readily available, and there was insensitivity to persistent violation of security rules." Hirsch's assessment reflects a widely held Cold War outlook on the war's inadequate security efforts, placing them in distressing contrast to the postwar era's more robust vigilance. This view has been accepted by scholars for decades. Twenty-five years ago, historian David Caute argued that "spy fever" originated in the Cold War, and as recently as 2003, Leonard Leshuk similarly identified a sharp break between the practices of World War II and the postwar era.[12] Such assessments largely overlook the efforts of a spy-obsessed FBI to hamper Communist agents and limit Soviet influence, especially in the atomic field, well before 1946—investigatory pressure that men like Feklisov, Hiskey, Kheifetz, Nelson, and Semyonov knew only too well. Reactions like Dibrell's, Deane's, Eisenhower's, and Hirsch's, though, certainly exemplify the intense Cold War reaction to wartime Soviet espionage and subversion, a response that led directly to that era's expansive security apparatus.

The 1930s, as Eisenhower was correct to note, were in contrast characterized by an open environment shaped by few security measures. Soviet agents took full advantage of this situation, assisted by many businessmen eager for orders. Moscow was free then to conduct a wide-scale effort to gather American industrial information from factory inspection tours and a network of strategically placed agents and contacts of the NKVD, both Russian and American. The limited U.S. response to this offensive in the decade of the Depression can be traced to an undeveloped security program, rooted in popular antipathy to manifestations of official investigatory power. After the war began in Europe, the declaration of an "emergency" in the United States vastly expanded the jurisdiction of internal security agencies like the FBI and soon led to the apprehension of such active spies as Gaik Ovakimian and Mikhail Gorin, even as many others, like Harry Gold and Jacob Golos, were overlooked.

After Pearl Harbor, Allied cooperation initially quashed counterintelligence efforts and fostered even greater access for Soviet agents to American military-industrial technology. In part, expanded access fulfilled the goals of the war: by materially supporting the industrial development of the Soviet Union, particularly in the area of aircraft and weapons technology, the United States made important contributions to the anti-Nazi effort. Even as Department of Justice officials and their counterparts at the War and Navy Departments pointed to the Soviets' insatiable appetite for information under lend-lease, the State Department and the Roosevelt administration rightly put a priority on good relations for the sake of Allied victory. Their commitment did bring Americans some concrete returns in information and access, especially as compared to those that Moscow granted the more suspicious and less helpful British.[13]

Notwithstanding the sensitive diplomacy of lend-lease and Allied relations, the FBI still succeeded in identifying a number of Soviet spies during World War II. And although FBI agent Robert Lamphere could lament at war's end that his agency was "not as knowledgeable or as sophisticated" as the Soviet intelligence service—and indeed it had failed to detect many of Moscow's most important agents—the Bureau's methods by that time were considerably more formidable than they had been earlier, as Soviet observers were the first to acknowledge.[14] Among members of the counterintelligence community, Soviet espionage had elicited a new approach in American relations with Russia.

In the immediate aftermath of the war, diplomatic considerations were initially deemed more important than catching Russian spies, as the unhindered departures of such agents as Andrei Shevchenko and Arthur Adams suggest. Strategic interests would soon change dramatically, as the nascent Cold War rapidly evaporated wartime unity and reluctance to offend the Russians. Soviet representatives had long been under tight surveillance, but in January 1946, Stepan Zakharovich Apresyan, Soviet vice consul in San Francisco, told Moscow that there had been a "sharp increase in the work of the FBI against [us]."[15] In March of that year, as Winston Churchill gave his Iron Curtain speech and Truman called for Russian troops to exit Iran, the FBI seized Lt. Nikolai Grigorevich Redin of the Soviet Purchasing Commission for military espionage in Portland.[16]

Nevertheless, not until the late 1940s, following the expansive probes of the Bentley and Gouzenko allegations, would the FBI broadly develop its army of investigative personnel and unleash a full arsenal of counterintelligence techniques in order to gain a better understanding of Soviet penetration of American military-industrial secrets and government agencies. Such

efforts signaled a far more comprehensive counterintelligence and counterespionage program at the Bureau than had been the case in World War II
or even its immediate aftermath. In 1947, when Lamphere transferred to FBI
headquarters to supervise cases in the espionage section of the Domestic
Intelligence Division, the section had only seven supervisors. By the end of
the decade, there were fifty. The threatening international atmosphere in the
late 1940s, signaled by the "fall" of China and the blast of the first Soviet
bomb, also led Director Hoover to push his agents to pursue their investigations and surveillance techniques more aggressively, to undertake additional
"black bag" operations, and to pressure more Eastern Europeans to defect.[17] In
February 1950, the same month that Joseph McCarthy read his famous "list"
of Communists in the government, the Bureau took offense at the campaign
of "an articulate minority to ridicule security"; this "minority" had compared
the work of investigative agencies to "witch hunts."[18] Its agents were no doubt
gratified when Truman urged Americans to cooperate with the FBI in its hunt
for spies and subversives after the outbreak of the Korean War (see illustra-
tion). But critics like Socialist Corliss Lamont did not hide their disgust with
Bureau methods: "Liberals and radicals throughout the U.S.A. are fearful that
the FBI is tapping their phone, has installed a secret microphone in their living room or car, opens their mail, or goes over the contents of their waste-
paper basket," he would complain in 1956.[19]

A year later, Senator McCarthy died of alcoholism, but Soviet espionage
remained a sobering prospect for many. In 1957, Russian scientists had
launched their first satellite, causing Americans to panic that the United
States had fallen behind the Soviet Union in military technology. For this
reason, Senators were eager to listen to the speculations of Lewisburg (Pa.)
Penitentiary chemist-in-residence Harry Gold, who informed his Sputnik-
shocked audience that Julius Rosenberg had told him during the war "that
the electronics industry of the Soviet Union was very, very poor . . . and that
Rosenberg was undertaking to get everything he possibly could to assist the
Soviets to build up their electronics system." Gold's old espionage contact,
machinist David Greenglass, also stepped out from behind bars to tell the
alarmed legislators that Rosenberg had told him after the war about obtaining material for Russia from "my boys" relating to a "space platform . . . a
closed vessel rotating as a satellite around the world." Lawmakers, seeing only
too clearly the links between these alleged espionage incidents and the creation of Sputnik, voted for a large increase in American defense spending.
Gold, however, was not discouraged about America's potential. Noting that

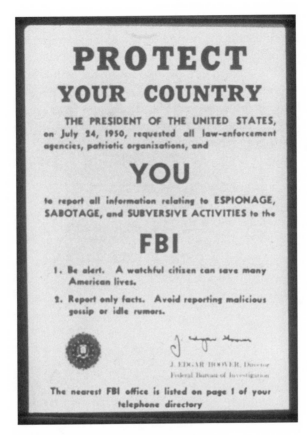

FBI poster, "Protect Your Country"

the Soviets "are waging a war on all fronts: it's espionage, it's diplomatic, and it is scientific," this Soviet expert still believed that "if we really wake up, we can fill the gap." Soon, of course, presidential candidate John F. Kennedy would be trumpeting another gap, a missile gap that, as it turned out, did not exist.[20]

In 1959, when membership in the CPUSA had dropped to a few thousand, a significant percentage of whom were FBI agents, members of the House Un-American Activities Committee remained concerned about "Communist Infiltration of Vital Industries and Current Communist Technique." As HUAC claimed, echoing J. Edgar Hoover's concern about the party "underground" ten years earlier, "the strategy and tactics of the Communist

Party are constantly changing for the purpose of avoiding detection and in an attempt to beguile the American people and the Government respecting the true nature of the conspiracy."[21] As events in the 1950s and after showed, an anti-Soviet outlook had quickly become official orthodoxy during the Cold War, not only among the counterintelligence community but the public's elected representatives as well. The discovery of Soviet spies in the war years continued to inflame the charged atmosphere of postwar America, leaving a legacy of suspicion that would last for decades.

ABBREVIATIONS IN TEXT AND NOTES

ACLU	American Civil Liberties Union
AEA	Atomic Energy Administration
AEC	Atomic Energy Commission
ATC	Amtorg Trading Corporation
BDM	British Diffusion Mission
BEW	Bureau of Economic Warfare
CINRAD	Communist Infiltration of the Radiation Laboratories, University of California, Berkeley
CIO	Congress of Industrial Organizations
COMRAP	Comintern Apparatus
COCOM	Coordinating Committee on Multilateral Export Controls
CPUSA	Communist Party, U.S.A.
DSS	Defense Security Service
DSM	Development of Substitute Materials
DOJ	Department of Justice
FDRL	Franklin Delano Roosevelt Library
FISA	Foreign Intelligence Surveillance Act
FARS	Foreign Agents Registration Section
FSU	Friends of the Soviet Union
G-2	U.S. Army Intelligence
HSOA	House Subcommittee on Appropriations
HSTL	Harry S. Truman Library
HUAC	House Committee on Un-American Activities
HUMINT	human intelligence
ILWU	International Longshoremen's and Warehousemen's Union
IMF	International Monetary Fund
IRR	Investigative Records Repository (RG 319)
JCAE	Joint Commission on Atomic Energy
JCS	Joint Chiefs of Staff
JRO	J. Robert Oppenheimer
MD	Morgenthau diary
MID	Military Intelligence Division
NACA	National Advisory Committee for Aeronautics
NARA	National Archives and Record Adminstration
NKGB	Soviet secret police (1943–46)

NKVD	Soviet secret police (1934–43)
NKVT	National Commissariat on Foreign Trade
NSA	National Security Agency
OF 10B	President's Official File 10B
OGPU/GPU	Soviet secret police (1923–34)
ONI	Office of Naval Intelligence
PSF	President's Secretary's File
RG	Record Group
RGAE	Russian State Archive of the Economy
RGASPI	Russian State Archive of Social and Political History
SACB	Subversive Activities Control Board
SAM	Substitute Alloy Material Lab
SCI	Systems Control Inc.
SHSW	State Historical Society of Wisconsin
SIGINT	signals intelligence
SIOP	Single Integrated Operation Plan
SVRR	Russian Foreign Intelligence Service
TASS	Telegraph Agency of the Soviet Union
WHCF	White House Confidential Files
WPB	War Production Board
YCL	Young Communist League

NOTES

INTRODUCTION

1. House Committee on International Relations, *Corporate and Industrial Espionage,* 1, 5.

2. See www.fbi.gov/priorities/priorities.htm (FBI Web site).

3. Schrecker, *Many Are the Crimes,* 166.

4. The act, whose name is an acronym for "Uniting and Strengthening America by Providing Appropriate Tools Required to Intercept and Obstruct Terrorism," was introduced less than a week after September 11. Because of the act, the government may more easily conduct surveillance on Americans and share between agencies the results of wiretaps and grand jury proceedings related to foreign intelligence or counterintelligence.

5. The notion of a clear division in U.S. attitudes and policies between World War II and the Cold War era is almost axiomatic in the literature of the postwar United States. See, for instance, Leshuk, *U.S. Intelligence Perceptions,* 254; Goldberg, *Enemies Within,* 25–26; Whittaker, "Cold War Alchemy," 177–80; Tanenhaus, *Chambers,* 203; Fariello, *Red Scare,* 24; Pessen, *Losing Our Souls,* 127; Hershberg, *Conant,* 265–66; Theoharis and Cox, *The Boss,* 222. For a lucid discussion of the scholarly tendency to downplay the contributions of World War II to American political and military institutions and ideologies, see Kimball, "Incredible Shrinking War," 347–65.

6. J. Edgar Hoover speech to American Legion's Annual Convention in San Francisco, September 30, 1946, file 2731, reel 235, ACLU Papers, Seeley Mudd Library. These "inroads" would be significantly reduced thereafter; the number of party members shrank from a peak of eighty thousand during the war to about three thousand by the late 1950s, in large part owing to FBI harassment and infiltration of the organization. The waning membership, of course, did not affect the director's publicly expressed concerns in the least.

7. On the role of German espionage in creating a more powerful and active FBI, see Batvinis, "In the Beginning," 2001. Batvinis focuses on the 1938 Rumrich case and the Duquesne case of 1940–42. Both are discussed in chapter 2.

8. FBI memo, June 2, 1940, box 12, OF 10B, FDRL. Few of these investigations, however, resulted in arrests. On the FBI's wartime expansion, see discussion in Theoharis and Cox, *The Boss,* chap. 9.

9. Batvinis, "In the Beginning," 340, chart 1; "Testimony of the Director before the House Subcommittee on Appropriations (HSOA) regarding the 1942 Regular and National Defense Appropriation Estimates of the FBI," 184, Appropriations Testimony,

FBI Office of Public Affairs. I am indebted to John Fox of the FBI for copies of these HSOA reports.

10. "Testimony of the Director on January 15, 1942, before the HSOA regarding the 1943 Appropriations Estimates for the FBI in the Amount of $29,636,787 (including a Supplemental 1943 National Defense Estimate in the Amount of $3,800,000)," 125; Davis, *Spying on America*, 29.

11. See Gallicchio, *African American Encounter*, chaps. 5 and 6, passim; Charles, "Informing FDR," 211–32; O'Reilly, *Hoover and the Un-Americans*, 23–25; Friedman, "There Goes the Neighborhood," 569–97, and "Nazis and Good Neighbors."

12. See Bernstein, "In the Matter of J. Robert Oppenheimer," 201. Bernstein acknowledges that security interviews were conducted with Oppenheimer in the war, yet begins his discussion of "earlier doubts about Oppenheimer" in 1947. Oppenheimer's wartime FBI file has recently received close attention in Herken's *Brotherhood*, especially chaps. 4–6. See also FBI JRO file, #1. *FBI file designations typically consist of three numbers separated by dashes: the classification number (61=treason, 65=espionage, 74=perjury, 100=domestic security); the case number; and the particular item number. References to FBI files in these notes are by the name of the file as it appears in the bibliography, followed by the number of the particular item that is cited (preceded by the symbol "#"). Furthermore, FBI files in the bibliography are arranged alphabetically under the FBI subheading, and each is followed by the classification and case number (e.g., the JRO files appears as "J. Robert Oppenheimer (100–17828)." Thus, "FBI JRO file, #1" is the equivalent of 100–17828–1. Multiple files on an individual are further distinguished here and in the bibliography by a letter enclosed in brackets (e.g., FBI Hiss-Chambers file [b], #3, which is the equivalent of 65–59549–3).*

13. See Albright and Kunstel, *Bombshell*, 94; Haynes and Klehr, *Venona*, 46.

14. Quoted in Sandilands, *Lauchlin Currie*, 149.

15. U.S. AEC, *In the Matter of J. Robert Oppenheimer*, 98.

16. Ibid., 358.

17. Books featuring such moles include, among others, Le Carré's *A Perfect Spy* (1986), *Tinker, Tailor, Soldier, Spy* (1974), and *The Spy Who Came in from the Cold* (1964), Frederick Forsyth's *The Fourth Protocol* (1985), Charles McCarry's *The Last Supper* (1983) and *The Miernik Dossier* (1973), Graham Greene's *The Human Factor* (1978), and Robert Littell's *The Defection of A. J. Lewinter* (1973).

18. Walsh interview, June 19, 2003.

19. Theoharis, *Chasing Spies*, 34; Peake interview, November 21, 2003.

20. Theoharis, *Chasing Spies*, 79–84; Schrecker, *Many Are the Crimes*, 174 (emphasis in original); Richard Gid Powers, "Introduction," to Moynahan, *Secrecy*, 49–55. Beyond the treatments of scholars like David Caute, who finds Bentley unreliable but at least discusses her claims (see his *The Great Fear*, 56–57), the whole subject of Soviet espionage in surveys of U.S. foreign relations has long been strikingly neglected. Robert Dallek's 670-page *Franklin Roosevelt and American Foreign Policy, 1932–1945* manages to omit the subject entirely, mentioning only German espionage, and a recent edition of Walter Lafeber's *America, Russia and the Cold War* names Bentley only once and says nothing about her case.

21. See, for example, White, *Hiss's Looking-Glass Wars;* Mark, "Who Was 'Venona's' 'Ales'?" 45–72; Haynes and Klehr, *In Denial;* Olmsted, *Red Spy Queen;* Schecter and Schecter, *Sacred Secrets;* Feklisov, *Man behind the Rosenbergs;* Romerstein and Breindel, *Venona Secrets;* Andrew and Mitrokhin, *Sword and the Shield;* Haynes and Klehr, *Venona;* Weinstein and Vassiliev, *Haunted Wood;* Albright and Kunstel, *Bombshell;* Tanenhaus, *Chambers;* Benson and Warner, *Venona;* Klehr et al., *Secret World.* These new assessments have not lacked detractors, including Boughton and Sandilands, "Politics and the Attack on FDR's Economists"; Lowenthal, "Venona and Alger Hiss"; Schrecker and Isserman, "The Right's Cold War Revisionism"; Wang, *American Science,* 291–94; and Schneir and Schneir, "Cryptic Answers," and "Cables Coming in from the Cold."

22. Lansdale-Oppenheimer interview, September 12, 1943, AEC, *In the Matter of JRO,* 873.

23. FBI report, "Soviet Espionage Activities," October 19, 1945, 10, FBI file, box 167, PSF, HSTL.

24. He and his wife had joined such suspected groups as the American League for Peace and Democracy and the League of Women Shoppers. See Haynes and Klehr, *Venona,* 131–33; Weinstein and Vassiliev, *Haunted Wood,* 161–62; Silvermaster investigation, November 16, 1945, November 26, 1945, FBI Silvermaster file, #26X2. Other substantiation of wartime suspicion of Silvermaster is in the March 29, 1943, to November 1, 1944, documentation included in the FBI's "Comintern Apparatus (COMRAP) Summary Report," San Francisco, FBI COMRAP file, #3702 (hereafter cited as "COMRAP Summary"); I am grateful to John Earl Haynes for a copy of this report. A later discussion, following Elizabeth Bentley's revelations about Silvermaster, is in "Silvermaster," attached to Hoover to Major Gen. Harry Hawkins Vaughan, February 1, 1946, FBI file, box 169, PSF, HSTL.

25. See reports of Silvermaster's information in Venona 1017, 1022 New York to Moscow, June 29–30, 1943; Venona 1469 New York to Moscow, October 17, 1944; Bentley, *Out of Bondage,* 98–99; Bentley testimony, in HUAC, *Hearings regarding Communist Espionage* (1948), 522–23; Bentley testimony, in Senate Committee on Expenditures, *Export Policy and Loyalty,* 14–15.

26. Venona 1388–1389 New York to Moscow October 1, 1944; Venona 14 New York to Moscow, January 4, 1945.

27. Venona 1456 Mikhailov to Director, September 8, 1943. Other evidence of their concern is in Venona 1431 New York to Moscow, September 2, 1943.

28. Venona 586 New York to Moscow, April 29, 1944.

29. Feklisov, *Man behind the Rosenbergs,* 105–6, 139.

30. Senate Select Committee, *Intelligence Activities,* bk. 2, 35–38, and *Supplementary Detailed Staff Reports,* bk. 3, 417. The NAACP investigation opened in 1941 after protests from African American mess attendants about conditions in the navy. The navy asked for the investigation that led to the FBI's spying on the NAACP to unearth its "connections with the Communist Party." The subsequent wartime investigation found "numerous contacts" between the NAACP and the CP, "but no evidence of CP control." See Rafalko, *Counterintelligence Reader,* 1:180–81.

31. See Charles, "Informing FDR," 232.

32. "COMRAP Summary," March 29, 1943, through Aug. 1, 1944, 3–4.

33. Whitehead, *FBI Story,* 228–29; Richard Gid Powers, *Secrecy and Power,* 271–72.

34. See Bradley F. Smith, *Sharing Secrets,* 186.

35. See, for instance, Martel, *Lend-Lease,* 53–54.

36. Chambers's allegations of Soviet espionage in the U.S. State and Treasury departments, as well as other New Deal–era agencies, first surfaced in a report he gave to A. A. Berle, head of State Department intelligence, in September 1939, as discussed in chapter 2. On Hoover's efforts to alert the White House, see "Memorandum for the Director," May 5, 1943, FBI Nelson file, #104; Hoover to White House, August 2, 1943, #157.

37. See Haynes and Klehr, *Venona,* 46.

38. Kansas City report, July 28, 1941, 5, FBI ATC file, #475.

39. J. Edgar Hoover to Harry Hopkins, May 7, 1943, cited in Warner and Benson, *Venona,* 49–50. The Soviet security agency was called the OGPU from 1923–34, the NKVD from 1934–43, and the NKGB for the rest of the war.

40. Comintern Apparatus report, May 7, 1943, 12, Nelson file, #112; "Recording No. 3, Nelson and 'X,' (Zubilin)," April 10, 1943, attached to D. M. Ladd to Director, Communist Infiltration at Radiation Laboratory (CINRAD) report, Nelson file, #201. See also FBI report, "Soviet Activities in the US," July 25, 1946, 21, box 15, Clifford Papers, HSTL; HUAC, *Report on Atomic Espionage,* 5.

41. See "Origin of Investigation," 3–5, 414–15, FBI Adams file, #715; CINRAD Summary Memo #1, March 5, 1946, 12, FBI CINRAD file, #2017 (hereafter cited as "CINRAD Summary." I am indebted to Gregg Herken for a copy of the latter report.

42. FBI report, "Soviet Activities in the US," 5.

43. Revel, *How Democracies Perish,* 161.

44. See Nicholas Lemann's profile of Dick Cheney, "The Quiet Man," in *The New Yorker,* May 7, 2001. Lemann cites the lasting influence of one of Cheney's college teachers, Yale historian H. Bradford Westerfield, who rued in 1963 that America, "buoyed by a congenital optimism" drawing from its "privileged historical experience," would be too late in developing a sense of the dangers of Communist inroads, whence "more and more Americans might conclude in panic that resistance was hopeless." Westerfield, *Instruments of America's Foreign Policy,* 2, 5.

CHAPTER 1

1. Oliphant to Henry Morgenthau Jr., November 13, 1933, and attached memo, November 8, 1933, Correspondence 1933–35, box 243, Morgenthau Papers, FDRL.

2. In doing so, scholars have often relied on the statements of such hard-line anti-Bolsheviks as Wilson's secretary of state, Bainbridge Colby, overlooking the way that his Republican successors, while equally committed to Wilsonian edicts on Moscow's illegitimacy, nevertheless slowly allowed for expanded trading opportunities with Russia. The view of Republican rigidity is best expressed in Wilson, *Ideology and Economics,* 29; Daniel M. Smith, *Aftermath of War,* 68; and William Appleman Williams, *American-Russian Relations,* 173. For an opposing view, see Siegel, *Loans and Legitimacy,* 4.

3. S. G. Bron, "Prospects of Soviet-American Trade," Report of the Chairman of the Board of Amtorg at the Presidium of the Supreme Council of National Economy of USSR, *Ekonomicheskya Zhizn*, June 10, 1928.

4. Sales were growing markedly: from $42 million in 1924 to $74 million in 1928 to $114 million in 1930. See American-Russian Chamber of Commerce, *Economic Handbook*, 352; Budish and Shipman, *Soviet Foreign Trade*, 10–11.

5. "Communist Activities," April 22, 1925, New York, FBI ATC file, #7.

6. "Memo for Mr. Hoover," [unreadable signature], April 28, 1925, ATC file, #10; "Communist Activities," May 5, 1925, New York, #8.

7. "Amtorg Trading Corp., Espionage," New York, May 24, 1941, 35, 49–53, ATC file, #319.

8. FBI report, November 27, 1945, 3, box 97, RG 233, NARA; J. Edgar Hoover to Adm. H. H. Hough, March 30, 1925, Mark Brooke to Hough, April 3, 1925, Hough to Brooke, April 6, 1925, Hoover to Brooke, September 17, 1925, file A8–5/EF61, RG 38, NARA; Col. James H. Reeves to Hoover, September 24, 1925, file 10110–G-42, RG 165, NARA; Streloff's report, 12–16, attached to W. R. Sayles to R. H. Grayson, December 16, 1926, file A-5/23, RG 38, NARA; "400 Smuggled Liberty Motors Traced to Soviet," *New York Herald Tribune*, November 26, 1930, box 8b, Gumberg Papers, SHSW. See also "Amtorg Trading Corp., Espionage," New York, May 24, 1941, 81–82, 84, ATC file, #319. It was illegal at the time to export Liberty Motors to Russia.

9. Simpson Thacher and Bartlett to Reeve Schley, January 22, 1930, box 7, Gumberg Papers; see also testimony from Louis Connick, Simpson Thacher, and Bartlett attorney, July 22, 1930, in House Committee on Rules, *Investigation into the Activities of Communists*, pt. 3, 3:91, 115–20.

10. House Committee on Rules, *Investigation into the Activities of Communists*, pt. 3, 3:118. See also 3:125–33 for a list of employees in 1930 and 3:135–207 for a list of visitors in 1929 and the first half of 1930.

11. Kelley memo, July 2, 1930, document file note, file 811.00B/1126, RG 59, NARA.

12. "Report on USA and USSR (Secret)," July 15 to August 15, 1930, *fond* 5240, *op.* 15c, *del.* 2283, *RGAE.*

13. Amtorg Trading Corp., May 3, 1929, re businessmen's trip to Russia, attached to M. Mendenson to Dvolaitsky, May 3, 1929, *fond* 413, *op.* 13, *del.* 100, *RGAE.*

14. House Committee on Rules, *Investigation into the Activities of Communists*, pt. 3, 3:113.

15. "Soviet Union as a Market for American Machinery," *Economic Review of the Soviet Union*, May 15, 1932, 224, *fond* 413, *op.* 13, *del.* 100, *RGAE.*

16. June 23, 1942, 9, FBI Feldman, Brandes, Ovakimian file, #743.

17. P. A. Foren to Glavmetall, Moscow, Attention Mr. Kalliballov, November 25, 1938, and Foren to Antipov, General Manager of the Gipromez, *fond* 7297, *op.* 16, *del.* 1, *RGAE.*

18. FBI report, New York, June 21, 1941, 8–9, Amtorg file, #372.

19. Amtorg press release, April 12, 22, 1929, *fond* 413, *op.* 13, *del.* 100, *RGAE.*

20. *Economic Review of the Soviet Union*, October 1, 1931; "Soviet Union as a Market for American Machinery," ERSU, May 15, 1932, 221–22.

21. See Weinstein and Vassiliev, *Haunted Wood*, 26.

22. Jerome Davis, "What Businessmen Think of Recognition," *The Nation*, May 18, 1932, *fond* 413, *op.* 13, *del.* 99, 567, 565, *RGAE*.

23. HUAC, *Investigation of Un-American Propaganda Activities* (1939), 9:5811.

24. Intelligence report, January 30, 1945, file 113673, Evaluation B-3, in Intelligence Reports ("Regular Series"), 1941–45, box 1288, entry 16, RG 226, NARA.

25. See Felix Cole, chargé d'affaires ad interim, Riga, to Secretary of State, Dispatch No. 438, June 10, 1932, Enclosure No. 12: "V. V. Kuibyshev's Report at the Seventeenth Conference of the All-Union Communist Party on the Second Five Year Plan," *Pravda*, February 8, 1932, reel 7, file 861, RG 59, NARA.

26. "Structure of Financial Capital in the USA," Planning and Economic Board of Amtorg, *fond* 413, *op.* 13, *del.* 775, *RGAE*; see also Ia. M. Budish, "Economic Review for 1935" attached to letter of B. Procin to Tov. Kaminsky, Trade Representative, NKVT, February 21, 1936, *fond* 413, *op.* 13, *del.* 3389, and Amtorg's Economic Bureau's study of American aviation, January 1939, *fond* 413, *op.* 13, *del.* 2145. On machine construction, see *Economic Review of the Soviet Union*, December 16, 1938, *fond* 413, *op.* 13, *del.* 2144.

27. E. H. Hunter to Commander Charles H. Shaw, September 9, 1932, file A8–5/EF61, RG 38, NARA. For a sampling of Soviet visits to plants, see files 307–W-3 through 307–W-70, RG 165, NARA.

28. Standley and Ageton, *Admiral Ambassador*, 39–40.

29. Rafalko, *Counterintelligence Reader*, 1:151.

30. House Committee on Rules, *Investigation into the Activities of Communists*, pt. 1, 4:2.

31. *New York Times*, May 4, 1930, 28; Corson and Crowley, *New KGB*, 299.

32. House Committee on Rules, *Investigation into the Activities of Communists*, pt. 3, 3:76.

33. Fish Committee, quoted by Hugh Cooper at American-Russian Chamber of Commerce luncheon, January 30, 1931, box 21, Gumberg Papers, SHSW. The American-Russian Chamber of Commerce, composed mainly of large manufacturing interests, had appointed a committee of its top officials to meet with Commerce Secretary Thomas P. Lamont to alert the government to the documents' lack of authenticity. See Reeve Schley to Robert P. Lamont, May 19, 1930, and S. R. Bertron, Allen Wardwell, Hugh L. Cooper, and H. H. Dewey to Members of the American-Russian Chamber, June 14, 1930, box 21, Gumberg Papers; Gumberg to Louis Fischer, August 20, 1930, box 8b, Gumberg Papers. See also "Report on USA and USSR (Secret)," July 15 to August 15, 1930, *RGAE*.

34. "Amtorg Trading Corp., Espionage," New York, May 24, 1941, 84–86, ATC file, #319; May 5, 1941, 3, #316.

35. House Committee on Rules, *Investigation into the Activities of Communists*, pt. 1, 4:209–12; "Amtorg Trading Corp., Espionage," New York, May 24, 1941, 87, Amtorg file, #319.

36. J. V. Ogan, Office of Naval Intelligence, by direction of Director of Naval Intelligence to Assistant Chief of Staff, G-2, [1930], file 2515–D-135/1, RG 165, NARA.

37. "The Pattern of Soviet Espionage in the United States," June 5, 1947, 5, file 383.4 USSR, Army Intelligence Project Decimal File, RG 319, NARA. See House Committee on Rules, *Investigation into the Activities of Communists*, pt. 3, 3:45; and Andrew and Gordievsky, *KGB*, 174–75.

38. House Committee on Rules, *Investigation into the Activities of Communists*, pt. 3, 3:43; "Amtorg Trading Corp., Espionage," New York, May 5, 1941, 4, ATC file, #316.

39. Editorial comment on report of Fish Committee, 88, *fond* 413, *op.* 13, *del.* 101, *RGAE*. See additional negative commentary in "Still the Fish Committee Nonsense!" ACLU pamphlet, May 1932, at www.debs.indstate.edu/a505s75_1932.pdf. The committee singled out the ACLU for its "'work to uphold Communists in spreading revolutionary propaganda and inciting revolutionary activities to undermine our American institutions.'"

40. Goodman, *The Committee*, 9. The lack of relations, of course, had not stopped the famous *Buford* deportation of 1919, with Emma Goldman among its passengers.

41. Hoover to Attorney General, January 2, 1932, cited in Rafalko, *Counterintelligence Reader*, 1:159.

42. "Report on USA and USSR (Secret)," July 15 to August 15, 1930, *RAEG*.

43. U.S. passports were very desirable, since many naturalized American immigrants also had foreign-sounding names and accents. As Whittaker Chambers wrote, without "boots," or passports, "a spy can get nowhere." Chambers, "The Soviet Passport Racket," 1938, manuscript submitted to journalist Herbert Solow but never published, box 25, Sam Tanenhaus Papers, Hoover Institution, Stanford, California (hereafter Tanenhaus Papers); *New York Times*, April 24, 1934.

44. In 1929, when Tilton was recalled to Moscow (and replaced by Mark Zilbert), he brought Dozenberg with him. For the next few years, Dozenberg worked to establish Soviet military intelligence operations in such countries as Germany, Rumania, and China until he broke with the Soviet Union in 1938. Dozenberg statement, November 8, 1949, in HUAC, *Hearings regarding Communist Espionage* (1951), 3540–41.

45. See "COMRAP Summary," 146–47; Dozenberg, later convicted in Earl Browder's passport fraud case, was sent to prison.

46. House Committee on Un-American Activities, *Hearings regarding Steve Nelson*, 186.

47. Alfred T. Smith, "Memorandum for the Chief of Staff," May 20, 1931, file 10110–2634/7, RG 165, NARA; Philip R. Faymonville to Chief of Ordnance, April 28, 1931, NYOD 201/11469 Dunckel Ralph L.

48. Assistant Attorney General Nugent Dodds to Pierre de L. Boal, May 30, 1932, file 811.108 Kantor, Solomon, et al./2, RG 59, NARA. See also Dallin, *Soviet Espionage*, 397–99.

49. Fred J. Edgar report, attached to R. B. Nathan, Acting Special Agent in Charge, Detroit Office, to director, FBI, August 29, 1932, attached to Nugent Dodds to Secretary of the Navy, September 8, 1932, file A8–2 QM/ Fred J. Edgar/Activities of Amtorg Trading Corp. file 202600–2806, RG 38, NARA.

50. See ibid.; Nugent Dodds to William Larson, July 22, 1932, file 2801–107/3, RG 165, NARA; Special Agent in Charge in Detroit to the Director of the Bureau of Investigation, July 14, 1932, September 8, 1932, file A8–2/QM/ Fred J. Edgar/Activities of Amtorg Trading Corp., file 202600–2806, RG 38, NARA.

51. R. B. Nathan, Acting Special Agent in Charge, Detroit Office, to director, FBI, August 29, 1932, attached to Nugent Dodds to Secretary of the Navy, September 8, 1932; Fred J. Edgar report, attached to Nathan to Director, August 29, 1932.

52. V. J. Dixon to Commandant, Ninth Naval District, August 29, 1932, Activities of

Amtorg Trading Corp., A8–2/QM/Amtorg Trading Corp, RG 38, NARA ; Fred J. Edgar report, attached to Nathan to Director, August 29, 1932.

53. Ellis to Commanding Officer, Submarine Base, New London, July 26, 1932, Director of Naval Intelligence Hayne Ellis to Commandant, Third Naval District, July 26, 1932, Activities of Amtorg Trading Corp., A8–2/QM/Amtorg Trading Corp., RG 38, NARA.

54. W. B. Phillips, Commandant Third Naval District, to the Chief of Naval Operations (Director of Naval Intelligence), April 24, 1936, A8–5/P9–2/Amtorg, RG 38, NARA.

55. Paul Paschal to Colonel Smith, November 9, 1932, Edward L. King to Chief of Staff, November 5, 1932, file 10110–2708, RG 165, NARA.

56. Special Agent M. H. Purvus, Chicago, to Director, Division of Investigation, May 28, 1932, cited in Rafalko, *Counterintelligence Reader*, 1:153.

57. See chapter 2 of Spolansky, *Communist Trail.*

58. MacArthur to King, November 14, 1932, King to MacArthur, November 5, 1932, file 10110–2708, RG 165, NARA.

59. While occasionally picking up Russian intelligence in pursuit of Japanese and German traffic, these efforts "remained infrequent and unsystematic" until World War II. See Alvarez, *Secret Messages,* 200.

60. Rafalko, *Counterintelligence Reader,* 1:153.

61. Sales fell from $104 million in 1931 to $12.6 million the following year. See American-Russian Chamber of Commerce, *Handbook of the Soviet Union,* 352.

62. Alter to I.N. Matveef, VP, Amtorg, November 12, 1941, Alter to ARCC, Oct 19, 1931, *fond* 413, *op.* 13, *del.* 99, *RGAE.*

63. Materials on Trade and Economic Relations with USA, April 12, 1931, 95, *fond* 413, *op.* 13, *del.* 101, *RGAE.*

64. Resolution of the meeting of the Press Department of the trade policy sector of NKVT on the activities of the Amtorg press, on report of Tov. Mendelson, June 30, 1931, 71, *fond* 413, *op.* 13, *del.* 99, *RGAE.*

65. Pavlov to Mendelson, January 29, 1931, 96, *fond* 413, *op.* 13, *del.* 96, *RGAE.* Of course, Dewey would not be sympathetic to Stalin's regime for long; in April 1937 he chaired a skeptical inquiry in Coyoacan, Mexico, into the Moscow trial of Leon Trotsky.

66. See, for instance, Purchases of principal groups of commodities, 110, *fond* 413, *op.* 13, *del.* 96, *RGAE.*

67. "Support and Defend the Soviet Union: Demand Recognition"; "Bonchi Friedman to All FSU Secretaries," December 2, 1932, 35, 37, *fond* 515, *op.* 1, *del.* 3027, *RGAE.*

68. "Report of N.H. Tallentire on National Speaking Tour for FSU, December 21, 1931 to April 23, 1932, inclusive," 50 ("Gen. Situation"), *fond* 515, *op.* 1, *del* 2977, *RGAE.*

69. Bennett, *Franklin D. Roosevelt,* 22–23.

70. *Economic Review of the Soviet Union,* January 1934, *fond* 413, *op.* 13, *del.* 1792, *RGAE;* on the earlier trade figures, which reached nearly $140 million in 1930, see discussion in Siegel, *Loans and Legitimacy,* 104.

71. Litvinov to chargé d'affaires August 4, 1937, *fond* 413, *op.* 13, *del.* 2134, *RGAE; New York Times,* August 7, 1938, box 9, RG 233, Dies Committee files, NARA.

72. Economic Dept of Amtorg, Ia. M. Budish, June 7, 1935, *fond* 413, *op.* 13, *del.* 3475, *RGAE.*

73. James B. Turner, "USSR in Construction," *Soviet Russia Today,* November 1935, 52, 56.

74. "Stalin on the Problem of Technique," *Economic Review of the Soviet Union,* January 1935, 4–5, box 2, RG 233, NARA. The Soviet Union experienced great gains in 1934, with a 22.2 percent increase in coal production from the previous year, and 37 percent increase in rolled steel (15). That same year, *Economic Review* reported that more than 40 percent of all tourists to Russia came from the United States.

75. Anna Louise Strong, "Two Economic Systems," *Soviet Russia Today,* November 1935, 32.

76. Weinstein and Vassiliev, *Haunted Wood,* 37.

77. "The Pattern of Soviet Espionage in the United States," June 5, 1947, 17, file 383.4 USSR, Army Intelligence Project Decimal File, RG 319, NARA.

78. June 23, 1942, 105, 162, FBI Feldman file, #743. Agents would be paid from $40–$75 for each "occasion" when material was obtained.

79. Senate Judiciary Committee, *Scope of Soviet Activity,* 1022–23; Gold, "The Circumstances Surrounding My Work as a Soviet Agent—A Report," in *Scope of Soviet Activity,* 1064 (hereafter cited as Gold, "Circumstances"). This report was excerpted from a 110–page handwritten report that Gold had given his lawyers in October 1950. See discussion in Radosh and Milton, *Rosenberg File,* 490n 23. Later in the decade, when Gold's industrial contacts proved less fruitful, he was reassigned temporarily to political espionage and ordered to find Trotskyite conspirators in Philadelphia, including a music teacher and a pharmacist. See *Scope of Soviet Activity,* 1020–21.

80. Andrew and Mitrokhin, *Sword and the Shield,* 131.

81. Kilmarx, *History of Soviet Air Power,* 163–65.

82. "National Defense," n.d. [ca. 1934], file 3850 USSR, RG 165, NARA.

83. Von Hardesty, "Early Flight in Russia," in Higham et al., *Russian Aviation,* 23.

84. See Melville, *Russian Face of Germany,* 78–79; translations from *Neue Berliner Zeitung, 8 Uhr Adenblatt,* and *B.Z. am Mittag,* Edward Carpenter, Military Attache, G-2 Report, Russia (Political) Subject: Soviet Espionage, June 14, 1928, 9944–D-38, file 2515–D-135/1, Correspondence of the MID, RG 165, NARA; Bergier, *Secret Armies,* 43.

85. See Stapfer, *Polikarpov Fighters,* 10. Also see John T. Greenwood, "The Designers: Their Design Bureaux and Aircraft," in Higham et al., *Russian Aviation,* 166. On comparisons with the I-16, see Nowarra, *Russian Fighter Aircraft,* 30.

86. Kilmarx, *Soviet Air Power,* 161.

87. Scanlon memorandum, Nov. 19, 1937, file 2090–319/2, RG 165, NARA. Kilmarx asserts that twenty American aircraft firms provided materials for the Soviet Union in this period. Among the planes purchased in the United States were the Seversky Pursuit Plane-U.S. Army P-35, Republic and Sikorsky amphibians, Douglas DC-2 Transport, Consolidated Long-range Flying Boat, and the Martin Ocean Transport.

88. Kilmarx, *Soviet Air Power,* 157; USSR Combat Estimate, 1938, February 15, 1939, U.S. Army Regional file USSR 9000, RG 165, NARA.

89. Reina Pennington, "From Chaos to the Eve of the Great Patriotic War, 1922–1941," in Higham et al., *Russian Aviation,* 41–42; "Aviation in Russia," for MID, May 1936, U.S. Army Regional file USSR 9000, RG 165, NARA.

90. *Economic Review of the Soviet Union,* January 1934, *fond* 413, *op.* 13, *del.* 1792, *RGAE.*

91. Luncheon, American-Russian Chamber of Commerce, Bankers Club, April 22, 1936, 66, *fond* 413, *op.* 13, *del.* 3389, *RGAE.*

92. Chargé d'Affaires ad interim of the USSR at Washington to the Secretary of State, December 11, 1935, December 30, 1935, W-47–3, W-47–5.

93. See C. M. Thiele to Commanding Officer, August 2, 1934, 307–W-10/2; Brig. Gen. H. J. Brees to C. Burnett, March 16, 1936, 307–W-8/7; C. Burnett to Paul Y. Oras, December 13, 1934, 307–W-10/7. On visits to bases and other military installations, see files 307–W-8/51 through /147, RG 165, NARA.

94. Zhuralev report, March 7–12, 1938, *fond* 7516, *op.* 2, *del.* 131, *RGAE.*

95. Director of Naval Intelligence to Director, Military Intelligence Division, October 14, 1935, file 183–Z-225/2, RG 165, NARA.

96. A.W. Brock Jr. to Chief of the Air Corps, July 8, 1936, 307–W-12/26; G. J. Brew to War Department General Staff, July 25, 1936, 307–W-12/25.

97. Larsen to War Department, Air Corps, December 21, 1934, 307–W-12/8.

98. C. Burnett to V. A. Burzin, March 13, 1936, J. D. Reardan to Foreign Liaison Officer, March 12, 1936, file 307–W-58/3, -58/2, RG 165, NARA; C. Burnett to Brig. Gen. H. J. Brees, March 23, 1936, 307–W-8/58.

99. V. A. Burzin to J. B. Coulter, April 7, 1936, Coulter to Burzin, April 17, 1936, files 307–W-8/59, /61, RG 165, NARA. On Aberdeen, see the discussion of Victor Franklin Reno below.

100. Secretary of War Harry H. Woodring to Everett L. Garner, White Motor Company, Indiana, June 8, 1937; Charles A. Walker, War Department, Ordnance Office, to Assistant Chief of Staff, G2, May 29, 1937, and handwritten note (signed H. B. R.), files 307–W-8/91, /81, RG 165, NARA.

101. E. R. W. McCabe to Secretary, General Staff, August 10, 1937, Begunov to Coulter, August 11, 1937, Coulter to Begunov, August 12, files 307–W-71/132, /135, /137, RG 165, NARA.

102. FBI report, New York, June 21, 1941, 1–5, 9, 22, ATC file, #372.

103. It was proved that although the documents had been typed on his typewriter, he had not mailed them. Instead, Robert Gordon Switz had. See Dallin, *Soviet Espionage,* 399–400; Kern, *Death in Washington,* 210. On the case see P.F. (Personnel File) 60379, Army Intelligence Project Decimal File, RG 319, NARA; FBI Levine file, 65–14720, 65–57792–48, in box 25, Tanenhaus Papers; Associated press report, March 20, 1934; Assistant Secretary of State R. Walton Moore to Secretary of War, August 11, 1934, file 351.1121 Switz, Robert/72, RG 59, NARA; U.S. Army Intelligence Center, *History of the Counter Intelligence Corps,* 59–60. Louis Waldman, Osman's lawyer, also discusses the case in his book *Labor Lawyer.* Whittaker Chambers sent $500 to the family of Switz after he was arrested in Paris. "Unknown Subject, 'Bill,' 'Johann,'" January 15, 1951, 1, 3, FBI Hiss-Chambers file [b], #3, in box 36, Tanenhaus Papers. After Switz served nine months in jail in France, he was deported back to the United States and became an informant for the FBI, sharing his knowledge of espionage at army bases until 1951. In the late 1930s, when he was already assisting the Bureau, its agents failed to learn about his earlier links

with Chambers, thus missing a chance to learn more about espionage in the government. Peake interview, November 21, 2003.

104. Luncheon, American-Russian Chamber of Commerce, Bankers Club, April 22, 1936, 66.

105. Luncheon Address by Troyanovsky, American-Russian Chamber of Commerce, May 25, 1938, *fond* 413, *op.* 13, *del.* 2134, *RGAE.*

106. Luncheon, American-Russian Chamber of Commerce, Bankers Club, April 22, 1936, 66.

107. See contract, February 25, 1935, *fond* 413, *op.* 13, *del.* 3543, *RGAE*; Kaganovich to Mikoyan regarding agreements with United Engineering and Foundry (1935–38) *fond* 7297, *op.* 17, *del.* 3, *RGAE.*

108. Dewey to Fin Sparre, April 19, 1929, accession 1662, box 35, Du Pont Papers, Hagley Museum and Library, Wilmington, Delaware.

109. See Siegel, *Loans and Legitimacy,* 130.

110. News from Amtorg, April 29, 1929; see also April 26, 1929, press release, *fond* 413, *op.* 13, *del.* 100, *RGAE.*

111. RCA agreement, September 20, 1935, signed by I. V. Boyeff, Chairman of Amtorg; R. G. Baker to Amtorg, April 23, 1935; David Sarnoff to Mr. Boyeff, October 2, 1935; all in *fond* 413, *op.* 13, *del.* 1046, *RGAE.*

112. J. A. Marcus to I. P. Serpkov, NKTP (Commissariat of Heavy Industry), October 12, 1938, *fond* 7297, *op.* 28, *del.* 128, *RGAE.*

113. Rosov memo, May 25, 1938, unsigned letter to E. D. Chvialev, "The Problems with Trade Relations with the Soviet Union," July 9, 1938, *fond* 413, *op.* 13, *del.* 2134, *RGAE.*

114. Andrew and Gordievsky, *KGB,* 81. On the Comintern's underground organizations, see also Klehr et al., *Secret World,* 20–21. On this topic, see also Valtin, *Out of the Night,* chap. 4, passim.

115. "COMRAP Summary," 4.

116. Chambers article, "Unpublished Ms. of 1938 on Soviet Espionage," by "Karl." Chambers submitted the article to Herb Solow, the author of a *New York Sun* series on the arrest in Moscow of an American couple, agents Arnold Ikal, aka Adolph Arnold Rubens and Donald Robinson, and his wife, who in the United States had been involved in the provision of false passports for Soviet representatives. Solow declined to publish Chambers's article because it lacked names. Ikal, along with Gen. Berzin, the former GRU chief, and Philip Rosenbliett, who had been a close contact of Chambers, were all charged as Trotskyists during the purges. Ikal died in a Soviet camp; Berzin, who led a Soviet military mission to Spain during its civil war, was executed; Rosenbliett provided dental services to privileged Soviet officials until being exiled to Novosibirsk in 1941. Ikal's wife was released but did not return to the United States. See box 25, Tanenhaus Papers; Haynes and Klehr, *Venona,* 84, and Haynes e-mail message, July 21, 2004; Andrew and Gordievsky, *KGB,* 173; Tanenhaus, *Chambers,* 126, 131.

117. "Unknown Subject, 'Bill,' 'Johann,'" January 15, 1951, 2, Hiss-Chambers file [b], #3, in box 36, Tanenhaus Papers; FBI report, February 21, 1950, 2, Levine file, #48; Tanenhaus, *Chambers,* 81–83.

118. James Bell, ms. for *Time,* 1949, box 36, Tanenhaus Papers.

119. See September 23, 1952, Hiss-Chambers file [d], #66; Hoover memo to the Attorney General, January 5, 1949, box 25, Tanenhaus Papers.

120. May 17, 1949, 375, May 11, 1949, 48–49, Hiss-Chambers file [c], #3220, #3221.

121. February 21, 1950, 3, Levine file [b], #48; "Unknown Subject, 'Bill,' 'Johann,'" January 15, 1951, 1–6, Hiss-Chambers file [b], #3, in box 36, Tanenhaus Papers.

122. Anderson testimony, January 31, 1949, Miller testimony, February 2, 1949, FBI Miller file, #2; and report, March 29, 1949, #3; all in box 25, Tanenhaus Papers. Later, Chambers was approached by Rosenbliett for blueprints on shell-loading equipment, but Bykov told Chambers to stay away from the dentist. See March 29, 1949, 5, Miller file, #3.

123. February 21, 1950, 3, Levine file, #48.

124. HUAC, Investigation of Propaganda Activities (1939), 9:5742.

125. Tanenhaus, Chambers, 111, 124. Chambers's allegations of Soviet sources at the State Department—if not their names—have been confirmed in the CPUSA archives in Moscow. See Klehr et al., Secret World, 110–18.

126. "FBI Chambers Allegations and Investigations Collected since November, 1948," April 15, 1949, box 25, Tanenhaus Papers. An FBI examination of the WPA records confirmed that Chambers held this job.

127. Ibid. Florence Tompkins, Silverman's maid, recalled the delivery of three rugs to the residence; she also recalled that White, Gregory Silvermaster, Ludwig Ullmann, and Priscilla Hiss were friends of the Silvermans. The rug story is convincingly detailed in Weinstein, Perjury, 212–16.

128. Tanenhaus, Chambers, 115; H. B. Fletcher to Mr. D. M. Lord, December 20, 1948, Hiss-Chambers file [a]; FBI report, Edwin O. Johnson, December 12, 1948, Hiss-Chambers file [c], #195; FBI report, SAC Denver to Director FBI, June 21, 1949, box 54, Tanenhaus Papers.

129. Reno's statement to FBI, December 13, 1948, was made after he had at first denied any connection with Chambers and then returned a day later to change his story. See FBI report, SAC Denver to Director FBI, June 21, 1949.

130. FBI background on Reno, box 54, Tanenhaus Papers. However, one of Reno's colleagues at Aberdeen, Herman Louis Meyers, remembered him as a man with a drinking problem. Moreover, he asserted that the material Reno gave Chambers was "worthless," with the firing tables dating from World War I. See Meyer interview, July 31, 1962, box 54, Tanenhaus Papers.

131. This was described as a "schematic drawing of the range trail diagram with a bar across the top." See FBI memo, December 13, 1948, and FBI report, November 7, 1949, box 54, Tanenhaus Papers; see also FBI report, December 20, 1948, FBI interview with Reno, March 1949, and FBI report, Edwin O. Johnson, December 12, 1948 (all in box 54, Tanenhaus Papers), and discussion in Weinstein, Perjury, 236–37.

132. Reno's statement to FBI, December 13, 1948; see also FBI report, SAC Denver to Director FBI, June 21, 1949, 15, 17.

133. FBI report, SA Frederick A. Johns, February 11, 1949, box 54, Tanenhaus Papers.

134. Reno's statement to FBI, December 13, 1948; FBI report, SAC Denver to Director FBI, June 21, 1949, 16; FBI report, Edwin O. Johnson, December 12, 1948.

135. Reno's statement to FBI, December 13, 1948; FBI report, SAC Denver to Director FBI, June 21, 1949, 18.

136. FBI interview with Reno, March 1949, 7–8; FBI report, December 20, 1948; FBI report, Edwin O. Johnson, December 12, 1948, 4. Poyntz, a longtime Communist activist, disappeared after leaving her apartment in early June 1937, shortly after a visit to Russia that had disillusioned her faith in the Soviet regime. She was almost certainly murdered by the NKVD. See discussion in Tanenhaus, *Chambers,* 131–33.

137. FBI report, SA Frederick A. Johns, February 11, 1949.

138. See coverage in *Denver Post,* February 27, 1952; *Washington Post,* July 2, 1952; *New York Times,* July 3, 1952; all in box 54, Tanenhaus Papers.

139. Gold, "Circumstances," 1013, 1018, 1066.

140. Ibid., 1060–62.

141. Ibid., 1063–64.

142. Black never did get to Russia; see his testimony in *Scope of Soviet Activity,* 1114–15. On Black, see also Venona 1430 New York to Moscow, October 10, 1944; Venona 1055 Kvasnikov to Fitin, July 5, 1945; Weinstein and Vassiliev, *Haunted Wood,* 174; Radosh and Milton, *Rosenberg File,* 29; Haynes and Klehr, *Venona,* 290–91; Gold, "Circumstances," 1063–64; *New York News,* May 18, 1956, FBI Rosenberg file [a], #234, and interview with Abraham Brothman, "Investigation of Original Allegations," May 29, 1947, FBI Brothman file, #47. Black also received information from Frank Jones Dziedzic; who also worked at National Oil Products Company.

143. Gold, "Circumstances," 1018, 1064.

144. Radosh and Milton, *Rosenberg File,* 25–29; Gold, "Circumstances," 1046.

145. Gold, "Circumstances," 1059–60.

146. Ibid., 1014–15.

147. See Radosh and Milton, *Rosenberg File,* 26–29; Gold testimony, *Scope of Soviet Activity,* 1016; Gold, "Circumstances," 1055; memorandum, interview with Harry Gold, October 16, 1957, in *Scope of Soviet Activity,* 4842.

148. "Summary Brief on Fuchs and Gold," February 12, 1951, Fuchs file, #1494X, 138.

149. Gold testimony, *Scope of Soviet Activity,* 1022; "Circumstances," 1071; memorandum, interview with Harry Gold, October 16, 1957, *Scope of Soviet Activity,* 4842.

150. Firms like Du Pont had been selling processes to the Soviet Union since 1929 and charging the Soviets a fraction of the development cost for the process. For example, Du Pont sold Chemstroi, the Soviet chemical agency, its process for ammonia oxidation, used in the making of fertilizer, for $150,000; researching and developing the process had cost the chemical giant $27 million. See Fin Sparre to T. S. Grasselli, March 21, 1930, president to Sparre, April 4, 1930, accession 1813, box 2, Willis F. Harrington Papers, Hagley Museum and Library; see also Sutton, *Western Technology,* 212–13.

151. Gold, "Circumstances," 1071, 1023.

152. Gold's boss at the sugar company, Gustav Reich, related that Gold worked on flue gas (for dry ice) from 1936–39, then on yeast fermentation, and finally on grain alcohol distillation to make synthetic rubber and solvents. See "Facts Concerning American Espionage Contact, Summary of Facts, Jurisdiction, Collaboration with British," in Fuchs file, #1494X, 181. Gold also attempted to recruit others to this work of helping the Soviet

Union during this time, as Radosh and Milton discuss in *Rosenberg File*, 26–29. See also Gold, "Circumstances," 1019.

153. Gold, "Circumstances," 1017–23, 1026. On Smilg, see also Weinstein and Vassiliev, *Haunted Wood*, 27.

154. "COMRAP Summary," 149.

155. Muir, "American Warship Construction," 337; Maddux, *Years of Estrangement*, 85; Bennett, *Franklin D. Roosevelt*, 117–18.

156. Maddux, *Years of Estrangement*, 86–87; Maddux, "United States-Soviet Naval Relations," 29–35, passim.

157. Joseph Green, head of the Office of Arms and Munitions Control, quoted in Muir, "American Warship Construction," 346 (see also the discussion on 344–46); Maddux, "United States-Soviet Naval Relations," 33–35; Joseph E. Davies, "Memorandum of Conference Had This Fifth Day of June, 1938, with Mr. Stalin, President Kalinin, and Premier Molotov, in the Kremlin at Moscow," Diplomatic Correspondence, Russia, 1937–1940, box 49, PSF, FDRL; Meeting between Morgenthau and Umanskii, June 30, 1939, Morgenthau diary (hereafter MD), 199:429–37, Morgenthau Papers, FDRL.

158. Muir, "American Warship Construction," 350–51; Bennett, *Franklin Delano Roosevelt*, 136.

159. Scott Ferris to J. Z. Dalinda, March 15, 1939, box 6, Dies Committee files. The U.S. "emergency" of 1939–41 is discussed further in the next chapter.

160. O. S. Wood to Assistant Chief of Staff, G2, San Francisco, December 14, 1936, file 307–W-84/7, RG 165, NARA.

161. Martin F. Scanlon memorandum, November 19, 1937, file 2090–319/2, Correspondence of the MID, RG 165, NARA.

162. HUAC, *Un-American Propaganda Activities* (1939), 9:5810.

163. Ibid., 9:5811–12.

164. Ibid., 9:5814–17.

165. Boston, May 28, 1941, ATC file, #340. His contact, an Armenian, may well have been Ovakimian, who was interested in the kinds of processes that Badger employed.

166. FBI report, untitled, attached to Captain E. B. Nixon to Director of Naval Intelligence, April 15, 1940, file A8–5/QM/Amtorg Trading Corp./Reports, RG 38, NARA.

167. Andrew, *President's Eyes Only*, 90; Haynes, *Red Scare or Red Menace?* chap. 2, passim. The Dies Committee also closely examined groups like William Pelley's Silver Shirts. See box 22, Dies Committee files.

168. See, for example, MacDonnell, *Insidious Foes*, 7–8, 77–81; Cohen, *When the Old Left Was Young*, chap. 9; Dies, *Trojan Horse*, 303. For a discussion of the negative effect that the Molotov-Ribbentrop pact and the Soviet invasion of Finland had upon U.S.-Soviet trade relations, see Libbey, "American-Russian Chamber of Commerce," 247.

169. See Goodman, *The Committee*, 10–24, passim; on Dickstein's work for the Soviets, which differed from others of this period in its financial motives, see Weinstein and Vassiliev, *Haunted Wood*, chap. 7.

170. *Congressional Record*, 73rd Cong., 2nd sess., June 27, 1934, 11.

171. The term "Third Period," which originated at the Sixth Comintern Congress in 1928, was linked with "both intensified class struggle and renewed imperialist war," inter-

nal and external threats that endangered the Soviet Union. See Jacobson, *Soviet Union Enters World Politics*, 268–69.

172. Ryan, *Browder*, 35; *Congressional Record*, June 27, 1934, 11–12, 36.

173. *Congressional Record*, June 27, 1934, 18.

174. Goodman, *The Committee*, 11–12; Weinstein and Vassiliev, *Haunted Wood*, 141.

175. Congress was not informed about the FBI's new counterintelligence responsibilities until 1939. See Senate Select Committee, *Intelligence Activities*, bk. 2, 25–29, and *Supplementary Detailed Staff Reports*, bk. 3, 393–94; Davis, *Spying on America*, 25–27; Spolansky, *Communist Trail*, chap. 2; O'Reilly, *Hoover and the Un-Americans*, 22–26.

176. Rafalko, *Counterintelligence Reader*, 1:161.

177. Talbert, *Negative Intelligence*, 256–58; Powers, *Secrecy and Power*, 218; see also FBI memo, June 2, 1940, box 11, OF 10B, FDRL); Theoharis and Cox, *The Boss*, 181–87; Peake interview, November 21, 2003.

178. See Batvinis, "In the Beginning," 47.

179. Ibid., 10–29, passim.

180. Ibid., 32–38, passim. The Bureau did take over immigration administration in May 1940 from the Labor Department. Frances Perkins's concerns about immigrants' sensitivities regarding fingerprinting, a legacy of the nation's long memory of the anti-immigrant excesses of World War I, were no longer tenable as the country reestablished a war footing (123–25).

181. Theoharis and Cox, *The Boss*, 179; see also Frank Murphy to Franklin D. Roosevelt, June 17, 1939, FDR to Secretaries of State, Treasury, War, Navy, Commerce, Attorney General, and Postmaster General, June 26, 1939, box 10, OF 10B. The 1938 allocation was three times what FDR recommended for the other two main counterintelligence agencies, the MID and the ONI. See Rafalko, *Counterintelligence Reader*, 1:163.

182. See discussion in Ryan, *Browder*, 108–13.

183. "Memorandum on the Political Situation in the USA and the Tasks of the CPUSA," January 9, 1938, *fond* 495, *op.* 14, *del.* 109, RGASPI.

184. Browder, quoted December 12, 1937, in *fond* 495, *op.* 14, *del.* 84, RGASPI.

185. Sidney Bloomfield, Referent, "America," January 1937, *fond* 539, *op.* 14, *del.* 75, *RGASPI* (emphasis added). The successful 1937 West Coast strike of longshoremen was led by Harry Bridges.

186. Davis Report, n.d., box 49, Dies Committee files.

187. "Memorandum on the Political Situation in the USA and the Tasks of the CPUSA," 5, 23–30, passim.

188. McDaniel, "Dies," 352–54, 368.

189. Goodman, *The Committee*, 18–19; MacDonnell, *Insidious Foes*, 4–9; McDaniel, "Dies," 355, 373–75.

190. Dies, *Trojan Horse*, 301.

191. McDaniel, "Dies," 413–17.

192. HUAC, *Investigation of Un-American Propaganda* (1938), 305. Steele's allegations filled more than four hundred pages in the committee's first volume of hearings. See O'Reilly, *Hoover and the Un-Americans*, 49.

193. See Goodman, *The Committee*, 29; MacDonnell, *Insidious Foes*, 79.

194. Quoted in McDaniel, "Dies," 375.

195. See Dies to Adolph Sabath, chairman of the Rules Committee, February 6, 1939, and *Muncie Morning Star,* May 25, 1943, both in box 38, Dies Committee files.

196. See *New York Times,* May 14, 1940, and Maynes deposition, December 1, 1939, both in box 25, Dies Committee files.

197. McDaniel, "Dies," 441–45.

198. On his speeches, for which he was paid handsomely, and on Hollywood, see McDaniel, "Dies,"432–41, 456–57, respectively.

199. Ibid., 694.

200. Los Angeles Police Department Red Squad report, n.d., box 39, Dies Committee files; C. H. Garrigues, "The Spotlight," *Los Angeles Daily News,* January 31, 1934, in LAPD Radical Squad, box 48, Dies Committee files. But a dissenting editorial vehemently argued that Communists should be limited to "Free speech zones" and afforded no protection because of their disagreement with American principles: "This is a period of war."

201. Los Angeles Red Squad report, "The Communist Situation in California," box 49, Dies Committee files. To this end, the police department spent $347.55 on its Intelligence Bureau in May 1934. "See Secret Service Monies, Intelligence Bureau Metropolitan Division, May 1934, LAPD," box 49, Dies Committee files.

CHAPTER 2

1. FDR statement, September 6, 1939, box 10, OF 10B; also quoted in report of the director of the Federal Bureau of Investigation, John Edgar Hoover, 1940, 152. I am grateful to John Fox of the FBI for copies of these reports.

2. See discussion in Ryan, *Browder,* 173–77; the State Department had been aware of Browder's passport irregularities for ten years. See also *Bristol Herald Courier,* October 23, 1939, FBI Bentley file [a], #A.

3. See T. J. Donegan, acting for E. J. Connelley, Assistant Director, FBI, to Special Agent in Charge, Chicago, May 7, 1941, ATC #323; report, Amtorg Trading Corporation espionage investigation file (hereafter ATC file), New York, May 5, 1941, 9, #316. The investigation stemmed from the directive of Connelley, who on June 13, 1941, "advised that the Bureau desired a complete and discreet investigation of the extent and ramifications of the trading and espionage activities of the ATC." See Philadelphia, Oct. 2, 1941, ATC file, #644.

4. Feklisov, *Man behind the Rosenbergs,* 54–55, 58.

5. Quoted in Batvinis, "In the Beginning," 46.

6. "Testimony of the Director on January 15, 1942, before the House Subcommittee on Appropriations (HSOA) regarding the 1943 Appropriation Estimates for the FBI in the Amount of $29,636,787 (including a Supplemental 1943 National Defense Estimate in the Amount of $3,800,000)," 108. Appropriations testimony, FBI Office of Public Affairs.

7. Frank Murphy to FDR, June 17, 1939; FDR to Secretaries of State, Treasury, War, Navy, Commerce, Attorney General, and Postmaster General, June 26, 1939; and FDR

statement, September 6, 1939, all in box 10, OF 10B; Hoover to FDR, June 3, 1940, box 11, OF 10B; Hoover to Watson, October 29, 1940, box 12, OF 10B.

8. FDR press release, November 27, 1940, box 10, OF 10B; quoted in Lowenthal, *Federal Bureau of Investigation*, 425.

9. "Testimony of the Director before the HSOA regarding the Bureau's Regular 1940 Appropriations," April 27, 1939, Justice Department Appropriation Bill, 1940, 100–126, passim.

10. "Emergency Supplemental Appropriation Bill, 1940," HSOA, November 30, 1939, 302–7, passim; see also "Testimony of the Director before the HSOA regarding the Regular 1941 and National Defense Appropriation Estimates of the FBI," January 5, 1940, 153.

11. "Testimony of the Director before the HSOA regarding the 1942 Regular and National Defense Appropriation Estimates of the FBI," 164.

12. Quoted in Lowenthal, *Federal Bureau of Investigation*, 425.

13. DOJ, "Annual Report, 1940," 153; appropriations testimony, FBI Office of Public Affairs; "Emergency Supplemental Appropriation Bill, 1940," November 30, 1939, 303, 306; "Testimony of the Director before the House Subcommittee on Appropriations regarding the 1942 National Defense Supplemental Estimate for the FBI in the Amount of $5,600,000," June 11, 1941, 265.

14. Hoover to Watson, December 26, 1939, box 11, OF File 10B.

15. "Testimony of the Director before the HSOA regarding the 1942 Regular and National Defense Appropriation Estimates of the FBI," 192; "Testimony of the Director on January 15, 1942 before the House Subcommittee on Appropriations regarding the 1943 Appropriation Estimates," 108.

16. DOJ, "Annual Report, 1940," 152.

17. "Testimony of the Director before the HSOA regarding the 1942 National Defense Supplemental Estimate," 265.

18. "Testimony of the Director before the HSOA regarding the 1941 Deficiency and Supplemental Appropriations in the Amount of $975,000," February 19, 1941, 184.

19. "Testimony of the Director before the HSOA regarding the 1942 National Defense Supplemental Estimate," 153. Today, the FBI has fifty-six field offices.

20. Rabaut put his encomiums in the record so that "they will be properly inscribed . . . as being the sentiments of this committee." See "Testimony of the Director before the HSOA regarding the 1942 Regular and National Defense Appropriation Estimates of the FBI," 160. Rabaut, incidentally, was the first congressman to introduce a measure adding the phrase "under God" to the Pledge of Allegiance. Proposed in 1952, the wording was adopted in 1954.

21. "Testimony of the Director before the HSOA regarding the 1941 Deficiency and Supplemental Appropriations," 179.

22. Ibid., 181, 182.

23. Ibid., 186–87, 194; DOJ, "Annual Report, July 1, 1940 to June 30, 1941," 3.

24. Ibid., 191; "Testimony of the Director before the HSOA regarding the 1942 National Defense Supplemental Estimate for the FBI in the Amount of $2,150,000, on January 27, 1942," 140.

25. "Testimony of the Director before the HSOA regarding the 1941 Regular and National Defense Appropriation Estimates of the FBI, January 5 1940," 157.

26. "Testimony of the Director before the HSOA regarding the 1942 National Defense Supplemental Estimate," 276.

27. Batvinis, "In the Beginning," 186–207, passim. According to Batvinis, one of the letters that Kent was charged with stealing was an MI-5 inquiry directed to the FBI regarding Armand Labis Feldman and Willie Brandes (204).

28. Ibid., chap. 7, passim.

29. "Testimony of the Director before the HSOA regarding the 1943 Appropriations Estimates for the FBI," 123.

30. Stone to Felix Frankfurter, February 9, 1925, quoted in Theoharis and Cox, *The Boss,* 91 (see also discussion on 91–94); "Memorandum on Division of Duties between Military Intelligence Division, Office of Naval Intelligence and the Federal Bureau of Investigation," May 29, 1940, quoted in Batvinis, "In the Beginning," 65. In 1924, Attorney General Stone stipulated that national security cases could be opened only when an individual seeking to overthrow the government was actually violating the law in order to bring about this goal. See Stone to Hoover, May 13, 1924, cited in Batvinis, 66fn. 15.

31. The world situation had clearly heightened concerns about the presence of foreign groups on U.S. soil, as an FBI file titled "Germans, Russians, Italians and Japanese Board the 'Asama Maru': Espionage" attested. See New York, May 24, 1941, 102, ATC file, #319.

32. See *Nardone et al. v. United States,* 1937. SCT.1233, 302 U.S. 379, 58 S. Ct. 275, 82 L. Ed. 314; the full text may be found on the Web at www.druglibrary.org/schaffer/legal/l1930/nardone_v_us_us_supreme_court.htm. FDR's order is in Roosevelt memorandum to Attorney General Robert Jackson, May 21, 1940, cited in Theoharis and Cox, *The Boss,* 171. See also discussion in Batvinis, "In the Beginning," 97–120, passim.

33. "Testimony of the Director before the HSOA regarding the 1942 Regular and National Defense Appropriation Estimates of the FBI," 195–96.

34. Haynes, *Red Scare or Red Menace?* 34–35; "'Moral Embargo' against Moscow," *New York Times,* December 2, 1939. On Soviet reactions to the embargo, see Steinhardt to Secretary of State, March 8, 1940, Safe file, Russia 1939–41, box 5, PSF, FDRL; J. Edgar Hoover to Edwin M. Watson, August 29, 1940, FBI Report #210, July 10, 1940, box 12, OF 10B. The embargo was lifted by early 1941; see FBI memo, January 28, 1941, box 13, OF 10B. On German-Soviet trade in this era, see Geoffrey Roberts, *Origins of the Second World War,* 175–78.

35. On the aircraft shipment, see White to Morgenthau, February 5, 1940, Herbert E. Gaston to Morgenthau, February 6, 1940, Group Meeting, February 6, 1940, MD, 239:239, 311, 419–20, Morgenthau Papers, FDRL; Basil Harris, memorandum for the Secretary, April 10, 1940, MD, 253:253; Alekseev and Rvachev, "The Problems of Our Import from the USA," May 20, 1940, *fond* 413, *op.* 13, *del.* 2870, *RGAE.*

36. Alekseev and Rvachev, "The Problems of Our Import from the USA."

37. May 5, 1941, 78, #319, ATC file.

38. Milwaukee, Wis., June 19, 1941, 12, 14, ATC file, #378; on export licenses, see also Cincinnati, July 11, 1941, ATC file, #449, #466.

39. Detroit, June 28, 1941, 5, ATC file, #406.

40. For example, forty Soviet engineers, some of whom were said to be "on good terms with Nazi circles," were at aircraft maker Curtis-Wright in 1941. See New York, May 24, 1941, 47, ATC file, #319.

41. New York, June 21, 1941, 132, ATC file, #372.

42. New York, May 24, 1941, 3, ATC file, #319. See also Donegan to Special Agent in Charge, Chicago, May 7, 1941, ATC file, #323.

43. New York, May 24, 1941, 4, 72, ATC file, #319; Kansas City, July 28, 1941, 5, ATC file, #475.

44. New York, June 21, 1941, 66, ATC file, #372. Among the names were 106 Americans and a "long list" of Soviets.

45. Ibid., 74–78, 85, 115–25, passim.

46. H. R. Stark to Inspector of Naval Aircraft, December 20, 1939, file A8–5/EF61, RG 38, NARA; Stark to Secretary of State, August 14, 1940, L11–4/QM/Wright Aeronautical Corp., RG 38, NARA; Loy Henderson to Mr. Welles, August 15, 1940, file 861.20111/2, RG 59, NARA.

47. May 5, 1941, 74, ATC file, #319. Former intelligence officer Pavel Sudoplatov has noted that Amtorg was one of four important centers of Soviet espionage in the United States during this period. The others were the Soviet embassy, the office of illegal agent Itzhak Akhmerov, and the San Francisco consulate. See Sudoplatov, *Special Tasks*, 217; Andrew and Mitrokhin, *Sword and the Shield*, 106–7. The American activities of the GRU, the Soviet military intelligence agency (which ran Alger Hiss, among other agents), remain more obscure, since most of its cables are still closed to researchers. See Weinstein and Vassiliev, *Haunted Wood*, 44n.

48. New York, November 3, 1941, 101, ATC file, #876.

49. However, a mail cover on the agency was ruled out, as Amtorg received 3,000 to 4,000 pieces of mail daily. New York, May 24, 1941, 107, 113, ATC file, #319.

50. FBI report, New York, June 21, 1941, 144, ATC file, #372; New York, May 24, 1941, 41–44, #319.

51. New York, September 26, 1941, ATC file, #620; October 6, 1941, #716. On the bank-account monitoring, also see FBI report, New York, June 21, 1941, 57, ATC file, #372.

52. For example, Budd Manufacturing, Brown Instrument, and Baldwin Locomotive Works all insisted that Amtorg representatives were given at best "short sightseeing tours." Philadelphia, October 2, 1941, 18–21, ATC file, #644.

53. New York, December 27, 1941, ATC file, #956; Cleveland, October 15, 1941, #673; Cleveland, September 30, 1941, 58, #651.

54. Cleveland, September 30, 1941, 1–2, ATC file, #651.

55. "Inspectors, Amtorg Corporation," Chicago, December 16, 1939, ATC file, #63X.

56. Detroit, Michigan, May 26, 1941, ATC file, #345.

57. Cleveland, September 30, 1941, 8–9, 45, ATC file, #651; Buffalo, June 26, 1941, #413, 2.

58. Detroit, June 22, 1941, 1–6, 12, ATC file, #457.

59. St. Paul, July 31, 1941, ATC file, #480.

60. Buffalo, December 9, 1941, ATC file, #413.

61. St. Paul, September 17, 1941, ATC file, #599.

62. Boston, October 25, 1941, ATC file, #730.

63. Milwaukee, June 19, 1941, 2, ATC file, #378.

64. Buffalo, October 1, 1941, ATC file, #624.

65. New York, May 24, 1941, 76–77, 97, ATC file, #319.

66. New York, May 27, 1941, 1–5, ATC file, #343. Subsequently, Brenner reported, Amtorg officials had gone to San Francisco to inspect such a motor.

67. New York City, June 12, 1941, 1, 8, 27, 28, ATC file, #352. This file was labeled "obscene" because of the recorded conversations' frequent referrals to women, although Rosenbaum divulged that he was "not a terribly over-sexed guy. . . . I got a sweet wife and I have been faithful to her" (46).

68. Ibid., 34–39, passim, 44–45, 52.

69. New York, [no month] 1941, 7, ATC file, 61–6351–646.

70. New York, October 21, 1941, 14, ATC file, #718; Newark, June 28, 1941, #411.

71. Hoover to Berle, November 2, 1940, and memo, November 2, 1940, file 2801–401/23, RG 165, NARA. See also Max G. Dice to Chief, Inspection Section, Air Plant Protection Control, October 28, 1940, file 2801–401/18.

72. George V. Strong, Memorandum of the Assistant Chief of Staff, G-2, February 15, 1940, files 2801–393/1, /2; Bresovitz FBI file, February 20, 1940, file 2801–393/4; Hoover to Colonel McCabe, Assistant Chief of Staff, G-2, February 20, 1940, file 2801–393/4. All in RG 165, NARA.

73. "Special Report on Subversive Situation, Headquarters Second Corps Area," November 20, 1940, 4, 5, 9, file 10110–2662/362, RG 165, NARA.

74. Lt. Col. John H. Wilson, Assistant Chief of Staff, G-2, "Report on Subversive Activities, 9th Corps Area," November 18, 1940, 1–8, passim, file 10110–2669/374, RG 165, NARA.

75. Hoover to Brig. Gen. Sherman Miles, May 4, 1940, Amtorg Trading Corporation, ATC file, #15; Hoover to Col. E. R. Warner McCabe, Asst. Chief of Staff, G2, Dec. 19, 1939, ATC file, #5; Hoover to Brig. Gen. Sherman Miles, Asst. Chief of Staff, G-2, May 22, 1940, 10104–1381/17; "Armed with Names, US Moves to Cleanse Unions of Communists," *Washington Post,* June 13, 1941, box 40, Ohly Papers, HSTL.

76. "USA: Communist Strategy," January 7, 1941, file 10110–1581/172, RG 165, NARA.

77. "Crouch Bares Spying at Atom Bomb Center," *Miami Daily News,* May 18, 1949, box 39, Tanenhaus Papers.

78. HUAC, *Investigation of Un-American Propaganda Activities* (1941), 10–11.

79. William P. Goodman, Chairman of the North American Aviation Unit Local 683 UAW CIO, to Dies, June 3, 1941, box 20, Dies Committee files.

80. Memo, Air Corps Matériel Division, Office of the Air Corps Representative, North American Aviation Inc, Inglewood, Calif., Subject: "Military Possession and Operation of North American Aviation Inc." to Secretary of War, with Col. Branshaw's report, "Report of Activities of US troops employed in opening North American Aviation Plant at Inglewood, Calif, June 7th to 11th inclusive," in Plant Seizures file, box 40, Ohly Papers; also see FDR's executive order, June 9, 1941, box 40, Ohly Papers. A "Report on Industrial Relations Activities North American Aviation Inc. during Operation by United States Government" noted unfairly differentiated wages scales contributed to employees' low

morale; Branshaw, however, refused to meet with the suspended men. Former union leader Sidney Hillman, who was then the Office of Price Management's associate director general in the labor division, supported FDR's order. See his press release, June 9, 1941, box 40, Ohly Papers.

81. *New York Times,* June 9, 1941; "Armed with Names, US Moves to Cleanse Unions of Communists," *Washington Post,* June 13, 1941, box 40, Ohly Papers. Today Bridges is lionized as a labor leader. See, for instance, the Web site of the University of Washington's Harry Bridges Center for Labor Studies, depts.washington.edu/pcls/.

82. "Party Line Before and After: Defends Russia's Run-Out," June 15, 1941, *Daily Worker,* box 38, Dies Committee files.

83. *Soviet Russia Today,* quoting TASS communiqué, February 1941, 5, box 6, Dies Committee files.

84. On monitoring of Soviet accounts and orders, see Andrew, *President's Eyes Only,* 92–93; Group Meeting, December 4, 1939, MD, 226:261–68; Harry Dexter White to Morgenthau, December 21, 1939, MD, 231:223; White to Morgenthau, January 9, 1940, MD, 234:86; Roosevelt to Morgenthau, January 10, 1940, and Hoover to Watson, January 6, 1940, MD, 235:52–53; Roosevelt to Morgenthau, February 8, 1940, Vincent Astor to President, February 5, 1940, and Captain W. D. Puleston to Morgenthau, February 8, 1940, MD, 240:117, 118, 121; FBI Memorandum, March 13, 1941, box 13, OF 10B.

85. See box 5, Dies Committee files and Libbey, "American-Russian Chamber of Commerce," 233–48.

86. "United States Exports to the Union of Soviet Socialist Republics," box 36, Dies Committee files.

87. May 5, 1941, 4, ATC file, #316; May 24, 1941, 27, #319.

88. Council newsletter, March 11, 1941, box 6, Dies Committee files.

89. See June 23, 1942, 23, 24, FBI Feldman file, #743; FBI report, November 27, 1945, 17, RG 233, NARA; FBI, "Underground Soviet Espionage Organization (NKVD) in Agencies of the U.S. Government, October 21, 1946," cited in Benson and Warner, *Venona,* 78. Documents to create passports to enable the entry of Soviet agents were obtained at such facilities as the New York Public Library (where useful birth certificates of people who died young were kept) and the State Department (where naturalization papers from those whose husbands or wives had died were available), as well as other locations, including the anthracite coal regions of Pennsylvania, where the rate of early death among miners, many of whom had Slavic surnames, was high. See "Karl" (Whittaker Chambers), "The Soviet Passport Racket," 1938 (never published), box 25, Tanenhaus Papers. On birth certificates, see Venona messages 2505–2512 Washington to Moscow, from Capt I. A. Egorichev (likely) to Captain M. A. Vorontsov, Dec 31, 1942.

90. *Washington Post,* September 2, 1949, FBI Bentley file [a], #A; Olmsted, *Red Spy Queen,* 21–22.

91. June 23, 1942, 61–69, passim, 134, Feldman file, #743.

92. Ibid., 2; Andrew and Gordievsky, *KGB,* 223–24. One of those captured was Percy Glading, who had taken an actual course in industrial espionage in 1929. See Bergier, *Industrial Espionage,* 46.

93. Andrew and Mitrokhin, *Sword and the Shield,* 107. Former special agent John J.

Walsh says Ovakimian also got material from a Department of Justice official who was later transferred to the Office of Price Administration. Walsh interview, June 19, 2003.

94. Schecter and Schecter, *Sacred Secrets*, 47. The Schecters further suggest that Ovakimian also was behind Soviet agent Vitali Pavlov's attempts to influence Harry Dexter White, who they claim advised Henry Morgenthau to call for the Japanese to withdraw troops from China and establish an oil embargo. According to the Schecters, this Soviet-influenced policy—when combined with the work of Soviet agents in Japan—was the spur that led to Pearl Harbor (4–6, 33–38). Bruce Craig's forthcoming book, *Treasonable Doubt* (Lawrence: University Press of Kansas, 2004) casts doubt on these assertions of White's influence regarding the Japanese, however. See idem, especially 246–51.

95. June 23, 1942, 61–69, passim, Feldman file, #743. A discussion of the FBI's monitoring of Ovakimian is in Weinstein and Vassiliev, *Haunted Wood*, 91. The Soviets were particularly interested in the Houdry process for cracking oil—and eventually built plants on this process with stolen plans. See p. 68, #743. Also see top-secret report, n.d., attached to FBI report, 5, Brothman file, #474.

96. June 23, 1942, 61, 66, Feldman file, #743; "Summary Brief on Fuchs and Gold," February 12, 1951, 186, FBI Fuchs file, #1494X (1998 supplemental release).

97. June 23, 1942, 3–4, 54–71, passim, Feldman file, #743. For more on Feldman's role, see Weinstein and Vassiliev, *Haunted Wood*, 91.

98. Walsh interviews, February 11, June 19, 2003.

99. Ironically, two of those who came to the United States in this exchange were the Russian wives of journalists and were "strongly suspected of being Soviet agents"; only one was an American citizen. See "Underground Soviet Espionage Organization (NKVD) in Agencies of the US Government," 14, Justice Department Confidential files, box 21, WHCF, HSTL.

100. Schecter and Schecter, *Sacred Secrets*, 88.

101. Rees became a double agent in 1971 and then committed suicide in 1976 when newspapers planned to publicize his past. He made one of his most important contributions to the Soviets in 1950, when he furnished them with a Mobil-designed converter for increasing the yield of gasoline from crude oil. See *New York Times*, March 1, 1976; Herbig and Wiscoff, *Espionage Against the United States*, 8.

102. American Council on Soviet Relations newsletter, April 11, 1941, 6, box 6, Dies Committee files; Batvinis, "In the Beginning," 42n63.

103. "COMRAP Summary," 148.

104. FBI Philbrick file, #31; see also D. M. Ladd to Director, June 20, 1951, #33.

105. "Underground Soviet Espionage Organization (NKVD)," 14; Peake, "Afterword," *Out of Bondage*, 221.

106. June 23, 1942, 24, 119, Feldman file, #743; World Tourists Inc. report, portion of New York report, n.d., Bentley file [a], #6221; Weinstein and Vassiliev, *Haunted Wood*, 86.

107. Toledano and Lasky, *Seeds of Treason*, 131. As FBI special agent Robert Thelan noted, "According to the surveillance logs of this case, Bentley, on two occasions, was surveilled after leaving World Tourists, Inc. when she went to Penn Station and entered the ladies rest room there and the surveillance was lost." The FBI report was also mentioned in Walter Winchell's column of March 20, 1950; in box 36, Tanenhaus Papers.

108. FBI New York to Washington, November 8, 1945, Silvermaster file, #1. The FBI confirmed that his name came up in the Ovakimian case. See Ladd to Director, November 15, 1945, #91. On the surveillance see also Weinstein and Vassiliev, *Haunted Wood*, 90–91; Olmsted, *Red Spy Queen*, 40–41.

109. Silvermaster report, December 17, 1945, 10:62, Silvermaster file, #248; SAC New York to Director, June 21, 1955, Bentley file [a], section 6; "Underground Soviet Espionage Organization (NKVD)"; Olmsted, *Red Spy Queen*, 38.

110. Weinstein and Vassiliev, *Haunted Wood*, 93.

111. Although Bentley showed plenty of savvy both as a spy dealing with difficult clients and later as a HUAC witness to Communist intrigue, she was a mediocre student. Her average at Vassar was a C+; and her master's thesis, "*Il bel Gherdino,*" was considered too sophisticated to have been written by a graduate student, and was most probably penned by an assistant of her Italian adviser. See May, *Un-American Activities*, 79; Olmsted, *Red Spy Queen*, 6–7. On her early years see also Peake, "Afterword," *Out of Bondage*, 222–29.

112. Olmsted, *Red Spy Queen*, 16; Peake, "Afterword," *Out of Bondage*, 229–30.

113. Report, November 16, 1945, re Pauline Rosen/Rogers, Silvermaster file, #26X1; Peake, "Afterword," *Out of Bondage*, 230–32.

114. "Underground Soviet Espionage Organization (NKVD)," in Agencies of the US Government," 218; "Personal History and Background Report," 7, attached to memo to [blank], December 4, 1950, in Brothman file, #482.

115. His seventeen articles had appeared in the *Journal of Chemical Physics, Physical Reviews,* and *Chemical and Metallurgical Engineering;* see also n.d., top-secret report, attached to FBI report, 2–3, Brothman file, #474.

116. Ibid.; "Summary Brief on Fuchs and Gold," February 12, 1951, 74, Fuchs file, #1494X (1998 supplemental release).

117. "Personal History and Background Report," 9; n.d., top-secret report, attached to FBI report, #474, 5, 17; "Underground Soviet Espionage Organization (NKVD)," 218; see also Ladd to Director, August 8, 1950, 15, Fuchs file, #426; J. Edgar Hoover to Rear Admiral Sidney W. Souers, May 24, 1950, 148, "FBI—G" file, box 168, PSF, HSTL; "John R. Murphy's Fuchs Report," March 9, 1950, 108, Fuchs file, #642.

118. "John R. Murphy's Fuchs Report," 109; T. G. Spencer report, Silverman et al., November 30, 1945, 6:13, Silvermaster file, #220.

119. See Weinstein and Vassiliev, *Haunted Wood*, 91–3. See also "Underground Soviet Espionage Organization (NKVD)," 12.

120. "Summary Brief on Fuchs and Gold," February 12, 1951, 202, Fuchs file, #1494X (1998 supplemental release); see also Brothman biography, 4–5, Rosenberg file; Hoover to Souers, May 24, 1950, FBI file, box 168, PSF, HSTL.

121. Congress believed the process had come from the United States Rubber Reserve Committee. See Senate Judiciary Committee, *Scope of Soviet Activity,* 4843. On Brothman's role as a Soviet source for Buna-S, see Venona 1390 New York to Moscow, October 1, 1944.

122. Batvinis, "In the Beginning," 150; Peake interview, November 21, 2003; Kern, *Death in Washington*, 180–81, 200–204. Krivitsky's July appeal to extend his visa—"the Soviet Government . . . would take measures to finish me off"—was for the moment successful. Quoted in Kern, 207.

123. Batvinis, "In the Beginning," 149–57; Kern, *Death in Washington*, 208–20, passim. Hoover, it seems, was upset with Krivitsky's reports of Soviet infiltration happening right under the FBI's nose, as well as the fact that the defector's closest confidants were in the State Department, not the Bureau. Kern, *Death in Washington*, 189–90. In the late 1940s, ironically, the deceased Krivitsky was cited repeatedly as a source in FBI records for identifying such OGPU agents as Boris Bykov. See Hoover to John A. Cimperman, April 14, 1949, FBI Bykov file, #38; FBI Bykov report, October 6, 1951, #95.

124. Peake interview, November 21, 2003. Orlov later wrote to Stalin that he would say nothing if his family in Russia were left alone. His tell-all book was *The Secret History of Stalin's Crimes* (New York: Random House, 1953). On the Orlov case, see John Costello and Oleg Tsarev, *Deadly Illusions*. On Massing's defection, see, for instance, Weinstein, *Perjury*, 175, 177; Haynes and Klehr, *Venona*, 203.

125. See D. C. Watt, "Francis Herbert King," 62–83; Kern, *Death in Washington*, 231–37, and pt. 3, chap. 10; Andrew and Mitrokhin, *Sword and the Shield*, 107.

126. See Kern, *Death in Washington*, 222, 287, 312–13. His death has always been mysterious; speculations of his assassination by either a German agent, or the NKVD, have never been laid to rest. See discussion in Kern, especially pt. 4, chaps. 5–7, and Tanenhaus, *Chambers*, 168–69.

127. Berle memo, September 4, 1939, 2, in box 211, Tanenhaus Papers. Also see Weinstein, *Perjury*, 57. Levine was described by Soviet agents as "an old-standing enemy of the Soviet Union and the Russian Revolution and the Communist International. He is a special feature writer on the Hearst Staff. At every period since the Russian revolution, he has written the most fantastic and vicious stories about the CP, CI and the Soviet Union." "The Trostskyist Literary Highwaymen in America," Bloomfield report, April 7, 1937, *fond* 539, *op.* 14, *del.* 75, RGASPI.

128. Berle and Jacobs, *Navigating the Rapids*, August 18, 1948, 583.

129. Weinstein, *Perjury*, 59; Tanenhaus, *Chambers*, 169; Haynes and Klehr, *Venona*, 92. Although Berle did follow up at least once in the intervening period, to warn the Bureau to be alert to Soviet actions, his correspondence apparently did not sufficiently sway the FBI to undertake an active investigation of Chambers. It was only after an informant told the Bureau about Chambers that he was at last contacted by special agents in his *Time* office in May 1942, a meeting that eventually led to Berle's turning over the detailed memo of his encounter with Chambers, although not until 1943. The Bureau, however, did little with the information at that point. Peake interview, November 21, 2003.

130. Walsh interview, June 19, 2003. Walsh was an assistant to Tamm during 1939.

131. Tanenhaus, *Chambers*, 203–4, 169–70; Haynes and Klehr, *Venona*, 91–92.

132. See Hoover to Assistant Attorney Gen Warren Olney, December 8, 1953, D. M. Ladd to Hoover, January 5, 1954, and Ladd to Director, September 3, 1948, box 63, Tanenhaus Papers; C. H. Carson to J. E. Hoover, September 3, 1948, box 36, Tanenhaus Papers; Tanenhaus, *Chambers*, 170; Berle and Jacobs, *Navigating the Rapids*, 249–50; FBI report, November 27, 1945, 47.

133. Berle and Jacobs, *Navigating the Rapids*, 598; Berle testimony, in HUAC, *Hearings regarding Communist Espionage* (1948), 1298.

134. Chambers statement to the FBI, Baltimore, Maryland, December 3, 1948, 7, box 27, Tanenhaus Papers.

135. Levine testimony, in HUAC, *Hearings regarding Communist Espionage* (1948), 1007; Weinstein, *Perjury,* 57. Berle's notes are in United States Court of Appeals for the Second Circuit, No. 78, October Term, 1950. *United States of America against Alger Hiss; Appeal from a Judgment of the District Court of the United States of the Southern District of New York. Affirmed. Transcript of Record* (Second Trial), 6:6:3325ff., cited in Weinstein, 57.

136. HUAC, *Investigation of Un-American Propaganda* (1938), 396–400; Goodman, *The Committee,* 110–13.

137. HUAC, *Investigation of Un-American Propaganda* (1941), 20–24.

138. CPUSA memo to U.S. Senators and Representatives, January 9, 1939, [signed by Browder], box 513, Taft Papers, Library of Congress, Washington, D.C.; Ryan, *Browder,* 172–73.

139. Goodman, *The Committee,* 67–68; Buckley et al., *The Committee and Its Critics,* 101.

140. HUAC, *Investigation of Un-American Propaganda* (1941), 20–23.

141. "The People Are with Dies," editorial, *Manassas (Va.) Journal,* November 28, 1940; HUAC, *Investigation of Un-American Propaganda* (1941), 1.

142. Andrew and Mitrokhin, *Sword and the Shield,* 107, 109; see also Weinstein and Vassiliev, *The Haunted Wood,* 173.

143. Feklisov, *Man behind the Rosenbergs,* 50.

144. Harry Gold statement, June 4, 1950, FBI file 65–4332–1A4; Sudoplatov, *Special Tasks,* 175; Black testimony, *Scope of Soviet Activity,* 1119. Black began cooperating with the FBI in 1950. He was not imprisoned; in fact, he maintained his job on a contract at Atlas Refining Company for the Percy Helie Company in Worcester, Massachusetts, and was assured assistance from the grateful senators to obtain a security clearance (1127).

145. Andrew and Mitrokhin, *Sword and the Shield,* 111, 129. The 1945 microfilm alone was the equivalent of 68,000 pages. See Haynes and Klehr, *In Denial,* 214.

146. Jeffreys-Jones, *Cloak and Dollar,* 126–28.

147. Batvinis, "In the Beginning," 277–78, chap. 9, passim; DOJ, "Annual Report, 1943," 3.

148. Feklisov, *Man behind the Rosenbergs,* 58.

CHAPTER 3

1. HUAC, *Shameful Years,* 22–23 (hereafter *Shameful Years*). See also Dallin, *Soviet Espionage,* 425–38, passim; "Report of Viktor Andreevich Kravchenko," July 31, 1944, file 383.4 USSR, Army Intelligence Project Decimal File, RG 319, NARA; "Spotlight on Spies," p. 112, reel 261, vol. 132, ACLU Papers, Seeley Mudd Library. Kravchenko's defection in 1944 was humiliating for his country and embarrassing for its ally, the United States; facing the prospect of being shipped back to Russia, he was closely watched by the FBI. See Haynes and Klehr, *Venona,* 254. Athan Theoharis, who has seen Kravchenko's recently released FBI file, confirms the Bureau's close monitoring of him. Theoharis, conversation with author, August 28, 2003.

2. Kravchenko testimony, in HUAC, *Hearings regarding Shipment of Atomic Material,* 1950, 1185, 1180.

3. Indeed, the commission's personnel were known as "probationers" or agents. See Venona 959 Zubilin to Fitin, July 8, 1942. However, the Purchasing Commission staff did not necessarily know who in the ranks were the NKVD representatives, and even Leonid Rudenko, head of the commission, did not control the NKVD. Kravchenko testimony, in HUAC, *Hearings regarding Shipments*, 1181–82.

4. See Kravchenko testimony, in HUAC, *Hearings regarding Shipments*, 1177–84, passim; see also "Report of Viktor Andreevich Kravchenko," July 31, 1944, 6–7.

5. Feklisov, *Man behind the Rosenbergs*, 58. He and his associates discovered that their phones were tapped, their homes tailed, and their offices watched (61).

6. Venona 586, 1755 New York to Moscow, April 29, 1944, December 14, 1944, respectively.

7. Ohly, memorandum for the Secretary of War, box 33, Ohly Papers, HSTL. "Secret," according to one government definition, meant "information and material (matter), the unauthorized disclosure of which would endanger national security, cause serious injury to the interests of prestige of the Nation, or would be of great advantage to a foreign Nation," with a lengthy list of particulars following. "Top secret" was described as "information and material (matter), the security aspect of which is paramount, and the unauthorized disclosure of which would cause exceptionally grave damage to the Nation." See "Secret Information," in Senate Committee on Government Operations, *Army Signal Corps-Subversion and Espionage*, 53, 54.

8. See Publications Section, PR Branch, Headquarters U.S. Army Air Forces, December 12, 1941, "Memorandum to Commanding Officers of All Army Air Forces Posts, Stations and Organizations, to Members of the Aircraft Industry and to the Aviation Writers Association," box 34, Ohly Papers; "Joint Statement by the Secretary of War, the Attorney General, the Secretary of the Navy, and the Chairman of the Maritime Commission, on 'The Employment of Aliens,'" June 7, 1943, box 7, Ohly Papers.

9. War Department, "Plant Protection for Manufacturers" (brochure), May 1, 1943, box 31, Ohly Papers.

10. "Testimony of the Director on January 15, 1942, before the House Subcommittee on Appropriations regarding the 1943 Appropriation Estimates for the FBI in the Amount of $29,636,787 (including a Supplemental 1943 National Defense Estimate in the Amount of $3,800,000)," 110.

11. "Security Policies of the Army Air Forces," January 1, 1942, box 34, Ohly Papers.

12. Ohly memo, "Contract Clause to Permit Discharge of Communists," box 33, Ohly Papers.

13. Ohly, "Employment of Communists," November 18, 1942, box 33, Ohly Papers.

14. See "Memo for the Provost Marshal General (Col. H. G. Reynolds) from James P. Mitchell," June 4, 1942, and "Memo re Procedure for Dealing with Subversive Elements in Defense Factories," November 10, 1941, box 33, Ohly Papers.

15. Ohly memo, "Removal of Subversives—Conference with Representatives of the UAW and the URW," September 2, 1943, box 33, Ohly Papers.

16. Albert Epstein, International Association of Machinists, and Nathaniel Goldfinger, Committee on Economics, CIO, "Communist Tactics in American Unions," *Labor and Nation* (Fall 1950), box 32, Ohly Papers.

17. Ryan, *Earl Browder*, 217–22, passim. These proposals generated enormous controversy in the movement and eventually led to Browder's downfall in April 1945. Through the vituperative pen of French Communist Jacques Duclos (conveniently provided with retranslated Russian versions of Browder's speeches) the Soviet Union denounced Browder's accommodation with capitalism and savaged him as practicing a "notorious revision of Marxism" (246–47).

18. Alexander Barmine, "The New Communist Conspiracy," *Reader's Digest*, October 1944, box 513, Taft Papers.

19. Bentley, *Out of Bondage*, 103; Weinstein and Vassiliev, *Haunted Wood*, 96.

20. Ryan, *Browder*, 240–41; see also Haynes and Klehr, *Secret World*, 236.

21. Interdepartmental Committee on Employee Investigations, General Memo No. 6 to Executive Heads of Departments, Etc., September 1, 1943; Executive Order 9300, "Establishing the Interdepartmental Committee to Consider Cases of Subversive Activity on the Part of Federal Employees," box 2, Vanech Papers; see also attorney general's form letter regarding subversive investigations, October 22, 1941, cited in "Testimony of the Director on January 15, 1942, before the HSOA regarding the 1943 Appropriations Estimates for the FBI," 127.

22. Gaston, chairman of the Interdepartmental Commitee, to the White House, n.d., box 2, Vanech Papers.

23. "Testimony of the Director on January 15, 1942, before the HSOA regarding the 1943 Appropriation Estimates for the FBI," 125–26.

24. "Testimony of Mr. Tolson, Assistant to the Director, June 9, 1942, before the HSOA Regarding a Supplemental Appropriations Estimate of $9,200,000 for the FBI for 1943, and a Supplemental Appropriations Estimate of $865,000 for 1942 for the FBI," 83.

25. DOJ, "Report of the Director of the FBI for the Fiscal Year 1943," 3, 8; Appropriations testimony, FBI Office of Public Affairs.

26. "Testimony of the Director on February 18, 1943, before the HSOA regarding the 1944 Appropriation Estimates for the FBI in the Amount of $42,768,000," 242.

27. "Testimony of the Director on January 15, 1942, before the HSOA regarding the 1943 Appropriations Estimates for the FBI," 126, 128.

28. DOJ, "Report of the Director of the FBI for the Fiscal Year 1943," 4.

29. "Testimony of the Director on January 15, 1942, before the HSOA regarding the 1943 Appropriations Estimates," 121.

30. As of June 30, 1945, 16,054 alien enemies had been apprehended, including 7,041 Germans and 1 Bulgarian. Of these, 5,653 had been released, 3,204 interned, and 1,150 repatriated. See DOJ, "Report of the Director of the FBI for the Fiscal Year 1945," 1.

31. DOJ, "Report of the Director of the FBI for the Fiscal Year 1943," 8.

32. "Testimony of Mr. Tolson, Assistant to the Director, before the HSOA, June 9, 1942," 78.

33. Kilmarx, *History of Soviet Air Power*, 211.

34. On January 8, 1943, FDR reiterated to law enforcement officials and the public his 1939 directive on the FBI's role, stating in part: "I suggested that all patriotic organizations and individuals likewise report such information relating to espionage and related matters to the Federal Bureau of Investigation." Quoted in DOJ, "Report of the Director of the FBI for the Fiscal Year 1943," 3.

35. DOJ, "Report of the Director of the FBI for the Fiscal Year 1942," 1–2, 5.

36. "Testimony of the Director on January 15, 1942, before the HSOA regarding the 1943 Appropriation Estimates," 94, 113.

37. "Testimony of the Director on February 18, 1943, before the HSOA Regarding the 1944 Appropriation Estimates," 240.

38. DOJ, "Report of the Director of the FBI for the Fiscal Year 1942," 3. The Duquesne case was mentioned in "Testimony of the Director on January 15, 1942, before the HSOA regarding the 1943 Appropriation Estimates," 123; "Testimony of Mr. Tolson, Assistant to the Director, June 9, 1942, before the HSOA," 82; "Testimony of the Director on February 18, 1943, before the HSOA regarding the 1944 Appropriation Estimates," 234; and "Testimony of the Director on December 3, 1943, before the HSOA regarding the 1945 Appropriation Estimates for the FBI in the Amount of $49,850,000," 229.

39. In one reference that could have referred to the Soviets, Hoover mentioned that "much information desired by . . . espionage agents deals directly with our war-production programs and the training and movement of our military personnel." "Testimony of the Director on February 18, 1943, before the HSOA regarding the 1944 Appropriation Estimates," 234.

40. Walsh interview, June 19, 2003.

41. DOJ, "Report of the Director of the FBI for the Fiscal Year 1942," 3; "Testimony of Mr. Tolson, Assistant to the Director, June 9, 1942, before the HSOA," 82.

42. DOJ, "Report of the Director of the FBI for the Fiscal Year 1942," 3.

43. DOJ, "Report of the Director of the FBI for the Fiscal Year 1943," 1, 5; "Report of the Director of the FBI for the Fiscal Year 1944," 1, 9.

44. "Testimony of the Director on February 18, 1943, before the HSOA regarding the 1944 Appropriation Estimates," 233.

45. HSOA, "Reports Submitted by House and Senate Appropriations Committees on First Supplemental Surplus Appropriation Rescission Act, 1946, Together with Testimony of the Director on October 2, 1945, before the HSOA regarding the Rescission of $3,240,000 from the Appropriations for the FBI," 716; DOJ, "Report of the Director of the FBI for the Fiscal Year 1943," 1, and "Report of the Director of the FBI for the Fiscal Year 1945," 4.

46. DOJ, "Report of the Director of the FBI for the Fiscal Year 1945," 6.

47. Walsh interview, June 19, 2003.

48. JCAE, *Soviet Atomic Espionage*, 185; "COMRAP Summary," 6. A comprehensive study of lend-lease policy is Leon Martel's *Lend-Lease, Loans, and the Coming of the Cold War*.

49. Standley and Ageton, *Admiral Ambassador*, 39–40.

50. "Soviet Government Purchasing Commission," March 29, 1946, November 5, 1946, FBI file, box 169, PSF, HSTL.

51. Hoover to Harry Vaughan, November 5, 1946, "Soviet Government Purchasing Commission," March 29, 1946, November 5, 1946; all in FBI file, box 169, PSF, HSTL.

52. Higham et al., *Russian Aviation*, 10 (introduction). See also *Die Zeit*, November 22, 1956, "The Russian Supersonic Bomber T-150—Deported German Specialists Who Had Done Their Duty, Could Go," in *Scope of Soviet Activity*, 4901.

53. Kilmarx, *Soviet Air Power*, 211–12.

54. Combined Chiefs of Staff, "Disclosure of Technical Information to the U.S.S.R., Memorandum by the Representatives of the British Chiefs of Staff, 29 December 1943," appendix, 2, folder JIC-CIC-Russia, vol. 18, box 91A, Donovan Papers, Military History Institute, Carlisle, Pa.

55. Burns to Hopkins, August 16, 1943, box 140, Hopkins Papers, FDRL; Spalding Oral History, 208; Annex C, "Soviet-U.S. Relations," attached to Raymond E. Lee, memo for the Chief of Staff, February 12, 1942, box 217, Hopkins Papers. On the same topic, see also War Department General Staff Military Attache Report, U.S.S.R., January 3, 1942, U.S. Army Regional file USSR 9000, RG 165, NARA; Gaddis, "Intelligence, Espionage, and Cold War Origins," 194–95, and discussions in Deane, *Strange Alliance,* and Bradley Smith, *Sharing Secrets.*

56. HUAC, Jordan testimony, *Hearings regarding Shipment,* 937–53, passim, 1055; David Sentner, *New York Journal-American,* September 7, 1948, box 15, Clifford Papers, HSTL; JCAE, *Report on Export of Atomic Materials to the Soviet Union,* January 9, 1950, cited in JCAE, *Soviet Atomic Espionage,* 184.

57. See discussion in Jordan, *Major Jordan's Diaries,* chap. 6, and idem, 135–37, 264–67; JCAE, *Soviet Atomic Espionage,* 184; Kravchenko testimony, in HUAC, *Hearings regarding Shipment,* 1182–85; "Report of Viktor Andreevich Kravchenko," July 31, 1944; Rhodes, *Dark Sun,* 98–99.

58. Jordan, *Major Jordan's Diaries,* 194; see also Jordan testimony, in HUAC, *Hearings regarding Shipment,* 914.

59. Jordan, *Major Jordan's Diaries,* 137–40.

60. Barney M. Giles to General A. I. Belyaev, October 6, 1943; Burns, memo for Hopkins, October 21, 1943; and Hopkins to Arnold, October 22, 1943; all in book 9, box 335, Hopkins Papers, Sherwood Collection.

61. Quoted in Jordan, *Major Jordan's Diaries,* 252.

62. Jordan, *Major Jordan's Diaries,* preface, 77–78.

63. JCAE, *Soviet Atomic Espionage,* 185; Rhodes, *Dark Sun,* 100–101.

64. Quoted in Jordan, *Major Jordan's Diaries,* 247–50.

65. "Report of Viktor Andreevich Kravchenko," 5–7; Kravchenko testimony, in HUAC, *Hearings regarding Shipments of Atomic Material,* 1180–84.

66. Fitin quoted in Weinstein and Vassiliev, *Haunted Wood,* 155.

67. Andrew and Mitrokhin, *Sword and the Shield,* 106, 109. Akhmerov claimed he had never met Browder. See Venona 588 New York to Moscow, April 29, 1944.

68. See Ladd to Hoover, November 25, 1945, Silvermaster file, #108X12; see also Haynes and Klehr, *Venona,* 210–11.

69. Comintern Apparatus (COMRAP) Report, May 7, 1943, 33, in Nelson file, #112; Andrew and Mitrokhin, *Sword and the Shield,* 108.

70. See, for instance, Venona 854 New York to Moscow, June 16, 1944; Venona 771 New York to Moscow, May 30, 1944.

71. The U.S. Army Security Agency's Signal Intelligence Service's code-breaking of Soviet cables, code-named Venona, began in 1943, in response to concerns about a possible separate peace between Russia and Germany. But the United States had begun collecting Soviet telegraphic traffic (along with that of Germany, Japan, and Italy) after the

Nazi-Soviet Pact. See Schecter and Schecter, *Sacred Secrets,* xxxiii–xxxv, 95–97. Only about 2 percent of the roughly two million messages sent from 1939 to1945 were at least partially decoded; they suggested the presence of two hundred collaborators with Soviet intelligence in military industry and the government.

72. See Benson and Warner, *Venona,* xxi–xxii; Schecter and Schecter, *Sacred Secrets,* chap. 5. The FBI initially resisted sharing its findings with the CIA, however, including the identifications. The fact that the "material . . . was primarily domestic in nature" was one reason, but so too was Hoover's own animus against the CIA: "In view of loose methods of C.I.A. and some of its questionable personnel, we must be most circumspect," he jotted on a memo from Ladd. See Belmont to Ladd, June 23, 1952, 2; Belmont to Ladd, May 23, 1952, 3; both at foia.fbi.gov/venona/venona.pdf. Because of the pressure applied by CIA director Walter Bedell Smith, the CIA eventually gained access in the spring of 1952. See Belmont to Boardman, February 1, 1956, 3, foia.fbi.gov/venona/venona.pdf.

73. See Belmont to Ladd, memo, May 15, 1950, 4, foia.fbi.gov/venona/venona.pdf; and Benson and Warner, *Venona,* xxiv–xxv.

74. Schwartz, *From West to East,* 337.

75. See Venona 446, 457 Kheifetz to Moscow, October 31, 1943, November 3, 1943. Kheifetz asked for $800 for York, who was identified as "in desperate need of funds for buying a house." FBI report, November 27, 1945, 36. He had begun spying for the Soviets at Northrop in 1935. See Weinstein and Vassiliev, *Haunted Wood,* 26–27; Benson and Warner, *Venona,* xxviii. Sabatini had also fought in the Spanish civil war with Soviet agent Morris Cohen. See Benson and Warner, op. cit., xxvi.

76. Schecter and Schecter, *Sacred Secrets,* 55–56.

77. See Belmont to Ladd, memo, May 15, 1950, foia.fbi.gov/venona/venona.pdf, 5. Weisband, who always denied he was a spy, was never prosecuted for espionage; in 1950, however, he served one year in prison for contempt. See discussion in Benson and Warner, *Venona,* xxviii.

78. Venona 1220, 1264 New York to Moscow, August 26, September 6, 1944.

79. Venona 512 Kheifetz to Moscow, December 7, 1943; Venona 32 Kharon to Moscow, January 17, 1944.

80. Indeed, Elizabeth Bentley's "'unsettled private life'" and drinking binges created much angst among her Soviet handlers. See KGB file 70545, 1:368–71, cited in Weinstein and Vassiliev, *Haunted Wood,* 102, 353n67.

81. Venona 1969 Capt. I. A. Egorichev, Sr. Naval Attaché in Washington [Naval-GRU] to Moscow, August 13, 1943. Three months later, a message confirmed that this material had been sent; see Venona 2933 Washington to Moscow, November 14, 1943.

82. As Venona relates, Soviet representatives in the United States hoped to use Rosenberg to obtain "leads from among people who are working on ENORMOZ [the atomic bomb] and in other technical fields," and Rosenberg had complied by convincing his sister-in-law, Ruth Greenglass, "to cooperate with us in drawing in KALIBR [Ruth's husband, David] with a view to ENORMOZ." David Greenglass's work on the bomb concerned "the mechanism which is to serve as the detonator." See Venona 1340 Stepan Apresyan to Fitin, September 21, 1944, Venona 1600 Kvasnikov to Fitin, November 14, 1944, and Venona 28 Kvasnikov to Fitin, January 8, 1945. A comprehensive study of

Greenglass and his role in espionage (which is especially critical of his contributions to the government's case against the Rosenbergs) is Sam Roberts's *The Brother,* which cites a Soviet cable from June 1944 dismissing the importance of Greenglass's first installment of information (132). Fuchs confessed in 1950; see discussion of his role in Robert Chadwell Williams, *Klaus Fuchs: Atom Spy,* and the 1998 supplemental release of the Klaus Fuchs FBI file. The lesser-known Hall, a nineteen-year-old graduate of Harvard University, with "an exceptionally keen mind" and a "politically developed" outlook, according to his Soviet contact, had volunteered himself as a source of information in 1944. See Venona 1585 New York to Moscow, November 12, 1944; FBI reaction is in Ladd to Hoover, February 28, 1950, 10–11, foia.fbi.gov/venona/venona.pdf. Hall denied this activity and later escaped to England, where he died in 1999. He is profiled in Albright and Kunstel, *Bombshell.* These were hardly the only atomic spies of the era. Recently, Alexander Feklisov divulged yet another source on atomic espionage who does not appear in Venona, "Monti," an engineer whose firm was constructing the Oak Ridge plant. See *Man behind the Rosenbergs,* 98–100. Soviet representatives, seeking authorization from Moscow to recruit still more spies, also proposed that Bernard Schuster, a Soviet contact in the American Communist Party, should contact Rosenberg "about leads from among people who are working on ENORMOZ and in other technical fields." See Venona 1340 Apresyan to Fitin, September 21, 1944.

83. Bentley testimony, *Julius Rosenberg and Ethel Rosenberg, Petitioners, vs. the United States of America* (US District Court, Southern District of NY, June 7, 1952) 2:1003–4, 1011; Bentley statement, 106, Silvermaster file, #220; Teletype to Bureau, August 11, 1950, Rosenberg file [b], #4297; New York report, SA Vincent J. Cahill, December 15, 1950, FBI file, 65–4873–254; Bentley file [b], #2; Haynes and Klehr, *Venona,* 295; New York report, Thomas G. Spencer, December 5, 1945, Re: N. Gregory Silvermaster, Rosenberg file [b], #264.

84. See discussion in Radosh and Milton, *Rosenberg File,* 230–34. At the Rosenberg trial, Bentley was attacked by the Rosenberg defense for conveniently making this up to link herself with the case and thus help the sale of her book, but her testimony in 1945 had certainly mentioned "Julius." Moreover, Max Elitcher testified at the Rosenberg trial that Rosenberg had mentioned he knew Bentley. See Peake, "Afterword," *Out of Bondage,* 261–63.

85. Rosenberg testimony, *Julius Rosenberg and Ethel Rosenberg, Petitioners, vs. the United States of America,* 2:1058–59; Report, Julius Rosenberg, July 18, 1950, attached to Hoover to Souers, July 18, 1950, FBI file, box 169, PSF, HSTL.

86. See report, February 14, 1950, "Joel Barr," FBI Sarant file, #1.

87. SAC Albany to Director FBI, August 7, 1950, 3:26, 71, 74, FBI Sarant file, #77; James H. Higdon Jr. report, January 25, 1951, vol. 11, #397.

88. James H. Higdon Jr., Newark report, October 26, 1950, vol. 3, FBI Sarant file, #320; George W. Hutchison report, February 10, 1951, #406.

89. See Greenglass testimony, *Scope of Soviet Activity,* 1107; Feklisov, *Man behind the Rosenbergs,* 131. After the war, Barr—then unable to get a job—pursued musical studies in Europe. Haynes and Klehr, *Venona,* 297.

90. SAC New York to J. Edgar Hoover, July 31, 1952, FBI Barr file [b], #147.

91. On Sarant, see Venona 628 Apresyan to Moscow, May 5, 1944; on Barr, see Venona 175 Kvasnikov to Fitin, December 5, 1944.

92. Venona 1600 Kvasnikov to Fitin, November 14, 1944; Venona 1749–1750 New York (unrecoverable signature) to Fitin, December 13, 1944.

93. See Feklisov, *Man behind the Rosenbergs,* 115, 136.

94. FBI interviews with former Steinmetz Club members indicated an active circle at CCNY in the late 1930s. A certain "Emmer" told agents that in the Young Communist League (YCL) Rosenberg and Barr, among others, were most active; another informant, Shapiro, also recalled that Rosenberg was very active in the discussions, Perl less so. Feklisov notes that "half the students at CCNY belonged to the YCL." Perl investigation, May 18, 1953, 31, 39, FBI Perl file [b], #791; Feklisov, *Man behind the Rosenbergs,* 130.

95. Director FBI to SAC New York, April 7, 1950, SAC New York to Director, April 17, 1950, Barr file [b], #41, #43, respectively.

96. Investigated subjects were often described in ways that accented their Semitic appearance; Joseph P. Green, for example, had a "large Roman Jewish and concave" nose and his general appearance was "New York Jew"; see Floyd L. Jones, Silvermaster report, December 13, 1945, 33, Silvermaster file, #234.

97. "Memo: re: William Perl, Espionage," July 27, 1950, New York City, Perl file [a], #NR, vol. 1; "Arrested as Liar in Atom Spy Case," *New York Mirror,* March 16, 1951, FBI Perl File [a], subfile b.

98. SAC New York to Director, February 28, 1952, 2–3, Perl file [b], #665.

99. See Radosh and Milton, *Rosenberg File,* 51; Venona 732 New York to Moscow, May 20, 1944; Venona 1314 Apresyan to Fitin, September 14, 1944; Venona 854 Fedosimov to Fitin, June 16, 1944. On Perl's "highly valuable" contributions, see also Venona 154 Fitin (Moscow) to New York, February 16, 1945.

100. Feklisov, *Man behind the Rosenbergs,* 139, 147, 160.

101. Venona 976 New York to Fitin, July 11, 1944; HUAC, *Shameful Years,* 70.

102. D. M. Ladd to Director, August 8, 1950, FBI Sobell file [a], #100.

103. See chap 5, note 174.

104. Ladd to Director, August 23, 1950, Sobell file [a], #236.

105. Elitcher interview with Congress, April 5, 1952, HUAC, 82nd Cong., 1st sess., Alethea Arceneaux, Official Reporter, 2–3, in FBI Elitcher file [a]; "Alertronic Protective Corp. of America," Morgan J. Lacey filing, Elitcher file [a], #60.

106. Transcript of Record, *United States of America against Julius Rosenberg, et al.,* U.S. District Court, Southern District of New York, June 1, 1952, 1:207–10; Radosh and Milton, *Rosenberg File,* 134.

107. Vincent J. Cahill memo on Elitcher, September 27, 1950, 2–3, FBI Sobell file [b], #531.

108. Venona 1053 Stepan Apresyan (New York) to Fitin, July 26, 1944.

109. William Perl investigation, October 19, 1953, FBI Perl file [a], #1162; Radosh and Milton, *Rosenberg File,* 130–34, 139; John M. O'Mara, SA, memo on Sobell, September 29, 1950, Sobell file [b], #558.

110. Report, August 21, 1950, Sobell file [a], #143 (supplemental release).

111. See D. M. Ladd to Director, March 23, 1951, 4, FBI Elitcher file [d], #31.

112. Radosh and Milton, *Rosenberg File,* 130, 134; Haynes and Klehr, *Venona,* 297; tes-

timony of Benjamin Mandel, Research Director, in *Scope of Soviet Activity,* 4875. As Radosh and Milton note, much of the FBI's observations of Sobell through the war concerned his propensity to mingle with African Americans and to be combative with other employees over politics (134).

113. Feklisov, *Man behind the Rosenbergs,* 110; Venona 1715 Kvasnikov to Fitin, December 5, 1944; Venona 200 Fitin to New York, March 6, 1945; Venona 736 New York to Moscow, May 22, 1944. Rosenberg may not have taken the money; according to Feklisov, he had a very difficult time getting Rosenberg to accept even $25 per month to cover expenses. See Feklisov, *Man behind the Rosenbergs,* 122.

114. Feklisov, *Man behind the Rosenbergs,* chap. 13, passim, 115–16.

115. Andriyve testimony, *Scope of Soviet Activity,* 1125–26.

116. See Michael Dobbs, "How Soviets Stole U.S. Atom Secrets," *Washington Post,* October 4, 1992. To this day many of the Soviet sources in the United States remain unknown, as the Venona messages' frequently unidentified codenames confirm—and these are only the unknown agents who appear in Venona.

117. Ibid.; June 23, 1942, 9, Feldman file, #743. The FBI's new understanding of the situation is spelled out in the FBI report of November 27, 1945, 51.

118. Duggan quoted in Weinstein and Vassiliev, *Haunted Wood,* 18. On his reluctance see 12–13, 295.

119. Steve Nelson report, July 17, 1943, Nelson file, #153; on informants in Pittsburgh, for instance, see Nelson report, November 30, 1949, Pittsburgh, 46–47, #498.

120. FBI report, November 27, 1945, 24; Haynes and Klehr, *Venona,* 44–46; Benson and Warner, *Venona,* xviin30. The letter, [anonymous] to Hoover, August 7, 1943, in both English and Russian, is in Benson and Warner, *Venona,* 51–54.

121. Additional evidence of Zarubin/Zubilin's role appears in Venona 846 Zubilin to Moscow, June 3, 1943; Elizabeta Zubilin is named also in Venona 1004 Zubilin to Fitin, June 25, 1943.

122. Sudoplatov et al., *Special Tasks,* 196–97. According to Sudoplatov, Zarubin and his wife were recalled to Russia on the basis of the letter, as was Mironov; the senior officials were cleared but the junior informant ended up in a mental institution. See also discussion in Schecter and Schecter, *Sacred Secrets,* 64–67. The defection of Purchasing Commission representative Viktor Kravchenko in April 1944 may have also contributed to Zarubin's departure. See Theoharis, *Chasing Spies,* 53. Mironov's letter apparently encouraged the Soviet Union to cut ties between American Communist agents and scientists at work on the atomic project; Moscow tried to use its own agents instead. See Merkulov to Beria, October 2, 1944, cited in Schecter and Schecter, *Sacred Secrets,* 50, 348n12.

123. Klarin appears as well in Venona 1164 Klarin to Fitin, July 18, 1943; Kheifetz is named in Venona 446–57 Grigorii Markovich Kheifetz to Moscow, October 31, 1943, November 3, 1943, respectively, and Venona 276 [unnamed Moscow agent] to San Francisco, August 29, 1944.

124. Kvasnikov is named also in Venona 793–94, 1055 Kvasnikov to Fitin, May 25, 1945, July 5, 1945, respectively.

125. Semyonov is mentioned in Venona 586 New York to Moscow, April 29, 1944.

126. Shevchenko is also named in Venona 780, 792 Kvasnikov to Fitin, May 25, 1945, May 26, 1945, respectively, and Venona 1054 New York to Fitin, July 5, 1945.

127. Tarasov appears as well in Venona 708 Fitin (Moscow) to Yurij (Mexico City), December 8, 1944.

128. Sudoplatov et al., *Special Tasks,* 196–97. The Germans first reported the Katyn massacre in 1943, blaming it on the Soviets, but Western correspondents, including Kathleen Harriman, the daughter of American ambassador W. Averell Harriman, did not see the evidence until the Soviets showed them the bodies in January 1944, when Moscow claimed the Nazis were responsible. Kathleen Harriman believed the Soviet account, and her report became the basis of her father's cable back to Washington. Ambassador Harriman, according to his biographer, "wanted to believe" the Soviet story; he was "more concerned with the diplomatic repercussions and working with the Soviets on the future of Poland" than delving further into the problem of these deaths. Mikhail Gorbachev finally acknowledged the Red Army's responsibility for the massacre during the *glasnost* era. See Abramson, *Spanning the Century,* 362–63. The Venona cable confirming Zubilin's role at Katyn is Venona 1033 New York to Moscow, July 1, 1943, cited in Haynes and Klehr, *Venona,* 45.

129. Benson and Warner, *Venona,* xvii–xviii; on Semyonov, see memo, Belmont to Ladd, May 15, 1950, 10, foia.fbi.gov/venona/venona.pdf.

130. "Summary Brief on Fuchs and Gold," February 12, 1951, 4g, Fuchs file, #1494X (supplemental release).

131. Feklisov, *Man behind the Rosenbergs,* 106, 138.

132. Venona 306 Fitin to San Francisco, September 20, 1944.

133. "The Red Army Intelligence—NKVD Inspection of 1944," in FBI report, "Soviet Activities in the US," July 25, 1946, box 15, Clifford Papers, HSTL; "The Pattern of Soviet Espionage in the United States," June 5, 1947, 6, file 383.4 USSR, Army Intelligence Project Decimal File, RG 319, NARA; FBI, "Soviet Espionage Activities," October 19, 1945, 12, FBI file, box 167, PSF, HSTL.

134. On COMRAP and CINRAD's origins, see Theoharis, *Chasing Spies,* 62–63; on techniques, see Senate Select Committee, *Intelligence Activities,* bk. 2, 35–38.

135. FBI report, "Soviet Activities in the US," 25. Summing up the case in 1944, the FBI wrote that Nelson "is shown as engaging in military and industrial espionage; to be active in political and Governmental aspects of the Apparatus; and is further shown as active in the gathering and dissemination of propaganda favorable to the Soviet Union." "COMRAP Summary," 59.

136. "COMRAP Summary," 6, 8.

137. Harriman to President, March 18, 1944, President's cable to Harriman, March 30, 1944, box 172, Harriman Papers, Library of Congress. I am indebted to David S. Foglesong for these documents. See also Whitehead, *FBI Story,* 228–29; Richard Powers, *Secrecy and Power,* 271–72.

138. Weinstein and Vassiliev, *Haunted Wood,* 156.

139. T. G. Spencer report, 84; "Underground Soviet Espionage Organization (NKVD) in Agencies of the U.S. Government," 289.

140. Weinstein and Vassiliev, *Haunted Wood,* 164–65.

141. "Underground Soviet Espionage Organization (NKVD)," 19.

142. T. G. Spencer report, 36.

143. "John R. Murphy's Fuchs Report," 109; Peake, "Afterword," *Out of Bondage,* 323.

144. Radosh and Milton, *Rosenberg File,* 36.

145. "Personal History and Background Report," 3.

146. Gold, "Circumstances," 1074–75.

147. "Personal History and Background Report," 12; Gold, "Circumstances," 1055–57; Abraham Brothman report, December 4, 1950, 4, #473.

148. "John R. Murphy's Fuchs Report," 107; see also October 1, 1944, message paraphrase, Summary Brief on Fuchs and Gold, February 12, 1951, Fuchs file, #1494X (supplemental release), 71. The Soviets were kept well informed of Brothman's various businesses and his inventions, as well as his sometimes challenging relationship with his partners. See October 1, 1944, message paraphrase, 54.

149. "Personal History and Background Report," 9. On Buna-S, see also FBI New York (Scheidt) to director, November 18, 1950, #363. Brothman apparently got some of his material from B. F. Goodrich and from the Hendrick Company, where he worked as an engineer developing chemical equipment in the late 1930s. See Scheidt to Director, November 18, 1950, #465; Scheidt to Hoover, November 21, 1950, #471.

150. Gold, "Circumstances," 1075; Brothman biography, FBI Rosenberg file 65–15185, 4–5; HUAC, *Shameful Years,* 69. Venona confirms this interest in synthetic rubber: see Venona 1609, 1621 Washington to Moscow, July 13, 1943, July 14, 1943, respectively; Venona 471 Director, Moscow, to Washington, March 18, 1943. Other cables that confirm Gold's work are Venona 195, 1797 Leonid Romanovich Kvasnikov (New York) to P. M. Fitin (Moscow), February 9, 1944, December 20, 1944, respectively.

151. Abraham Brothman report, December 4, 1950, Brothman file, #473.

152. Undated top-secret report, attached to FBI report, 2–3, 16, Brothman file, #474.

153. "Personal History and Background Report," 9–11.

154. Bergier, *Secret Armies,* 49; Haynes and Klehr, *Venona,* 290; Gold, "Circumstances," 1056–57, 1076; discussion of Gold testimony in *Scope of Soviet Activity,* 4864; *US News & World Report,* November 24, 1950, cited in JCAE, *Soviet Atomic Espionage,* 214–16. Slack was later arrested and pleaded guilty to providing information on explosives from the Holston Ordnance Works in Kingsport, Tennessee, and received a fifteen-year prison term; see "Summary Brief on Fuchs and Gold," February 12, 1951, Fuchs file, #1494X (supplemental release), 4h; Roberts, *The Brother,* 233.

155. An interesting semi-fictional account of Gold's career that also provides a compelling creation of his inner life and turmoil as a spy is Millicent Dillon's *Harry Gold.*

156. Gold, "Circumstances," 1068, and testimony in *Scope of Soviet Activity,* 1021, 1029; see also Radosh and Milton, *Rosenberg File,* 30.

157. "Summary Brief on Fuchs and Gold," February 12, 1951, 170, Fuchs file, #1494X (supplemental release).

158. JCAE, *Soviet Atomic Espionage,* 11.

159. Haynes and Klehr, *Venona,* 289; Venona 1390 New York to Moscow, October 1, 1944; "Facts concerning American Espionage Contact, Summary of Facts, Jurisdiction, Collaboration with British," 213, Fuchs file, #1494X (supplemental release).

160. Hugh H. Clegg and Robert J. Lamphere to the Director, June 4, 1950, Fuchs file, #1412 (1998 supplemental release).

161. See discussion in Roberts, *The Brother*, 130, 144, 184; Weinstein and Vassiliev, *Haunted Wood*, 213.

162. Gold, "Circumstances," 1072.

163. "Summary Brief on Fuchs and Gold," February 12, 1951, 4g, Fuchs file, #1494X (supplemental release). Gold worked for Semyonov between late 1941 and early 1944.

164. Weinstein and Vassiliev, *Haunted Wood*, 177.

165. Radosh and Milton, *Rosenberg File*, 31; Gold, "Circumstances," 1074.

166. Gold, "Circumstances," 1024, 1029; Summary Brief on Fuchs and Gold, February 12, 1951, 71, Fuchs file, #1494X (supplemental release).

167. Radosh and Milton, *Rosenberg File*, 31; Gold, "Circumstances," 1083–84.

168. Venona 1327 New York (signature unrecoverable) to Fitin, September 15, 1944; HUAC, *Soviet Espionage Activities*, 102, 104. Haynes and Klehr note that Venona messages 941, 1048 New York to Moscow, July 4, July 25, 1944, respectively, confirm that Franey had already sent at least one set of secret information; the FBI, they point out, did not contact her until August. *Venona*, 293–94.

169. Hoover to Hopkins, July 18, 1942, box 16, OF 10B; FBI memo, June 2, 1940, box 11, OF 10B; Haynes and Klehr, *Venona*, 293.

170. Franey testimony, in HUAC, *Soviet Espionage Activities*, 104.

171. Ibid., 104–5, 127–28; FBI agent Jacob Spolansky insisted that "not a particle of information that might hurt the United States was allowed to trickle out." Spolansky, *Communist Trail*, 161.

172. Venona 780, 792 Kvasnikov to Fitin, May 25, 1945, May 26, 1945, respectively. The FBI remained unsure, however, in 1950 about Beiser; see Ladd to Hoover, February 28, 1950, 14, foia.fbi.gov/venona/venona.pdf.

173. HUAC, *Soviet Espionage Activities*, 116–19; see also likely initial contact with Haas referenced in Venona 705 New York to Moscow, May 18, 1943. See also discussion of Shevchenko's meetings with "Shtamp," who was probably Haas, in Venona 1327 New York (signature unrecoverable) to Fitin, September 15, 1944; Venona 1607–1608 Anton (Kvasnikov) to Viktor (Fitin), November 16, 1944.

174. FBI report, "Soviet Activities in the US," 29.

175. HUAC, *Soviet Espionage Activities*, 120–22. Or, as Henry Wallace put it, "[S]cience is universal. You can't bottle science up, and when you do you condemn your own nation to backwardness." See HUAC, *Hearings regarding Shipment*, 1095.

176. Venona 736 New York (signature unrecoverable) to Fitin, May 22, 1944. The Soviets purchased German cameras in Mexico; see Venona 976 New York to Fitin, July 11, 1944. See also HUAC, *Soviet Espionage Activities*, 107–9; FBI report, November 27, 1945, 50.

177. On Ostrovsky and Curtiss-Wright, see Venona 941 New York to Moscow July 4, 1944; Professor Alexander Nicholas Petroff of the Curtiss-Wright Aircraft Corporation was also noted as supplying some "highly valuable" as well as "not valuable" information. See Venona 134, 305 Moscow to New York, February 16, 1945, April 4, 1945, respectively. On Mazurin see Venona 1657 New York to Moscow, November 27, 1944, and Ladd to Hoover, February 28, 1950, 12, foia.fbi.gov/venona/venona.pdf. On Plourde see Venona

1151 New York to Moscow, August 12, 1944; on Pinsly, see also Ladd to Hoover, February 28, 1950, 13. On the source at Republic Aircraft and the German buzz bomb, see Venona 780, 792 Kvasnikov to Fitin, May 25, 1945, May 26, 1945, respectively; Venona 1327 New York to Moscow, September 15, 1944, cited in Haynes and Klehr, *Venona*, 295; and Ladd to Hoover, February 28, 1950, 14.

178. Belmont to Ladd, espionage memo, May 15, 1950, 5, foia.fbi.gov/venona/venona.pdf.

179. Venona 854 Fedosimov to Fitin, June 16, 1944.

180. See discussion in Ladd to Hoover, February 28, 1950, 12, as well as FBI report, "Soviet Activities in the US," 29.

181. HUAC report (see recovered document), in JCAE, *Soviet Atomic Espionage*, 164.

182. HUAC, *Soviet Espionage Activities*, 115, 126.

183. Weinstein and Vassiliev, *Haunted Wood*, 104–7, passim.

184. With this new understanding of U.S. counterintelligence, Feklisov had a hair-raising moment in February 1946 when a former agent offered him two fat packages of material related to aircraft carriers. Throwing caution to the wind, Feklisov decided to accept them—and turned out to be very lucky. See Feklisov, *Man behind the Rosenbergs*, 86–91.

185. See D. M. Ladd to Hoover, August 24, 1948, Nathan Gregory Silvermaster report, Silvermaster file; Hoover to Attorney General, November 28, 1945, #94; Clyde Tolson to R. C. Hendon, November 26, 1945, #108X11; Washington to ASAC Donegan, November 21, 1945, #53; G. C. Callan to Evans, November 25, 1945#75; memo, November 28, 1945, #85; Hoover memo, November 21, 1945, #108X4. FBI wiretaps on her sources, however, were inadmissible in court. See Theoharis, *Chasing Spies*, 43–44.

186. Olmsted, *Red Spy Queen*, 105–6.

187. FBI report, November 27, 1945, 47; Klehr et al., *Secret World*, 309–17.

188. Hayden Peake does an effective job of demolishing the claims of one of Bentley's accused, William H. Taylor, that she was substantially inaccurate. See Peake, "Afterword," *Out of Bondage*, 237–47, as well as the FBI's own listing of her corroborating evidence in appendix b. On the FBI's difficulties in proving her allegations of espionage, see May, *Un-American Activities*, 88–89. On her exaggerations, see, for instance, Olmsted, *Red Spy Queen*, 162–63.

189. Weinstein and Vassiliev, *Haunted Wood*, 95–96; Venona 973 New York to Moscow, July 11, 1944.

190. May, *Un-American Activities*, 82–83.

191. Bentley testimony, in HUAC, *Hearings regarding Communist Espionage* (1948), 541. She got her revenge on Browder, telling her Moscow bosses he had attacked Soviet espionage as "dirty blackmail." Weinstein and Vassiliev, *Haunted Wood*, 99.

192. Olmsted, *Red Spy Queen*, 68; Weinstein and Vassiliev, *Haunted Wood*, 98.

193. Olmsted, *Red Spy Queen*, 72; "Underground Soviet Espionage Organization (NKVD)," 20.

194. Haynes and Klehr, *Venona*, 122; Weinstein and Vassiliev, *Haunted Wood*, 95–100; FBI report, "Soviet Activities in the US," in Clifford Report (July 25, 1946).

195. Senate Committee on Expenditures, *Export Policy and Loyalty*, 20, 36.

196. T. G. Spencer report, 84; July 13, 1948, *Washington Post*, box 36, Tanenhaus Papers; "Underground Soviet Espionage Organization (NKVD)," 289; Senate Committee on

Expenditures, *Export Policy and Loyalty,* 20–21. Bentley told the Senate that these offers represented a "very cynical" Russian attitude toward Americans. "They behaved somewhat like cheap gangsters," she complained, as they offered her more and more money (from $50 to $300 a week) and urged her to give cash to her sources.

197. "Underground Soviet Espionage Organization (NKVD)," 289; T. G. Spencer report, 6:85, Silvermaster file, #220.

198. Gold, "Circumstances," 1075; Weinstein and Vassiliev, *Haunted Wood,* 98–100.

199. Weinstein and Vassiliev, *Haunted Wood,* 100–101; "Underground Soviet Espionage Organization (NKVD)," 290; Senate Committee on Expenditures, *Export Policy and Loyalty,* 21; T. G. Spencer report, 6:85; Olmsted, *Red Spy Queen,* 76–77; D. M. Ladd to Hoover report, "Nathan Gregory Silvermaster et al. ESPIONAGE- R" August 24, 1948. Ladd insisted that "Heller was an individual of no political significance who had no connection with this case."

200. Weinstein and Vassiliev, *Haunted Wood,* 100–101.

201. T. G. Spencer report, 84–86; Venona 1673 Pavel Ivanovich Fedosimov to Fitin, November 30, 1944.

202. See World Tourists Incorporated, US Service and Shipping Corporation, John Hazard Reynolds, Elizabeth Terrill Bentley, Max L. Spector file, March 28, 1945, FBI Bentley file [a], #25.

203. SAC New York to Director, FBI, November 15, 1944, Bentley file [a], #21. See also World Tourists Incorporated, US Service and Shipping Corporation, John Hazard Reynolds, Elizabeth Terrill Bentley, Max L. Spector file, July 12, 1945, Bentley file [a], #26.

204. See "Underground Soviet Espionage Organization (NKVD)," 289; T. G. Spencer report, 84. In late 1946, World Tourists was still advertising that it sent "new and old clothing" to Russia and would "fumigate and supply a Board of Health Certificate" on shipments of used clothes. See World Tourist ad in *The Worker,* December 1, 1946, section 3, Bentley file [a], #A.

205. "Underground Soviet Espionage Organization (NKVD)," 291.

206. T. G. Spencer report, 86.

207. Weinstein and Vassiliev, *Haunted Wood,* 98, 102–3; Olmsted, *Red Spy Queen,* 97; Bentley testimony, in HUAC, *Hearings regarding Communist Espionage* (1948), 812; "Underground Soviet Espionage Organization (NKVD)," 292. Bentley turned the money over to the FBI, who held onto it until Bentley blackmailed them to give it back to her in the fall of 1951, which they did for "assistance and services." As Olmsted notes, this became a precedent for Bentley's weekly payments by the FBI, which began in 1952. See Olmsted, *Red Spy Queen,* 174, 179.

208. Senate Committee on Expenditures, *Export Policy and Loyalty,* 44. Her confession was based on no animus against those Americans she had worked with, she said. She argued that "these poor devils" (her sources) "were roped into Soviet espionage."

209. Bentley testimony in HUAC, *Hearings regarding Communist Espionage* (1948), 540.

210. Senate Judiciary Committee, *Communist Activities among Aliens and National Groups,* 122; Olmsted, *Red Spy Queen,* 98–99.

211. Senate Committee on Expenditures, *Export Policy and Loyalty,* 40; Bentley testimony, in HUAC, *Hearings regarding Communist Espionage* (1948), 811.

212. D. M. Ladd to Director, November 9, 1945, Silvermaster file, #8; New York to Director, Washington, November 8, 1945, #1; see also FBI's material from Bentley, November 8, 1945, box 169, PSF, HSTL; Olmsted, *Red Spy Queen,* 99–100.

213. Olmsted, *Red Spy Queen,* chap. 5, passim; May, *Un-American Activities,* 77.

214. Senate Committee on Expenditures, *Export Policy and Loyalty,* 24.

215. "Underground Soviet Espionage Organization (NKVD)," 65.

216. Bentley's meetings with Browder are referenced in Venona 2011 Zubilin to Fitin, December 11, 1943, which notes that "Good Girl has twice seen Helmsman." Golos's meetings with him are mentioned in Venona 325 Moscow to Washington, May 17, 1942, and in FBI report, November 27, 1945, 32.

217. "Underground Soviet Espionage Organization (NKVD)," 6. Her "accurate" story, however, changed over the ensuing years, as Bentley embellished her tale with even more damning accusations. See Peake, "Afterword," *Out of Bondage,* 236–37. In some cases, Bentley tailored her story to suit the more outrageous allegations of sensational journalists, as she did when discussing Harry Dexter White's provision of currency plates to the Soviet Union during World War II. See Olmsted, *Red Spy Queen,* 185–86. On White's role, see the full discussion in Craig, *Treasonable Doubt,* chap. 5.

218. "Underground Soviet Espionage Organization (NKVD)," 18.

219. Bentley's allegations first appeared in public in Nelson Frank and Norton Mockridge, "Red Ring Bared by Its Blond Queen," *New York World Telegram,* July 21, 1948. See discussion in Olmsted, *Red Spy Queen,* 123–29.

220. T. G. Spencer report, 18.

221. Bentley testimony, in HUAC, *Communist Activities among Aliens and National Groups,* 112; T. G. Spencer report, 19–21. On dues, see Ladd to Hoover, November 25 1945, Silvermaster file, #108X12.

222. T. G. Spencer report, 22–23.

223. Ibid., 19; Louis J. Russell testimony, in HUAC, *Hearings regarding Communist Espionage* (1948), 614.

224. "Underground Soviet Espionage Organization (NKVD)," 21; Weinstein and Vassiliev, *Haunted Wood,* 161. Silvermaster had long been involved in Communist Party activities, dating back to his days as an undergraduate at the University of Washington.

225. "Underground Soviet Espionage Organization (NKVD)," 22; Russell testimony, in HUAC, *Hearings regarding Communist Espionage* (1948), 614. See also Sandilands, *Lauchlin Currie,* 145.

226. Russell testimony, in HUAC, *Hearings regarding Communist Espionage* (1948), 613–15; Senate Judiciary Committee, *Communist Activities among Aliens and National Groups,* 116.

227. Senate Judiciary Committee, *Communist Activities among Aliens and National Groups,* 119; Silvermaster investigation, November 26, 1945, Silvermaster file, #26X2.

228. Russell testimony, in HUAC, *Hearings regarding Communist Espionage* (1948), 615; Sandilands, *Lauchlin Currie,* 146; Weinstein and Vassiliev, *Haunted Wood,* 161; Schecter and Schecter, *Sacred Secrets,* 161; Haynes and Klehr, *Venona,* 132–33. In 1948, Currie defended himself vigorously against the charges that he had protected Silvermaster, declaring both that it was Patterson, as well as General Strong, who had made the decision on

Silvermaster's job and that to imply that Currie had pressured them was "calumny." Currie testimony, in HUAC, *Hearings regarding Communist Espionage* (1948), 854–55; see also *Washington Post*, August 13, 1948, box 36, Tanenhaus Papers. According to the KGB archives, however, Silvermaster told Zarubin that Currie "made every effort to liquidate his case ... [Currie] managed to persuade the majority of members of this [investigatory] committee to favor repealing this investigation." See Weinstein and Vassiliev, *Haunted Wood*, 163. Although Currie admitted "I was probably too accessible" with Communists and fellow travelers during the war years, his biographer Roger Sandilands argues that he was tarred with "guilt by association ... without taking [his] record as a whole." *Lauchlin Currie*, 149. Mentioned in nine Venona cables, the involvement of Lauchlin Currie in Soviet espionage, however "limited," remains controversial. See Haynes and Klehr, *Venona*, 146–49, and posts on H-Diplo on-line discussion board, June 1999.

229. Venona 732, 735 Zubilin (New York) to Fitin (Moscow), May 21, 1943: "William Ludwig Ullman," "Abraham George Silverman," February 1, 1946, attached to Hoover to Vaughan, February 1, 1946, FBI file, box 169, PSF, HSTL. On Silvermaster's background, see also "Underground Soviet Espionage Organization (NKVD)," 23.

230. Haynes and Klehr, *Venona*, 133; see Venona 1431 New York to Moscow, September 2, 1943. Weinstein and Vassiliev's Soviet research shows extensive documentation of the Silvermaster investigation. See *Haunted Wood*, 358nn28–33.

231. T. G. Spencer report, 23. When the FBI later explored the basement, they discovered photoflood bulbs with attachments, the bellows of a camera, light reflectors, an enlarger, photographic developing equipment and fluids, pans, printing paper, drying frames, negatives, electric dryers, photograph trimmings. and empty film cartons in the trash. See report, December 13, 1945, 7:158–59, Silvermaster file, #234; see also Floyd L. Jones, report, December 13, 1945, vol. 7, #234, and "Underground Soviet Espionage Organization (NKVD)," 24.

232. Bentley, *Out of Bondage*, 98; Olmsted, *Red Spy Queen*, 46.

233. T. G. Spencer report; Bentley, *Out of Bondage*, 96, 98.

234. See, for instance, Venona 794–799 New York to Moscow, May 28, 1943.

235. Bentley testimony, in HUAC, *Communist Activities among Aliens and National Groups*, 117.

236. Weinstein and Vassiliev, *Haunted Wood*, 163–64; FBI report, November 27, 1945, 47; Venona 211, 212 Stepan Zakharovich Apresyan to Fitin, February 10, 1945; "Silvermaster" report, February 1, 1946, attached to Hoover to Vaughan, February 1, 1946, FBI file, box 169, PSF, HSTL; "Underground Soviet Espionage Organization (NKVD)," 73.

237. Report on White, November 16, 1945, Silvermaster file, #108. He would make a similar protest later in front of HUAC in 1948, in response to Bentley's allegations, and then suffer a heart attack three days later. White's name, along with George Silverman's, also came up in an anonymous letter to FDR that the FBI received in April 1944 and traced to Victor Perlo's ex-wife. A former Communist, she told the FBI that she had indeed written the letter, identifying "the underground Communist group in Washington, D.C."

238. Craig, "Treasonable Doubt," 560, 585; Olmsted, *Red Spy Queen*, 48–50.

239. Bentley, *Out of Bondage*, 99; T. G. Spencer report, 27. Although this was her story in 1945, when testifying to a grand jury in March 1948, Bentley played down the signifi-

cance of the B-29 information she received from Silvermaster. See Olmsted, *Red Spy Queen,* 123.

240. Bentley, *Out of Bondage,* 98; Venona 1635 New York to Moscow, November 21, 1944.

241. Weinstein and Vassiliev, *Haunted Wood,* 164–69; T. G. Spencer report, 27, 53. The relationship between the Silvermasters and Ullman did not end, however; the three left Washington and went into real estate on the New Jersey shore. See Weinstein and Vassiliev, *Haunted Wood,* 170.

242. Some of these men, including Hiss and Kramer, had been members of Harold Ware's group, which Whittaker Chambers had named as his main source in the mid-1930s. See FBI report, November 27, 1945, 48; Weinstein, *Perjury,* 156. The Ware group included members of several New Deal agencies, among them the Agricultural Adjustment Administration, the Labor Department, and the National Labor Relations Board. Perlo group members' names, including Perlo, Kramer, Charles Flato, Harold Glasser, and Edward Joseph Fitzgerald, appear in Venona 588 New York to Moscow, April 29, 1944; see also Venona 771 New York to Moscow, May 30, 1944; Venona 3708, 3713–15 Gromov (Washington) to Moscow, June 29, 1945; "Harry Dexter White," February 1, 1946, FBI file, box 169, PSF, HSTL. Also on Glasser, see Weinstein and Vassiliev, *Haunted Wood,* 265–72.

243. T. G. Spencer report, 6:16–17; FBI report, November 27, 1945, 47–48; HUAC, *Hearings regarding Communist Espionage* (1948), 688.

244. See HUAC, *Hearings regarding Communist Espionage* (1948), 688–89, 849; T. G. Spencer report, 53.

245. Bentley report, November 7, 1945, attached to Ladd to Hoover, August 24, 1948, box 36, Tanenhaus Papers; Ladd to Hoover, December 12, 1945, vol. 8, Silvermaster file, #235. Browder served as a useful mask for Soviet activities; many spies, such as Remington, thought their information was going only to him. Senate Committee on Expenditures, *Export Policy and Loyalty,* 31.

246. Ladd to E. A. Tamm, November 19, 1945, Silvermaster file, #37. There was some controversy over whether so many men could be made available; SAC Hottel in Washington field resisted the calls for more men, declaring the effort impossible, but Hoover insisted, noting that "the tempo on this case everywhere was entirely too slow and in order to get it done . . . a special assignment had to be made out of it." See A. C. Hendon to Mr. Tolson, November 19, 1945, Silvermaster file, #38; Ladd to Tamm, November 21, 1945, #54.

247. In Silvermaster file, see Hoover, memo for the Attorney General, November 17, 1945, #27X; Washington to the attention of SAC Donegan, November 21, 1945, #53; JEH Memo, November 21 1945, #108X-4; Evans to G. C. Callan, Callan to Evans, November 25, 1945, #75; Clyde Tolson to R. C. Hendon, subject Gregory Silvermaster, November 26, 1945, #108X11; memo, November 28, 1945, #85; J. Edgar Hoover to Attorney General, November 28, 1945, #94; Floyd L. Jones report, December 18, 1945, #269. On June 26, 1945, Chambers had also spoken about Hiss being part of an underground headed by Harold Ware. Bentley confirmed Hiss's name in her lengthy November 30 statement to the FBI. See T. G. Spencer report. On Hiss, see also memo for Attorney General, November 30, 1945, Silvermaster file, #94. Although the FBI investigation found no evidence that Hiss was spying, Hoover hoped to ease him out of his job. Lacking proof of his Communist Party membership, this was not possible. See Theoharis, *Chasing Spies,* 38–41.

248. "Justification for Personnel Request for Fiscal Year 1947" (FBI budget estimates), November 30, 1945, FBI file, box 167, PSF, HSTL.

249. Washington to Director and SAC URGENT, November 8, 1945, Silvermaster file, #4.

250. Telegram, New York to Washington, November 21, 1945, Silvermaster file, #56.

251. Ibid.

252. This point is well made in Olmsted, *Red Spy Queen*, 105–8. As she notes, if Bentley had been able to resume her life as a Soviet agent, "the FBI could have collected damning evidence against dozens of spies." Although other historians, like Athan Theoharis, have argued that FBI methods (such as wiretapping) were the key obstacle to arrests of Soviet spies, the "intelligence coup" effected by Philby was the first insurmountable problem for the FBI. See Theoharis, *Chasing Spies*, chap. 4.

253. Telegram, New York to Washington, November 21, 1945, Silvermaster file, #56; Weinstein and Vassiliev, *Haunted Wood*, 104–6; *Washington Post*, July 13, 1948. Bentley apparently didn't know of his recall, as she came to a prearranged meeting on March 23, 1946, for which he never arrived. See Peake, "Afterword," *Out of Bondage*, 267.

254. Silvermaster report, 11:5, 9, Silvermaster file, #249. Browder was doing economic research for a bulletin, *Distributors Guide*, which he planned to publish beginning in 1946. From what Bentley could tell, he no longer had any Soviet connections. Indeed, he told her with "bitter feeling" that "he has absolutely no connection with any Communists at this time" (11:10). He claimed party membership had fallen off by half and pointed out, with some satisfaction, that this would create difficulties for the new party leaders, William Z. Foster and Eugene Dennis. Browder remained convinced that Stalin was not responsible for his disgraceful treatment.

255. See discussion in Olmsted, *Red Spy Queen*, 108–11.

256. Ladd to Hoover, December 12, 1945, Silvermaster file, #235; Hoover to Attorney General, November 28, 1945, #94; Theoharis, *Chasing Spies*, 239.

257. Ladd to Tamm, November 23, 1945, Silvermaster file, #108; Ladd to Hoover, December 12, 1945, #235. This did not stop the Bureau from conducting "at least three break-ins." See Theoharis, *Chasing Spies*, 43.

258. Ladd to Director, December 12, 1945, Silvermaster file, #235.

259. May, *Un-American Activities*, 89; Olmsted, *Red Spy Queen*, 203.

260. Hoover to George E. Allen, June 7, 1946, FBI file, box 169, PSF, HSTL.

261. Memo, December 5, 1945, Silvermaster file, #118; Memo, July 29, 1948, 1, 3, 10, FBI Remington file, #X10; T. G. Spencer report, 48.

262. Latham, *Communist Controversy*, 160.

263. See discussions in Weinstein and Vassiliev, *Haunted Wood*, chaps. 5, 10, 11, and Klehr et al., *Secret World*, 309–17.

264. See Olmsted, *Red Spy Queen*, 134–38, and Olmsted, "'I Think She Is One Hundred Percent Our Woman': Elizabeth Bentley and Female Agency" (paper, AHA Pacific Coast Branch Conference, Honolulu, August 1, 2003).

265. Schrecker, *Many Are the Crimes*, 172. Bentley was indeed an alcoholic and had a number of other noticeable character flaws, from lying to plagiarism; see discussion in May, *Un-American Activities*, 138–39; Olmsted, *Red Spy Queen*, 6–7.

266. See *Washington Post*, May 23, 1942, box 46, Dies Committee files.

267. *The Nation*, May 14, 1942, box 46, Dies Committee files.

268. "A Message to the House of Representatives," January 1943, box 15, Dies Committee files.
269. Ibid.
270. See discussion in Goodman, *The Committee*, 166–70.
271. On the Nazi movement, see, for example, HUAC, *Investigation of Un-American Propaganda Activities in the United States: Report on the Axis Front Movement in the US.*
272. Frank Kingdon to Joe Starnes, July 6, 1942, box 44, Dies Committee files; Goodman, *The Committee*, 141.
273. Walter Winchell script on Dies Committee (on Blue Network [ABC radio]), January 31, 1943, and Mark Woods to Dies Committee, January 11, 1944, box 49, Dies Committee files; "The Private Papers of a Cub Reporter," *New York Daily Mirror*, March 2, 1944, box 59, Dies Committee files.
274. *William Schneiderman vs. The United States of America*, Supreme Court of the United States, No. 2, October Term 1942, June 21, 1943, box 32, Dies Committee files.
275. "House Group Will Look Into 'Reds' in Army," *New York Times*, February 23, 1945; see also reaction from I. F. Stone, *The Nation*, March 3, 1945, in ACLU Clippings, 1945, vol. 2649, microfilm reel 229, ACLU Papers.
276. Stettinius to Truman, April 13, 1945, Cabinet File, box 159, PSF, HSTL.
277. On Fahy, see Venona 901, 360 Washington to Moscow, Moscow to Washington, April 27, 1943, February 26, 1943, respectively, and Haynes and Klehr, *Venona*, 186–88; on payments, see Venona 115 Moscow to Washington, January 20, 1943.

CHAPTER 4

1. "COMRAP Summary," 9.
2. See Sherwin, *A World Destroyed*, 85–89, chap. 4, passim; Kimball, *Forged in War*, 220–21. Feklisov points to a May 1942 agreement between Russia and Britain that called for sharing "all information, including specifications . . . concerning weapons, blueprints or procedures . . . for the pursuit of war against the common enemy." Cited in Feklisov, *Man behind the Rosenbergs*, 194.
3. Roosevelt to Oppenheimer, June 29, 1943, quoted in AEC, *In the Matter of JRO*, 30.
4. Schecter and Schecter, *Sacred Secrets*, 47; Rhodes, *Dark Sun*, 52–54; Weinstein and Vassiliev, *Haunted Wood*, 180; Andrews and Gordievsky, *KGB*, 261–62; Haynes and Klehr, *Venona*, 317–21; Albright and Kunstel, *Bombshell*, 150–51. "Perseus" remains a sketchy character; much of what is known about him comes from an account by Vladimir Chikov, "How the Soviet Secret Service Split the American Atom." Haynes and Klehr suggest Perseus may be a combination of two other scientists, the unidentified "Fogel/Pers" and Ted Hall ("Youngster"), and add that the Cohens were certainly key Soviet agents, as attested by the Kremlin's willingness to ransom them in 1967 from Britain, where they were imprisoned. Fogel is mentioned in Venona 854 New York to Moscow, June 16, 1944, which notes that "two secret plans of the layout of the ENORMOUS plant received from FOGEL." Another unidentified source on the atomic separation process was "Kvant," mentioned in Venona 972, 979, 983 New York to Moscow, June 22–23, 1943.

5. Lansdale-Oppenheimer interview, September 12, 1943, in AEC, *In the Matter of JRO*, 871.

6. Memorandum for the Director, May 5, 1943, Nelson file, #104; Hershberg, *Conant*, 157–58.

7. Schweber, *In the Shadow of the Bomb*, 60; AEC, *In the Matter of JRO*, 31.

8. AEC, *In the Matter of JRO*, 173; Groves quoted in *Christian Science Monitor*, n.d., Summer 1948, in box 27, Tanenhaus Papers.

9. Herken, *Brotherhood*, 102; Feklisov, *Man behind the Rosenbergs*, 202–3; Lansdale quoted in AEC, *In the Matter of JRO*, 261.

10. Oppenheimer quoted in AEC, *In the Matter of JRO*, 28; FBI Rosenberg file, 65–15185, 6.

11. See Hershberg, *Conant*, 164–65. In 1944, Americans would learn that the German effort was "at least two years behind" the Anglo-American program. See Jungk, *Brighter Than a Thousand Suns*, 164. The Germans actually abandoned the project in 1942. See Thomas Powers, "Letter from Copenhagen," 55.

12. *History of the Soviet Atomic Project, 1938–1949* (Moscow: Ministry of Atomic Energy, 1999), 1:223, cited in Schecter and Schecter, *Sacred Secrets*, 88; Herken, *Brotherhood*, 90.

13. Weinstein and Vassiliev, *Haunted Wood*, 183–84; Schecter and Schecter, *Sacred Secrets*, 47; Sudoplatov, *Special Tasks*, 174–75.

14. Schecter and Schecter, *Sacred Secrets*, 55–56. Pontecorvo's name had not come up in the earlier Gouzenko revelations of Moscow's Canadian espionage. See also JCAE, *Soviet Atomic Espionage*, 8.

15. See Schecter and Schecter, *Sacred Secrets*, 47–50, the quote (50) is from Merkulov's letter to Beria, October 2, 1944; Herken, *Brotherhood*, 93. Weinstein and Vassiliev, moreover, state flatly that "Oppenheimer was not a Soviet agent." *Haunted Wood*, 216. Kheifetz had reasons to puff up his results, not the least of which was his vulnerability as a Jew in an anti-Semitic agency and as a former victim of Stalin's purges in 1938. See Schecter and Schecter, *Sacred Secrets*, 81–82.

16. Weinstein and Vassiliev, *Haunted Wood*, 184.

17. Herken, *Brotherhood*, 54; "COMRAP Summary," 26; "Communist Infiltration of Radiation Laboratory, University of California, Berkeley, California," July 7, 1943, FBI file 100–16980, 1; "CINRAD Summary," Memo #1, March 5, 1946, FBI file 100–190625–2017, 7.

18. "COMRAP Summary," 25.

19. Julius Robert Oppenheimer, February 17, 1947, FBI background, attached to Hoover to Vaughan, February 28, 1947, box 167, PSF, HSTL; see also Julius Robert Oppenheimer report, March 18, 1946, attached to Hoover to George Allen, May 29, 1946, box 169, PSF, HSTL; HUAC, *Report on Atomic Espionage*, 5. William Branigan, one of the FBI's agents who listened in on the Nelson conversations, confirmed he could understand nothing that the speakers were talking about. Romerstein interview, November 21, 2003.

20. Proceedings, September 11, 1939, ONI, G-2, quoted in "Nelson, Steve," report, Naval Criminal Investigative Service Records, Department of the Navy, released as part

of Nelson FBI FOIA request. Some of Nelson's views likely were unwelcome to U.S. officials, thus encouraging them to keep a close eye on him. For instance, he suggested that the "CP policy in U.S. in case of war . . . [is to] encourage the soldiers to turn their guns on their own leaders of capitalist countries and not upon the poor working men in the opposite trenches." See "Confidential Report," November 9, 1939, ONI, Washington, DC, FBI file 61–7559–5625, quoted in ONI, "Nelson, Steve" report.

21. Pieper to Director, FBI, May 29, 1941, September 22, 1941, San Francisco, Calif., Nelson file, #3, #5, respectively; Hoover to Attorney General, October 31, 1941, #6.

22. "USA: Communist Strategy," January 7, 1941, file 10110–1581/172, RG 165, NARA.

23. Hoover to Attorney General, February 17, 1942, 14, and E. G. Fitch to D. M. Ladd, March 12, 1942, Nelson file, #20, #21, respectively; D. M. Ladd to E. A. Tamm, November 24, 1942, #46; on physical surveillance, see N. J. L. Pieper to Hoover, October 6, 1942, March 9, 1943, #31, #58, respectively.

24. "CINRAD Summary," 5.

25. Wendell Berge to Director, FBI, February 16, 1943, and Hoover to Berge, June 29, 1942, April 1, 1943, Department of Justice, Criminal Records Division.

26. Pieper to Hoover, April 28, 1943, Nelson file.

27. Report, July 17, 1943, Nelson file, #152; HUAC, *Report on Atomic Espionage*, 1–2; report, May 14, 1943, #125.

28. Pieper to Director FBI, May 25, 1943, Nelson file, #135; Steve Nelson file, 65–1136, Philadelphia, June 7, 1943, 2, 6, in Nelson file, #134. By 1944, the Bureau definitively identified his parents as Jewish, but recorded him as being born in Yugoslavia in 1903, when of course that nation did not exist until 1919. "COMRAP Summary," 58.

29. L. Whitson to H. B. Fletcher, January 30, 1950, Nelson file, #505; COMRAP report, May 7, 1943, 31, #112.

30. HUAC, *Report on Atomic Espionage*, 2; Report, September 12, 1945, 5, Nelson file, #285.

31. Report, June 25, 1945, 15, Nelson file, #271. Subjects included "Marxian Economics," "Military Science," and "How to Take Over a City." September 12, 1945, 5, #285.

32. Report, August 21, 1945, 2, Nelson file, #281; Nelson New York file, April 3, 1947, 30, #402; Steve Nelson report, June 25, 1945, 45, #271.

33. Ladd to Director, August 31, 1948, Nelson file, #463.

34. *Daily Worker*, November 10, 1937, quoted in ONI report, "Steve Nelson," in Nelson file, #14; Report, August 21, 1945, 3, #281. Louis Budenz wrote that Nelson worked hard in "stamping out Trotskyites for the secret police." *Men without Faces*, 36. Another view is in Rosenstone, *Crusade of the Left*, 128–29.

35. Eby, *Between the Bullet and the Lie*, 163, 170; Johnston, *Legions of Babel*, 124.

36. HUAC, *Report on Atomic Espionage*, 3; Ladd to Director, August 31, 1948, Nelson file, #463.

37. Report, June 25, 1945, 20–25, Nelson file, #271.

38. Report, November 28, 1941, Nelson file, #14; ONI report, "Steve Nelson," #14; HUAC, *Report on Atomic Espionage*, 3–4; "COMRAP Summary," 60–61; Steve Nelson, report, June 25, 1945, 28, FBI Nelson file, 100–2696.

39. HUAC, *Hearings regarding Communist Infiltration*, 826–27.

40. Harry M. Kimball, SAC San Francisco to Director, FBI, September 19, 1946, Nelson file, #354; July 4, 1946, July 19, 1946, surveillance log, 5:67, #394. At his 1954 security hearings, however, Oppenheimer said he knew that Nelson was "an important Communist." AEC, *In the Matter of JRO*, 195.

41. Julius Robert Oppenheimer, February 17, 1947, FBI background, attached to Hoover to Vaughan, February 28, 1947, box 167, PSF, HSTL.

42. "CINRAD Summary," 8; Oppenheimer's brother, sister-in-law, and wife were all former Communists, as was former paramour Jean Tatlock. On monitoring of Kitty Oppenheimer, see FBI report, November 27, 1945, 39; on Frank, see Richard Connolly, Special Agent, CIC, Memo for the Officer in Charge, July 19, 1943, Boris T. Pash, Military Intelligence, Chief, Counter Intelligence Branch, to Major George B. Dyer, Director, Intelligence Division, Headquarters Third Service Command, Baltimore, July 10, 1943, *Washington Post*, June 15, 1949, all in Frank Friedman Oppenheimer file, E2037207, Records of the Army Staff, Records of the Office of the Assistant Chief of Staff, G-2, Intelligence, Records of the Investigative Records Repository, Security Classified Intelligence and Investigative Dossiers, 1939–76 (hereafter IRR), RG 319, NARA.

43. Julius Robert Oppenheimer, February 17, 1947, FBI background, attached to Hoover to Vaughan, February 28, 1947, box 167, PSF, HSTL; Oppenheimer, vol. 1, 1941/Character of case, Internal Security, Oppenheimer file, #1.

44. See Hoover to N. J. L. Pieper, February 10 and April 15, 1942, Oppenheimer, vol. 1, 1941/Character of case, Internal Security, 6–7, Oppenheimer file, #1. The FBI director got quite testy about Pieper's requests for surveillance, pointing out that they must be made "telephonically" to Clyde Tolson, a policy that dated to September 1941.

45. Memo to Boardman, April 16, 1954, Oppenheimer file, #1208; "COMRAP Summary," 38–9.

46. Report on J. R. Oppenheimer, February 5, 1950, "Summary Brief on Fuchs," February 6, 1950, 2, Fuchs file, #1202 (1998 supplemental release). As this report shows, Oppenheimer had told the FBI in June 1947 that before the war he "had dabbled in Communist front organizations to learn what they proposed as a panacea for governmental ills of the United States."

47. AEC, *In the Matter of JRO*, 11.

48. See FBI letter to David Lilienthal, April 23, 1947, and memo, April 21, 1947, cited in Schecter and Schecter, *Sacred Secrets*, appendix 1. Berkeley professor Haakon Chevalier reported his and Oppenheimer's membership in the same unit of the party from 1938 to 1942. Chevalier to Oppenheimer, July 13, 1964, cited at www.brotherhoodofthe bomb.com.

49. Memorandum for the Director, May 5, 1943, Nelson file, #104; Haynes and Klehr, *Venona*, 327.

50. Employment of Oppenheimer had been considered a "calculated risk" during World War II. The notion of "calculated risk" allowed for giving clearance despite security issues to a candidate who "is a man of great attainments and capacity and has rendered outstanding services." Oppenheimer's hearing board felt that such a standard only applied during times of "Critical national need," certainly not in the Cold War; the physicist had been consulted for his expertise only two and a half days in 1953. See "Findings

and Recommendation of the Personnel Security Board in the Matter of J. Robert Oppenheimer, May 27, 1954," and "Recommendations of the General Manager (K. D. Nichols) to the US Atomic Energy Commission in the Matter of J. Robert Oppenheimer, June 12, 1954," in AEC, *In the Matter of JRO,* 15/1013, 43/1041, respectively. See also Groves, *Now It Can Be Told,* 63.

51. FBI report, November 27, 1945, 39.

52. AEC, *In the Matter of JRO,* 260, 270; Pash to Lansdale, September 6, 1943, cited in *In the Matter of JRO,* 273.

53. Ibid., 262, 264.

54. Pash to Lansdale, June 29, 1943, cited in ibid., 822; See discussion of Pash's "Alsos" mission in Jungk, *Brighter Than a Thousand Suns,* 158; on Pash's bodyguard surveillance, see Herken, *Brotherhood,* 100.

55. HUAC, *Shameful Years,* 31; FBI report, September 27, 1945, 40. On the surveillance of Nelson, see also D. M. Ladd to the Director, April 16, 1943, Re: CINRAD, Nelson file, #201; "Communist Infiltration of Radiation Laboratory, University of California, Berkeley, California," FBI file 100–16980, July 7, 1943, 1; report, June 25, 1945, 28, Nelson file, 100–2696.

56. "COMRAP Summary," 19; "Communist Infiltration of Radiation Laboratory, University of California, Berkeley, California," July 7, 1943, 2–4, FBI file 100–16980.

57. Recorded transcript, August 20, 1945, 3, Nelson file, #NR.

58. COMRAP report, May 7, 1943, 3, 4, Nelson file, #112.

59. "CINRAD Summary," 6; Memorandum for the Director from D. M. Ladd, May 5, 1943, Nelson file, #104; COMRAP report, May 7, 1943, 5, Nelson file, #112.

60. Report, August 20, 1945, 17, Nelson file, #NR.

61. COMRAP report, May 7, 1943, 5, Nelson file, #112.

62. Quoted in HUAC, *Report on Atomic Espionage,* 5.

63. Report, August 20, 1945, 8–20, passim, Nelson file, #NR.

64. Memorandum for the Director, May 5, 1943, Nelson file, #104; COMRAP report, May 7, 1943, 6, Nelson file, #112.

65. "COMRAP Summary," 25. Rossi Lomanitz, too, had wanted to leave the lab and "come into the open with his Communist Party activities" by working at a shipyard, but Nelson dissuaded him, arguing that "the research work at the Radiation Laboratory was just as important as Party work." Memorandum for the Director, May 5, 1943, Nelson file, #104.

66. August 20, 1945, 18, Nelson file, #NR; COMRAP report, May 7, 1943, 5, Nelson file, #112; FBI report, "Soviet Activities in the United States," July 25, 1946, 26, box 15, Clifford Papers, HSTL.

67. The FBI deduced that these were "possibly Charlotte Serber, a clerical employee, and Robert Server [actually also Serber] a scientist." Ladd to Director, April 16, 1943, 2, Nelson file, #201.

68. August 20, 1945, 19, Nelson file, #NR.

69. Ibid., 15.

70. Ibid., 4–7. Lansdale agreed with this; Kitty Oppenheimer's "strength of will was a powerful influence in keeping him away from what we would regard as dangerous associations." AEC, *In the Matter of JRO,* 266.

71. "CINRAD Summary," 7; Ladd Memorandum for the Director, May 5, 1943, FBI Nelson File, #104; COMRAP report, May 7, 1943, Nelson file, #112.

72. COMRAP report May 7, 1943, Nelson file, #112, 9; see also Fletcher to Ladd, September 17, 1948, and attached memorandum, Nelson file, #462. This did not stop speculation that Nelson had handed Ivanov "a sheath [sic?] of papers . . . [with] one of the most important formulas in the production of the atomic bomb." Donald Robinson, "Steve Nelson: Unwelcome Guest," The American Legion Magazine, February 1950.

73. Pieper to Director, March 31, 1943, Nelson file, #202.

74. "Summary of Facts, Jurisdiction, Collaboration with British," Fuchs file, #14949X, 7.

75. Report on J. R. Oppenheimer, February 5, 1950, Summary Brief on Fuchs, February 6, 1950, 1, Fuchs file, #1202; George M. Langdon report, JRO file, #16; SAC San Francisco to Director, Washington, May 8, 1946, May 14, 1946, JRO file, #33. As Gregg Herken notes, the revelations of Canadian atomic espionage in February 1946 created new momentum for investigations of those involved in atomic research. Brotherhood, 160.

76. See Fletcher to Ladd, September 17, 1948, and attached memorandum, "Communist Party Activity," Nelson file, #462.

77. "CINRAD Summary," 7. See also FBI, "Summary Brief on Fuchs," February 6, 1950, Fuchs file, #1202 ; "Summary of Facts, Jurisdiction, Collaboration with British," 7, #1494X.

78. Herken, Brotherhood, 99–102. It would not be until 1947, with the passage of the Atomic Energy Act, that the FBI received full responsibility for "investigations with reference to character, associations, and loyalty of all applicants for positions with, and employees of, the AEA." See Hoover to Honorable Brian McMahon, Chairman, Joint Congressional Committee on Atomic Energy, April 6, 1950, Fuchs file, #1079; "Summary Brief on Fuchs," February 6, 1950, Fuchs file, #1202.

79. Report, August 20, 1945, Nelson file, #NR, 23, 48; Herken, Brotherhood, 109.

80. HUAC, Report on Atomic Espionage, 6–7, 7–11; see also HUAC, Hearings regarding Communist Infiltration, 802–4.

81. Herken, Brotherhood, 109–10; HUAC, Hearings regarding Communist Infiltration, 808–9, 811; "CINRAD Summary," 12.

82. Lomanitz's statement at draft board hearing, August 12, 1943, quoted in HUAC, Hearings regarding Communist Infiltration, 293, 295. Under pressure from Groves, the CIO shut down the FAECT local at the laboratory in October 1943. Herken, Brotherhood, 106–7.

83. AEC, In the Matter of JRO, 126, 129, 206, 276; Strout, Conscience, Science, and Security, 9.

84. Lansdale memo, Groves's conversation with Oppenheimer, September 14, 1943, in AEC, In the Matter of JRO, 277.

85. Lomanitz testimony, in HUAC, Hearings regarding Communist Infiltration, 329. Lomanitz eventually became a popular math teacher at New Mexico State University, where he worked for many years. He died in January 2003.

86. FBI report, July 25, 1946, 20; "The Pattern of Soviet Espionage in the United States," June 5, 1947, 11, file 383.4 USSR, Army Intelligence Project Decimal File, RG 319, NARA. The FBI's use of microphone surveillance here is discussed in Klehr et al., Secret World, 216–17n5.

87. In 1943, the Germans first reported having discovered evidence of the massacre of thousands of Polish officers in the Katyn Forest near Smolensk and blamed the Soviets, who had occupied the region. The Soviets, in turn, credited the Germans with the massacre. Some fifteen thousand Poles had been murdered. During the *glasnost* era, Mikhail Gorbachev finally acknowledged what was by then long suspected: the Red Army had executed the victims. See Abramson, *Spanning the Century*, 362–63. The cable confirming Zubilin's role at Katyn is Venona 1033 New York to Moscow, July 1, 1943, cited in Haynes and Klehr, *Venona*, 44–45.

88. Hoover to John A. Cimperman, Legal Attaché, American Embassy, London, January 8, 1947, Nelson file, #379; "The Pattern of Soviet Espionage in the United States," 11, June 5, 1947, 383.4 USSR Army Intelligence Project Decimal File.

89. HUAC, *Report on Atomic Espionage*, 5; J. Edgar Hoover to Harry Hopkins, May 7, 1943, cited in Warner and Benson, *Venona*, 49–50.

90. COMRAP report, May 7, 1943, Nelson file, #112, 12; Recording No. 3, Nelson and "X" (Zubilin), April 10, 1943, attached to DM Ladd to Director, CINRAD report, #201; FBI report, July 25, 1946, 21.

91. Ladd to Director, April 16, 1943, CINRAD report, 2, 3, Nelson file, #201; FBI report, July 25, 1946, 20. Schneiderman, who had been threatened with deportation back to Russia in 1939, may have been thinking of his own self-preservation here. When the Supreme Court cancelled the order in 1943, he became more open to working with Soviet intelligence once again, as Venona suggests. See Venona San Francisco to Moscow, April 18, 1945, February 20, 1946, cited in Romerstein and Breindel, *Venona Secrets*, 258–59.

92. "Recording #2, Nelson and 'X' (Zubilin)," April 10, 1943, attached to DM Ladd to Director, CINRAD report, Nelson file, #201.

93. COMRAP report, May 7, 1943, 25–29, Nelson file, #112.

94. Ibid., 12; "Recording No. 3, Nelson and 'X' (Zubilin)," April 10, 1943, attached to D. M. Ladd to Director, CINRAD report, Nelson file, #201. See also FBI report, "Soviet Activities in the US," 21.

95. Memorandum for the Director, May 5, 1943, Nelson file, #104; COMRAP report, May 7, 1943, Nelson file, #112. Hopkins has been charged as a Soviet agent by some because of his meetings with NKVD agent Akhmerov, but Gordievsky's assertion that he was an "unconscious agent" rather than a conscious one, who saw Akhmerov as simply an "intermediary" for Stalin rather than as representing the secret police, seems most compelling. Andrew and Gordievsky, *KGB*, 287–88.

96. "COMRAP Summary," 59. Summing up the case in 1944, the agency wrote that Nelson "is shown as engaging in military and industrial espionage; to be active in political and Governmental aspects of the Apparatus; and is further shown as active in the gathering and dissemination of propaganda favorable to the Soviet Union."

97. Hoover to SAC San Francisco, September 1943, and Piper to Hoover, September 13, 1943, Nelson file, #169; Herken, *Brotherhood*, 100.

98. COMRAP report, May 7, 1943, 22, 28, 37–40, Nelson file, #112. Aware he was being watched, Zarubin engaged in a number of diversionary tactics, including bumping into people on purpose so that he could turn around to see if he were being followed (21).

99. Steve Nelson report, July 17, 1943, Nelson file, #153.

100. AEC, *In the Matter of JRO,* 825.

101. See discussion in Herken, *Brotherhood,* 56–57, 108. By 1944, overwhelmed by a policy that had required investigation of every Communist the Bureau identified, the FBI limited its new investigations to the most significant party leaders. See Senate Select Committee, *Supplementary Detailed Staff Reports,* bk. 3, 421.

102. FBI Director to Attorney General, October, 28, 1948, Nelson file, #463.

103. Schecter and Schecter, *Sacred Secrets,* 105.

104. Margaret Gertrude Nelson report, March 14, 1945, Nelson file, #257; see discussion of the wiretap evidence problem in Theoharis, *Chasing Spies,* chap. 4. As a result, Nelson was able to maintain the fiction in his 1981 biography, coauthored by two academics, that he had not spied. Nelson et al., *Steve Nelson,* 294.

105. CINRAD report, July 7, 1943, 5–7, CINRAD file, #222.

106. FBI background on Julius Robert Oppenheimer, February 17, 1947, attached to Hoover to Vaughan, February 28, 1947, box 167, PSF, HSTL.

107. Quoted in HUAC, *Hearings regarding Communist Infiltration,* 3495; see also HUAC, *Report on Soviet Espionage,* 182; John Lansdale Jr. to J. Edgar Hoover, August 27, 1943, December 13, 1943, file 383.4 USSR, U.S. Army Intelligence Project Decimal File, RG 319, NARA; FBI report, November 27, 1945, 39–40; Holloway, *Stalin and the Bomb,* 103. Eltenton's argument was also made by spies like Ted Hall. See Albright and Kunstel, *Bombshell,* 89–90.

108. "COMRAP Summary," 39–40. Eltenton, when interviewed in June 1946, confirmed that he had been asked by Peter Ivanov to investigate what was happening "up on the hill." He had contacted Chevalier, knowing of his friendship with Oppenheimer, who had agreed but "then subsequently advised that there was no chance whatsoever of obtaining the information." Report on J. R. Oppenheimer, February 5, 1950, Summary Brief on Fuchs, February 6, 1950, 5, Fuchs file, #2.

109. Chevalier, *Oppenheimer,* 53–54. Chevalier's discomfort was not so apparent to Eltenton, however. Herken, *Brotherhood,* 92.

110. AEC, *In the Matter of JRO,* 130; Chevalier, *Oppenheimer,* 19.

111. Oppenheimer's reply to Nichols, March 4, 1954, cited in AEC, *In the Matter of JRO,* 14. Despite Oppenheimer's sympathy toward better relations with the Soviet Union, few accounts accuse him of espionage. Sudoplatov's *Special Tasks* and the Schecters' *Sacred Secrets* are the notable exceptions. Relying on Chevalier's version of events, Sudoplatov speculates that Oppenheimer may have called Eltenton's entreaties "treason" to a Communist (Chevalier) in order "to establish a record of separation from his Communist friends," while the Schecters assert that Oppenheimer was cooperating with Soviet agents as early as December 1941. *Special Tasks,* 187n13; *Sacred Secrets,* 47–51. On Oppenheimer's "passivity" in taking action on what he did know, see Haynes and Klehr, *Venona,* 330.

112. Report on J. R. Oppenheimer, February 5, 1950, Summary Brief on Fuchs, February 6, 1950, 3, Fuchs file, #1202.

113. Julius Robert Oppenheimer, February 17, 1947, FBI background, attached to Hoover to Vaughan, February 28, 1947, box 167, PSF, HSTL; Oppenheimer to Nichols, March 4, 1954, in AEC, *In the Matter of JRO,* 14.

114. "Chevalier Conspiracy," pt. 2, August 20, 1945, 34–35, Nelson file, 100–16980.

115. AEC, *In the Matter of JRO*, 137–38, 145–49.

116. Ibid., 148, 815.

117. Ibid., 143.

118. Pash-Oppenheimer interview, August 26, 1943, quoted in AEC, *In the Matter of JRO*, 297.

119. Ibid., 847.

120. AEC, *In the Matter of JRO*, 816; see also letter from Pash to General Groves, September 2, 1943, cited in *In the Matter of JRO*, 816.

121. De Silva to Pash, September 2, 1943, quoted in AEC, *In the Matter of JRO*, 274–75.

122. Ibid., 274.

123. AEC, *In the Matter of JRO*, 89.

124. In this connection, Lansdale mentioned "the Weinberg case." AEC, *In the Matter of JRO*, 263.

125. Lansdale-Oppenheimer interview, September 12, 1943, quoted in AEC, *In the Matter of JRO*, 874–75.

126. Ibid., 879–80.

127. Lansdale memo, Groves's conversation with Oppenheimer, September 14, 1943, quoted in AEC, *In the Matter of JRO*, 277

128. Bernstein, "In the Matter of J. Robert Oppenheimer," 246.

129. Lansdale-Oppenheimer interview, September 12, 1943, quoted in AEC, *In the Matter of JRO*, 871; Jungk, *Brighter Than a Thousand Suns*, 152.

130. AEC, *In the Matter of JRO*, 270.

131. Ibid., 172–73.

132. Ibid., 261, 279.

133. "Chevalier Conspiracy," pt. 2, August 20, 1945, 36, Nelson file, 100–16980; Julius Robert Oppenheimer, February 17, 1947, FBI background, attached to Hoover to Vaughan, February 28, 1947, box 167, PSF, HSTL.

134. Herken, *Brotherhood*, 113–14; "CINRAD Summary," 14–15. Despite his vow of secrecy to Oppenheimer, General Groves told Colonel Lansdale, who told the FBI. As Herken relates, Oppenheimer's reporting on Chevalier was "comeuppance" for the French professor's attempt to recruit his brother (120). The War Department's Military Intelligence Division had opened an investigation on Frank Oppenheimer in July 1943, in response both to his attendance at Communist meetings in 1940 and to his brother's leadership of the Manhattan Project. Frank also was a physicist at the Radiation Laboratory. According to Lieutenant Colonel Pash, who instigated the probe, Frank Oppenheimer was "reliably reported to be a Communist and possibly engaged in espionage." Pash called for an investigation of "Oppenheimer's associates, activities, and political sympathies." But one of his former teachers, G. H. Dieke of Johns Hopkins, saw Frank as a shy and retiring type and dismissed his political leanings, only to say that as a "Hebrew," Frank Oppenheimer would not have any warm feelings about Nazism. Boris T. Pash, Lt. Col., Military Intelligence, Chief, Counter Intelligence Branch, to Major George B. Dyer, Director, Intelligence Division, Headquarters Third Service Command, Baltimore, July 10, 1943; Richard Connolly, Special Agent, CIC, Memo for the Officer in Charge, July 19, 1943; *Washington Post*, June 15, 1949, all in Frank Friedman Oppenheimer file, E2037207,

IRR, RG 319, NARA. On Frank Oppenheimer, see also HUAC, *Hearings regarding Communist Infiltration*, 359–60.

135. AEC, *In the Matter of JRO*, 831.

136. Report on J. R. Oppenheimer, February 5, 1950, Summary Brief on Fuchs, February 6, 1950, 4–5, #1202; Branigan to Belmont, March 31, 1954, JRO file, #1279.

137. "COMRAP Summary," 18–19.

138. Herken, *Brotherhood*, 122; HUAC, *Report on Soviet Espionage*, 12; FBI report July 25, 1946, 25.

139. HUAC, *Report on Soviet Espionage*, 17, 24.

140. See "CINRAD Summary," 15; Hoover to SAC San Francisco, August 27, 1945, ONI, "Nelson, Steve," report; see also FBI report, "Soviet Activities in the US," 25.

141. HUAC, *Report on Soviet Espionage*, 18–19, 40; Herken, *Brotherhood*, 123.

142. HUAC, *Report on Soviet Espionage*,16–22, passim, 34.

143. Ibid., 20–34, passim.

144. Ibid., 25, 41, 46.

145. Ibid., 43.

146. HUAC, *Report on Soviet Espionage*, 182.

147. "COMRAP Summary," 78; HUAC, *Report on Soviet Espionage*, 12.

148. HUAC, *Report on Soviet Espionage*, cited in JCAE, *Soviet Atomic Espionage*, 165–66.

149. June 20, 1950, 362–63, Adams file, #715.

150. Ibid., 294; HUAC, *Hearings regarding Clarence Hiskey*, 402.

151. June 20, 1950, 278, Adams file, #715.

152. HUAC, *Report on Soviet Espionage Activities*, cited in JCAE, *Soviet Atomic Espionage*, 165; June 20, 1950, 300, Adams file.

153. Weinstein and Vassiliev, *Haunted Wood*, 179–80.

154. HUAC, *Report on Soviet Espionage*, cited in JCAE, *Soviet Atomic Espionage*, 166.

155. June 20, 1950, 279, 280, Adams file, #715.

156. "CINRAD Summary," 12. Adams may well have been the agent "Achilles," who is identified in Venona as obtaining technical information at the University of Chicago in 1941–43. Haynes and Klehr, *Venona*, 340.

157. June 20, 1950, 188, 433, Adams file, #715.

158. "CINRAD Summary," 18; "100 Things You Should Know About Communism," 108, reel 261, vol. 132, ACLU Papers; 414–15, 486–87, Adams file, #715. In addition to material on the "1000 KW plant," notes in Adams's apartment on the "production of salt" and the "operating of ISO Diffusion" were also said to be "without a doubt, information concerning the DSM project." "COMRAP Summary," 12.

159. June 20, 1950, 10–14, 26, 56, 64, Adams file, #715.

160. Ibid., 69.

161. Ibid., 57.

162. On Novick's assistance see ibid., 24, 161–63. Novick received up to $6 million in government contracts during the war for "highly secret electronic devices used in connection with radar installations." Yet he had a history of giving large donations to Communist causes, such as the Friends of the Soviet Union, the National Council for American-Soviet Friendship, and the Abraham Lincoln Brigade. HUAC, *Report on Soviet*

Espionage, 177. Adams's applications for entry into the United States were not always approved. His February 1938 application to join Novick was denied, for example, because he was judged to be a mere "contract laborer" competing in a field full of laid-off men; Adams protested that he was in fact a "technical adviser and business man" who would develop other projects with Novick. See his letter, 165–67, in Adams file, #715. Adams made several attempts to enter the United States thereafter, eventually procuring an immigration visa by arguing that he would assist in the production of a cream whipper, apparently a desirable skill in the Depression. He entered through Buffalo on May 17, 1938, filing his official "Declaration of Intention" on March 15, 1940 (4, 170, 452–53).

163. 279–80, Adams file, #715. The firm operated from 1938 to 1943. It had no lab equipment except for a microscope and two magnifying glasses. Ibid., 81.

164. Ibid., 8.

165. "CINRAD Summary," 19; June 20, 1950, 87, Adams file, #715, 177, 217. Though he regularly spent two hours a day at the firm, he seems to have done little work for it.

166. "COMRAP Summary," 12; HUAC, *Report on Soviet Espionage Activities*, cited in JCAE, *Soviet Atomic Espionage*, 166.

167. See Haynes and Klehr, *Venona*, 324; HUAC, *Testimony of Murray and Manning*, 877–99; HUAC, *Hearings regarding Hiskey*, 385; HUAC, *Hearings regarding Communist Infiltration*, 2:878–79. Hiskey later went to Hawaii to work on flame-throwing equipment. "CINRAD Summary," 12.

168. 344–45, 490, Adams file, #5; one of Adams's expense sheets for 1944 noted $50 for "Marcia" (418). Marcia Hiskey's visits to Adams are covered in Adams file, 488–92.

169. HUAC, *Report on Soviet Espionage*, 64; ibid., cited in JCAE, *Soviet Atomic Espionage*, 166–67; "CINRAD Summary," 17. Chapin was then assigned to a project that was monitoring the progress of German atomic bomb research, in which the Soviets had great interest.

170. 332–33, Adams file, #715; HUAC, *Report on Soviet Espionage*, 67.

171. 133–34, 329–32, Adams file, #715; "CINRAD Summary," 17; HUAC, *Report on Soviet Espionage Activities*, 56.

172. 284–85, 317, 343, Adams file, #715; HUAC, *Testimony of Murray and Manning*, 889–90.

173. HUAC, *Testimony of Murray and Manning*, 887.

174. A former associate of Manning's, Samuel Steingiser, was his correspondent. 344, Adams file, #715. Despite his professions of Hiskey's discretion, Manning told the FBI that Hiskey was probably Adams's source (134).

175. Ibid., 134–35.

176. Manning's statement to FBI, March 27, 1949, 348, Adams file, #715; HUAC, *Testimony of Murray and Manning*, 891–92.

177. Ibid., 496.

178. Ibid., 135, 368–69. Perlowin remarked that he had not provided Adams with documents nor had Adams taken notes; yet, he added, "knowing Adams, it was easily possible that the latter could probably recall entire conversations between [them]."

179. Hoover to Vaughan, January 16, 1948, FBI file, box 167, PSF, HSTL.

180. HUAC, *Report on Soviet Espionage*, quoted in JCAE, *Soviet Atomic Espionage*, 164.

On FBI informants attempts to find Adams at the end of January 1946, see Adams file 100–331280–715, 436–39.

181. Adams file, #715, 131–32.

182. Ibid., 280, 337.

183. Nelson report, San Francisco, June 25, 1947, Nelson file, #408, 6.

184. Spender, "The Inner Meaning of the Fuchs Case," *New York Times Magazine*, March 12, 1950, 13; Robert Williams, *Klaus Fuchs*, 19, 103–4.

185. FBI American Embassy Lish Witson to Hoover, March 7, 1950, Fuchs file, #640.

186. Report of Clegg and Lamphere, June 4, 1950, Fuchs file, #1412, 8–9; Feklisov, *Man behind the Rosenbergs*, 193–94.

187. Perrin quoted in Hoover to Sumner Pike, Acting Chairman, AEC, March 2, 1950, Fuchs file, #504.

188. Lish Whitson to Hoover, March 7, 1950, Fuchs file, #640, 2. Similar to the way in which Groves saw Oppenheimer, the British government believed Fuchs's importance to the nuclear project was more important than his political history. Robert Williams, *Klaus Fuchs*, 42.

189. Feklisov, *Man behind the Rosenbergs*, 195; Fletcher to Ladd, September 27, 1949, Fuchs file, #7, 7; "John R. Murphy's Fuchs Report," 17. On Fuchs's clearance, see letter in summary memo, by W. A. Akers of British Ministry of Supply Mission, December 10, 1943. Another letter from D. Dean to Jones, August 6, 1947, reiterated Fuchs's clearance status. See Summary Brief on Dr. E. J. K. Fuchs, February 6, 1950, Fuchs file, #1202 (1998 supplemental release).

190. J. P. Mohr to Tolson, February 12, 1950, in Fuchs file, #32, 479 (1998 supplemental release).

191. J. Edgar Hoover to Sidney W. Souers, February 6, 1950, February 21, 1950, May 7, 1950, FBI file, box 168, PSF, HSTL; Robert Williams, *Klaus Fuchs*, 40, 124.

192. Perrin quoted in Hoover to Sumner Pike, Acting Chairman, AEC, March 2, 1950, Fuchs file, #504, 2–3.

193. Venona 195 Kvasnikov to Fitin, February 9, 1944. The United States actually used three methods to separate isotopes to make uranium-235: electromagnetic separation, thermal diffusion, and gaseous diffusion, all of which the Soviets tried.

194. Gold testimony, *United States of America vs. Julius Rosenberg et al.* (US District Court, Southern District of NY, March 15, 1951, cited in JCAE, *Soviet Atomic Espionage*, 148–49). It is not clear why Gold cites in his testimony the June visit as his first contact, when Venona records the initial meeting as having taken place in February.

195. Report of Clegg and Lamphere, June 4, 1950, Fuchs file, #1412, 12, 47.

196. Ibid., 13; Hoover to Souers, May 24, 1950, FBI file, box 168, PSF, HSTL.

197. Hoover to Sumner Pike, Acting Chairman, AEC, March 2, 1950, Fuchs file, #504, 2.

198. Venona 2344 New York to Moscow, August 29, 1944; Hoover to Souers, May 24, 1950, FBI file, box 168, PSF, HSTL.

199. Feklisov, *Man behind the Rosenbergs*, 105–6, 200; Gold, "Circumstances," 1076. "Summary Brief on Fuchs and Gold," February 12, 1951, 135, Fuchs file, #1494X; Holloway, *Stalin and the Bomb*, 108; Dobbs, "How Soviets Stole U.S. Atom Secrets"; Haynes et al., *Secret World*, 222.

200. Gold testimony, *United States of America vs. Julius Rosenberg et al.* (US District Court, Southern District of NY, March 15, 1951, cited in JCAE, *Soviet Atomic Espionage,* 147.

201. Paraphrase of Venona cable in Summary Brief on Fuchs and Gold, February 12, 1951, 54, Fuchs file, #1494X. In February 1945, the New York station was asked "exactly where and in what capacity CHARLES [Fuchs] is working at the PRESERVE [Los Alamos]" and "what he has been doing since August." Venona 183 Moscow to New York, February 27, 1945.

202. JCAE, *Soviet Atomic Espionage,* 23–24.

203. Report of Clegg and Lamphere, June 4, 1950, 31, Fuchs file, #1412.

204. Perrin quoted in Hoover to Sumner Pike, Acting Chairman, AEC, March 2, 1950, 3–4, Fuchs file, #504.

205. Gold testimony, *Julius Rosenberg and Ethel Rosenberg, Petitioners, vs. the United States of America* (US District Court, Southern District of NY, June 7, 1952) 2:818.

206. According to Venona, Julius Rosenberg had convinced his sister-in-law, Ruth Greenglass, "to cooperate with us in drawing in KALIBR [David Greenglass] with a view to ENORMO." Venona 1600 Kvasnikov to Fitin, November 14, 1944.

207. Greenglass was unusual in his eagerness for monetary compensation; he received $850 for his material, plus $5,000 in enticement for him to go to Mexico after the case was opened in 1950. JCAE, *Soviet Atomic Espionage,* 11.

208. Gold testimony, *Julius Rosenberg and Ethel Rosenberg, Petitioners, vs. the United States of America,* 2:818–22. According to Sudoplatov, it was Semyonov and Ovakimian who had permitted Gold's contact with Greenglass; this led the United States to discover the Rosenberg connection once Gold identified Greenglass. After the Rosenberg case broke in 1950, Semyonov lost his job for allowing the contact and Ovakimian was demoted. According to Sudoplatov, Semyonov's Jewish background, a major liability in the final years of Stalin's life, contributed to his scapegoating. *Special Tasks,* 214–15.

209. Paraphrase of Venona cable, New York to Moscow, December 13, 1944, "Summary Brief on Fuchs and Gold," February 12, 1951, 54, Fuchs file, #1494X.

210. Greenglass testimony, *United States of America vs. Julius Rosenberg et al.* (US District Court, Southern District of NY, March 9, 1951, cited in JCAE, *Soviet Atomic Espionage,* 68–72, passim.

211. Report of Clegg and Lamphere, June 4, 1950, 32, Fuchs file, #1412.

212. Gold testimony, *Julius Rosenberg and Ethel Rosenberg, Petitioners, vs. the United States of America,* 2:824–31.

213. Report of Clegg and Lamphere, June 4, 1950, 33, Fuchs file, #1412.

214. "Summary Brief on Fuchs and Gold," February 12, 1951, 145E, Fuchs file, #1494X.

215. Gold testimony, *Julius Rosenberg and Ethel Rosenberg, Petitioners, vs. the United States of America,* 2:836, 838. He did see Fuchs again (see my chapter 5).

216. Holloway, *Stalin and the Bomb,* 108, 137–38; Feklisov, *Man behind the Rosenbergs,* 201.

217. "Summary Brief on Fuchs and Gold," February 12, 1951, 4, Fuchs file, #1494X. I am indebted to John Earl Haynes for the information regarding the unidentified atomic sources.

218. See Hoover to Sumner Pike, Acting Chairman, AEC, March 2, 1950, 8, Fuchs file, #504.

219. Truman to Byrnes, November 17, 1945, FBI file, box 167, PSF, HSTL. "Corby," Gouzenko's code name, was the name of a whiskey that he particularly enjoyed.

220. Dean Acheson to Truman, December 22, 1945, General File, box 114, PSF, HSTL.

221. *New York Times,* February 20, 1946, and *Montreal Gazette,* February 19, 1946, box 87A, Donovan Papers, Military History Institute, Carlisle, Pennsylvania.

222. Schrecker, *Many Are the Crimes,* 170–71. Schrecker notes that Groves may also have been Pearson's source, in order to hinder discussion of international control of atomic energy.

223. FBI report, "Soviet Activities in the United States," 5.

224. War Department General Staff, "Soviet Espionage in Canada," *Intelligence Review,* October 3, 1946, 18.

225. Hoover to Matthew Connelly, September 24, 1945, box 167, PSF, HSTL; FBI report, "Soviet Activities in the United States," July 25, 1946.

226. FBI, "Soviet Espionage Activities," October 19, 1945, 10, FBI file, box 167, PSF, HSTL.

227. FBI, "Justification for Personnel Request for Fiscal Year 1947" (budget estimates), November 30, 1945, FBI file, box 167, PSF, HSTL.

228. FBI report, "Soviet Activities in the United States," July 25, 1946. The War Department alleged that the Labour Progressive Party, the Canadian Communist Party, did not encourage open membership in the party, but instead urged more secretive affiliation, through which members could be "developed" into spies. See War Department General Staff, "Soviet Espionage in Canada," 21.

229. FBI report, November 27, 1945, 49.

230. FBI, "Soviet Espionage Activities," October 19, 1945, 5–8, FBI file, box 167, PSF, HSTL.

231. Cited in *Montreal Gazette,* February 21, 1946, box 87A, Donovan Papers. The Soviet statement referred to published documents including the "well-known" works of Henry D. Smyth, head of Princeton's physics department and consultant to the Manhattan Project.

232. See Extracts of Report of Royal Commission on Spying Activities in Canada (Kellock-Taschereau Commission), 87, file 424.67, box 87A, Donovan Papers.

233. War Department General Staff, "Soviet Espionage in Canada," 20.

234. Summary on Allan Nunn May, Ladd to Director, February 6, 1950, no file no.; FBI report, November 27, 1945, 44; JCAE, *Soviet Atomic Espionage,* 51.

235. FBI, "Soviet Espionage Activities," October 19, 1945, 8–9, FBI file, box 167, PSF, HSTL.

236. Rhodes, *Dark Sun,* 127; Summary on Allan Nunn May, Ladd to Director, February 6, 1950, no file no., 3. May had received $700, plus two bottles of whiskey that he took "against [his] will." JCAE, *Soviet Atomic Espionage,* 59.

237. Summary on Allan Nunn May, Ladd to Director, February 6, 1950, no file no., 3; JCAE, *Soviet Atomic Espionage,* 52, 55–57.

238. JCAE, *Soviet Atomic Espionage,* 57–58.

239. On the allegations against May, see Hoover to Matthew Connelly, September 12, 1945, quoted in Benson and Warner, *Venona,* 61–62; JCAE, *Soviet Atomic Espionage,* 2–3, 58–59; FBI report, "Soviet Activities in the US," July 25, 1946; Extracts of Report of Royal Commission, 615–20; Granatstein and Stafford, *Spy Wars,* 63–64; Rhodes, *Dark Sun,* 128; Gouzenko, *Iron Curtain,* 239–42. May, who died in 2003, was sentenced to ten years at hard labor. He was released in six for good behavior and later ended up in Ghana, where he taught physics and kept abreast of nuclear developments in Africa.

240. JCAE, *Soviet Atomic Espionage,* 52–53.

241. Gouzenko, *Iron Curtain,* 261; Granatstein and Stafford, *Spy Wars,* 62.

242. Gouzenko, *Iron Curtain*, 223, 230–31.

243. Stanley Camache's testimony, "Inquiry under P.C. 411," 1946, 23–25, file 424.62, box 87A, Donovan Papers; Gouzenko, *Iron Curtain*, 236.

244. Camache testimony, 23–25; Report of Royal Commission Extracts, 616–20.

245. War Department General Staff, Intelligence Division, "The Soviet Union," 60, box 187, PSF, HSTL.

246. "The Pattern of Soviet Espionage in the United States," June 5, 1947, 12, box 284, 383.4 USSR Army Intelligence Project Decimal File.

247. FBI report, "Soviet Activities in the US."

248. Sudoplatov, *Special Tasks*, 217–18; War Department General Staff, Intelligence Division, "The Soviet Union," 59–60 (emphasis in original).

249. JCAE, *Soviet Atomic Espionage*, 11–12.

250. Hoover to Sauers, March 7, 1950, FBI file, box 168, PSF, HSTL.

CHAPTER 5

1. See Benson and Warner, *Venona*, xxi–xxvii.

2. US Military Mission, Moscow, to War Department, June 13, 1945, Subject file: Foreign Affairs, Russia, box 187, PSF, HSTL; Zhukov to Eisenhower, October 20, 1945, file 220, box 823, President's Official File, HSTL.

3. House Committee on Foreign Affairs, *European Study Trip*, 19. The delegation, the first to go to Russia since 1939, included Representatives Thomas S. Gordon, Joseph Ryter, Karl Mundt, and Frances Bolton.

4. Venona 781–87 Pravdin to Fitin, May 25–26, 1945.

5. Stoler, *Allies and Adversaries*, 215–19, 268–69. Stoler discusses the post-Yalta developments in chap. 12 of his book.

6. Ibid., 270.

7. "Long Telegram," February 22, 1946. The full text is in Department of State, *Foreign Relations of the United States* 6:696–709. Kennan's gendered and pathological references have been highlighted by Frank Costigliola, who notes Kennan's likening the Soviet Union to a "rapist," with "insistent, unceasing pressure for penetration and command" as well as its "psychosis which permeates and determines [the] behavior of [the] entire Soviet ruling caste." Kennan quoted in Costigliola, "Unceasing Pressure for Penetration," 1310.

8. Winston Churchill, Iron Curtain Speech, March 5, 1946.

9. Harbutt, *Iron Curtain*, 281.

10. CINRAD Summary Memo #1, 1–2.

11. See Weinstein and Vassiliev, *Haunted Wood*, 216–22, passim, 220 (NKGB file).

12. Leab, "Red Menace and Justice," 83, 84.

13. Ibid., 83, 85.

14. Ibid., 86–91; on Redin's seizure, see Venona 34 Apresyan to Moscow (Fitin), January 30, 1946; Venona 123 Viktor Vasilyevich Afanasyev to Semen (unidentified), March 27, 1946; FBI report, November 27, 1945, 51; see also FBI report, "Soviet Activities in the US," July 25, 1946, box 15, Clifford Papers, HSTL.

15. Clifford to Admiral William D. Leahy, July 18, 1946, box 63, Elsey Papers, HSTL.

16. Report is from William Leahy, Fleet Admiral, US Navy, Chief of Staff to the Commander in Chief of the Army and Navy (President) Joint Chiefs of Staff, Memo for the President, "Texts of the Military Agreements Made between the US and the SU from 1941 to the Present," July 26, 1946, box 15, Clifford Papers.

17. Robert Patterson to Truman, July 27, 1946, box 63, Elsey Papers.

18. See Kennan, "Draft of Information Policy on Relations with Russia," July 22, 1946, State Department Russia 1948 file, box 27, Acheson Papers, HSTL.

19. Clark Clifford to Attorney General, July 18, 1946, box 63, Elsey Papers; FBI report, "Soviet Activities in the US."

20. Hoover to George E. Allen, Director, Reconstruction Finance Corporation, May 29, 1946, Subject file: FBI, box 167, PSF, HSTL.

21. Clark Clifford, Report to the President by the Special Counsel to the President, "Summary of Relations with the Soviet Union," September 24, 1946, chap. 5 ("Soviet Activities Affecting American Security"), box 15, Clifford Papers.

22. Rosenberg continued his secret service, despite official discouragement, "maintaining contact with comrades . . . while gathering valuable scientific and technical information." See Soviet intelligence files cited in Weinstein and Vassiliev, *Haunted Wood,* 222; see also Feklisov, *Man behind the Rosenbergs,* 219. Judith Coplon also was an active spy throughout this era (she began spying in early 1945 but was not caught until 1948). See Venona 27 New York to Moscow, January 8, 1945, and Marcia and Tom Mitchell, *Spy Who Seduced America.* Soviet espionage had hardly ended, of course; it would reach its next peak of activity forty years later, during the Reagan administration, as discussed in chapter 6.

23. Elsey draft for Clifford Report, "Summary of Relations with the Soviet Union," August 3, 1946, box 63, Elsey Papers.

24. Clifford Report, 73–74, Clifford Papers.

25. Truman quoted in Hamby, *Man of the People,* 339.

26. So incendiary were the report's contents, however, that Truman locked it in a drawer. The report remained secret throughout his term.

27. "The Pattern of Soviet Espionage in the United States," June 5, 1947, 15, 383.4 USSR, Army Intelligence Project Decimal File, RG 319, NARA.

28. Ibid., 21, 26.

29. See Willoughby memo, October 17, 1947, and Willoughby to Commander in Chief, June 30, 1947, November 20, 1947, files ZF016130, ZF106135, IRR, RG 319, NARA.

30. John H. Lichtblau, Headquarters, Sub-region Bayreuth, Counterintelligence Corps (CIC) Region VI, memo for the officer in charge, November 13, 1946; Chaucer, Special Intelligence Memo, December 6, 1946; Albert Holman, Headquarters CIC Region VIII, Zehlendorf Field Office, January 13, 1947; Bill Grubert, Headquarters Sub Region Goeppingen, CIC Region III, Memo for the Officer in Charge, "German Specialist Deported to Russia," March 1947; all in file XE 169886, IRR, RG 319, NARA.

31. "Soviet Importation of German Technicians and Industry," *Intelligence Review* (November 27, 1946): Naval Aide files, Alphabetical files, War Department, box 17, HSTL. Also see Shabinsky testimony, in Senate Judiciary Committee, *Scope of Soviet Activity,* 4892. See also V. L. Sokolov, "Soviet Uses of German Science and Technology, 1945–46," in *Scope of Soviet Activity,* 4905ff.

32. See Internal Route Slip, January 29, 1947, file no. 350.09, IRR, RG 319, NARA, for example, regarding experts from the Helmholts Institute. R. D. Wentworth noted, "Plans are underway for a partial transfer to the United States of scientific personnel and some equipment from the Helmholts Institute under project Paperclip." File XE 169886, IRR, RG 319, NARA. Paperclip brought 150 German scientists to assist in U.S. guided missile research.

33. Special Memorandum No. 18, Headquarters Berlin District U.S. Army, Office of the Assistant Chief of Staff, G-2, October 31, 1946, file XE 169886, IRR, RG 319, NARA.

34. Tokaev, *Stalin Means War*, 98, 100.

35. Ibid., 123, 118.

36. "Soviet Measures to Stimulate Scientific Research and Development," *Intelligence Review* (November 14, 1946): 38–39. See discussion of this issue in Leshuk, *U.S. Intelligence Perceptions*, 2, chap. 6, passim.

37. Gold testimony, *Julius Rosenberg and Ethel Rosenberg, Petitioners, vs. the United States of America*, (US District Court, Southern District of New York, June 7, 1952), 2:839.

38. "Summary Brief on Fuchs and Gold," February 12, 1951, 4g, 145, Fuchs file, #1494X.

39. Gold testimony, *Julius Rosenberg and Ethel Rosenberg, Petitioners, vs. the United States of America*, 2:843–44; Gold, "Circumstances," 1070, 1076; Weinstein and Vassiliev, *Haunted Wood*, 218–19. Yakovlev would be tried in absentia at the Rosenberg trial.

40. "Personal History and Background Report," 13; "Summary Brief on Fuchs and Gold," 4a, Fuchs file, #1494X. Gold and Brothman's grand jury performance required coordination: before the hearings, the two "walked the streets in the neighborhood of Brothman's home from 3:30 to 5:30 am discussing the story about how Gold met Golos in order to get their stories straight." Brothman, interestingly, had been tempted to tell the truth to the jury but Gold effectively pressured Brothman's partner, Miriam Moskowitz, to get him to stick with Gold's story. But when Gold finally left Brothman's firm in 1948, Brothman told him, "Don't pull a Louis Budenz," a reference to the defector who told all in front of HUAC. In 1950 it was Brothman who was indicted for "willfully influencing Gold to give false testimony." See "Personal History and Background Report," #14; Radosh and Milton, *Rosenberg File*, 35–36; New York to Washington teletype, November 18, 1950, Brothman file, #463. In 1947 Gold told the jury that Carter Hoodless of Pennsylvania Sugar had introduced him to Golos, and that Golos told him he needed a "recognized chemist" to get blueprints from Brothman for possible purchase. In fact, as Gold told the FBI in 1950, he had never met Golos and had been sent to Brothman by Semyon Semyonov, his Soviet handler. Hoodless was conveniently dead in 1947 and could not deny the tale. See "Facts Concerning American Espionage Contact, Summary of Facts, Jurisdiction, Collaboration with British," 120, Fuchs file, #1494X; "Personal History and Background Report," 8; "Summary Brief on Fuchs and Gold," 4a, 4g, 121. In the event, because of Gold's changed testimony in 1950, Brothman received a seven-year sentence for obstructing justice and a $15,000 fine, and Moskowitz received a two-year term and $10,000 fine. "Summary Brief on Fuchs and Gold," 4h.

41. "Summary Brief on Fuchs and Gold," 4h; Gold testimony, in *Scope of Soviet Activity*, 1058.

42. Greenglass testimony at Lewisburg Penitentiary, answers to Roy Cohn, David Schine, witnessed by Greenglass's attorney, O. John Rogge, October 1953, in *Scope of Soviet Activity*, 4866. On G&R Engineering, see Rosenberg testimony, *Julius Rosenberg and Ethel Rosenberg, Petitioners, vs. the United States of America*, 2:1060. However, U.S. authorities did not believe that the Soviets had a proximity fuse in 1946. "Soviet Active and Passive Air Defense," *Intelligence Review* (August 15, 1946):24. G&R Engineering, with a $7,000 capitalization, made little money; nor did its successor, Pitt Machine Products. Sam Roberts, *The Brother*, 163.

43. Greenglass testimony at Lewisburg Penitentiary, in Senate Committee on Government Operations, *Army Signal Corps-Subversion and Espionage*, 20, 21.

44. Weinstein and Vassiliev, *Haunted Wood*, 218–22; Sam Roberts, *The Brother*, 228.

45. Report of Clegg and Lamphere, June 4, 1950, 33–38, Fuchs file, #1412. See also Hoover to Sumner Pike, Acting Chairman, AEC, March 2, 1950, 5–6, Fuchs file, #504; Feklisov's meetings with Fuchs are discussed in Feklisov, *Man behind the Rosenbergs*, chap. 25.

46. Hoover to Sumner Pike, 6–7, Fuchs file, #504; Schecter and Schecter, *Sacred Secrets*, 140.

47. See "Spymaster Rudolf Abel," www.timmonet.co.uk/html/body_rudolf_abel.htm; "Rudolf Ivanovich Abel (Hollow Nickel Case)," www.fbi.gov/libref/historic/famcases/abel/abel.htm.

48. Those named who held sensitive positions were vulnerable, even if the charges could not be proven. As a result of Chambers's testimony, Felix Inslerman, a General Electric airplane designer and draftsman in Schenectady, New York, came under investigation in late 1948 as a security risk, for occupying a position in which he had "access to secret information." Authorities determined that he had removed technical data from his previous employer, Republic Aircraft Company, and they found thirty-six rolls of unprocessed film on his property. Determining that "The subject's previous subversive and espionage activities are such as to present a serious threat of compromising the security interests of the United States," the military revoked his clearance. See "Inslerman, Felix August, Summary of Information," December 28, 1948, and Army Navy A/F Personnel Security Board, memo, January 19, 1949, file X843973, IRR, RG 319, NARA. On Wadleigh and Pigman, see FBI report, January 18, 1949, Bykov file; *New York Times*, June 10, 1949; Chambers, Whittaker, file X8138683, box 28, RG 165.

49. As early as February 1946, Hoover had intervened with Truman in an unsuccessful effort to halt White's confirmation as a delegate to the International Monetary Fund (IMF); Truman was not impressed with Hoover's accusations or their sources. See Hoover to Harry Hawkins Vaughan, February 1, 1946, FBI file, box 169, PSF, HSTL. An excellent discussion of White's culpability is in Bruce Craig's dissertation, "Treasonable Doubt," 406, 410, 411n18. Craig argues convincingly that White was not responsible for some of the more notorious charges against him, such as transferring German occupation currency plates to the Soviets and thus looting the American treasury for $100 million; nor was he guilty of other "policy subversion" initiatives for which he has been accused, such as sparing the Soviets war with Japan before World War II and bringing on Pearl Harbor instead, or pushing Germany into the hands of Moscow by promoting the Morgenthau plan (iii). (These charges are made most recently in Schecter and Schecter, *Sacred Secrets*,

especially chap. 2, passim, and 124–25.) Craig argues, nevertheless, that White was guilty of a "species of espionage." Moreover, he was "clearly and openly . . . a trusted friend of the Soviet Union"; see "Treasonable Doubt," 15. Further elaboration is in Craig's forthcoming book by the same title, especially chap. 12, which appeared as this book was going to press.

50. Rob T. Albright, "Stolen Papers Meant Codes Were Broken, State Aide Says; New Red Spy Suspects Sought," *Washington Post,* December 8, 1948; Truman quoted in Powers, *Secrecy and Power,* 297; see also *New York Times,* December 16, 1948, quoted in Tanenhaus, *Chambers,* 324. Truman persisted in doubting the espionage accusations, referring to "a crook and a louse[:] Mrs. Bentley and Whittaker Chambers." Truman note, November 17, 1953, quoted in Craig, "Treasonable Doubt," 411n18.

51. Along with HUAC's retracing the history of the apartment and car the two men had shared, the FBI's painstaking recovery of Hiss's typewriter, on which the documents were composed, is a classic tale in forensic history. See Weinstein, *Perjury,* 31–48, passim, 386–97.

52. Elsey to Clifford, August 16, 1948, in Benson and Warner, *Venona,* 117.

53. See Olmsted, *Red Spy Queen,* 178–79. Considering her value to the Bureau, it is telling that she had to beg the agency for this financial support. Her difficulty in finding secure employment in the 1950s, along with her alcoholism, no doubt contributed to her poor health and her early death at fifty-five. At the same time, CPUSA official Morris Childs, who became a double agent for the FBI in 1951 and continued in that capacity until 1980 (along with his brother Jack), was put in the Mayo Clinic courtesy of Hoover when he got sick. Defectors today, of course, like the agent who received $7 million for giving the United States the file on Robert Hanssen in 2001, are generally treated even better. Romerstein interview, November 21, 2003; Andrew and Mitrokhin, *Sword and the Shield,* 288–93.

54. *Washington Post,* September 9, 1949; Peake, "Afterword," *Out of Bondage,* 255–58; Senate Committee on Expenditures, *Export Policy and Loyalty,* 38–39.

55. Memo, 10, Remington file, #X10; Peake, "Afterword," *Out of Bondage,* 249; Senate Committee on Expenditures, *Export Policy and Loyalty,* 39.

56. Memo, 7, Remington file, #X10; May, *Un-American Activities,* 95, 112–20; Peake, "Afterword," *Out of Bondage,* 250.

57. Memo, 6–7, 10, Remington file, #X10; Ladd to Director, Sept. 6, 1948, Remington file, #X1.

58. Report, May 24, 1950, 5, Remington file, #NR; Peake, "Afterword," *Out of Bondage,* 25; May, *Un-American Activities,* 163–65.

59. Report, 8–14, Remington file, #NR.

60. See Olmsted, *Red Spy Queen,* 162–163. Bentley's propensity to exaggerate is clear in a comment that she made in August 1949 at a speech at the Beverly Hills Hotel; she pronounced that the Soviet Union "probably has an even stronger espionage organization in this country today than she did during the war when, as an ally, she received a great deal of valuable data." "Elizabeth Bentley Tells How Intellectuals Help Red Plots," *L.A. Herald and Express,* August 31, 1949; George Dixon, "Washington Scene," *Washington Post,* September 3, 1949.

61. For example, an FBI investigation unearthed that he had been "associated closely with known Communists" while at the TVA in the 1930s. Memo, 4, Remington file, #X10; May, *Un-American Activities*, 109.

62. Remington's letter to supporters, June 8, 1948, quoted in May, *Un-American Activities*, 105.

63. May, *Un-American Activities*, 135; *New York Journal American*, February 1, 1950, Bentley file [a], #A.

64. The 1953 trial also found him guilty of "giving Bentley information to which she was not entitled." May, *Un-American Activities*, 288. On his murder, see F. L. Price to Mr. Rosen, November 22, 1954, FBI Remington file, 70–22845, #3, #7; see also Peake, "Afterword," *Out of Bondage*, 252. He was murdered not because of his beliefs, but because of prison gang rivalry, according to the *Washington Post*, November 26, 1954.

65. Ladd to Hoover, February 28, 1950, 1, foia.fbi.gov/venona/venona.pdf.

66. See discussion in Benson and Warner, *Venona*, xxiv–xxv.

67. See Theoharis, *Chasing Spies*, especially chap. 4.

68. Mitchell and Mitchell, *Spy Who Seduced America*, 20.

69. Her meeting with Apresyan is in Venona 27 New York to Moscow, January 8, 1945. She also appears in an earlier message, Venona 1014 New York to Moscow, July 20, 1944, when she was working at the BEW.

70. For a discussion of her arrest, see Lamphere, *FBI-KGB War*, chap. 7.

71. SAC Robert Granville quoted in Mitchell and Mitchell, *Spy Who Seduced America*, 65.

72. Clark to Truman, March 16, 1949, Justice Department Papers, box 21, WHCF, HSTL; Schrecker, *Many Are the Crimes*, 176.

73. Mitchell and Mitchell, *Spy Who Seduced America*, 60–61, 118–19, 145–47.

74. Ibid., 134–39, passim.

75. Ibid., 88–89.

76. Ibid., 102–14.

77. Ibid., 187.

78. J. Howard McGrath to Truman, December 7, 1949, FBI file, box 168, PSF, HSTL.

79. See Kai Bird and Max Holland, "The Taping of 'Tommy the Cork,'" *The Nation*, February 8, 1986,144; *The Washington Monthly*, February 1987, 41, in Vertical File, Thomas G. Corcoran 1945–47, FBI file, box 168, PSF, HSTL. While Corcoran was chiefly an opportunist, in at least one instance his work affected the administration's attempts to stop "subversion." In June 1945, Philip Jaffe, editor of the *Amerasia* journal, was accused, along with five associates, of stealing 1500–1700 "secret" State Department documents to support the journal's editorial policy against recognition of Nationalist China. Close to seventy-five FBI agents were involved in handling the case over the course of three months, breaking into the magazine, grabbing files, and interviewing the men, but the investigation led to only two convictions at the time. Corcoran, as Hoover's bug revealed, had helped "fix" the case—he wanted to avoid embarrassment for Chiang's Kuomintang government, his clients—and had pressed State Department "China hand" John Stewart Service, who was to be a witness in the grand jury investigation, to keep quiet. Service cooperated with Corcoran—although he always denied his connections with the lobbyist—and was rewarded by only "perfunctory" questions by the grand jury.

As Klehr and Radosh note, Service missed a chance thereby to condemn America's China policy, the reason he had conferred with Jaffe in the first place. Hoover, meanwhile, could not admit to the bug's existence without embarrassing Truman, so thus was unable to demonstrate Corcoran's actions. See Klehr and Radosh, *Amerasia Spy Case*, 112 –27; "Amerasia Case Costly to FBI," *Washington Daily News,* May 10, 1950; "Amerasia Case Was Fixed at a Very High Level," *Kansas City Star,* April 20,1986; and "Summaries of Conversations: Thomas G. Corcoran," August 2, 1945, box 335, PSF, where Corcoran's pressure on Service not to testify is evident. The *Amerasia* case finally cost Service his position on December 14, 1951 (see letter from Carlisle H. Humelsine to Service, December 27, 1951), because "there is a reasonable doubt as to your loyalty to the Government of the United States . . . based on the intentional and unauthorized disclosure of documents and information of a confidential and non-public character." See Loyalty Investigation of John Stewart Service, Papers of John S. Service and Charles E. Rhetts, HSTL.

80. Mitchell and Mitchell, *Spy Who Seduced America,* 209–18, passim.

81. Ibid., 272–73.

82. Lamphere, *FBI-KGB War,* chap. 7. Hand's decision was quoted in a recent case, *U.S.A. v. Stephen Flemmi,* US District Court of the District of Massachusetts, CR 94–10287, Boston, Mass., August 21, 2001.

83. Mitchell and Mitchell, *Spy Who Seduced America,* 305. Earlier, the State Department had recommended deportation of Gubitchev before trial, but the Attorney General insisted on his presence. See Tom Clark, memo for President, March 16, 1949, box 21, WHCF.

84. See Director FBI to Assistant Attorney General Warren Olney III, May 1, 1953, and Director, FBI to Assistant Attorney General, February 15, 1952, Perl file [b], #773, #660, respectively.

85. Belmont to Boardman, February 1, 1956, 4–10, foia.fbi.gov/venona/venona.pdf.

86. Benson and Warner, *Venona,* xxvii; as they note, William Weisband, a spy inside the Armed Forces Security Agency, had likely informed Moscow even earlier about the project. See also Weinstein and Vassiliev, *Haunted Wood,* 291–93.

87. Perrin quoted in Hoover to Sumner Pike, 5, Fuchs file, #504.

88. Ladd to Director, August 8, 1950, Fuchs file, 4, #426.

89. Director FBI to SAC New York, January 9, 1950, Fuchs file, #53; J. Edgar Hoover to Sidney W. Souers, February 6, 1950, February 21, 1950, FBI file, box 168, PSF, HSTL; Fuchs confession to Skardon, January 27, 1950, cited in Williams, *Klaus Fuchs,* 184–85; Report on Emil Fuchs, November 7, 1949, Fuchs file, #32 (1998 supplemental release). Also see "Fuchs Hearing in London," *New York Times,* in JCAE, *Soviet Atomic Espionage,* 31. On Venona's assistance in the case, see H. B. Fletcher to D. M. Ladd, October 21, 1949, and Personal: British Headquarters to Mr. Ladd, October 29, 1949, Fuchs file, #24, #33 (both in 1998 supplemental release). On the document, see "Summary Brief on Fuchs and Gold," 53, Fuchs file, #1494X; "Summary Brief on Fuchs," February 6, 1950, 19, Fuchs file, #1202 (1998 supplemental release). Venona 850 Moscow to New York, June 15, 1944, referred to Fuchs's information as having been received. A month later, the resident agent at the Soviet consulate recommended a $500 bonus for Fuchs.

90. Ladd to Director, August 8, 1950, 4, Fuchs file, #426.

91. Hoover to Souers, March 7, 1950, FBI file, box 168, PSF, HSTL; Williams, *Klaus*

Fuchs, 135. See Hoover's reaction handwritten on cablegram from Belmont to Ladd, February 28, 1950, Fuchs file, #456 (1998 supplemental release).

92. "Summary Brief on Fuchs and Gold," 11b, Fuchs file, #1494X; see also "Summary of Facts, Jurisdiction, Collaboration with British," 7, in #1494X.

93. Fletcher to Ladd, February 1, 1950, Fuchs file, #84.

94. "John R. Murphy's Fuchs Report," 16. As the FBI analyst put it, "It is not likely that Goose would have obtained such an interpretation of any business differences of Brothman from a third party."

95. See John R. Murphy Report, E. J. K. Fuchs, March 9, 1950, Fuchs file, #642 (1998 supplemental release).

96. Fuchs's confession, February 23, 1950, accompanying letter, Lish Whitson to American Embassy, 2, Fuchs file, #328. See also Clegg and Lamphere to the Director, June 4, 1950, Fuchs file, #1412 (1998 supplemental release). In 1959, Fuchs was released for good behavior and quickly flown to East Germany. Peter F. Maxson report, E. J. K. Fuchs, February 17, 1950, Fuchs file, #326 (1998 supplemental release).

97. "Summary Brief on Fuchs and Gold," 4a, 127–28, Fuchs file, #1494X.

98. Gold, "Circumstances," 1069, 1082–84.

99. Hoover to Souers, May 24, 1950, FBI file, box 168, PSF, HSTL.

100. "Summary Brief on Fuchs and Gold," 226C, Fuchs file, #1494X.

101. Ladd to Hoover, February 28, 1950, 3, foia.fbi.gov/venona/venona.pdf.

102. JCAE, *Soviet Atomic Espionage,* 5.

103. Supreme Court of the United States, October Term, 1951, Transcript of Record, *Julius Rosenberg and Ethel Rosenberg vs. The United States of America, Morton Sobell vs. The United States of America,* 1952, published by the Committee to Secure Justice for Morton Sobell, vol. 1, bk. 1, 183.

104. Benson and Warner, *Venona,* xxvi.

105. See Venona 1585 New York to Moscow, November 12, 1944; FBI reaction is in Ladd to Hoover, February 28, 1950, 10–11, foia.fbi.gov/venona/venona.pdf. More documents are at www.bombshell-1.com.

106. See Albright and Kunstel, *Bombshell,* 89–90.

107. Report re Joel Barr, October 27, 1950, September 28, 1950, and Edward J. Cahill, memo re Joel Barr, September 6, 1950, in FBI Barr file [a], #154, #245, #118, respectively; Senate Judiciary Committee, *Scope of Soviet Activities,* 4866–67.

108. Feklisov, *Man behind the Rosenbergs,* 287–88.

109. Frederick G. Bauckham report, August 11, 1950, Barr file [b], #60.

110. SAC Albany to Director FBI, August 7, 1950, 75, James H. Higdon Jr., Newark, February 26, 1950, and FBI Albany teletype, June 28, 1950, FBI Sarant file, #77, #320, #3, respectively.

111. SAC Albany to Director FBI, SAC Phoenix, SAC Boston, August 23, 1950, and Laughlin to Belmont, August 23, 1950, Sarant file, #194, #203, respectively.

112. A. M. Belmont to D. M. Ladd, October 28, 1950, Sarant file, #309. By January 25, 1951, there was a grand jury subpoena outstanding for Sarant, but it was never carried out. See Belmont to Ladd, January 25, 1951, Sarant file, #390.

113. Radosh and Milton, *Rosenberg File,* 118; SAC San Francisco to Director, October

10, 1950, and FBI Buffalo to Director FBI, October 31, 1950, Sarant file, #294, #332, respectively.

114. SAC Albany to Director FBI, August 7, 1950, John B. O'Donoghue report, October 24, 1950, Report to SAC New York, April 23, 1951, "Examination of Toolmarks—Misc.," Sarant file, #77, #307, #444, respectively; Radosh and Milton, *Rosenberg File*, 114.

115. SAC New York to Director, February 28, 1952, 2–3, Perl file [b], #665.

116. See Radosh and Milton, *Rosenberg Case*, 298–99; FBI lab report, to SAC New York from Hoover, January 23, 1952, Perl file, #652; William Perl investigation, October 19, 1953, Perl file [a], #1162.

117. L. B. Nichols to Tolson, April 30, 1953, and New York to Director, May 15, 1953, Perl file [b], #785, #833, respectively.

118. See Director FBI to Assistant Attorney General Warren Olney III, May 1, 1953, and Director, FBI to Assistant Attorney General, February 15, 1952, Perl file [b], #773, #660, respectively. Hoover had hoped that the Rosenbergs would talk, thus enabling him to pursue the espionage charge.

119. SAC New York to Director, May 20, 1953, Perl file [b], #803.

120. See William Perl investigation, October 19, 1953, Perl file [a], #1162; Maurice W. Corcoran, recording, May 18, 1953, Perl file [b], #791.

121. New York to Director, May 20, 1953, Perl file [b], #803.

122. New York to Director, May 19, 1953, Perl file [b], #834; William Perl investigation, October 19, 1953, Perl file [a], #1162; New York to Director, May 21, 1953, Perl file [b], #841. Glassman confirmed this meeting with Perl. See William Perl memo, September 2, 1952, Perl file [b], #730.

123. C. E. Henreich to A. H. Belmont, May 22, 1953, Perl file [b], #845.

124. *New York World Telegram and Sun*, May 21, 1953, *New York Mirror*, May 22, 1953; *New York Journal American*, June 5, 1953; *New York Mirror*, June 6, 1953; report, Washington City News Service, June 5, 1953, Perl file [b], #854; Radosh and Milton, *Rosenberg File*, 299–303. David Greenglass had also testified that Rosenberg had told him he had an intelligence source who was an adviser on the Aswan Dam project; William Perl was indeed hired as a consultant by Hugh L. Cooper & Company, an engineering firm, to work on aerodynamics calculations for the dam. Perl memo, June 9, 1953, Perl file [b], #857; Senate Judiciary Committee, *Scope of Soviet Activities*, 4867.

125. See "MiG Plans Linked to Rosenberg Ring," *New York World Telegram and Sun*, July 9, 1953, cited in Perl file [a], #b75, and Radosh and Milton, *Rosenberg File*, 303–4. Radosh and Milton, who also note that the FBI was aware of these allegations as early as April 1951, cite a 1952 FBI memorandum quoting defector Grigorii Tokaev, who recalled seeing "original NACA data sheets, diagrams, and descriptive data'" concerning designs for jet engine testing (538).

126. See Schneir and Schneir, "Cables Coming in from the Cold," who cite U.S. Air Force historian Richard Hallion's assertions that the Rolls-Royce engine, sold to the Soviets in 1946, was the chief foreign contribution to the MiG-15. Hallion, however, does argue that Soviet espionage did contribute to the MiG-19 of 1953. See also debate of Till Geiger, Wesley Yang, and John Earl Haynes and Harvey Klehr on H-Diplo on-line discussion list, September 3–5, 2003.

127. Branigan to Belmont, June 1, 1953, Perl file [b], #856.

128. Radosh and Milton, *Rosenberg File,* 303; see reports, 1967 and 1970, Perl file [a], vol. 13.

129. Radosh and Milton, *Rosenberg File,* 131–32, 139; *Rosenbergs vs. U.S., Morton Sobell vs. U.S.,* June 1, 1952, 1:210–11; Bernice Levin Colen, February 28, 1956, FBI Myers file, #18. See additional discussion of Sobell's role in chap. 3.

130. D. M. Ladd to Director, August 8, 1950, Sobell file [a], #100 (supplemental release). Sobell left New York on June 22, 1950, and spent the next few weeks at a boarding house in Mexico City. He was found by the Mexican police, acting on FBI orders, on August 16, 1950, and turned over to the FBI two days later. Sobell was charged with violating the Federal Conspiracy Statute "in that he did conspire with Julius Rosenberg to transmit information relating to the National Defense of the United States contrary to the provisions of Section 32A of Title 50." August 21, 1951, Sobell file [a], #143. At the same time, Greenglass reported he had been offered $5,000 to disappear by Rosenberg, just as Vivian Glassman had offered $2,000 to William Perl. D. M. Ladd to Director, August 8, 1950, Sobell file [a], #100.

131. Ladd to Director, August 23, 1950, Sobell file [a], #236. The Bureau, especially its Office of the Legal Attaché in Mexico, had of course expended a great deal of effort in the search for Sobell; special agents Edwin L. Sweet and John J. Creeden exhaustively checked ads for rooms for rent to find the neighborhood where Sobell was located, checked ships at Tampico and Veracruz, and worked closely with the Mexican Security Police and its head, Gen. Marcelino Inurreta. The FBI also used the Mexican Security Police to patrol the ports mentioned, as well as Yucatan and the Mexico City Airport. Russian ships at Veracruz were thought a likely destination for Sobell. In addition, agents closely watched restaurants, especially the Kuku establishment where Sobell had been spotted, supermarkets, and a Sears Roebuck store. It was the supermarket monitoring that led the police to Sobell's neighborhood and thus made possible his arrest. In his neighborhood canvassing, SA Sweet told the "humble folk" that Sobell's step-daughter, Sidney Gurewitz Sobell, had been kidnapped, which "consistently enlisted the sympathetic attention of the neighborhood people" and helped them overcome their distrust of law enforcement officials. After one such visit, an elderly woman called the security police and alerted them to the location of Sobell's apartment. The Bureau gave no credit to the Mexican police in this manhunt, declaring that they "fall far short of the standards of reliability which a case like this requires." Yet the task of arresting the highly combative Sobell fell to the security police. After the struggle, General Inurreta, with some reluctance, agreed to have his men take Sobell the 750 miles to Laredo, followed by two special agents. Except for "abrupt stops" so that the "extremely" carsick female Sobells could relieve themselves, they drove without interruption. Legation, Mexico City office, to Director, April 4, 1951, 7–12, Sobell file [a], #991.

132. So associated is Sobell with Alcatraz that a 2001 reissue of his book, *On Doing Time,* was published by the Golden Gate National Park Association, which manages the prison site today.

133. See Sobell, *On Doing Time,* passim, and his discussions of the Venona releases and his role at www2.h-net.msu.edu/~diplo/Sobell.htm. The author's attempts to interview Sobell were unsuccessful.

134. George M. Langdon Report, JRO file, #16; San Francisco Office to Washington Director, May 8, 1946, #33; SAC San Francisco to Director, May 14, 1946, #33. The FBI took over the Manhattan District files on Oppenheimer in the summer of 1946. AEC, *In the Matter of JRO*, 417.

135. Oppenheimer had been an adviser to Bernard Baruch in the latter's eponymous plan for internationalizing atomic energy, and he contributed to the Acheson-Lilienthal Report for the control of atomic energy. Julius Robert Oppenheimer, February 17, 1947, FBI background, attached to Hoover to Vaughan, February 28, 1947, box 167, PSF, HSTL.

136. Oppenheimer Memo, March 18, 1946, 2, JRO file, #22.

137. Memo on Oppenheimer, April 16, 1954, JRO file, #1208.

138. Hoover to Vaughan, February 28, 1947, FBI file, box 167, PSF, HSTL; see discussion of Frank Oppenheimer's investigation in Herken, *Brotherhood*, 181.

139. W. A. Branigan to A. H. Belmont, April 7, 1954, JRO file, 1055.

140. FBI memo, April 21, 1947, cited in Schecter and Schecter, *Sacred Secrets*, appendix 2. This memo cited "a highly confidential and reliable source of information having access to certain records of the Communist Party in San Francisco" as claiming that a November 1946 party financial report listed a certain "X-1 (Berkeley Professor)" as the contributor of monthly payments. Gregg Herken agrees with the Schecters that Oppenheimer was a member of the party, and he cites a letter that Haakon Chevalier wrote Oppenheimer, discussing their membership in the same unit of the party from 1938 to 1942. See Chevalier to Oppenheimer, July 13, 1964, on the Web site for Herken's *Brotherhood of the Bomb*: www.brotherhoodofthebomb.com.

141. Memo on Oppenheimer attached to Ladd to Director, March 18, 1946, 6, JRO file, #51.

142. Ibid.; see also Belmont to Boardman, April 15, 1954, and Memo to Boardman, April 16, 1954, JRO file, #1159, #1208, respectively.

143. Strickland to Ladd, March 26, 1946, JRO file, #24.

144. W. A Branigan to A. H. Belmont, March 31, 1954, JRO file, #1279. Branigan was quoting Lewis Strauss, chairman of AEC, via David Teeple, Lewis's assistant, on Eisenhower's view of Oppenheimer. See also Schecter and Schecters, *Sacred Secrets*, 196–99; Wang, *American Science*, 268–70. The events leading to the suspension are discussed in Herken, *Brotherhood*, chs. 15–16. Also see Polenberg, *In the Matter of J. Robert Oppenheimer*.

145. AEC, *In the Matter of JRO*, 136.

146. Belmont to Boardman, and Memo on Oppenheimer, April 16, 1954, JRO file, #1158, #1208, respectively; see also Report on J. R. Oppenheimer, February 5, 1950, in "Summary Brief on Fuchs," 6, Fuchs file, #1202; Belmont to Boardman, May 7, 1954, JRO file, #1431.

147. Belmont to Ladd, January 5, 1954, and W. A. Branigan to A. H. Belmont, April 7, 1954, JRO file, #587, #1055, respectively.

148. FBI Newark to Director, FBI, July 13, 1954, and Belmont to Boardman, August 24, 1954, JRO file, #1880, #1974, respectively; see also Hoover's earlier request for a wiretap, in which he justified the request based on Oppenheimer's "contact with individuals reported to be Soviet agents." April 26, 1946, memo to the Attorney General, JRO file, #29.

149. Belmont to Boardman, August 24, 1954, and Hoover memo, October 15, 1954, JRO file, #1974, #2072, respectively.

150. D. M. Ladd to J. Edgar Hoover, December 1, 1953, regarding "the Fort Monmouth Situation," FBI Elitcher file [b], #505.

151. Edward Scheidt to Col. William Mayer, September 21, 1950, vol. 8, Sobell file [b], #471A; "Ft. Monmouth Investigation," December 1, 1953, 1B-1H, passim, Elitcher file [b], #505; Belmont to Ladd, April 25, 1951, Elitcher file [e], #129. In 1951, as Kitty came forward to talk about his role at Fort Monmouth, and in order to glean names of "all members of the Young Communist League whom he recalls," Belmont wanted it very clear that there would be "no promises" in return for his turning over evidence. As Hoover wrote, emphatically, "Be certain FBI agrees to no deal even if [Justice] Dept. does."

152. "Ft. Monmouth Investigation," December 1, 1953, 1K, Elitcher file [b], #505.

153. Hoover to Allen, July 18, 1946, on the National Committee Plenum of the CPUSA, New York City, July 16 to July 18, 1946, FBI file, box 167, PSF, HSTL.

154. See discussion in Richard Powers, *Secrecy and Power*, 285–91.

155. See Whitehead, *FBI Story*, 279.

156. S. J. Chamberlin, G2, to Devitt Vanech, February 11, 1947, box 2, Vanech Papers. Still, less than two hundred employees lost their jobs because of this program. See O'Reilly, *Hoover and the Un-Americans*, 63. On Hoover's role, see discussion in Schrecker, *Many Are the Crimes*, 210.

157. Chamberlin to Vanech, February 11, 1947.

158. See Richard Powers, *Secrecy and Power*, 285; Report, President's Temporary Commission on Employee Loyalty, November 25, 1946, box 1, Vanech Papers.

159. Report of President's Temporary Commission on Employee Loyalty, March 1947, 21, 22, box 2, Vanech Papers.

160. Schrecker, *Many Are the Crimes*, 210; Report, PCTEL, November 25, 1946, 24.

161. Vanech Memo, December 26, 1946, box 2, Vanech Papers.

162. Richard Powers, *Secrecy and Power*, 285–90. The order stated that "investigations of persons entering the competitive service shall be conducted by the Civil Service Commission, except in such cases as are covered by a special agreement between the Commission and any given department or agency." Box 1, Vanech Papers.

163. According to Executive Order 9835, the Justice Department was supposed to furnish the Loyalty Board with "the name of each foreign or domestic organization, association, movement, group or combination of persons which the Attorney General, after appropriate investigation and determination, designates as totalitarian, fascist, communist or subversive, or as having adopted a policy of advocating or approving the commission of acts of force or violence to deny others their rights under the Constitution of the United States, or as seeking to alter the form of government of the United States by unconstitutional means." Seth W. Richardson, Chairman, Loyalty Review Board, April 25, 1949, to All Executive Departments and Agencies. XE 333886, box 17, IRR, RG 319, NARA.

164. Hoover to Attorney General, March 31, 1947, box 1, Vanech Papers.

165. Richard Powers, *Secrecy and Power*, 290–91. On the bill, see Acting Attorney General Douglas W. McGregor to Chairman, Committee on Post Office and Civil Service, House of Representatives, June 4, 1947, box 1, Vanech Papers. On AEA, see Hoover to Honorable Brian McMahon, Chairman Joint Congressional Committee on Atomic Energy, April 6, 1950, Fuchs file, #1079 (1998 supplemental release); "Summary Brief on Fuchs," #1202.

166. Schrecker, *Many Are the Crimes*, 211–12; Tom Clark Memo to Vanech, February 14, 1947, box 2, Vanech Papers; Statement by Seth Richardson, Chairman of Loyalty Review Board, December 23, 1947, box 2,Vanech Papers.

167. "Bad Medicine," *New York Times*, July 17, 1947; "Civil Liberties and the Reds," *Washington Post*, August 22, 1947; see also "700 State Employees Probed a Month," *Washington Daily News*, June 12, 1947, box 2, Vanech Papers. Indeed, a proposed query letter began, "The [Civil Service Commission] has received information to the effect that you have been a member of the Communist Party and the Communist Political Association," citing details of meetings attended and recruitment effected and requesting information on current party affiliation. See US Civil Service Commission, "Interrogation (model)," box 1, Vanech Papers.

168. Hoover to Attorney General, March 28, 1947, box 1, Vanech Papers. A congressional committee backed him up on the fingerprints and also called for a commission composed of members of the Department of Justice, the War Department, the Naval Department, the State Department, the Treasury Department, and the Civil Service Commission to explore the issues and "to present to the Congress . . . a complete and unified program that will give adequate protection to our Government against individuals whose primary loyalty is to governments other than our own." See House Committee on the Civil Service, *Report of Investigation with Respect to Employee Loyalty*, cited in box 2, Vanech Papers.

169. Seth Richardson statement, December 23, 1947.

170. *New York Times*, March 23, 1947; see discussion of Marzani in Andrew and Mitrokhin, *Sword and the Shield*, 226–27. Marzani went on to run the pro-Soviet Liberty Book Club, which published such works as Joachim Joesten's *Oswald: Assassin or Fall-Guy* (1964), a polemic that claimed Oswald was connected with the FBI and CIA and doing the bidding of wealthy, right-wing zealots who disliked Kennedy's moderate approach to the Soviet Union.

171. "In Times of Challenge, U.S. Liberties: 1946–47" (ACLU annual report), 4, box 2, Vanech Papers; Clark to Seth W. Richardson, November 24, 1947, quoted in Edward F. Witsell and Dwight D. Eisenhower, Department of the Army memo, December 15, 1947, XE338886, IRR, RG 319, NARA.

172. "Court Holds That the Word 'Communist' Is Too Vague to Use in Accusing a Person," *New York Times*, February 20, 1941, box 34, Ohly Papers.

173. "A Statement to Accompany the Report the President by His Committee on Loyalty, by Herbert E. Gaston, Chairman of the Interdepartmental Committee of Employee Investigations Created by Executive Order 9300," n.d., box 2, Vanech Papers.

174. Hoover to A. Devitt Vanech, January 3, 1947, box 1, Vanech Papers.

175. "List of Criteria for Designating Organizations under Section 3 of Part III of 9835," July 1947, box 1, Vanech Papers.

176. "Asks Tighter Laws for Espionage," *Washington Herald*, August 15, 1948, box 56, Elsey Papers.

177. "Suggestions for Improvement of AEC Security," February 5, 1950, in "Summary Brief on Fuchs," 3, Fuchs file, #1202. For current espionage laws, see, for instance, U.S. Code, Title 10, Section 906, Article 106a, which applies to members of the armed forces and states possible penalties (including death) for any person transmitting defense-related

material "with intent or reason to believe that it is to be used to the injury of the United States or to the advantage of a foreign nation."

178. Some actions emanated from the executive branch. In 1947, for instance, the Atomic Energy Commission prevented shipments of electrical equipment that Russia had ordered for "general industrial development" because of fears they would be used for atomic research. See *Washington Times-Herald,* October 17, 1947, 1.

179. Funigiello, *American-Soviet Trade,* 32–36; HUAC, *Hearings regarding Shipments of Atomic Material,* 1182–84; "Report of Viktor Andreevich Kravchenko," July 31, 1944, 6–7, file 383.4 USSR, Army Intelligence Project Decimal File, RG 319, NARA.

180. Hoover to Vaughan, October 20, 1948, FBI file, box 169, PSF, HSTL.

181. Funigiello, *American-Soviet Trade,* 38–44, passim.

182. Ibid., 46, 49, 68; for further discussion, see De Pauw, *Soviet-American Trade Relations.*

183. See Robinson, "Steve Nelson: Unwelcome Guest."

184. Margaret Gertrude Nelson file, March 14, 1945, and Ladd to Director, January 30, 1950, Nelson file, #257, #509, respectively. See discussion of the wiretap problem in Theoharis, *Chasing Spies,* chap. 4.

185. N. J. L. Pieper to Hoover, July 10, 1945, Nelson file, #276, vol. 3; see discussion of the Duclos attack in Ryan, *Browder,* chap. 10.

186. See, for instance, February 2–3, 1946, July 4, 1946, July 19, 1946, surveillance log, Steve Nelson, Nelson file, #394, vol. 5 (unfortunately, much of the material is blacked out); FBI San Francisco to Director and SACS, Chicago, October 1945, #303; J. W. Vincent to Director, FBI, November 5, 1945, #305. On his foreign language groups work, and for examples of extensive evidence of surveillance in 1946, see #394, vol. 4.

187. SAC Philadelphia to Director, FBI, March 1, 1946, Nelson file, #327.

188. Quotation from an FBI informant's version of Nelson's speech at Communist Party meeting at D'Quine hall in Scranton, Penn., February 9, 1946; another informant at the same meeting, who admitted he had not heard the whole speech, disagreed that Nelson would have called for "mass pressure," as these were the tactics of ex-CP leader Earl Browder—and Nelson had only attacked Browder in his speech. Nelson file, #368, 4:9–11.

189. SAC Milwaukee to Director FBI, February 27, 1946, Nelson file, #337: FBI report, "Soviet Activities in the US."

190. SAC New York to Director FBI, April 3, 1947, Nelson file, #400; Hoover to SAC New York, February 28, 1947, #392, vol. 4; Director FBI to SAC New York, October 15, 1947, #414.

191. See, for instance, Hoover to SAC New York, March 11, 1948, Nelson file, #424; Director to SAC Miami, April 26, 1948, #425.

192. Hoover to SAC New York, December 13, 1947, Nelson file, #418; Ladd to Director, August 31, 1948, #463; Victor Riesle, "Inside Labor," *New York Post,* December 8, 1948, in Nelson file, #466; Nelson report, New York, Sept. 22, 1948, #451.

193. Hoover to SAC New York, May 24, 1948, Nelson file, #430.

194. Steve Nelson, Witness Special Agent, FBI, Miami, April 24, 1948, Nelson file, #426X.

195. Nelson report, New York, September 22, 1948, Nelson file, #451, 6, 9; SAC Pittsburgh to Director FBI, January 16, 1948, #420; Director FBI to SAC NY, May 8, 1947, #405.

196. Nelson File, New York, April 3, 1947, 30–42, Nelson file, #402. The sources for some of this material included numerous "active, paid" informants, many of whom were mem-

bers of the Communist Party, were "considered reliable," and had "never been compromised" (51). The published sources are mentioned in HUAC, *Hearings regarding Steve Nelson*, 146–47.

197. HUAC, *Hearings regarding Steve Nelson*, ix; Nelson et al., *Steve Nelson*, 294.

198. Nelson report, Pittsburgh, January 14, 1949, Nelson file, #469, quoting Nelson on September 17, 1948; Venona 1328 Pavel P. Mikhailov (New York) to the Director (Moscow), August 12, 1943.

199. *Washington Times Herald*, October 8, 1948, Nelson file, #458; Citation of contempt is in "Proceedings against Steve Nelson," August 10, 1950, 81st Cong., 2nd sess., cited in Nelson file, #542. The citation made Nelson subject to a $1,000 fine or one year in jail or both. The Supreme Court would uphold the right of defendants to take the Fifth Amendment regarding their Communist membership based on the fact that testifying to membership could result in incriminating consequences stemming from the Smith Act. See Schrecker, *Many Are the Crimes*, 323.

200. C. E. Hendrich to A. H. Belmont, August 2, 1950, Nelson file, #540.

201. Pittsburgh to Director, December 5, 1950, Nelson file, #578; Pittsburgh to Director and SAC Washington Field, December 6, 1950, #579; Washington to Director, December 8, 1950, #577.

202. Soucy to FBI Director and SAC New York, September 30, 1950, Nelson file, #556; Soucy to Director, October 17, 1950, #565.

203. Sedition meant "any writing, etc., the intent of which is: A. To cause any outbreak or demonstration of violence against Pennsylvania or the United States. B. To encourage any person to take any action with a view to overthrowing or destroying by threat or force the government of Pennsylvania or the United States." See Nelson report, Pittsburgh, November 6, 1950, 11, Nelson file, #572.

204. Rabinowitz, *Unrepentant Leftist*, 132–33; Leab, *I Was a Communist*, 67–68.

205. "Police Raid Bares Red's Top Secrets," *Washington Times-Herald*, October 3, 1950, Nelson file, #570; Rabinowitz, *Unrepentant Leftist*, 132. In addition to these instructions, as the *Times-Herald* article noted, cadres were informed how to "Employ the output of left wing columnists and authors in attempting to show that the United States was to blame for the Korean war." The Communist Party's FBI report, "Memorandum of the State Review Commission," noted that the FBI "has compiled lists and records of individuals and organizations who have even in the mildest manner shown some enthusiasm for the New Deal. This governmental Gestapo represents one of the most important agencies of the intimidation and persecution of all Americans who stand for peace and are opposed to fascism."

206. I. F. Stone, in Fast et al., *Steve Nelson*, 4; Leab, *I Was a Communist*, 68; FBI Pittsburgh to Director, September 14, 1950, Nelson file, #554.

207. Howard Fast, Milton Wolff, in *Steve Nelson*, 2, 14; Nelson report, Pittsburgh, November 6, 1950, 13, Nelson file, #572.

208. Rabinowitz, *Unrepentant Leftist*, 134–39; Leab, *I Was a Communist*, 88.

209. Belmont to Ladd, September 12, 1950, Nelson file, #549.

210. Director of FBI to Assistant Attorney General James M. McInerney, September 12, 1950, Nelson file, #549. Nelson's bail was set at $100,000, later reduced to $50,000 and

then $10,000. Soucy, FBI Pittsburgh to Director, September 16, 1950, September 28, 1950, #552, #559, respectively. The raid on the Communist Party headquarters left the facilities padlocked so that officials could return later for more material. L. B. Nichols to Mr. Tolson, October 3, 1950, #561. The use of the padlock was later declared invalid. Blank to Belmont, October 3, 1950, #571. Nelson had also been arrested in August for disorderly conduct at a city council meeting in McKeesport, Pennsylvania, while protesting against an ordinance requiring the registration of Communists. Nelson report, Pittsburgh, November 6, 1950, 14, #572.

211. See Herken, *Brotherhood of the Bomb,* 189. Wiretapped evidence was often introduced as coming from "a very reliable and highly confidential informant." See, for instance, HUAC, *Annual Report, 1949,* 5.

212. HUAC, *Report on Atomic Espionage,* 11.

213. Schrecker, *Many Are the Crimes,* 169; 282, Adams file, #715.

214. HUAC, *Report on Soviet Activities,* 162.

215. HUAC, *Annual Report, 1949,* 1; HUAC, *Hearings regarding Communist Espionage* (1951), 3563.

216. "Spotlight on Spies," 113–16, reel 261, vol. 132, ACLU Papers, Manuscript Collection, Seeley Mudd Library, Princeton University.

217. In grade school fashion, it posed such questions as, "How can a Communist be identified?" The answer: "It is easy. Ask him to name ten things wrong with the United States. Then ask him to name two things wrong with Russia. *His answers will show him up even to a child.* Communists will denounce the President of the United States but *they will never denounce Stalin.*" "100 Things You Should Know About Communism," 15, reel 261, vol. 132, ACLU Papers, emphasis in original.

218. Ibid., 102–3.

219. "Spotlight on Spies," 114–16, 123–24.

220. Ibid., 114, 123, 125.

221. HUAC, *Annual Report, 1949,* 18–19.

222. Weinstein and Vassiliev, *Haunted Wood,* 297–99.

223. See McGohey's notes on April 29, 1948, meeting with Attorney General Tom Clark, and July 20, 1948, grand jury Smith Act indictment, in John F. X. McGohey papers, Smith Act Case file, box 1, HSTL.

224. See Schrecker, *Many Are the Crimes,* 196–99.

225. Wm. Z. Foster, Chairman, and Eugene Dennis, General Secretary, CP, telegram to Truman, November 8, 1947, box 100, WHCF, HSTL.

226. SACB, No. 51–101, *James P. McGranery, Attorney General of the U.S., Petitioner, v. The Communist Party of the United States of America, Respondent,* 133–35; *Herbert Brownell Jr., Attorney General of the U.S., Petitioner, v. The Communist Party of the United States of America, Respondent,* 191, box 39, Dies Committee Files.

227. *Subversive Activities Control Board vs. CPUSA, Herbert Brownell, Jr., Attorney General of the U.S.A., Petitioner, vs. CPUSA, Respondent,* April 20, 1953, Dies Committee Files, box 39.

228. See "A Report to the President Pursuant to the President's Directive of January 31, 1950," April 7, 1950, in Department of State, *Foreign Relations of the United States* (Washington: GPO, 1977), 1:237–92; Acheson quoted in "Meeting of the President with Con-

gressional Leaders in the Cabinet Room," December 13, 1950, box 164, PSF, HSTL. For NSC-68's significance, see Cumings, *Origins of the Korean War*, vol. 2, *Roaring of the Cataract*, 177–81, 747; Gaddis, *Strategies of Containment*, especially chap. 4. For earlier signs of a harder line, see Mitrovich, *Undermining the Kremlin*, 36; the quotes are from his citations of "U.S. Objectives with Respect to the USSR to Counter Soviet Threats to U.S. Security," NSC 20/4, November 23, 1948.

229. "COMRAP Summary," 18–19.

CHAPTER 6

1. Of course, nor did the United States arrest its attempts to learn more about Russia. For a fascinating look at some of the U.S. efforts against the Soviet Union during its waning years, see Bearden and Risen, *Main Enemy*, pt. 1, passim.

2. See Herbig and Wiskoff, *Espionage against the United States*, xii.

3. See Nicholas Lemann's profile of Dick Cheney, "The Quiet Man," in *The New Yorker*, May 7, 2001, and discussion above on page 254, note 44; also see testimony of Council on Foreign Relations Senior Fellow and Columbia University professor Stephen Sestanovich in U.S. House Committee on International Relations, "U.S.-Russia Relations in Putin's Second Term," 108th Congress, 2d session, March 18, 2004, http://www.cfr.org/pub6869/stephen_r_sestanovich/congressional_testimony_usrussian_relations.php. Sestanovich was ambassador at large and Special Adviser to the Secretary of State for the New Independent States from 1997–2001.

4. U.S. Department of Defense, "Hostile Intelligence Threat—U.S. Technology," 3–13, passim; on the use of conferences and trade fairs, Western journals and official information, as well as exchange students, see Brian Freemantle, *The Steal*, 59–61; Metcalfe, *New Wizard War*, 151; Tuck, *High Tech Espionage*, 161.

5. See discussion in Herbig and Wiskoff, *Espionage against the United States*, 7–8. Two famous examples were Robert Lee Johnson and James Allen Mintkenbaugh, U.S. Army sergeants and friends who were both stationed in Europe. They began spying for the Soviets in the early 1950s but were not discovered until the mid-1960s. A full list of U.S. espionage cases from 1945 to 1989 is in West, *Games of Intelligence*, 57–60.

6. Charles Whittaker, letter to author, November 11, 2003.

7. See Bell, *Taking Care of the Law*, 100–101.

8. See "Rudolf Ivanovich Abel (Hollow Nickel Case)," www.fbi.gov/libref/historic/famcases/abel/abel.htm. Despite Abel's notoriety, Nigel West argues that his U.S. espionage career was insignificant and that he had never gained access to classified materials. *Games of Intelligence*, 90–91. Ronald Kessler, however, argues that because the Soviets were willing to trade Powers for Abel, he "was a very important spy," although Kessler notes that his activities remain mysterious. *Spy vs. Spy*, 235.

9. See discussion on Morros and Soble in Weinstein and Vassiliev, *Haunted Wood*, chap. 6, and Haynes and Klehr, *Venona*, 268–76.

10. Bamford, *Puzzle Palace*, 177–96, passim. The two men, fed up with life in the Socialist paradise, tried to return to the United States in the late 1970s but were not admitted.

11. Ibid., 196–200; West, *Games of Intelligence*, 30.

12. See discussion in Bearden and Risen, *Main Enemy*, 21–23. It was Soviet defector Anatoli Golitsyn, a somewhat unstable individual with similar "indications of paranoia," who convinced Angleton of the existence of a KGB Strategic Deception Plan and a mole inside the CIA. Richelson, *Century of Spies*, 288–90.

13. Wise, *Cassidy's Run*, 32–51, passim.

14. Bell, *Taking Care of the Law*, 100–101, 119–23; Herbig and Wiskoff, *Espionage against the United States*, 10–11.

15. Herbig and Wiskoff, *Espionage against the United States*, 10–11; on 2002 FISA requests, see John Ashcroft to L. Ralph Mecham, April 29, 2003, www.usdoj.gov/04foia/ readingrooms/2002fisa-ltr.pdf. This 2002 figure, not surprisingly, reflects a significant increase in the government's counterintelligence activity after the events of September 11, 2001.

16. This reference may be found, for instance, in Polmar and Allen, "Decade of the Spy," 104–9.

17. See DSS Web site, http://www.dss.mil/training/espionage/index.htm#date%20 of%20arrest; see also Defense Security Service, *Recent Espionage Cases*; Barron, *Breaking the Ring*, 101.

18. "Espionage in the Defense Industry," www.fbi.gov/libref/historic/famcases/petrov/ petrov.htm. The FBI Web site gives Markelov the alias "Sergei Viktorovich Petrov." West, *Games of Intelligence*, 29–30.

19. "2 Arrested by FBI On Spying Charges," *Washington Post*, June 28, 1975; see also www.dss.mil/training/espionage/industry.htm.

20. Herbig and Wiskoff, *Espionage against the United States*, 7–8; "Alleged Ex-Agent Reported Suicide," *New York Times*, March 1, 1976.

21. "Soviet Alien Arrested in Jersey on Spy Charges," and "Accused Soviet Spy Known as a Drifter," *New York Times*, January 8, 1977, January 9, 1977, respectively; see also www.dss.mil/training/espionage/industry.htm.

22. Bell, *Taking Care of the Law*, 113–16; "2 Russians Arrested by F.B.I. for Spying," *New York Times*, May 21, 1978; www.dss.mil/training/espionage/industry.htm.

23. Statement of Stanislav Levchenko, April 29 and May 7, 1992, House Judiciary Committee, *Hearings before the Subcommittee on Economic and Commercial Law*, 146, 148. In 1983, the year of the "Evil Empire" speech, public interest in Soviet economic espionage also peaked. See, for instance, P. Mann, "Soviet Action Spurs Technology Policy," *Aviation Week and Space Technology*, January 24, 1983, 25–27; Margaret Murray, "The Real Goal of Soviets' Global Spy Network," *U.S. News and World Report*, April 18, 1983, 31–32; H. Eason, "Soviet Spies: Your Firm Could Be Their Next Target," *Nation's Business*, June 1983, 22–25.

24. Freemantle, *The Steal*, 61.

25. Robert Lindsey, "Young, Rich." Lindsey is also the author of *The Falcon and the Snowman: A True Story of Friendship and Espionage* (New York: Simon and Schuster, 1979), the best-selling book about the Boyce-Lee case. The "black vault" was hardly the secure hold its name was meant to imply; as Boyce recalls, it was a site where he and his fellow employees "partied and boozed it up during working hours." Quoted in Andrew and Mitrokhin, *Sword and the Shield*, 217. Boyce's leaks were not as damaging as they

might have been, because the satellite system he was working on was in an early stage of development. Peake interview, November 21, 2003.

26. Lindsey, "Young, Rich," 106; "Alleged Soviet Spy Testifies He Was Blackmailed After Telling a Friend of CIA 'Deception' of Australia," *New York Times*, April 27, 1977; West, *Games of Intelligence*, 50–51.

27. See Court TV Web site www.crimelibrary.com/terrorists_spies/spies/boyce_lee/8.html?sect=23.

28. Quoted in "The Falcon and the Fallout," *Los Angeles Times*, March 2, 2003.

29. Freemantle, *The Steal*, 7, 56–58; www.dss.mil/training/espionage/industry.htm. One reason that Poles and other East bloc agents were used to obtain secrets was that they did not face the kinds of travel restrictions Soviet agents did. Kessler, *Spy vs. Spy*, 146.

30. "California Man Charged with Spying," *Washington Post*, October 18, 1983. See also discussion in Freemantle, *The Steal*, 52–55.

31. "Engineer Is Held in Scheme to Sell Secrets," *New York Times*, December 19, 1984; www.dss.mil/training/espionage/industry.htm. It was Cavanaugh's bad luck to be sentenced four days after John Walker's arrest in a mammoth Soviet espionage plot, a development that surely threw the California engineer's role into a worse light. See Kessler, *Spy vs. Spy*, 167.

32. "Sailor Sentenced after Bid to Sell Plans to Soviets," *Washington Post*, January 14, 1983.

33. "Agent Tells of Meeting Spy Suspect," *Washington Post*, December 22, 1985; Kessler, *Spy vs. Spy*, chap. 16.

34. The year is so described in such books as Bearden and Risen, *Main Enemy*, chap. 1, and Wise, *Inside Story*, 44.

35. Pollard received a life sentence, a particularly stringent punishment for someone who spied for an ally, or even for one who spied for an enemy. Miller, in contrast, received twenty years and was out in six.

36. "Pollard Was No Pelton," *The Forward*, December 8, 2000; see also discussion in Bearden and Risen, *Main Enemy*, 325.

37. Wise, *Inside Story*, 45; Barron, *Breaking the Ring*, 145–47; Weiner et al., *Betrayal*, 54; Kessler, *Spy vs. Spy*, chap. 15; Office of the National Counterintelligence Executive Web site, www.ncix.gov/pubs/misc/screen_backgrounds/spy_bios/ronald_pelton_bio.html.

38. See Bearden and Risen, *Main Enemy*, 84–88; Weiner et al., *Betrayal*, 52–54; Barron, *Breaking the Ring*, 143–45.

39. Earley, *Family of Spies*, 73; "Ex-Army Warrant Officer Accused of Being Soviet Spy," *New York Times*, July 16, 1981. A more detailed discussion of the cipher systems is in Barron, *Breaking the Ring*, 26–28.

40. Earley, *Family of Spies*, 108, 131, 144, chap. 30, chap. 58; Barron, *Breaking the Ring*, 126–28.

41. Barron, *Breaking the Ring*, 164 (Clark quote), 211.

42. Earley, *Family of Spies*, 207–8, 289.

43. Ibid., 10–11; J. P. Lenner, "Soviet Spies: Fool Friends & Colleagues; Steal Secrets During 70s, 80s," *Spokesman Online*, September 2002, aia.lackland.af.mil/homepages/pa/spokesman/Sep02/heritage.cfm.

44. Quoted in Earley, *Family of Spies*, 358. See also Barron, *Breaking the Ring*, 148.

Yurchenko was an interesting case. After defecting and telling the United States enough information for it to tip off the British that their MI-6 agent in the KGB, Oleg Gordievsky, was about to be uncovered, as well as telling the CIA about their own spy, Edward Lee Howard, and the NSA's Ronald Pelton, he then redefected to the KGB, who claimed he'd been "drugged and kidnapped by American agents." More likely, he was upset by his treatment at CIA hands. See Maas, *Killer Spy*, 64–79, passim; Barron, *Breaking the Ring*, 141–57, passim; Weiner et al., *Betrayal*, 69–71; West, *Games of Intelligence*, 19–22.

45. Earley, *Family of Spies*, 12.

46. Weiner et al., *Betrayal*, 102. See also Herbig and Wiskoff, *Espionage against the United States*, v.

47. Wise, *Inside Story*, 21, 46; Vise, *Bureau and the Mole*, 47. Interestingly, the Soviets did not pursue "Tophat" until Aldrich Ames revealed him a second time in 1985. Polyakov was executed in 1988. See Wise, *Inside Story*, 23–24.

48. Wise, *Inside Story*, 23, 50–59, passim. Ames had walked into the Soviet embassy to offer his services just six months earlier. In a much shorter spy career, he received far more money ($2.7 million) from the Soviets than Hanssen did. See Wise, *Inside Story*, 272. Wise notes Ames was offered an additional $1.9 million, bringing his potential earnings to $4.6 million. *Nightmover*, 325.

49. Senate Committee on Governmental Affairs, "Soviet Acquisition of Western Technology," April 1982, exhibit no. 1, in *Hearings before the Permanent Subcommittee on Investigations of the Senate Committee on Governmental Affairs, May 4, 5, 6, 11, and 12, 1982*, 97th Cong., 2nd sess., quoted in Fialka, *War by Other Means*, 9; see also Fialka, chap. 6; Philip Hanson, "Soviet Industrial Espionage: Some New Information," Royal Institute of International Affairs Discussion Papers, 1987, 2; and Andrew and Mitrokhin, *Sword and the Shield*, 215, 218. For more on Vetrov, and especially his sangfroid in the face of a KGB execution squad later, see Bearden and Risen, *Main Enemy*, 135–36.

50. Statement of Levchenko, *Hearings before the Subcommittee on Economic and Commercial Law*, 145; Fialka, *War by Other Means*, 70.

51. *UN and Conflict Monitor*, 6 (Winter 2000), www.bradford.ac.uk/acad/confres/monitor/mntr6_comment.html; "Putin's Career Rooted in Russia's KGB," *Washington Post*, January 30, 2000.

52. Andrew and Mitrokhin, *Sword and the Shield*, 220.

53. Hon. Henry J. Hyde, "Trade with the Soviets," *Congressional Record* (June 29, 1989): E2387.

54. Statement of Levchenko, *Hearings before the Subcommittee on Economic and Commercial Law*, 146, 148; Freemantle, *The Steal*, 9.

55. Maas, *Killer Spy*, 6–12, 95, 101; Wise, *Nightmover*, 266–71; Weiner et al., *Betrayal*, 39–41. Six disappeared in just half a year. Three others named by Ames—Oleg Gordievsky, Boris Yuzhin, and Sergei Fedorenko—escaped execution. Gordievsky was rescued by the British, and Yuzhin and Fedorenko were saved by the demise of the Soviet Union. See Bearden and Risen, *Main Enemy*, 157, 237–39.

56. Wise, *Nightmover*, 213. By contrast, when the FBI tried to determine who killed Martynov and Motorin in 1986, the CIA had given them no assistance. Weiner et al., *Betrayal*, 103.

57. Maas, *Killer Spy,* 83; Wise, *Nightmover,* 211, 225. As Bearden and Risen note, CIA chief William Casey did little despite the losses piling up in Moscow. *Main Enemy,* 165–66.

58. Weiner et al., *Betrayal,* 114–17; Barker, *Dancing with the Devil,* 313–15. The KGB was extremely effective at such deceptions, convincing the CIA that its own Edward Lee Howard, too, was behind many of the botched operations. Bearden, to his credit, had wanted to transfer Ames, whom he considered "lazy," out of the Soviet division in 1989, but Ames managed to stay in his position. Wise, *Nightmover,* 185.

59. "Prosecutors Say Official at CIA Spied for Russia," *New York Times,* February 24, 1994.

60. "Report Says Bad Supervision Helped FBI Spy Flourish," *New York Times,* August 14, 2003. A government panel also attacked the FBI for its lax security in Hanssen's case, suggesting that the agency's concerns about Russian espionage had dangerously waned in recent years. *Philadelphia Inquirer,* April 5, 2002.

61. "Retired U.S. Army Reserve Colonel Accused of Selling Secrets to Soviet Union," June 14, 2000, www.cnn.com/2000/US/06/14/military.espionage.03/; Dong-Phuong Nguyen, "Trofimoff Guilty of Spying," *St. Petersburg Times,* June 27, 2001.

62. See Section 3281 of Title 18 of the U.S. Code. I am indebted to Mark Kramer and John Earl Haynes for enlightening me about the changing espionage laws.

63. Maas, *Killer Spy,* 50–51, 242; Weiner et al., *Betrayal,* 33; Wise, *Inside Story,* 264–65.

64. "FBI Arrests Ex-Soldier as Mysterious KGB Spy in Supersecret NSA," *Washington Post,* February 24, 1996.

65. PBS Online Newshour, December 18, 1996, www.pbs.org/newshour/bb/law/december96/fbi_12-18.html; Office of the National Counterintelligence Executive Web site, nacic.gov/pubs/misc/screen_backgrounds/spy_bios/earl_pitts_bio.html.

66. Joint CIA-FBI Press Release on Arrest of Harold James Nicholson, November 18, 1996, www.fas.org/irp/cia/news/pr111896.html; www.nacic.gov/pubs/misc/screen_backgrounds/spy_bios/harold_james_bio.html.

67. See DSS Web site, www.dss.mil/training/espionage/nsa.htm.

68. *Sixty Minutes,* February 1, 2000, at www.cbsnews.com/stories/2000/01/31/60II/main155216.shtml; Wise, *Inside Story,* 193–94.

69. Wise, *Inside Story,* 4, 8.

70. Ibid., 79, 81, 107.

71. Ibid., 95, 132; Vise, *Bureau and the Mole,* 239–43. Much of this material on U.S. intelligence gathering came from the NSA, and thus his activity may have been even more damaging to that agency than to the FBI.

72. This amazing tale is well told in Wise, *Inside Story,* chap. 25.

73. Ibid., 273–78, passim; Vise, *Bureau and the Mole,* 80–81; Bearden and Risen, *Main Enemy,* 132.

74. Vise, *Bureau and the Mole,* 184–89.

75. "U.S. Set to Seek Death in Spy Case," *Washington Post,* April 20, 2002; "Spy Trial Opens, Death Penalty Result Possible," http://hollandsentinel.com/stories/012803/new-012803029.shtml; January 28, 2003; "Convicted Spy Accepts Life Sentence: Sudden Sentencing Deal Will Prevent Prosecution of Ex-Air Force Analyst's Wife," *Washington Post,* March 21, 2003; U.S. Attorneys' Office, Department of Justice, Press Release, July 30, 2003.

76. Ronald Radosh, "Cuba's Top Spy," frontpagemagazine.com/Articles/ReadArticle. asp?ID=1467; *Washington Post,* March 20, 2002; *Miami Herald,* October 16, 2002.

77. Jim Wagner, "Protecting Proprietary Property from Espionage," www.esecurity-planet.com/trends/article.php/1498871; Sorojini J. Biswas, "The Economic Espionage Act of 1996," www.myersbigel.com/ts_articles/trade_secret4.htm.

78. See discussion in Schweizer, *Friendly Spies,* 4–5.

79. Biswas, "Economic Espionage Act of 1996"; www.nnsi.doe.gov/C/Courses/CI_ Awareness_Guide/T1threat/Legal.htm.

80. FBI director Louis Freeh, statement before the Senate Select Committee on Intelligence, January 28, 1998, and Department of Justice press release, "Taiwanese Firm, Its President and His Daughter Indicted in Industrial Espionage Case," October 1, 1997, both quoted on USDA Web site, www.usda.gov/da/ocpm/Security%20Guide/Spystory/Industry.htm#1.

81. An extensive discussion of this case is in Fink, *Sticky Fingers;* see also "Ask the FBI: Economic Espionage," *USA Today,* April 12, 2003.

82. Fink, *Sticky Fingers,* 38; Fialka, *War by Other Means,* 86; Federation of American Scientists, Intelligence Resource Program, John Pike, ed., "SVR Operations," http://www.fas.org/irp/world/russia/svr/ops.htm; Andrew and Mitrokhin, *Sword and the Shield,* 215; Gold testimony, in Senate Judiciary Committee, *Scope of Soviet Activity,* 1022–23.

83. "FBI Tries to Stem Economic Espionage," Associated Press, August 4, 2003; FBI Web site, www.fbi.gov/priorities/priorities.htm; Bush identified the governments of Iraq, Iran, and North Korea as part of an "axis of evil" in his State of the Union Address on January 29, 2002.

CONCLUSION

1. Morton Sobell Security Index report, Sobell file [a], #1761; W. A. Branigan to C. D. Brennan, June 10, 1971, #1759. Feklisov claims that he had met with "Morty" in Moscow in the 1970s, when he offered to work for the Soviets again! *Man behind the Rosenbergs,* 334.

2. In 1977, the FBI finally cancelled the lookout notice for Barr; see Memo, re Joel Barr, Special Agent in Charge (SAC) New York to Director FBI, August 8, 1973, FBI Barr file [b], #297; Robert G. Kunkel to Miss [blank], U.S. Department of State Passport Office, #734; Nick F. Stames to Passport Office, September 28, 1977, #748. Barr, alias Josef Berg, did return to the United States in 1992; he died in St. Petersburg, Florida, in 1998.

3. Affidavit of William O. Studeman, Director of Naval Intelligence, U.S. vs. John Anthony Walker, November 4, 1986, in Hunter, *Spy Hunter,* 224.

4. For a discussion of Acheson's transformation, see Beisner, "Patterns of Peril." Beisner suggests that the pivotal moment for Acheson came during the Turkish Straits crisis in August 1946, but does not discount the influence of "political expediency" for the undersecretary of state, whose shift came in a six-week period that included Truman's commissioning of the Clifford Report as well as his firing of Commerce Secretary Henry

Wallace (347). Truman quote is from his January 5, 1946, letter to James Byrnes, quoted in Hamby, *Man of the People,* 339.

5. Dibrell's allegations appeared in the *San Antonio Evening News,* August 24, 1948.

6. On this issue see Olmsted, *Red Spy Queen,* 116; Haynes and Klehr, *In Denial,* 220; Theoharis, *Chasing Spies,* 43. Examples of continued skepticism about major World War II spy cases include Caute, *The Great Fear,* 56; Schrecker, *Many Are the Crimes,* 172; and Lerner, *Fireweed,* 328–33. See also discussion in Haynes and Klehr, *In Denial,* chaps. 4–5, passim.

7. *Newsweek,* November 23, 1953, 30, cited in Peake, "Afterword," *Out of Bondage,* 234.

8. "COMRAP Summary," 59. Summing up the case in 1944, the agency wrote that Nelson "is shown as engaging in military and industrial espionage; to be active in political and Governmental aspects of the Apparatus; and is further shown as active in the gathering and dissemination of propaganda favorable to the Soviet Union."

9. Deane, *Strange Alliance,* 89.

10. U.S. Army Intelligence Center, *History of the Counter Intelligence Corps,* 81–84.

11. Eisenhower, *Crusade in Europe,* 32, quoted in U.S. Army Intelligence Center, *History of the Counter Intelligence Corps,* 96.

12. "PSB General Staff Meeting," September 26, 1952, box 27, PSB files, HSTL; Caute, *Great Fear,* 54; Leshuk, *U.S. Intelligence Perceptions,* 10.

13. Bradley F. Smith, *Sharing Secrets,* chap. 9, passim.

14. Lamphere, *FBI-KGB War,* 26; Weinstein and Vassiliev, *Haunted Wood,* 280.

15. Venona 34 Apresyan to Moscow (Fitin), January 30, 1946.

16. Venona 123 Viktor Vasilyevich Afanasyev to Semen (unidentified), March 27, 1946.

17. Lamphere, *FBI-KGB War,* 78.

18. FBI document, "Suggestions for Improvement of Atomic Energy Commission Security, 'Need for Security Consciousness,'" February 5, 1950, Fuchs file, #1202 (1998 supplemental release.

19. Quoted in Bertrand Russell letter to *Manchester Guardian,* April 5, 1956, attached to Nichols to Tolson, April 24, 1956, Elitcher file [c], #16.

20. Senate Judiciary Committee, *Scope of Soviet Activity,* 5002, 4865; Special Agent William J. McDonnell to SAC New York, November 22, 1957, Barr file [a], #634. Kennedy's thoughts on the missile gap are in the *Congressional Record* (February 29, 1960): 3801–3, cited in Merrill and Paterson, *Major Problems,* 351–52.

21. HUAC, *Hearings before the Committee,* 514.

BIBLIOGRAPHY

PRIMARY SOURCES

Archives

Department of Justice, Washington, D.C.
    Criminal Records Division
Federal Bureau of Investigation, Washington, D.C.
    Arthur Adams (100–331280)
    Amtorg Trading Corporation (61–5381). This was an espionage investigation, despite
        its "treason" classification.
    Elizabeth Bentley ([a] 61–6328; [b] 65–15639)
    Joel Barr ([a] 65–15392; [b] 65–59453)
    Abraham Brothman (100–365040)
    Boris Bykov (100–287685)
    Communist Infiltration of Radiation Laboratories (CINRAD) (100–190625)
    Comintern Apparatus (COMRAP) (100–203581)
    Max Elitcher ([a] 65–60731; [b] 65–61685; [c] 100–148352; [d] 100–357297; [e]
        100–367116)
    Armand Labis Feldman, William Brandes, Gaik Ovakimian (61–7574)
    Klaus Fuchs (65–58805)
    Harry Gold
    Alger Hiss and Whittaker Chambers ([a] 65–14920; [b] 65–59549; [c] 74–1333; [d]
        100–18830)
    Harry Arthur Levine ([a] 65–14720; [b] 65–57792)
    Isador Miller (65–58428)
    Wilfred E. Myers (100–351334)
    Steve Nelson (100–16847)
    J. Robert Oppenheimer (100–17828)
    William Perl ([a] 65–15387; [b] 65–59312)
    Herbert Philbrick (100–365248)
    William Walter Remington (74–1379)
    Julius and Ethel Rosenberg ([a] 65–15338; [b] 65–14603; [c] 100–365040)
    Alfred Sarant (65–59242)
    Nathan Gregory Silvermaster (65–56402)
    Morton Sobell ([a] 100–2483; [b] 100–37158)

Franklin D. Roosevelt Library, Hyde Park, New York
    Harry Hopkins Papers
    Henry Morgenthau Jr. Papers
    President's Official File
    President's Secretary's File
Hagley Museum and Library, Wilmington, Delaware
    E. I. Du Pont de Nemours and Company Papers
    Willis F. Harrington Papers
Harry S Truman Library, Independence, Missouri
    Dean Acheson Papers
    Thomas C. Clark Papers
    Clark Clifford Papers
    George M. Elsey Papers
    John F. X. McGohey Papers
    John M. Ohly Papers
    John Stewart Service and Charles E. Rhetts Papers
    Devitt Vanech Papers
    Papers of Harry S Truman
      Naval Aide File
      President's Official File
      President's Secretary's File
      Psychological Strategy Board File
      White House Confidential File
Hoover Institution on War, Revolution, and Peace, Stanford, California
    Sam Tanenhaus Papers
Library of Congress, Washington, D.C.
    Averell Harriman Papers
    Robert Taft Papers
Military History Institute, Carlisle, Pennsylvania
    William J. Donovan Papers
    Sidney R. Spalding Oral History File, 1889–1981
National Archives and Records Administration, Washington, D.C.
    Record Group 38, Office of Naval Intelligence (ONI) Central Administration Correspondence, 1930–1948
    Record Group 59, Records of the Department of State
    Record Group 165, Records of the War Department's General and Special Staffs
    Records of the Military Intelligence Division, 1918–41
    Record Group 226, Records of the Office of Strategic Services, Research and Analysis Branch Divisions
    Record Group 233, Records of the U.S. House of Representatives, Special Committee on Un-American Activities (Dies), Exhibits, Evidence, etc. re Committee Investigations
      Communism Subject Files, 1930–45

Record Group 319, Records of the Army Staff
  Army Intelligence Project Decimal File, 1941–45
  Records of the Office of the Assistant Chief of Staff, G–2, Intelligence, Records of
    the Investigative Records Repository, Security Classified Intelligence and Inves-
    tigative Dossiers, 1939–76
  Department of the Navy. Naval Criminal Investigative Service Records.
National Security Agency
  Venona cables, 1942–46
Rossiskii Gosudarstvennyi Arkhiv Ekonomiki (Russian State Archive of the Economy),
Moscow, Russia
  fond 413
  fond 5240
  fond 7297
  fond 7516
Rossiiskii Gosudarstvennyi Arkhiv Sotsialno-Politicheskoi Istorii (Russian State Archive of
Social and Political History), Moscow, Russia
  fond 495
  fond 515
  fond 539
Seeley Mudd Library, Princeton University, Princeton, New Jersey
  American Civil Liberties Union Papers
State Historical Society of Wisconsin, Madison, Wisconsin
  Alexander Gumberg Papers

Congressional and Administrative Publications

U.S. Congress. House. Committee on Appropriations. Subcommittee on Appropriations.
  [Regular, emergency, and national defense appropriation estimates of the FBI,
  1940–45], Appropriations Testimony, FBI Office of Public Affairs.
———. Committee on Foreign Affairs. Subcommittee No. 2. *European Study Trip.* 79th
  Cong., 1st sess., 1946.
———. Committee on International Relations. *Corporate and Industrial Espionage and
  Their Effects on American Competitiveness.* 106th Cong., 2nd sess., 2000.
———. Committee on Rules. *Investigation into the Activities of Communists in the United
  States.* 71st Cong., 2nd sess., 1930.
———. Committee on the Civil Service. *Report of Investigation with Respect to Employee
  Loyalty and Employment Policies and Practices in the Government of the United States.*
  79th Cong., 2nd sess., 1946.
———. Committee on the Judiciary. *Hearings before the Subcommittee on Economic and
  Commercial Law of the Committee on the Judiciary.* 102nd Cong., 2nd sess., 1992.
U.S. Congress. House. Committee on Un-American Activities [HUAC]. *Annual Report
  of the Committee on Un-American Activities, House of Representatives, for the Year
  1949.* 81st Cong., 1st. sess., 1949.

———. *Hearings before the Committee on Un-American Activities.* 86th Cong., 1st sess., 1959.

———. Hearings regarding Clarence Hiskey Including Testimony of Paul Crouch. 81st. Cong., 1st sess., 1949.

———. *Hearings regarding Communist Espionage.* 81st Cong., 1st, 2nd sess., 1951.

———. *Hearings regarding Communist Espionage in the U.S. Government.* 80th Cong., 2nd sess., 1948.

———. *Hearings regarding Communist Infiltration of Radiation Laboratory and Atomic Bomb Project at the University of California, Berkeley, Calif.* 81st Cong., 1st, 2nd sess., 1949–51.

———. *Hearings regarding Shipment of Atomic Material to the Soviet Union during World War II.* 81st Cong., 1st sess., 1950.

———. *Hearings regarding Steve Nelson.* 81st Cong., 1st sess., 1949.

———. *Report on Atomic Espionage: Steve Nelson (Nelson-Weinberg and Hiskey-Adams Cases).* 81st Cong., 1st sess., 1950.

———. *Report on Soviet Espionage Activities in Connection with the Atom Bomb; Investigation of Un-American Activities in the United States.* 80th Cong., 2nd sess., 1948.

———. *The Shameful Years: Thirty Years of Soviet Espionage in the United States.* 82nd Cong., 2nd sess., 1952.

———. *Soviet Espionage Activities in Connection with Jet Propulsion and Aircraft.* 81st Cong., 1st sess., 1949.

———. *Testimony of James Sterling Murray and Edward Tiers Manning.* 81st Cong., 1st sess., 1950.

U.S. Congress. House. Special Committee on Un-American Activities [HUAC]. *Investigation of Un-American Propaganda Activities in the United States.* 75th Cong., 2nd sess., 1938.

———. *Investigation of Un-American Propaganda Activities in the United States.* 76th Cong., 1st sess., 1939.

———. *Investigation of Un-American Propaganda Activities in the United States.* 77th Cong., 1st sess., 1941.

———. *Investigation of Un-American Propaganda Activities in the United States: Report on the Axis Front Movement in the US.* 78th Cong., 1st sess., 1943.

U.S. Congress. Joint Committee on Atomic Energy. *Soviet Atomic Espionage.* 82nd Cong., 1st sess., 1951.

U.S. Congress. Senate. Committee on Expenditures in the Executive Departments. *Export Policy and Loyalty.* 80th Cong., 2nd sess., 1948.

———. Committee on Government Operations. *Army Signal Corps-Subversion and Espionage.* 83rd Cong., 1st sess., 1954.

———. Committee on the Judiciary. *Communist Activities among Alien and National Groups.* 81st Cong., 1st sess., 1949.

———. Committee on the Judiciary. *Scope of Soviet Activity in the United States.* 84th Cong., 2nd sess., 85th Cong., 1st sess., 1956–57.

———. Select Committee to Study Government Operations with Respect to Intelligence Activities. Bk. 2. *Final Report: Intelligence Activities and the Rights of Americans.* Bk. 3.

Supplementary Detailed Staff Reports on Intelligence Activities and the Rights of Americans. 94th Cong., 2nd sess., 1976.
U.S. Department of Justice. [Reports of the Director of the Federal Bureau of Investigation, 1940–45], Appropriations Testimony, FBI Office of Public Affairs.
U.S. Department of State. *Foreign Relations of the United States.* 1977.

Court Records

Eugene Dennis et al. v. United States. Supreme Court of the United States, October term, 1951.
Julius Rosenberg and Ethel Rosenberg, Petitioners, vs. the United States of America. U.S. District Court, Southern District of New York, June 7, 1952.
Nardone et al. vs. United States, 1937. SCT.1233, 302 U.S. 379, 58 S. Ct. 275, 82 L. Ed. 314.
Subversive Activities Control Board vs. CPUSA, Herbert Brownell, Jr., Attorney General of the U.S.A., Petitioner, vs. CPUSA, Respondent, April 20, 1953.
Transcript of Record, *Julius Rosenberg and Ethel Rosenberg vs. The United States of America, Morton Sobell vs. The United States of America,* 1951. Published by the Committee to Secure Justice for Morton Sobell, 1960.

Interviews

Hayden Peake
Herb Romerstein
John J. Walsh

SECONDARY SOURCES

Books, Articles, and Dissertations

Abramson, Rudy. *Spanning the Century: The Life of W. Averell Harriman, 1891–1986.* New York: William Morrow, 1992.
Albright, Joseph, and Marcia Kunstel. *Bombshell: The Secret Story of America's Unknown Atomic Spy Conspiracy.* Web site, www.bombshell–1.com. New York: Times Books, 1997.
Alvarez, David. *Secret Messages: Code Breaking and American Diplomacy, 1930–1945.* Lawrence: University Press of Kansas, 2000.
American-Russian Chamber of Commerce. *Economic Handbook of the Soviet Union.* New York: self-published, 1936.
Andrew, Christopher, *For the President's Eyes Only: Secret Intelligence and the American Presidency from Washington to Bush.* New York, 1995.
———, and Oleg Gordievsky. *KGB : The Inside Story of Its Foreign Operations from Lenin to Gorbachev.* New York: HarperCollins, 1990.
———, and Vasili Mitrokhin. *The Sword and the Shield: The Mitrokhin Archive and the Secret History of the KGB.* New York: Basic Books, 1999.

Bamford, James. *Body of Secrets: Anatomy of the Ultra-Secret National Security Agency from the Cold War through the Dawn of a New Century.* New York: Doubleday, 2001.

———. *The Puzzle Palace: Inside the National Security Agency, America's Most Secret Intelligence Organization.* New York: Penguin Books, 1983.

Barker, Rodney. *Dancing with the Devil: Sex, Espionage, and the U.S. Marines; The Clayton Lonetree Story.* New York: Simon and Schuster, 1996.

Barron, John. *Breaking the Ring.* Boston: Houghton Mifflin, 1987.

Batvinis, Raymond J. "'In the Beginning' . . . An Investigation of the Development of the Federal Bureau of Investigation's Counterintelligence Program, 1936 to 1941." PhD diss., Catholic University, 2001.

Bearden, Milt, and James Risen. *The Main Enemy: The Inside Story of the CIA's Final Showdown with the KGB.* New York: Random House, 2003.

Beisner, Robert L. "Patterns of Peril: Dean Acheson Joins the Cold Warriors, 1945–56." *Diplomatic History* 20 (Summer 1996): 321–55.

Bell, Griffin B., with Ronald J. Ostrow. *Taking Care of the Law.* New York: William Morrow, 1982.

Bennett, Edward M. *Franklin D. Roosevelt and the Search for Security: American-Soviet Relations, 1933–1939.* Wilmington, Del.: Scholarly Resources, 1985.

Benson, Robert Louis, and Michael Warner, eds., *Venona: Soviet Espionage and the American Response, 1939–1957.* Washington, D.C.: National Security Agency/Central Intelligence Agency, 1996.

Bentley, Elizabeth. *Out of Bondage.* New York: Devin-Adair, 1951. Reprint. New Rochelle, New York: Conservative Book Club, n.d.

Bergier, Jacques. *Secret Armies: The Growth of Corporate and Industrial Espionage.* Translated by Harold J. Salemson. Indianapolis: Bobbs-Merrill, 1975.

Berle, Beatrice Bishop, and Travis Beal Jacobs, eds. *Navigating the Rapids, 1918–1971: From the Papers of Adolf A. Berle.* New York: Harcourt Brace, 1973.

Bernstein, Barton L. "In the Matter of J. Robert Oppenheimer." *Historical Studies in the Physical Sciences* 12, no. 2 (1982).

Bird, Kai, and Max Holland. "The Taping of 'Tommy the Cork.'" *The Nation,* February 8, 1986, 129, 142–45.

Boughton, James M., and Roger J. Sandilands. "Politics and the Attack on FDR's Economists: From the Grand Alliance to the Cold War." *Intelligence and National Security* 18 (Autumn 2003): 73–99.

Buckley, William F., et al. *The Committee and Its Critics: A Calm Review of the House Committee on Un-American Activities.* New York: Putnam's, 1962.

Budenz, Louis. *Men without Faces: The Communist Conspiracy in the U.S.A.* New York: Harper's, 1950.

Budish, J. M., and Samuel S. Shipman. *Soviet Foreign Trade: Menace or Promise.* New York: H. Liveright, 1931.

Caute, David. *The Great Fear: The Anti-Communist Purge under Truman and Eisenhower.* New York: Simon and Schuster, 1978.

Charles, Douglas M. "Informing FDR: Political Surveillance and the Isolationist-Interventionist Foreign Policy Debate, 1939–1945." *Diplomatic History* 24, no. 2 (Spring 2000): 211–32.

Chevalier, Haakon. *Oppenheimer: The Story of a Friendship.* New York: George Braziller, 1965.

Chikov, Vladimir. "Kak Sovyetskaya Razvyedka 'Rashchepila' Americanskii Atom" ("How Soviet Intelligence 'Split' the American Atom.") *Novoye Vremia* 16–17 (April 23 and April 30, 1991).

Churchill, Winston. "Iron Curtain Speech." In *A Treasury of the World's Great Speeches,* edited by Houston Peterson, 804–6. New York: Simon and Schuster, 1954.

Cohen, Robert. *When the Old Left Was Young: Student Radicals and America's First Student Movement, 1929–1941.* New York: Oxford University Press, 1993.

Corson, William R., and Robert T. Crowley. *The New KGB: Engine of Soviet Power.* New York: Quill, 1986.

Costello, John, and Oleg Tsarev. *Deadly Illusions: The KGB Orlov Dossier Reveals Stalin's Master Spy.* New York: Crown, 1993.

Costigliola, Frank. "'Unceasing Pressure for Penetration': Gender, Pathology, and Emotion in George Kennan's Cold War." *Journal of American History* 84 (March 1997): 1309–39.

Craig, Bruce. "Treasonable Doubt: The Harry Dexter White Case, 1948–1953." PhD diss., American University, 1999.

Cumings, Bruce. *The Roaring of the Cataract, 1945–1950. Vol. 2 of The Origins of the Korean War.* Princeton, N.J.: Princeton University Press, 1990.

Dallek, Robert. *Franklin Roosevelt and American Foreign Policy, 1932–1945.* New York: Oxford, 1995.

Dallin, David. *Soviet Espionage.* New Haven, Conn.: Yale University Press, 1955.

Davis, James Kirkpatrick. *Spying on America: The FBI's Domestic Counterintelligence Program.* Westport, Conn.: Praeger, 1992.

Deane, John R. *The Strange Alliance: The Story of Our Efforts at Wartime Cooperation with Russia.* New York: Viking Press, 1947.

Defense Security Service. *Recent Espionage Cases: Summaries and Sources.* Richmond, Va.: DSS, May 1996.

De Pauw, John W. *Soviet-American Trade Relations.* Westport, Conn.: Praeger, 1979.

Dies, Martin. *The Trojan Horse in America.* New York: Dodd, Mead, 1940.

Dillon, Millicent. *Harry Gold.* New York: Overlook Press, 2000.

Earley, Pete. *Family of Spies: Inside the John Walker Spy Ring.* New York: Bantam, 1988.

Eason, H. "Soviet Spies: Your Firm Could Be Their Next Target." *Nation's Business,* June 1983, 22–25.

Eby, Cecil. *Between the Bullet and the Lie: American Volunteers in the Spanish Civil War.* New York: Holt, Rinehart, and Winston, 1969.

Fariello, Griffin. *Red Scare: Memories of an American Inquisition.* New York: Norton, 1995.

Fast, Howard, I. F. Stone, Milton Wolff, et al. *Steve Nelson: A Tribute by 14 Famous Authors.* New York: Provisional Committee to Free Steve Nelson, n.d.

Feklisov, Alexander. *The Man behind the Rosenbergs.* New York: Enigma Books, 2001.

Fialka, John J. *War by Other Means: Economic Espionage in America.* New York: Norton, 1997.

Fink, Steven. *Sticky Fingers: Managing the Global Risk of Economic Espionage.* Chicago: Dearborn Trade, 2002.

Freemantle, Brian. *The Steal: Counterfeiting and Industrial Espionage.* London: Michael Joseph, 1986.

Friedman, Max Paul. "Nazis and Good Neighbors: The United States Campaign against the Germans of Latin America in World War II," PhD diss., University of California, Berkeley, 2000.

———. "There Goes the Neighborhood: Blacklisting Germans in Latin America and the Evanescence of the Good Neighbor Policy." *Diplomatic History* 27 (September 2003): 569–97.

Funigiello, Philip J. *American-Soviet Trade in the Cold War.* Chapel Hill: University of North Carolina Press, 1988.

Gaddis, John Lewis. "Intelligence, Espionage, and Cold War Origins." *Diplomatic History* 13 (Spring 1989): 191–212.

———. *Strategies of Containment: A Critical Appraisal of Postwar American National Security Policy.* New York: Oxford University Press, 1982.

Gallicchio, Marc. *The African American Encounter with Japan: Black Internationalism in Asia, 1895–1945.* Chapel Hill: University of North Carolina Press, 2000.

Goldberg, Robert Alan. *Enemies Within: The Culture of Conspiracy in Modern America.* New Haven, Conn.: Yale University Press, 2001.

Goodman, Walter. *The Committee: The Extraordinary Career of the House Committee on Un-American Activities.* New York: Farrar Straus and Giroux, 1968.

Gouzenko, Igor. *The Iron Curtain.* New York: Dutton, 1948.

Granatstein, J. L., and David Stafford. *Spy Wars: Espionage and Canada from Gouzenko to Glasnost.* Toronto: Key Porter Books, 1990.

Groves, Leslie. *Now It Can Be Told: The Story of the Manhattan Project.* New York: Harper, 1962.

Hamby, Alonzo L. *Man of the People: A Life of Harry S Truman.* New York: Oxford University Press, 1995.

Hanson, Philip. "Soviet Industrial Espionage: Some New Information." Royal Institute of International Affairs Discussion Papers, 1987.

Harbutt, Fraser. *The Iron Curtain: Churchill, America, and the Origins of the Cold War.* New York: Oxford University Press, 1986.

Haynes, John Earl. *Red Scare or Red Menace? American Communism and Anticommunism in the Cold War Era.* Chicago: Ivan R. Dee, 1996.

Haynes, John Earl, and Harvey Klehr. *In Denial: Historians, Communism and Espionage.* San Francisco: Encounter Books, 2003.

———. *Venona: Decoding Soviet Espionage in America.* New Haven, Conn.: Yale University Press, 1999.

Herbig, Katherine L., and Martin F. Wiscoff. *Espionage against the United States by American Citizens, 1947– 2001.* Monterey, Calif.: Defense Personnel Security Research Center, 2002.

Herken, Gregg. *Brotherhood of the Bomb: The Tangled Lives and Loyalties of Robert Oppenheimer, Ernest Lawrence, and Edward Teller.* Web site: www.brotherhoodofthebomb.com. New York: Holt, 2002.

Hershberg, James B. *James B. Conant: Harvard to Hiroshima and the Making of the Nuclear Age.* New York: Knopf, 1993.

Higham, Robin, John T. Greenwood, and Von Hardesty, eds. *Russian Aviation and Air Power in the Twentieth Century.* London: Frank Cass, 1998.

Holloway, David. *Stalin and the Bomb: The Soviet Union and Atomic Energy, 1939–1956.* New Haven, Conn.: Yale University Press, 1994.

Hunter, Robert W. *Spy Hunter: Inside the FBI Investigation of the Walker Espionage Case.* Annapolis, Md.: Naval Institute Press, 1999.

Jacobson, Jon. *The Soviet Union Enters World Politics.* Berkeley and Los Angeles: University of California Press, 1994.

Jeffreys-Jones, Rhodri. *Cloak and Dollar: A History of American Secret Intelligence.* New Haven, Conn.: Yale University Press, 2002.

Johnston, Verle B. *Legions of Babel: The International Brigades in the Spanish Civil War.* University Park: Pennsylvania State University Press, 1967.

Jordan, George Racey. *From Major Jordan's Diaries.* New York: Harcourt Brace, 1952.

Jungk, Robert. *Brighter Than a Thousand Suns: The Moral and Political History of the Atomic Scientists.* London: Victor Gollancz Ltd., 1958.

Kern, Gary. *A Death in Washington: Walter G. Krivitsky and the Stalin Terror.* New York: Enigma Books, 2003.

Kessler, Ronald. *Spy vs. Spy: Stalking Soviet Spies in America.* New York: Scribner's, 1988.

Kilmarx, Robert A. *A History of Soviet Air Power.* New York: Praeger, 1962.

Kimball, Warren F. *Forged in War: Roosevelt, Churchill, and the Second World War.* New York: William Morrow, 1997.

———. "The Incredible Shrinking War: The Second World War, Not (Just) the Origins of the Cold War." *Diplomatic History* 25 (Summer 2001): 347–65.

Klehr, Harvey, and Ronald Radosh. *The Amerasia Spy Case : Prelude to McCarthyism.* Chapel Hill: University of North Carolina Press, 1996.

Klehr, Harvey, John Earl Haynes, and Fridrikh Igorevich Firsov. *The Secret World of American Communism.* New Haven, Conn.: Yale University Press, 1995.

Lafeber, Walter. *America, Russia and the Cold War.* 7th ed. New York: McGraw Hill, 1993.

Lamphere, Robert, with Tom Schachtman. *The FBI-KGB War: A Special Agent's Story.* New York: Random House, 1986.

Latham, Earl. *The Communist Controversy in Washington: From the New Deal to McCarthy.* Cambridge, Mass.: Harvard University Press, 1966.

Leab, Daniel J. *I Was a Communist for the FBI: The Unhappy Life and Times of Matt Cvetic.* Pittsburgh: University of Pittsburgh Press, 2000.

———. "The Red Menace and Justice in the Pacific Northwest: The 1946 Trial of the Soviet Naval Lieutenant Nikolai Grigorevitch Redin." *Pacific Northwest Quarterly* 87 (Spring 1996): 82–94.

Lemann, Nicholas. "The Quiet Man," *The New Yorker,* May 7, 2001, 56–71.

Lerner, Gerda. *Fireweed: A Political Autobiography.* Philadelphia: Temple University Press, 2002.

Leshuk, Leonard. *U.S. Intelligence Perceptions of Soviet Power, 1921–1946.* London and Portland, Ore.: Frank Cass, 2003.

Libbey, James K. "The American-Russian Chamber of Commerce." *Diplomatic History* 9 (Summer 1985): 233–48.

Lindsey, Robert. *The Falcon and the Snowman: A True Story of Friendship and Espionage.* New York: Simon and Schuster, 1979.

Lowenthal, John. "Venona and Alger Hiss." *Intelligence and National Security* 15 (Autumn 2000): 98–130.

Lowenthal, Max. *The Federal Bureau of Investigation.* Westport, Conn: Praeger, 1950.

Maas, Peter. *Killer Spy: The Inside Story of the FBI's Pursuit and Capture of Aldrich Ames, America's Deadliest Spy.* New York: Warner Books, 1995.

MacDonnell, Francis. *Insidious Foes: The Axis Fifth Column and the American Home Front.* New York: Oxford University Press, 1995.

Maddux, Thomas R. "United States-Soviet Naval Relations in the 1930's: The Soviet Union's Efforts to Purchase Naval Vessels." *Naval War College Review* 29 (Fall 1976).

———. *Years of Estrangement: American Relations with the Soviet Union.* Tallahassee: University Press of Florida, 1980.

Mann, P. "Soviet Action Spurs Technology Policy." *Aviation Week and Space Technology,* January 24, 1983, 25–27.

Mark, Eduard. "Who Was 'Venona's' 'Ales?' Cryptanalysis and the Hiss Case." *Intelligence and National Security* 18 (Fall 2003): 45–72.

Martel, Leon. *Lend-Lease, Loans, and the Coming of the Cold War: A Study of the Implementation of Foreign Policy.* Boulder, Colo.: Westview Press, 1979.

May, Gary. *Un-American Activities: The Trials of William Remington.* New York: Oxford University Press, 1994.

McDaniel, Dennis Kay. "Martin Dies of Un-American Activities: His Life and Times." PhD diss., University of Houston, 1988.

Melville, Cecil F. *The Russian Face of Germany: An Account of the Secret Military Relations between the German and Soviet-Russian Governments.* Somerset and London: Wishart, 1932.

Merrill, Dennis, and Thomas G. Paterson. *Major Problems in American Foreign Relations.* 5th ed. Boston: Houghton Mifflin, 2000.

Metcalfe, Robyn Shotwell. *The New Wizard War: How the Soviets Steal U.S. Technology—And How We Give It Away.* Redmond, Wash.: Tempus Books, 1988.

Mitchell, Marcia, and Tom Mitchell. *The Spy Who Seduced America: Lies and Betrayal in the Heat of the Cold War; The Judith Coplon Story.* Montpelier, Vt.: Invisible Cities Press, 2002.

Mitrovich, Gregory. *Undermining the Kremlin: America's Strategy to Subvert the Soviet Bloc, 1947–1956.* Ithaca, N.Y.: Cornell University Press, 2000.

Muir, Malcolm, Jr. "American Warship Construction for Stalin's Navy Prior to World War II: A Study in Paralysis of Policy." *Diplomatic History* 5 (Fall 1981): 337–51.

Murray, Margaret. "The Real Goal of Soviets' Global Spy Network." *U.S. News and World Report,* April 18, 1983, 31–32.

Nelson, Steve, James R. Barrett, and Rob Ruck. *Steve Nelson: American Radical.* Pittsburgh: University of Pittsburgh Press, 1981.

Nowarra, Heinz J. *Russian Fighter Aircraft, 1920–1941.* Atglen, Pa.: Schiffer Publishing, 1997.

Olmsted, Kathryn S. *Red Spy Queen: A Biography of Elizabeth Bentley.* Chapel Hill: University of North Carolina Press, 2002.

O'Reilly, Kenneth. *Hoover and the Un-Americans: The FBI, HUAC, and the Red Menace.* Philadelphia: Temple University Press, 1983.

Peake, Hayden. Afterword. In *Out of Bondage,* by Elizabeth Bentley. New York: Ivy Books, 1988.

Pessen, Edward. *Losing Our Souls: The American Experience in the Cold War.* Chicago: Ivan R. Dee, 1993.

Polenberg, Richard, ed. *In the Matter of J. Robert Oppenheimer: The Security Clearance Hearing.* Ithaca, N.Y.: Cornell University Press, 2002.

Polmar, Norman, and Thomas B. Allen. "Decade of the Spy." *U.S. Naval Institute Proceedings* 115, no. 5 (1989): 104–9.

Powers, Richard Gid. "Introduction." In *Secrecy: The American Experience,* by Daniel Patrick Moynahan, 49–55. New Haven, Conn.: Yale University Press, 1998.

———. *Secrecy and Power: The Life of J. Edgar Hoover.* New York: Free Press, 1987.

Powers, Thomas. "A Letter from Copenhagen." *New York Review of Books,* August 14, 2003.

Rabinowitz, Victor. *Unrepentant Leftist: A Lawyer's Memoir.* Urbana: University of Illinois Press, 1996.

Radosh, Ronald, and Joyce Milton. *The Rosenberg File: A Search for the Truth.* New York: Holt, Rinehart, and Winston, 1983.

Rafalko, Frank J., ed. *A Counterintelligence Reader.* Vol. 1, *American Revolution to World War II.* Washington, D.C.: National Counterintelligence Center, 1996.

Revel, Jean François. *How Democracies Perish.* New York: Doubleday, 1983.

Rhodes, Richard. *Dark Sun: The Making of the Hydrogen Bomb.* New York: Simon and Schuster, 1995.

Richelson, Jeffrey T. *A Century of Spies: Intelligence in the Twentieth Century.* New York: Oxford University Press, 1995.

Roberts, Geoffrey. *The Soviet Union and the Origins of the Second World War: Russo-German Relations and the Road to War, 1933–1941.* New York: St. Martin's, 1995.

Roberts, Sam. *The Brother: The Untold Story of Atomic Spy David Greenglass and How He Sent His Sister, Ethel Rosenberg, to the Electric Chair.* New York: Random House, 2001.

Robinson, Donald. "Steve Nelson: Unwelcome Guest." *The American Legion Magazine,* February 1950.

Romerstein, Herb, and Eric Breindel. *The Venona Secrets: Exposing Soviet Espionage and America's Traitors.* Washington: Regnery Gateway, 2000.

Rosenstone, Robert. *Crusade of the Left: The Lincoln Battalion in the Spanish Civil War.* New York: Pegasus Books, 1969.

Ryan, James G. *Earl Browder and the Failure of American Communism.* Tuscaloosa: University of Alabama Press, 1997.

Sandilands, Roger. *The Life and Political Economy of Lauchlin Currie: New Dealer, Presidential Adviser, and Development Economist.* Durham, N.C.: Duke University Press, 1990.

Schecter, Jerrold, and Leona Schecter. *Sacred Secrets: How Soviet Intelligence Operations Changed American History.* Washington, D.C.: Brassey's, 2002.

Schneir, Walter, and Miriam Schneir. "Cables Coming in from the Cold." *The Nation,* July 5, 1999, 25–31.

————. "Cryptic Answers." *The Nation*, August 21, 1995, 152–53.

Schrecker, Ellen. *Many Are the Crimes: McCarthyism in America.* Princeton, N.J.: Princeton University Press, 1998.

————, and Maurice Isserman. "The Right's Cold War Revisionism: Current Espionage Fears Have Given New Life to Liberal Anti-Communism." *The Nation*, July 24, 2000, 22–25.

Schwartz, Stephen. *From West to East: California and the Making of the American Mind.* New York: Free Press, 1998.

Schweber, Silvan S. *In the Shadow of the Bomb.* Princeton, N.J.: Princeton University Press, 2000.

Schweizer, Peter. *Friendly Spies: How America's Allies Are Using Economic Espionage to Steal Our Secrets.* New York: Atlantic Monthly Press, 1986.

Sherwin, Martin J. *A World Destroyed: Hiroshima and the Origins of the Arms Race.* New York: Vintage, 1987.

Siegel, Katherine A. S. *Loans and Legitimacy: The Evolution of Soviet-American Relations, 1919–1933.* Lexington: University Press of Kentucky, 1996.

Smith, Bradley F. *Sharing Secrets with Stalin: How the Allies Traded Intelligence, 1941–1945.* Lawrence: University Press of Kansas, 1996.

Smith, Daniel M. *Aftermath of War: Bainbridge Colby and Wilsonian Diplomacy, 1920–1921.* Philadelphia: American Philosophical Society, 1970.

Sobell, Morton. *On Doing Time.* New York: Scribner's, 1974.

Spender, Stephen. "The Inner Meanings of the Fuchs Case." *New York Times Magazine*, March 12, 1950, 13, 71–76.

Spolansky, Jacob. *The Communist Trail in America.* New York: Macmillan, 1951.

Standley, Adm.William, and Rear Adm. Arthur A. Ageton. *Admiral Ambassador to Russia,* Chicago: Regnery, 1955.

Stapfer, Hans-Heiri. *Polikarpov Fighters in Action Part II.* Carrollton, Tex.: Squadron/ Signal Publications, 1996.

Stoler, Mark A. *Allies and Adversaries: The Joint Chiefs of Staff, the Grand Alliance, and U.S. Strategy in World War II.* Chapel Hill: University of North Carolina Press, 2000.

Strout, Cushing. *Conscience, Science, and Security: The Case of Dr. J. Robert Oppenheimer.* Chicago: Rand McNally, 1963.

Sudoplatov, Pavel, and Anatoli Sudoplatov, with Jerrold L. and Leona P. Schecter. *Special Tasks: The Memoirs of an Unwanted Witness, a Soviet Spymaster.* Boston: Little Brown, 1994.

Sutton, Antony. *Western Technology and Soviet Economic Development, 1917–1930.* Stanford, Calif.: Hoover Institution on War, Revolution and Peace, 1968.

Talbert, Roy, Jr. *Negative Intelligence: The Army and the American Left, 1917–1941.* Jackson: University Press of Mississippi, 1991.

Tanenhaus, Sam. *Whittaker Chambers: A Biography.* New York: Random House, 1999.

Theoharis, Athan G. *Chasing Spies: How the FBI Failed in Counterintelligence but Promoted the Politics of McCarthyism in the Cold War Years.* Chicago: Ivan R. Dee, 2002.

Theoharis, Athan G., and John Stuart Cox. *The Boss: J. Edgar Hoover and the Great American Inquisition.* Philadelphia: Temple University Press, 1988.

Tokaev, Grigorii A. *Stalin Means War*. London: George Weidenfeld & Nicolson, 1951.

Toledano, Ralph D., and Victor Lasky. *Seeds of Treason: The True Story of the Hiss-Chambers Tragedy*. New York: Funk and Wagnalls, 1950.

Tuck, Jay. *High Tech Espionage: How the KGB Smuggles NATO's Strategic Secrets to Moscow*. London: Sidgwick and Jackson, 1986.

U.S. Army Intelligence Center. *History of the Counter Intelligence Corps: The Counter Intelligence Corps between the World Wars, 1918–1941*. Fort Holabird, Baltimore: U.S. Army Intelligence Center, 1960.

U.S. Atomic Energy Commission. *In the Matter of J. Robert Oppenheimer: Transcript of Hearing before Personnel Security Board and Texts of Principal Documents and Letters*. Cambridge, Mass.: MIT Press, 1971.

U.S. Department of Defense. *Hostile Intelligence Threat—U.S. Technology* (November 1988). DOD 5200. 1-PH-2.

U.S. Department of State. *Foreign Relations of the United States, 1946*. Vol. 6. *The Soviet Union*. Washington, D.C.: GPO, 1969.

Valtin, Jan. *Out of the Night*. New York: Alliance Book Corp., 1941.

Vise, David A. *The Bureau and the Mole: The Unmasking of Robert Philip Hanssen, the Most Dangerous Double Agent in FBI History*. New York: Atlantic Monthly Press, 2002.

Waldman, Louis. *Labor Lawyer*. New York: E. P. Dutton, 1944.

Wang, Jessica. *American Science in an Age of Anxiety: Scientists, Anticommunism, and the Cold War*. Chapel Hill: University of North Carolina Press, 1999.

War Department General Staff. "Soviet Espionage in Canada." *Intelligence Review* (October 3, 1946).

Watt, D. C. "Francis Herbert King: A Soviet Source in the Foreign Office." *Intelligence and National Security* 3 (October 1988): 62–83.

Weiner, Tim, David Johnston, and Neil A. Lewis. *Betrayal: The Story of Aldrich Ames, an American Spy*. New York: Random House, 1995.

Weinstein, Allen. *Perjury: The Hiss-Chambers Case*. New York: Knopf, 1978.

———, and Alexander Vassiliev. *The Haunted Wood: Soviet Espionage in America; The Stalin Era*. New York: Random House, 1999.

Westerfield, H. Bradford. *The Instruments of America's Foreign Policy*. New York: Thomas Y. Crowell, 1963.

West, Nigel. *Games of Intelligence: The Classified Conflict of International Espionage*. New York: Crown Publishers, 1989.

White, G. Edward. *Alger Hiss's Looking-Glass Wars: The Covert Life of a Soviet Spy*. New York: Oxford University Press, 2004.

Whitehead, Don. *The FBI Story: A Report to the People*. New York: Random House, 1956.

Whittaker, Reg. "Cold War Alchemy: How America, Britain and Canada Transformed Espionage into Subversion." *Intelligence and National Security* 15 (Summer 2000): 177–210.

Williams, Robert Chadwell. *Klaus Fuchs: Atom Spy*. Cambridge: Harvard University Press, 1987.

Williams, William Appleman. *American-Russian Relations, 1781–1947*. New York: Rinehart, 1952.

Wilson, Joan Hoff. *Ideology and Economics: Soviet-American Relations, 1917–1933.* Columbia: University Press of Missouri, 1974.

Wise, David. *Cassidy's Run: The Secret Spy War over Nerve Gas.* New York: Random House, 2000.

———. *The Inside Story of How the FBI's Robert Hanssen Betrayed America.* New York: Random House, 2002.

———. *Nightmover: How Aldrich Ames Sold the CIA to the KGB for $4.6 Million.* New York: HarperCollins, 1995.

INDEX

Substitute Alloy Material Lab (SAM), 157, 158,
160, 161, 165
Subversion, 10, 46, 53, 60
in military, 68–72
responding to, 87–92
in war plants, 68–72
Subversive Activities Control Board (SACB),
219
Subversives, 46, 51–52, 59, 64, 159, 179
countering, 45, 55, 91
described, 89
investigation of, 23
looking out for, 56
registration of, 78
Sudoplatov, Pavel, 184, 305n208
on Amtorg, 269n47
on Mironov, 106
on Oppenheimer, 300n111
on Zarubin, 283n122
Sugar, David, 172
Sullivan Machine Company, 17
"Summary of U.S. Relations with the Soviet
Union," Elsey and, 178
Superior Court, 215
Supreme Court of Canada, 173
Surveillance, 3, 60, 83, 108, 114, 148
electronic, 222
microphone, 7, 298n86
physical, 127, 178, 203
technical, 127, 139, 141, 145, 202, 203
telephone, 138
Susemihl, Igor Vladimirovich, 234
SVRR. See Russian Foreign Intelligence Service
Sweet, Edwin L., 316n131
Switz, Marjorie Tilley, 29, 78
Switz, Robert Gordon, 29, 32, 78, 260n103
Syndar Corporation, 110
Synthetic rubber, 110, 133, 285n150
Systems Control Inc. (SCI), 228
Szczechowski, Clarence. See Hiskey, Clarence

Taft, Robert, 176
Talbert, Roy, Jr., 46
Tallentire, N. H., 24
Tamm, Edward, 68, 80
Tanenhaus, Sam, 80
Tanks, 25, 26, 32
Tarasov, Leonid, 106, 284n127.
Tartakow, Jerome, 197
Taschereau, Robert, 171
TASS, 176
Tatlock, Jean, 142, 200, 296n42

Tavenner, Frank S., 216
Taxol, 240
Taylor, William H., 287n188
Taylor Winfield Company, 63
Technical Service Bureau (Chicago), 65
Technological Laboratories Inc., 159
Technology, 16, 25, 27, 80, 85, 171, 172, 236
acquisition of, 23, 31, 40, 232–33
adhesive, 240
advanced, 24
aircraft, 102, 198
chemical warfare, 17
communications, 223
defense, 13, 227
experimental, 39
film, 98
German, 181
industrial, 2, 17, 65, 66, 68, 245
loss, 222, 233, 239–40
military, 2, 17, 65, 66, 68, 178, 237, 245
radar, 104
rocket, 182
satellite, 222
Stealth, 228, 229
theft of, 51, 209
weapons, 245
"Teheran Thesis," 88
Teller, Edward, 183
Temple, Shirley, 130
Temporary Commission on Employee Loyalty,
205, 206
Tenney, Helen, 125, 127
Terrorism, 1, 12, 221, 238, 240
Thelan, Robert, 272n107
Theoharis, Athan, 4, 59, 275n1, 292n252
Theoretical Physics Division (Los Alamos),
165
Third Period, 45, 46, 48
Thomas, Norman, 36
Thomas, Parnell, 214
Tilton, Alfred, 20, 21, 257n44
Time, Chambers and, 274n127
Timken Detroit Axle Company, 60
Tito, Josip Broz, 213
TNT, 66, 111, 168
Tokaev, Grigorii A., 181, 182, 315n125
Tolson, Clyde, 89, 91, 296n44
photo of, 90
Tompkins, Florence, 262n127
Trade, 13–14, 30
agreements, 13, 24
Cold War and, 211